Evangelical Christianity
and Democracy in Asia

EVANGELICAL CHRISTIANITY
AND DEMOCRACY
IN THE GLOBAL SOUTH

Series Editor
Timothy Samuel Shah

Evangelical Christianity and Democracy in Latin America
Edited by Paul Freston

Evangelical Christianity and Democracy in Africa
Edited by Terence O. Ranger

Evangelical Christianity and Democracy in Asia
Edited by David H. Lumsdaine

Evangelical Christianity and Democracy in Global Perspective
Edited by Timothy Samuel Shah

Evangelical Christianity and Democracy in Asia

Edited by
DAVID H. LUMSDAINE

2009

OXFORD
UNIVERSITY PRESS

Oxford University Press, Inc., publishes works that further
Oxford University's objective of excellence
in research, scholarship, and education.

Oxford   New York
Auckland   Cape Town   Dar es Salaam   Hong Kong   Karachi
Kuala Lumpur   Madrid   Melbourne   Mexico City   Nairobi
New Delhi   Shanghai   Taipei   Toronto

With offices in
Argentina   Austria   Brazil   Chile   Czech Republic   France   Greece
Guatemala   Hungary   Italy   Japan   Poland   Portugal   Singapore
South Korea   Switzerland   Thailand   Turkey   Ukraine   Vietnam

Copyright © 2009 by Oxford University Press, Inc.

Published by Oxford University Press, Inc.
198 Madison Avenue, New York, New York 10016

www.oup.com

Oxford is a registered trademark of Oxford University Press

All rights reserved. No part of this publication may be reproduced,
stored in a retrieval system, or transmitted, in any form or by any means,
electronic, mechanical, photocopying, recording, or otherwise,
without prior permission of Oxford University Press.

Library of Congress Cataloging-in-Publication Data
Evangelical Christianity and democracy in Asia /
edited by David Halloran Lumsdaine.
    p. cm. (Evangelical Christianity and democracy in the Global South)
Includes bibliographical references and index.
ISBN-13 978-0-19-530824-2; 978-0-19-530825-9 (pbk.)
1. Evangelicalism—Political aspects—Asia.
2. Democracy—Religious aspects—Christianity.
3. Christianity and politics—Asia.   I. Lumsdaine, David Halloran.
II. Series.
BR1642.A78 E93 2006
322'.1095—dc22   2005031886

9 8 7 6 5 4 3 2 1

Printed in the United States of America
on acid-free paper

For
Vinay Kumar Samuel,
on the fortieth anniversary of his ordination to ministry
in the Church of South India
(1967–2007)

And for all the churches of Asia, Africa, and Latin America
it remains his joy to serve

Preface

The research project that generated this volume began as an effort in evangelical self-understanding. The globally minded and globally active International Fellowship of Evangelical Mission Theologians (INFEMIT), together with its research and study arm, the Oxford Centre for Mission Studies (OCMS), based in Oxford, England, undertook numerous efforts in the 1980s and 1990s to develop sophisticated evangelical analyses of a host of global issues, including modernity and modernization, market economics, population growth, and human disability.[1] Toward the end of the 1990s it occurred to INFEMIT's director, Indian theologian Vinay Samuel, that international evangelicalism itself merited a critical analysis, particularly because of its growing social and political prominence in the developing countries of the "global South" (i.e., Asia, Africa, and Latin America).

Evangelical politics merited analysis, Samuel believed, not only because evangelical political efforts were increasingly organized and consequential but also because their impact on global South politics seemed so varied and ambivalent. After all, some of the best known instances of evangelical politics include the military dictatorship of Efraín Ríos Montt in Guatemala in the early 1980s as well as the support many white evangelicals gave to apartheid in South Africa until the early 1990s. On the other hand, the evangelical wing of Kenya's Anglican Church proved to be authoritarian president Daniel arap Moi's most vocal critic in the 1980s and 1990s.

In this variety and ambiguity global South evangelicals are not unlike their evangelical counterparts in the United States. Major political figures (such as former president Jimmy Carter, former senator Mark Hatfield, and former attorney general John Ashcroft) and movements (such as the Moral Majority and the Christian Coalition) suggest the enormous growth and influence of American evangelical political activism during the last thirty years. But they also underscore evangelicals' deep differences in political philosophy, their divergent policy goals, and the uncertainty of their long-term political achievements.[2] The fact that American evangelicals have remained consistent and enthusiastic supporters of George W. Bush—a president otherwise deeply and increasingly unpopular both inside and outside the United States—only deepens the sense that global evangelicalism has bequeathed an ambiguous political legacy that evangelicals bear a special responsibility to scrutinize.[3]

To launch this project of critical self-understanding, Vinay Samuel gathered a small team of evangelical scholars, including myself, in 1997. For the necessary funding, we turned to The Pew Charitable Trusts, which had an impressive track record of supporting scholarship on, and by, evangelicals. Luis Lugo, head of Pew's Religion Program at the time, and Susan Billington Harper, program officer with the Religion Program, provided indispensable encouragement and guidance at this early stage. As a first step in Pew's support, they provided a seed grant to conduct a preliminary "mapping" of the basic patterns of evangelical political activism across the global South as well as the most promising avenues for long-term research on the subject. Paul Freston, an outstanding sociologist specializing in the study of pentecostalism in Brazil and a member of our team, agreed to produce this mapping, and in a few short months performed the major miracle of writing a booklength overview of evangelical politics in nearly thirty countries in Africa, Asia, and Latin America, complete with an exhaustive bibliography. Freston's study, first in manuscript form and later as a published monograph, became a constant point of reference as we designed the project and, later, as we conducted the research.[4] It also made a compelling case to our prospective funders that the subject deserved more systematic and sustained examination. So in June 1999, The Pew Charitable Trusts provided our INFEMIT research team with a generous grant to conduct field research on politically engaged evangelicals on three continents—Asia, Africa, and Latin America—over three years.

We focused our critical analysis of evangelical politics in these regions of the global South in two ways. First, we identified what seemed to be the most significant cases of evangelical political mobilization and influence in each region's most significant countries: Brazil, Mexico, Guatemala, Nicaragua, Chile, and Peru in Latin America; Nigeria, Kenya, South Africa, Mozambique, Zambia, and Zimbabwe in Africa; and China, India, Indonesia, South Korea, and the Philippines in Asia.

Second, to give our research a sharper analytical and evaluative edge, we decided to pay special attention to the relationship between evangelical politics and democracy in each region. How has the overall trend toward democratization in all the regions of the global South, especially during the "third wave" of democratization (1974–1991), given evangelicals new incentives and opportunities for political mobilization and influence?[5] And, more important for our critical purposes, what has been the impact of politically engaged evangelicalism on democratization? To what extent has it contributed to the inauguration and consolidation of democratic regimes? And in countries where democratic transitions have not occurred, to what extent have evangelicals promoted the norms and practices of democratic politics, whether at the local, regional, or national level? Conversely, to what extent have politically engaged evangelicals blocked, slowed, or otherwise undermined democratization in the global South?

Evangelicalism's impact on democratization compelled our attention not only because of our interest in assessing the level and quality of evangelical political activism. It also seemed worthy of study because democratization in the global South, despite dramatic advances, remained so limited and fragile—particularly insofar as democracy in its most robust and valid form requires not only free and fair elections but also effective respect for basic human rights and freedoms. Democracy in Asia, Africa, and Latin America needed all the help it could get, and we wanted to know how much help, if any, evangelicals were giving. Since the start of our research, just how much the overall social and economic development of the global South requires the establishment of more effective, transparent, and democratic governance has become even more painfully obvious. Yet in Asia and Africa in particular, according to a 2007 Freedom House report, democratization has stagnated or even reversed since 2005.[6]

Furthermore, recent studies of religion and democratization had included almost no broad, comparative treatment of evangelical influences. Numerous scholars noted the important roles Catholic and mainline Protestant churches played in democratic transitions throughout the global South during the "third wave" of democratization, particularly in the 1980s and early 1990s. Indeed, the pro-democratic activism of such churches continues to provoke scholarly and journalistic interest. In July 2007 it was widely noted that the Roman Catholic bishop of Hong Kong, Cardinal Joseph Zen Ze-kiun, was in the forefront of a pro-democracy march marking the tenth anniversary of the island's return to Chinese rule.[7] And the vocal opposition of Zimbabwe's Catholic bishops to the increasingly repressive regime of Robert Mugabe received considerable attention in the press in early 2007.[8] But mainstream scholarship on religion and democratization, whether focused on Africa, Asia, or Latin America, tended to ignore or downplay the burgeoning evangelical sector of global South Christianity.[9] Granted that bishops and archbishops, clergy and laity, as well as a globe-trotting pope mobilized Catholic and mainline Protestant churches to battle authoritarian regimes and support democratic transitions throughout the global South, what about evangelical churches, denominations, and political parties? What about evangelical movements within mainline churches? After all, many of these churches in the global South, if not in their counterpart churches in Europe and North America, remain animated by the biblicist theology and missionary activism that are the hallmarks of evangelicalism.[10] Finally, we were eager to investigate the political contributions of the pentecostal subsector of evangelicalism in particular, which has become the most dynamic and demographically dominant force not only in global South evangelicalism but in global South Protestantism as a whole.

Demographic trends also recommended a focus on evangelical contributions to global South democratization. Throughout the 1950s and 1960s leading scholars and other observers, such as Indian historian and diplomat K. M. Panikkar, predicted with breathtaking confidence and uniformity that Christianity in Asia and Africa would collapse once the coercive pressures of Western colonialism were removed.[11] As it happens, Christianity and especially Protestantism saw continuing expansion, not contraction, in the last decades of the twentieth century. According to religion demographers David Barrett and Todd Johnson, Christians in Asia grew from 22 million in 1900 to 101 million in 1970 and then to 351 million by 2005 (thus growing from 2 percent to 9 percent of Asia's total population between 1900 and 2005). In Africa, likewise, Christians numbered 10 million in 1900 and 30 million in 1945, but then jumped to 144 million by 1970 and to 411 million by 2005.[12] In other words, Christianity's *postcolonial* growth in both Asia and Africa was at least as dramatic as its colonial growth.

Protestantism in particular has seen significant postcolonial growth across the global South, more than doubling from about 4 percent of the overall global South population in 1970 to about 10 percent by 2000. In comparison, Roman Catholicism saw its overall share of the global South population increase by only a little more than one percentage point during the same thirty-year period, from 13 percent to 14 percent, and Islam's share also grew rather modestly, from 19 percent to 23 percent. As a result of this exponential growth, the Protestant proportion of the population in Asia was ten times greater at the end of the twentieth century than at its beginning, in Africa thirteen times greater, and in Latin America six times greater.[13] No other major religious group came close to experiencing such a dramatic, sustained, and extensive demographic expansion across the global South during this period.

The most important driver and beneficiary of Protestantism's demographic expansion across the global South has clearly been evangelicalism—particularly, in recent years, in its pentecostal expressions. Within most of the global South's thriving mainline Protestant churches, evangelicalism is the dominant, driving element, which of course is what increasingly separates

Protestants from their fellow Anglicans, Episcopalians, Methodists, Lutherans, and Presbyterians in Europe and North America, among whom, to put it plainly, a gospel of political inclusion has increasingly displaced a gospel of spiritual conversion. Evangelicalism is thus not a denominational category, as our research takes pains to emphasize. Evangelical Methodists in Mozambique may have far more in common with evangelical Presbyterians in South Korea or with evangelical pentecostals in Brazil than with fellow Methodists in Maine, Minnesota, or Manchester, England.

Evangelicalism in its Spirit-filled pentecostal form has proven particularly contagious, constantly spreading across otherwise well-defended ecclesiastical borders. Numerous Protestant churches in the global South, not to mention the Roman Catholic Church, have succumbed to pervasive "pentecostalization" in the form of highly successful charismatic movements, even as pentecostal denominations such as the Assemblies of God expand and multiply with remarkable velocity in virtually every corner of Asia, Africa, and Latin America. A ten-country public opinion survey of global pentecostalism conducted by the Pew Forum on Religion and Public Life in 2006 found that nearly half or more of all Protestants interviewed in Brazil, Chile, Guatemala, Nigeria, and Kenya were members of pentecostal churches, while more than a quarter of Protestants interviewed in South Korea, the Philippines, South Africa, and Guatemala were Protestant charismatics (i.e., people who identified with the pentecostal label or with pentecostal practice such as speaking in tongues but remained members of nonpentecostal churches).[14] In Asia, for example, according to 2006 figures from the World Christian Database, pentecostals and charismatics now represent more than 4 percent, or about 163 million, of the population of nearly four billion people, whereas they represented less than 1 percent in 1970.[15] When one considers that both pentecostal and nonpentecostal evangelicals generally have higher rates of religious observance than other Christians, the conclusion that evangelicalism has become the dominant form of Christian practice in much of the global South is inescapable.

Further arguing in favor of a focus on evangelicalism's contributions to democracy is an impressive body of recent research on the democratic potential of this burgeoning form of Protestantism. Distinguished sociologist David Martin and a number of other scholars have painted a picture of global South evangelicals in the late twentieth century reminiscent of Alexis de Tocqueville's picture of American Christians in the early nineteenth century: voluntarist, independent of the state, and assiduous practitioners of the "art of association."[16] In their churches and small prayer and Bible study groups, evangelicals carve out what Martin terms "autonomous social spaces" within which believers receive Word and Spirit directly, without priestly mediation, and are empowered to share them with others. Amid degradation and exploitation, they experience stability, dignity, and equality.[17] In addition, Martin and others document how conversion to evangelicalism involves the acquisition of a

"Protestant ethic" that transforms drunken and indolent men into sober and responsible householders, which in turn provides their families with a modicum of economic stability.[18] As the pioneering sociologist of religion Peter Berger likes to say, "Max Weber is alive and well and living in Guatemala."[19]

In documenting these cultural, social, moral, and economic transformations, Martin and other scholars argue that they may well suggest that evangelicalism enjoys an intrinsic tendency to promote both the kind of moral and purposeful individualism and the kind of robust associational life that are conducive to democratization. But these somewhat tentative claims concerning evangelicalism's long-term democratic potential could and should be empirically tested, it seemed to us, against the actual political activism and performance of evangelicals across the global South. If the "evangelical ethic" really does promote the spirit of capitalism through microlevel moral and cultural change, does it also promote the spirit of democracy through macrolevel political change? The increasing number of cases of evangelical political activism in Asia, Africa, and Latin America enabled us to investigate whether evangelicals were living up to their democratic potential.

To direct the research on Asian evangelicals and democracy that generated this volume, we turned to distinguished scholar of international politics David H. Lumsdaine. Formerly professor of international relations and international political economy at Yale University (1986–1998) and at the Graduate School of Public Policy and Management of the Korea Development Institute in Seoul, Korea (1998–2004), and now professor of political studies at Gordon College in Wenham, Massachusetts, Lumsdaine guided an outstanding team of Asian scholars as well as one U.S.-based scholar as they conducted field research in key areas of a vast continent: Sushil Aaron on Gujarat, India; Bambang Budijanto on Indonesia; Kim-Kwong Chan on China; Sujatha Fernandes on Northeast India; Young-gi Hong on South Korea; and David Lim on the Philippines.

The insightful studies of these scholars probe the impact of evangelicals on democracy and democratization at local, regional, and national levels. More than the studies of Africa and Latin America in the accompanying volumes, in fact, the Asian case studies focus on local and regional politics as much as on national politics. Chan's chapter on China contains a number of local and regional case studies of evangelical activism and the ways in which activism fosters greater civic participation and sometimes pressures district-level political authorities to be more responsive and accountable to their religious constituents. Aaron's chapter on Gujarat state in western India focuses on the social and civic effects of the Christian work of preaching the Gospel on the part of evangelicals working and living among indigenous tribal peoples. Though many scholars and observers attack such activity as a paradigm case of cultural imperialism and social disenfranchisement, Aaron makes a persuasive (though highly nuanced and qualified) case that at least some of it empowers tribal converts to evangelicalism with a robust sense of agency and an assertive and engaged civic identity profoundly in keeping with our standard sense of what democratic citizenship entails. As Lumsdaine notes in his introduction, grassroots activism may be the most important way evangelical Christianity promotes democracy in Asia.

In the region's national-level politics, however, evangelical activism faces formidable challenges. Christians in general and evangelicals in particular are usually too few in number to launch national political movements or to secure significant representation in national assemblies or parliaments. Furthermore, in some Asian countries, such as India, Indonesia, and Sri Lanka, majority religious communities regard evangelical "proselytization" and expansion as a threat to religion-based national identities. (Aaron describes the struggle between Hindu nationalists and evangelical missionaries in his case study of Gujarat.) In these and other countries, including Myanmar and Vietnam, Protestantism is historically linked with separatist ethnic movements—among the Degar (or Montagnard) and Karen peoples, for example—and is thus considered a threat to national unity and territorial integrity. Partly because of such ethnoreligious separatism and partly because of the history of Western colonialism, the perception that Christians and especially evangelicals are "foreign," "anti-national," and U.S.-backed "neo-imperialists" is probably more entrenched and pervasive in Asia than in Africa or even Latin America.[20]

Despite frequently unfavorable circumstances, Lumsdaine's scholars note that evangelicals participated in national and regional politics with important consequences for democracy and civil society in several parts of Asia, including the Philippines, Korea, Indonesia, and Northeast India. In the Philippines, Korea, and Northeast India, evangelical politics has proven especially significant largely because evangelicals have been more numerous than in almost all other parts of Asia. Protestants are about 20 percent of the South Korean population and about 10 percent of the Philippine population. Of Northeast India's seven states, three have large Christian majorities: Nagaland, which is 90 percent Christian; Mizoram, 87 percent; and Meghalaya, 70 percent. The vast majority of Northeast India's Christians are not only evangelicals but also Baptists, though they have splintered (partly along ethnic lines) into a variety of denominations and para-church organizations.[21] As with the Karen in Myanmar and the Degar in Vietnam, Sujatha Fernandes chronicles how missionary Protestantism has deepened an already distinct sense of ethnic identity on the part of many tribal groups in Northeast India and fueled their long and frequently violent struggle for greater political independence from majority-Hindu India—though with mixed consequences for democracy and civil society. Lim's study of the Philippines, Budijanto's study of Indonesia, and Hong's study of South Korea all document how formerly quiescent evangelicals became increasingly assertive civic actors in the 1980s and 1990s. In each of these three cases, evangelicals both contributed to and capitalized on dramatic democratic openings at the national level.

Though this research has in many ways been an exercise in evangelical self-criticism, it is important to note that many of the researchers who have been involved in it do not identify personally with evangelical Christianity. To conduct field research and produce the country case studies, we sought scholars who were based in the countries they were studying and who had ample experience investigating evangelicalism in these countries, regardless of whether they were "card-carrying" evangelicals, as it were. In a number of cases, the most impressive scholars we could find *were* evangelicals. But that was not the point. Precisely because we wanted to offer the evangelical world a nondistortive picture of evangelical politics in the global South, warts and all, our overriding criterion in selecting our research team was not theological correctness but a proven ability to provide intelligent access to the phenomenon at hand.

Just as our research was produced by a religiously diverse team of scholars, however, we expect that it will be of interest to a religiously diverse audience. Evangelicals and nonevangelicals alike have a stake in understanding the political intentions and influences of this burgeoning, global movement, especially when a growing number of studies are sounding the alarm about the political dangers of religion in general and evangelical religion in particular.[22] The politics of global evangelicalism can be understood at the most basic level, however, only if one pays close attention to the politics of global South evangelicalism, which accounts for the vast majority of the world's evangelicals. At the same time, our research is an essential starting point even for those with no particular interest in global evangelical politics per se but who seek a deeper understanding of, say, American or Canadian or British evangelical political activism. For one cannot distinguish the constant and characteristically evangelical features of any of these movements from contingent features arising from the accidents of time, place, and political opportunity without systematically comparing them with forms of evangelical activism prevalent elsewhere. "And what should they know of England who only England know?"[23] Understanding evangelical politics anywhere requires at least some familiarity with evangelical politics everywhere.

Our somewhat fanatical insistence on the cardinal importance of broad and comparative inquiry leads us to believe that this volume is best read in conjunction with its companion volumes on Africa and Latin America. These three volumes were not generated by three separate projects, after all, but by one project motivated from the start by a common set of concerns and questions about the adequacy of evangelicalism's "political witness"—to use an evangelical phrase—in the countries of the global South. We developed common approaches to our key concepts, particularly evangelicalism and democracy, and we immersed ourselves in a common body of literature on religion and democratization. In the course of the project, there was significant interaction between the directors of the regional research teams, which encouraged significant intellectual cross-fertilization. And in June 2002, all the project participants gathered in Potomac, Maryland, to present our research to a distinguished gathering of scholars from around the world. The answers to the questions that launched our project lie in the totality of this cross-regional research and should not be inferred from any one volume or case study.

When seen in its totality, this body of research not only provides a broad survey of evangelical politics in nearly twenty countries but also offers insights into the wider trend that Peter Berger aptly terms the "desecularization of the world": the process whereby all the world's major religious communities—Islam, Hinduism, Buddhism, and Christianity—have surged in vitality and political influence from the early 1970s right up to the present, thus weakening the hold of secularist political regimes and ideologies across the globe and filling otherwise secular public spaces everywhere with religious voices.[24] Just as no case of evangelical politics can be properly studied in isolation from other cases, no case of religion's global political resurgence can be properly understood apart from this broad spectrum of politically mobilized religions. Any minimally adequate understanding of the causes and consequences of the Islamic political resurgence, for example, requires rigorous comparison with other cases of religion's political resurgence. And perhaps no case provides a more apt comparison than the worldwide evangelical political upsurge. Evangelical Protestantism, like Islam, is an egalitarian, scripture-based religion without a central hierarchy that has achieved impressive global expansion and political influence largely through grassroots mobilization. Yet I am aware of no systematic and sustained attempt to compare these powerful forms of religious political activism, despite the fresh insights into both movements such a study would be bound to generate. Perhaps our research can facilitate this and other potentially fruitful comparisons between the world's politically resurgent religions.

In coordinating such a massive project over so many years, I have incurred almost innumerable and certainly unrepayable debts. David Battrick, Darin Hamlin, Matthew Fesak, and Anne Fontenau provided crucial support as the project was launched in 1999 and early 2000. David Fabrycky, Laura Fabrycky, Scott Bond, and particularly Dawn Haglund offered various forms of assistance, with Dawn Haglund taking on the monumental task of organizing numerous research workshops throughout the world as well as the project's large international conference in June 2002. In this massive undertaking, Eric Naus and Cara Farr were a tremendous and cheerful help. At a later stage, Sarah Mehta and Stephen Joyce offered invaluable assistance. Abey George helped coordinate the arduous task of organizing and cleaning up the bibliographies of all three volumes, assisted admirably by Laura Fabrycky.

In the last two years, no single person has contributed more to the seemingly endless task of preparing the volumes for publication than Rachel Mumford. She happily immersed herself in the minutiae of each volume to an extent that would have driven lesser mortals insane. I can explain this only by her repeated affirmation that she made the project her own. I cannot thank her enough. Working closely with Rachel Mumford, Patricia Barreiro contributed her tremendous skills as a copyeditor and in the process gave up more tears and sweat than our meager recompense could justify. Without this dynamic duo, the volumes might never have seen publication.

Several institutions provided crucial support at points. The Ethics and Public Policy Center (EPPC) offered me and the project an extremely happy and hospitable base of operations from the moment The Pew Charitable Trusts decided to fund our research in June 1999 until I left the Center in July 2004. Elliott Abrams took a personal interest in the project and saw to it that I received all the help EPPC could muster. Markus Österlund was an unexpected and enormously delightful and stimulating intellectual companion. Above all, EPPC vice president Michael Cromartie gave me the warmest possible welcome and made himself an instant and continuing friend of this project with his characteristic combination of sharp advice and strong encouragement. Fieldstead and Company gave valuable financial support, enabling us to considerably expand our June 2002 conference, thus helping to make it a great success.

In his new capacity as director of the Pew Forum on Religion and Public Life, Luis Lugo offered me and the project generous support when I joined the Forum in August 2004. Thanks to his remarkable generosity and consistent belief in the importance of the subject matter, I enjoyed tremendous freedom to work on the project as well as outstanding assistance from Forum staff. Among Forum staff, the most notable assistance came from Julia Kirby, who worked closely with Rachel Mumford in the summer of 2005 to prepare the manuscripts for their original review by Oxford University Press. Most recently, Boston University's Institute on Culture, Religion and World Affairs (CURA) and the Council on Foreign Relations have provided the perfect institutional settings for thinking through the long-term significance and geopolitical consequences of evangelical expansion in the global South. My friends at these institutions, Peter Berger at CURA and Walter Mead at the Council, are the most perceptive, encouraging, and stimulating interlocutors on the issues addressed by this project that one could possibly hope for.

Numerous other individuals offered incisive commentary and valuable guidance at various stages of the project: Philip Jenkins, David Martin, Samuel Huntington, Mark Noll, Robert Woodberry, Paul Gifford, Daniel Levine, Susanne Rudolph, Christian Smith, Christopher Sugden, Haddon Willmer, Richard John Neuhaus, Virginia Garrard-Burnett, Jeffrey Klaiber, David Maxwell,

Lamin Sanneh, Daniel Philpott, Ken Woodward, Paul Marshall, Ron Sider, Jim Skillen, Keith Pavlischek, Oliver O'Donovan, Joan Lockwood O'Donovan, N. J. Demerath, José Míguez Bonino, Paul Sigmund, Timothy Steigenga, Hannah Stewart-Gambino, John Green, Dennis Hoover, Ruth Melkonian-Hoover, Hillel Fradkin, Daniel Bays, Marc Plattner, Carol Hamrin, David Aikman, Rosalind Hackett, John Wolffe, Matthews Ojo, Uwe Siemon-Netto, John Wilson, and Phil Costopoulos.

At Oxford University Press, Cynthia Read has been marvelously encouraging and unfailingly patient at every stage, despite the fact that the process of seeing the volumes to publication proved much more time-consuming and difficult than she ever dreamed possible. Christine Dahlin handled the volumes in the final stages with extraordinary efficiency and professionalism. We are also grateful for Theodore Calderara's and Julia TerMaat's assistance.

There would of course be no project and no volumes without our dedicated team of scholars. It has been a particular honor to work with our abundantly talented regional research directors: Vikram Chand, the first director of the Asian research, who had to give up his responsibilities with the project when he assumed a senior position with the World Bank in New Delhi in 2000; Terence Ranger, director of the African research; Paul Freston, director of the Latin American research; and, as I have already noted, David Lumsdaine, director of the Asian research. Each of these outstanding scholars contributed immeasurably to the project as a whole and not merely to his own piece of it. Above all, however, the chapter authors have been the heart and soul of this project. They have all produced rich and insightful case studies, and many braved considerable danger and difficulty in conducting their fieldwork. Special thanks go to Dino Touthang, who conducted many interviews for chapter 3 in this volume during a period when it became impracticable for outsiders to travel to the region. Along with the Asia scholars already mentioned, our Latin America scholars were Alexandre Brasil Fonseca, Felipe Vázquez Palacios, Darío López Rodriguez, Clay Matthew Samson, Roberto Zub, and David Muñoz Condell; and our Africa scholars were Cyril Imo, John Karanja, Anthony Balcomb, Isabel Phiri, Isabel Mukonyora, and Teresa Cruz e Silva.

This project has had its highs and lows, with many of the lows falling thickly in the last two years prior to publication. Through it all, no one has proven a more constant and energetic encouragement than my wife, Becky. Though she has had every right to be exasperated by a project that I have been working on longer than we have been married, she has instead been consistently herself: ferociously loyal and supportive and adamantly uncomplaining about the additional psychic burdens this project placed on me and therefore on her. I am deeply grateful.

Finally, let me reiterate that this ambitious project began as an idea in the fertile and deeply evangelical mind of Vinay Samuel. Without his leadership, at once visionary and practical, no such project would have been organized, funded, or even imagined. On behalf of all those who have participated in the project, I therefore gratefully dedicate the project volumes to the Rev. Dr. Vinay Kumar Samuel and to the simultaneously struggling and thriving churches of the global South he intended the volumes to serve.

—Timothy Samuel Shah
Council on Foreign Relations,
Boston University
August 15, 2007

NOTES

1. Philip Sampson, Vinay Samuel, and Chris Sugden, eds., *Faith and Modernity* (Oxford: Regnum, 1994); Herbert Schlossberg, Vinay Samuel, and Ronald J. Sider, eds., *Christianity and Economics in the Post–Cold War Era: The Oxford Declaration and Beyond* (Grand Rapids, Mich.: Eerdmans, 1994); and D. G. R. Belshaw, Robert Calderisi, and Chris Sugden, eds., *Faith in Development: Partnership between the World Bank and the Churches of Africa* (Oxford: Regnum, 2001). Major INFEMIT-sponsored analyses also appeared in the international evangelical journal *Transformation: An International Journal of Holistic Mission Studies*, started in 1984, including a special 1998 issue on human disability edited by Rebecca Samuel Shah (October–December 1998; volume 15, number 4).

2. For an outstanding collection of sympathetic yet critical appraisals of the political activism of American evangelicals in recent years, see Michael Cromartie, ed., *A Public Faith: Evangelicals and Civic Engagement* (Lanham, Md.: Rowman & Littlefield, 2003). See also Christian Smith's powerful analysis in *American Evangelicalism: Embattled and Thriving* (1998).

3. Seventy-eight percent of white evangelical voters supported Bush in 2004, giving him 40 percent of his winning vote share, and in the 2006 congressional elections, 72 percent of white evangelicals voted Republican in races for the U.S. House nationwide. See John C. Green, Corwin E. Smidt, James L. Guth, and Lyman A. Kellstedt, "The American Religious Landscape and the 2004 Presidential Vote: Increased Polarization," available at http://pewforum.org/publications/surveys/post election.pdf, last accessed on August 14, 2007; and the Pew Forum on Religion and Public Life, "Religion and the 2006 Elections," available at http://pewforum.org/docs/ ?DocID=174, last accessed on August 14, 2007.

4. Freston (2001).

5. Huntington (1991).

6. Arch Puddington, "Freedom in the World 2007: Freedom Stagnation amid Pushback against Democracy," January 2007, available at http://www.freedomhouse .org/template.cfm?page=130&year=2007, last accessed on August 9, 2007.

7. Keith Bradsher, "Hong Kong Marks an Anniversary with Fanfare and Protests," *The New York Times*, July 2, 2007.

8. *The Economist*, "The Hogwash of Quiet Diplomacy," April 4, 2007.

9. See, for example, Tun-jen Cheng and Deborah A. Brown, eds., *Religious Organizations and Democratization: Case Studies from Contemporary Asia* (Armonk, N.Y.: M. E. Sharpe, 2006), and Kang, *Christ and Caesar in Modern Korea* (1997), both of which emphasize the political contributions of the Catholic Church and more liberal mainline Protestant churches to the neglect of conservative evangelicals and pentecostals.

10. "As products of Evangelical enterprise, mainline churches in Africa uphold basic Evangelical doctrine with varying degrees of consciousness and conformity," notes Jehu J. Hanciles, "Conversion and Social Change: A Review of the 'Unfinished Task' in West Africa," in Donald M. Lewis, ed., *Christianity Reborn: The Global Expansion of Evangelicalism in the Twentieth Century* (Grand Rapids, Mich.: Eerdmans, 2004), 171. On the evangelical and even fundamentalist tendencies of many mainline churches in other parts of the global South, including Asia, see Lionel Caplan, *Class and Culture in Urban India: Fundamentalism in a Christian Community* (Oxford: Clarendon Press, 1987) and Philip Jenkins, *The New Faces of Christianity: Believing the Bible in the Global South* (Oxford: Oxford University Press, 2006).

11. K. M. Panikkar, *Asia and Western Dominance: A Survey of the Vasco Da Gama Epoch of Asian History, 1498–1945* (London: Allen & Unwin, 1959). Paul Gifford notes the predominance of this view among scholars of Africa during the era of decolonization in his introduction to Paul Gifford, ed., *The Christian Churches and the Democratisation of Africa* (Leiden: E. J. Brill, 1995), 2.

12. David B. Barrett and Todd M. Johnson, "Annual Statistical Table on Global Mission: 2004," *International Bulletin of Missionary Research* 28 (January 2004): 25. However, the figures in the text for 1900, 1970, and 2005 reflect revised and updated statistics accessed from the World Christian Database, directed by Todd M. Johnson, as quoted in The Pew Forum on Religion and Public Life, "Overview: Pentecostalism in Africa," available at http://pewforum.org/surveys/pentecostal/africa, last accessed on August 9, 2007, and Pew Forum, "Overview: Pentecostalism in Asia," available at http://pewforum.org/surveys/pentecostal/asia, last accessed on September 28, 2007.

13. Barrett, Kurian, and Johnson (2001), 4, 13–15; Woodberry and Shah (2004): 49.

14. The Pew Forum on Religion and Public Life, "Spirit and Power: A Ten-Country Survey of Pentecostals," October 2006, p. 3; available at http://pewforum.org/publications/surveys/pentecostals-06.pdf, last accessed on August 9, 2007.

15. Quoted in The Pew Forum on Religion and Public Life, "Overview: Pentecostalism in Asia," available at http://pewforum.org/surveys/pentecostal/asia, last accessed on August 14, 2007.

16. Alexis de Tocqueville, *Democracy in America*, translated by Harvey Mansfield and Delba Winthrop (Chicago: University of Chicago Press, 2000).

17. David Martin, *Tongues of Fire: The Explosion of Protestantism in Latin America* (Oxford: Blackwell, 1990); David Martin, *Pentecostalism: The World Their Parish* (Oxford: Blackwell, 2001).

18. Cecília Mariz, *Coping with Poverty: Pentecostals and Christian Base Communities in Brazil* (Philadelphia: Temple University Press, 1994).

19. Peter L. Berger, "The Desecularization of the World: A Global Overview," in Berger (1999), 16.

20. Jenkins (2002), 175–77, 182–85; Brouwer, Gifford, and Rose (1996).

21. See the "Religious Demographic Profiles" compiled by the Pew Forum on Religion and Public Life on South Korea (http://pewforum.org/world-affairs/countries/?CountryID=194), the Philippines (http://pewforum.org/world-affairs/countries/?CountryID=163), and India (http://pewforum.org/world-affairs/countries/?CountryID=94), last accessed on October 1, 2007.

22. For recent examples, see Christopher Hitchens, *God Is Not Great: How Religion Has Poisoned Everything* (New York: Twelve, 2007); Sam Harris, *Letter to a Christian Nation* (New York: Knopf, 2006); and Randall Balmer, *Thy Kingdom Come: How the Religious Right Distorts the Faith and Threatens America, an Evangelical's Lament* (New York: Basic Books, 2006).

23. Rudyard Kipling, "The English Flag," 1891.

24. Berger (1999).

Contents

Preface, vii
Timothy Samuel Shah

Contributors, xxiii

Abbreviations, xxvii

Evangelical Christianity and Democratic
Pluralism in Asia: An Introduction, 3
David H. Lumsdaine

1. The Christian Community in China: The Leaven Effect, 43
   Kim-Kwong Chan

2. Emulating Azariah: Evangelicals and Social Change
   in the Dangs, 87
   Sushil J. Aaron

3. Ethnicity, Civil Society, and the Church: The Politics
   of Evangelical Christianity in Northeast India, 131
   Sujatha Fernandes

4. Evangelicals and Politics in Indonesia:
   The Case of Surakarta, 155
   Bambang Budijanto

5. Evangelicals and the Democratization of South
   Korea Since 1987, 185
   Rev. Dr. Joshua Young-gi Hong

6. Consolidating Democracy: Filipino Evangelicals between People Power Events, 1986–2001, 235
David S. Lim

References, 285

Index, 317

Contributors

Sushil J. Aaron, an independent researcher based in New Delhi, was the 2004–2005 Sir Ratan Tata Fellow at the Asia Research Centre of the London School of Economics. His previous publications include *Christianity and Political Conflict in India* (2002) and *Straddling Faultlines: India's Foreign Policy in the Greater Middle East* (2003). He received his Ph.D. from Jawaharlal Nehru University.

Bambang Budijanto is the area director for Asia at Compassion International. He was the founder and executive director of the Pesat Foundation in Indonesia from 1987 to 1997 and was the founder and director of the Institute for Community and Development Studies from 1997 to 1999. He currently serves on the boards of the Pesat Foundation, the Institute for Community and Development Studies, the Oxford Centre for Mission Studies, and the Consortium for Graduate Programs in Christian Studies (CCS). He received his Ph.D. from the Oxford Centre for Mission Studies and the University of Wales.

Kim-Kwong Chan is executive secretary of the Hong Kong Christian Council and a research fellow at the Universities Service Center of China Studies at the Chinese University of Hong Kong. He is also a justice of the peace appointed by the Hong Kong government. He has authored or coauthored ten books on China, including *Protestantism in Contemporary China* (1993), *Witness to Power: Stories of God's Quiet Work in a Changing China* (2000), *Holistic Entrepreneurs in China* (2002), and *Religious Freedom in China: Policy, Administration, and Regulation: A Research Handbook* (2005). He holds a Ph.D. from the University of Ottawa and a Th.D. from St. Paul University.

Sujatha Fernandes is assistant professor of sociology at Queens College, City University of New York. Prior to joining Queens College she was a Wilson-Cotsen postdoctoral fellow at Princeton University's Society of Fellows in the Liberal Arts. Her research interests include the politics of art; the interconnections of gender, race, and class; state-society relations; and the role of culture in social movements. She is the author of *Cuba Represent! Cuban Arts, State Power, and the Making of New Revolutionary Cultures* (2006). She is writing a book based on her field research in Venezuela, entitled *In the Spirit of Negro Primero: Urban Social Movements in Chávez's Venezuela*, as well as a memoir, *Close to the Edge: Reflections on Race, Politics, and Global Hip Hop*. She received her Ph.D. in political science from the University of Chicago.

Rev. Dr. Joshua Young-gi Hong has published *Charis and Charisma: David Yonggi Cho and the Growth of Yoido Full Gospel Church, Gift Code*, and numerous other books and articles. He is president of the Institute for Church Growth in Seoul, South Korea; an ordained pastor of the Yoido Full Gospel Church; the senior pastor of Church Growth Mission Society; and a teacher at Hansei University. He often travels internationally, speaking about church growth and leadership. He earned his Ph.D. from the Oxford Centre for Mission Studies and the University of Wales.

David S. Lim is executive director of China Ministries International (Philippines). He teaches at the Asian Theological Seminary and the Haggai Institute in Singapore. He has authored four books and written on theological contextualization and holistic mission. He also serves on the boards of Asia Missions Network, the National Coalition for Urban Transformation, the Philippine Missions Association, and the Asian School for Development and Cross-cultural Studies. He is the national council chairman of a faith-based political party and is the treasurer of Christian Convergence for Good Governance. He received his M. Div. from the Asian Theological Seminary in Quezon City, his M.Th. from the Asian Center for Theological Studies and Mission (Seoul, Korea), and his Ph.D. in Theology (N.T.) at the Fuller Theological Seminary.

David H. Lumsdaine is interested in questions of fostering human dignity and liberty, in ways of alleviating poverty and human distress, in how ideas shape international relations and domestic politics for good and ill, and in the role of ethics and religion in politics. After receiving his Ph.D. from Stanford, he taught at Yale, in Korea and in England, and at Wheaton College. He is now professor of political studies at Gordon College. The questions examined in this volume continue lines of analysis begun in his previous book, *Moral Vision in International Politics: The Foreign Aid Regime, 1949–1989*, which examined the effects of humanitarian ideas on the macrostructure of the international system.

Timothy Samuel Shah is senior research scholar at the Institute on Culture, Religion, and World Affairs at Boston University; adjunct senior fellow for religion and foreign policy at the Council on Foreign Relations; and formerly senior fellow in religion and world affairs at the Pew Forum on Religion and Public Life. He also serves as a principal researcher for the Religion in Global Politics research project at Harvard University. Shah's work on religion and politics has appeared in the *Journal of Democracy*, *SAIS Review of International Affairs*, *Political Quarterly*, and *Foreign Policy*. His Harvard government department Ph.D. dissertation was awarded the Aaron Wildavsky Award for Best Dissertation in Religion and Politics by the American Political Science Association in 2003.

Abbreviations

Chapter 1
- CCC   China Christian Council
- CCP   Chinese Communist Party
- CPPCC   Chinese People's Political Consultative Conference
- NATO   North Atlantic Treaty Organization
- PRC   People's Republic of China
- RAB   Religious Affairs Bureau
- SARA   State Administration for Religious Affairs
- TSPM   Three-Self Patriotic Movement
- UFWD   United Front Work Department

Chapter 2
- AG   Amos for Gujarat (pseudonymous)
- BJP   Bharatiya Janata Party (Indian People's Party)
- FIRs   first information reports
- FLCS   Forest Labor Cooperative Societies
- GCS   Gujarati Christi Seva
- GCW   Gujarat Christian Workers (pseudonymous)
- RPI   Republican Party of India
- RSS   Rashtriya Swayamsevak Sangh (National Volunteers Organization)
- VHP   Vishwa Hindu Parishad (World Hindu Confederation)

Chapter 3
- ASA   Assam State Archives
- BJP   Bharatiya Janata Party (Indian People's Party)

EFICOR	Evangelical Fellowship of India Commission on Relief
KNA	Kuki National Army
KPM	Kuki Punitive Measures
MBC	Manipur Baptist Convention
MKHC	Mizoram Kohran Hruaitute Committee (Committee of Church Leaders in Mizoram)
MNF	Mizo National Front
NSCN	National Socialist Council of Nagaland
RSS	Rashtriya Swayamsevak Sangh (National Volunteers' Association)

Chapter 4

CSIS	Center for Strategic and International Studies
FKKI	Indonesia Christian Communication Forum
NPN	National Prayer Network
NU	Nahdlatul Ulama (Revival of Ulama; Muslim scholars' organization)
PDI	Partai Demokrasi Indonesia (Indonesian Democratic Party)
PDIP	Indonesian Democratic Party of Struggle
Perti	Pergerakan Tarbijah Islamijah (Islamic Educational Movement)
PKI	Communist Party of Indonesia
PNI	Partai Nasional Indonesia (Nationalist Party)
PPP	Partai Persatuan Pembangunan (United Development Party)
SI	Serikat Islam (Islamic League)

Chapter 5

BPMNA	Breakfast Prayer Meeting of the National Assembly
CCEJ	Citizens' Coalition for Economic Justice
CCFE	Christian Committee for Fair Elections
CCPDG	Christian Coalition for Producing Democratic Government
CEM	Christian Ethics Movement
CISJD	Christian Institute for the Study of Justice and Development
GNP	Grand National Party
JPF	Justice Politics Forum
KACP	Korean National Association of Christian Pastors
KEF	Korean Evangelical Fellowship
KNCC	Korean National Council of Churches
MDP	Millennium Democratic Party
PMCDR	People's Movement Coalition for Democracy and Reunification
SNU	Seoul National University
ULDP	United Liberal Democrat Party
YMCA	Young Men's Christian Association
YWCA	Young Women's Christian Association

Chapter 6

ACDA	Alliance of Christian Development Agencies
ACTS	ATS Center for Transformation Studies
APPEND	Alliance of Philippine Partners in Enterprise Development
ATS	Asian Theological Seminary
CBCP	Catholic Bishops Conference of the Philippines
CCGG	Christian Convergence for Good Governance
CDOs	Christian development organizations
CfC	Couples for Christ (a Catholic charismatic group)
CLAP	Christian Leaders' Alliance of the Philippines
CLCP	Christian Leaders Conference on the Philippines
CTN	Christian Teachers' Network
EDSA	Epifanio de los Santos Avenue
EJR	Evangelicals for Justice and Righteousness
FEBC	Far East Broadcasting Company
FOCIG	Fellowship of Christians in Government
GPCR	God's People's Coalition for Righteousness
GRACE	Grand Alliance for Christian Education
IFP	Intercessors of the Philippines (prayer arm of PJM)
INC	Iglesia Ni Cristo
ISACC	Institute of Studies in Asian Church and Culture
IVCF	Inter-Varsity Christian Fellowship
JIL	Jesus Is Lord
JMC	Jesus Miracle Crusade
KOMPIL 2	Konsensiya ng Mamamayang Pilipino (Conscience of Filipino Citizenry)
KONFES	Konsensiya ng Febrero Siete" (Conscience of February 7)
MNT	Movement for National Transformation
NCCP	National Council of Churches in the Philippines
NCUT	National Coalition for Urban Transformation
OQC	Operation Quick Count
PCEC	Philippine Council of Evangelical Churches
PJM	Philippines for Jesus Movement
SWS	Social Weather Stations; Web site: www.sws.org.ph
TransDev	Foundation for Transformational Development
UCCP	United Church of Christ in the Philippines

Evangelical Christianity and Democracy in Asia

Evangelical Christianity and Democratic Pluralism in Asia: An Introduction

David H. Lumsdaine

The six case studies in this volume contribute to our understanding of religion and politics in Asia and the world in various ways; this introduction seeks to highlight both the importance of the individual case studies and of their common themes and implications. Each study stands alone as an independent piece of scholarship, based on detailed field research *in situ* as well as on careful historical inquiry. The volume as a whole highlights various political impacts that evangelical Christianity has had in Asia and is part of a series exploring evangelical Christianity's effects on democracy and democratization in Latin America, Africa, and Asia.[1] Taken as a whole, common themes in these case studies suggest important hypotheses concerning evangelical Christianity and democracy—which neither their authors nor I anticipated—and in particular identify a range of specific dynamics whereby evangelical Christianity may enhance political democracy, equality, and pluralism, despite frequently inauspicious conditions.

What are these possible democratizing dynamics? In the cases assembled here, first, the embrace of evangelical Christianity has often enabled poor and marginalized people to have greater prosperity, self-confidence, and civic skills and a more vital associational life and has consequently pushed societies toward more open and democratic processes. These processes have had roots in the faith content of the people involved. Second, evangelical churches have assumed a growing role in democratic transition and consolidation, which explicitly reflects theological development and maturity. Third, in countries where there are democratic institutions, evangelical participation in civic organizations and citizen formation has played a key role in strengthening democracy. In some ways, this parallels the development, just noted, of tacitly democratic processes in societies where democratic participation is not possible. Such grassroots development of democratic action, processes, and values may well be the most important way evangelicalism affects democracy, at least in the countries studied in this volume. These dynamics are discussed in more detail in the final section of this chapter, which considers the possible evangelical roots of democratic pluralism in general.

In each of these respects the processes—the democratizing dynamics—discussed by the authors of the case studies, and theorized in this chapter, are advances simply as significant hypotheses generating questions for further research, which must determine how widespread such processes are and how reliably they occur even in the countries studied, and place any dynamics borne out by further research in the context of other political dynamics and influences.

The Design of the Studies

The studies in this volume and series were designed with two objectives in mind: to provide basic empirical material concerning evangelical Christianity's political effects worldwide, and to generate useful hypotheses about causal impacts of evangelical Christianity on democracy and democratization. The role of religion in world politics is almost certain to become increasingly important in the twenty-first century (Jenkins 2002; Berger 1999; Huntington 1996; Casanova 1994; Kepel 1994). Evangelical Protestantism's often dramatic political interventions in countries as diverse as Guatemala and South Korea, and its explosive numerical expansion in Asia, Africa, and Latin America during the twentieth century (Woodberry and Shah 2004, 47–61), sometimes estimated as a tenfold expansion in the second half of the twentieth century, especially demanded a serious program of research. Although detailed empirical research in this area has increased in recent years,[2] there remains a need for further systematic comparative study of evangelical politics, especially in Asia.

The project therefore recruited scholars to conduct carefully researched, field-based, literature-informed, and historically grounded studies of contemporary evangelical Christian influences on democracy—for good or ill—throughout the global South. Seventeen scholars, mostly based in the countries studied, produced studies for Asia, Africa, and Latin America.[3]

The studies could not be comprehensive. In Korea or the Philippines, a single study might, perhaps, address most aspects of contemporary evangelicalism and politics; in China or India, this is inconceivable. Yet even in South

Korea, volumes could be written on various aspects of the topic. Thus, the chapters in this volume had to be focused, providing as much as possible an in-depth treatment of some important features as well as a reasonably accurate overview.

We agreed to treat evangelicalism mainly as an independent variable, a cause of political outcomes, providing broad historical and religious context, but focusing on *the impact* of evangelical Christianity on politics in general and on democracy in particular. However, there was no attempt to reach common conclusions or similar findings. There were sustained efforts to develop a set of case studies that would be comparable, allowing focused comparison useful for theory development.[4] Contributors were strongly encouraged to define their own topics, make their own arguments, and draw their own conclusions. We sought well-researched studies that would establish an improved empirical foundation grounded in previous literature and detailed field observation.

Yet, the volume was a team effort. Contributors met together to discuss the logic, consistency, evidence, and development of their arguments. Editors of the Latin America and Africa volumes attended some meetings of the Asia research team and vice versa. We invited scholars and religious and political leaders from Asia to comment on the drafts, and scholars and leaders from around the world to review and critique Asian, African, and Latin American studies at a conference in June 2002 to receive the broadest possible input. And, indeed, far more research material was collected than could be presented in the studies. We sought to hold the volume to a manageable length while preserving the rich, detailed observations to serve as a resource for subsequent scholarship.

The overall research design, generously funded by the Pew Foundation, intended to facilitate comparison and theory building by examining a range of cases spanning the globe. However, we could not possibly *cover* the globe with seventeen case studies. The African cases are all sub-Saharan and all but one is Anglophone. We were particularly constrained in the Asia volume, given that Asia includes many more countries, people, and (arguably) cultural diversity than any other continent. For this reason, only East, Southeast, and South Asia are represented; we have no chapters on Central and West Asia or on mainland Southeast Asia. Rather than comprehensiveness, we hoped to attain enough diversity to suggest regional variation and enough commonality to make meaningful comparison possible.

We had to sample widely without hoping for comprehensiveness in individual studies, too. India and China are vast: each is more a continent than a country, and together they comprise over a third of the human family. Two separate chapters on India look at different and geographically distant regions: the Dangs in Gujarat and northeastern India (particularly the states of Manipur, Mizoram, and Nagaland). In China, Kim Chan managed to include studies of seven different groups across the country, so that his chapter itself presents a set of comparative case studies. Nevertheless, Chan's cases do not touch on Christianity among intellectuals, a phenomenon of great interest (Aikman 2003), and most of his studies concern relatively remote rural or tribal areas. These chapters, like the volume as a whole, provide good bases for forming hypotheses rather than testing hypotheses or assessing systematically how widely they obtain.

The Distinctiveness of the Asian Context

Asia differs from the other regions of the global South. First, Christianity in general and evangelical Christianity in particular occupies a tiny minority position. Only in the Philippines and now in independent East Timor, both Roman Catholic, is Christianity a majority religion. Only in South Korea are Protestants as much as a quarter of the population.

However, Asia's Protestant minority is fast-growing and significant in absolute numbers. The 200 million Protestants in Asia today constitute only about 5.5 percent of Asia's 3.7 billion people, but this figure is more than ten times larger than Protestantism's share in 1900, which was only 0.5 percent. This entire Protestant population is largely evangelical, with much of this century's growth occurring among burgeoning pentecostal and charismatic churches, treated here as a subset of evangelical Protestants.[5] The Asian evangelical Protestant population, then, may well be larger than the population of Brazil, Pakistan, or Russia.[6]

Asia also differs from Latin America and sub-Saharan Africa in the level of organized state and societal opposition to Christianity. In Latin America, constitutional and legal restrictions on Protestant churches and activities were gradually removed in recent decades and all but disappeared in the 1990s (Sigmund 1999). In sub-Saharan Africa, systematic repression of Christianity is the exception, not the rule, though where it exists—in the Sudan and northern Nigeria, for example—it is significant and egregious (An-Na'im 1999). In contrast, concern about violent repercussions, specifically about the possibility of physical violence affecting a study's author or its subjects, was a factor in four of the six case studies in this volume. In these cases, possible violence against Christians or religiously linked armed conflict affecting Christians there, restricted field observations, or required authors to mask informants' identities and restrict some information lest publication provoke attacks on Christians in the areas studied.

China, India, and Indonesia have all witnessed strong societal opposition to Christianity and to those adopting it. In China (perhaps decreasingly) and in India and Indonesia (perhaps increasingly), state power is used at least in some areas to restrict or punish Christian belief, even where it poses no direct challenge or threat to the state or public order. Systematic opposition to Christianity is not unique to Asia, but it may be more intense, more pervasive, and more diverse (taking communist, Hindu, Buddhist, and Islamic forms) there than elsewhere.

Defining Evangelicalism and Democracy

The word "evangelicalism" is used in a wide variety of ways. British Anglicans use the term to refer to the kind of liturgy that is celebrated on Sunday. Many elites in the United States use the term as a polite substitute for "fundamentalism" and consider it an unreasonable, militant, backward, and uneducated Protestantism (C. Smith 1998, 2000; Stark 2001, 250–256). In some Asian countries, the term refers to any churches that adhere to traditional Protestant faith (sometimes including "charismatic" churches).

Four defining characteristics set out by Bebbington (1989) are standard in many sociological studies. Freston (2001, 2) employs Bebbington's definition, and the volumes in this series do likewise. Bebbington defines evangelicalism as a form of Christianity that makes the cross of Christ central (crucicentrism), places strong emphasis on the authority of the Bible and on the importance of Bible reading and study (biblicism), insists that being a Christian requires a substantial and personal change of life (conversionism), and seeks to propagate the Christian faith to others in various forms of outreach (activism).[7] Although this definition need not exclude Roman Catholicism and Eastern Orthodoxy, most, including Bebbington, implicitly assume that it refers to Protestant Christianity; these volumes adhere to that convention. Sensitivity to context further commends this approach in the set of countries being studied in the project. In historically Catholic countries, such as the Philippines and Latin America, the term *evangélico* signifies Protestant, and most evangelicals draw a strong (sometimes invidious) definitional distinction, referring to coreligionists as Christians or evangelicals and to Roman Catholics as Catholics.

The term "democracy" is used far more widely than evangelical and with at least as much diversity. Studies of democratization often follow the definition of Robert Dahl's (1971) *Polyarchy: Participation and Opposition*, making periodic elections that determine effective national political authority the criterion. Dahl coined the word "polyarchy" to denote democracy in this restricted electoral and procedural sense. Dahl, and students of democratic transition and consolidation (e.g., Linz and Stepan 1996) who have built on Dahl's definition (often terming it "democracy" for sound research purposes), did not ignore other dimensions of democracy, such as liberty, equality, and civic association, but treat these other elements as causal factors that contribute to the consolidation and deepening of democracy.

Important lines of research about what makes democracies function effectively, from Gabriel Almond and Sidney Verba's (1963) *Civic Culture* through the recent work of Robert Putnam,[8] have also emphasized the democratizing role of various kinds of civic association, citizen involvement, and individual perceptions of civic efficacy and empowerment—lines of thinking that reflect the tradition of Tocqueville (1840)[9] or older traditions emphasizing republican virtue. These approaches reflect a desire to pinpoint the causal sequences involved in democratization and to craft well-defined and measurable variables to facilitate comparative research.

This volume's research purposes are different. Rather than considering general theories of democratization and its causes, the chapters aim to explore the range of democracy-enhancing effects that evangelical Christianity can have at diverse levels of analysis and in widely differing circumstances. Several studies address situations where current political or social contexts preclude effective electoral involvement, or situations where evangelicals form a minute minority amid populations indifferent or hostile to Christianity. Where circumstances discourage direct or effective electoral involvement by evangelicals, the possibility that evangelical Christianity's beliefs, content, or organizational form exert *indirect* democratizing effects becomes more important. Therefore, rather than select any single indicator of democracy, this volume considers various social and political domains in which evangelicalism might enhance democratic values and processes.

For example, various chapters look at the evangelical contributions to democratic accountability, liberty, dignity of the person, civility, equality, civil society, deliberation, and the like:

- Democratic *accountability* includes making public decisions lawful, transparent, and subject to scrutiny, whether through the selection of officeholders by elections or otherwise.
- *Liberty* includes the freedom to express opinions and act freely, subject to established laws that do not unduly restrict choices, particularly in matters of conscience.
- The *dignity of the person* refers to the basic human rights of liberty and security of the person against the arbitrary or intrusive exercise of state (or private) power and to the notion that respect and dignity are to be accorded to persons whatever their background and status.
- *Civility* refers to processes and norms of interaction and contention that are nonviolent, nonmanipulative, and generally involve "bridging social capital" as well as "bonding capital" (Putnam 2000), those that foster social unity and cooperation, particularly between ethnically or religiously different groups.
- *Equality* signifies greater access to resources by relatively marginalized groups, including respect, effective voice, and capacities enabling

them to be relatively secure, independent, and better off economically. This includes formal equality before the law, but also the broad availability of the means of meaningfully participating in society—especially for minorities in multicultural contexts—and ways of overcoming economic and social marginality.
- The idea of *civil society* here includes all areas of associational life that are spontaneous and unsupervised either by government or profit-making firms. The development of strong associational life is closely allied to the strengthening of effective citizenship and citizen participation, including civic awareness and involvement and responsible behavior as a member of the community.
- Finally, *deliberation* signifies the collective capacity of members of a group to question, debate, and engage in rational consideration of community problems.

Thinking of democracy in terms of such contributory and constituent values and practices suggests how ideas and practices arising from evangelical Protestantism could play a democratizing role even in contexts where electoral input and direct political participation are insignificant, ineffective, or absent from the country's political framework.

The Range of Cases in the Asia Volume

One might study the democratic impact of evangelical Christianity, or of any religious or social movement, in two different ways. One way focuses on local or grassroots contexts, primarily involving local issues, churches, and believers. Such situations are often implicitly rather than explicitly political. This approach might be thought of as focusing on the "microstructure" of politics and democracy. At the other pole are studies where the research is focused on national or regional situations that are more directly and explicitly political, sometimes called "high politics." This approach might be thought of as focusing on the "macrostructure" of politics and democracy.

The chapters by Sushil Aaron and Kim-Kwong Chan essentially adopt the first, microstructural or micropolitical, approach; those by David Lim and Young-gi Hong largely adopt the second, macrostructural or macropolitical, approach. Chapters by Sujatha Fernandes and Bambang Budijanto lie somewhere in between. The grassroots focus and the implicitly political predominate in Aaron's study of the Dangs region in Gujarat as well as in most of Chan's Chinese cases. These two studies have an ethnographic character and tend to focus on the effects of evangelical Christianity on individuals or small groups. Fernandes's study of northeast India and Budijanto's study of Surakarta in Indonesia deal with regional politics. Explicit political efforts are discussed, but evangelical Christianity is more concerned with liberty and the development of civil society. Lim's study of the Philippines and Hong's study of Korea chiefly concern national-level politics and include interviews with past presidents of those countries, Fidel Ramos and Kim Young-Sam, who were Protestants and arguably evangelicals.

The rapid spread of evangelicalism in Asia, Africa, and Latin America in recent decades has been predominantly a locally transmitted, grassroots phenomenon (Sanneh 2003; Walls 1996). In the six studies in this volume on Asia, the first and most important effect of evangelical Christianity on democracy—and on the polity, the economy, and society in general—occurred at the grassroots level. This grassroots effect involved both the strengthening of individuals' initiative and agency (a Weberian effect) and also the strengthening of societies' associational life (a Tocquevillian effect). Although this theme is echoed in different ways in the chapters on northeast India, Indonesia, South Korea, and the Philippines, it is particularly salient in the chapters on China and Gujarat, India, which focus on Christianity at a local, small-scale level.

Kim-Kwong Chan's Study of China

Chan's China chapter comprises seven small case studies of evangelical communities throughout the country. This approach helps capture the character of the small church groups that have spread throughout China, despite official disapproval. Chan's local focus on the lives of ordinary individuals illuminates how evangelicalism spreads to remote and unexpected locations and also its democratizing impact on the microstructure of Chinese society.

Political action, unless directed by the state and Communist Party, is generally forbidden. Even nonregistered, nonpolitical groups of three or more people are forbidden. Yet evangelical Christian commitment acts as an energetic and autonomous force locally, often spreading spontaneously from person to person. Chan aptly dubs this reproduction and diffusion, and the resulting creation of local and autonomous social space, the "leaven effect."

Christianity and church life in some instances helped people to overcome pervasive local social ills: alcohol and drug abuse, family problems and infidelity, and costly rituals that debilitate local economies. Communities sometimes arise that question state practices constraining worship or proclamation of the Christian message. Civic involvement by ordinary citizens often gradually pushes the state toward a more open, responsive posture. This ongoing process of small-scale change moves the micropolitical structure of post-totalitarian China toward a greater popular voice and increased political accountability.

In Fugong County and Baipidezai, tribal peoples were enmeshed in dysfunctional cultural and economic patterns; embracing Christianity seems to have helped them overcome these. To some extent, intoxication and animal sacrifices subside, lifestyles become more frugal, literacy spreads, crime decreases, marriages improve, and, perhaps the main attraction initially, these "Weberianized" people become noticeably more prosperous.

Changed individual and collective behavior reflects a changed sense of identity that, in turn, arises from a changed cosmic picture. As belief in a loving God's personal care, often initially demonstrated by perceived healings, replaces belief in malignant spiritual forces that need placation, people find encouragement to change from destructive to constructive habits, acquire new skills, enhance individual prosperity and happiness, and support community organization in the church. Rapid, spontaneous diffusion of beliefs may occur where changes of mind-set and practice sustain new ways of life that people find more satisfactory but otherwise difficult to achieve.

The growth of grassroots evangelical groups sometimes leads directly to political influence. In Baipidezai and surrounding areas the improved prosperity, relative freedom from addictions, and decreased crime attributed to Christian activity have brought favorable notice even among government and Communist Party circles. Church networks here and in Fugong County are notably influential, but Chan cautions that the extent of the evangelical community's influence in these ethnic enclaves is very atypical.

These effects are arguably democratizing in at least three ways. First, they represent the spread of skills, literacy, personal efficacy, and greater prosperity to poor and marginalized peoples. Second, they foster organizational and leadership skills within the villages. Third, they promote the development of civil society structures and communities independent of the Communist Party and government—structures and communities that include links to Christians in other villages and even beyond the tribal area.

Yangshan and Qingyuan Provinces, remote rural areas with ethnic Han populations, also display autonomous diffusion of evangelical Christianity. Chance personal encounters led to the rapid formation of a church in Yangshan and nearby areas. Desire for healing and inner peace attracted people to the church, whose structures and activities quickly expanded to include Bible studies, an organization to aid the poor, and visits to elderly care hostels. Here evangelical groups "earned respect in their communities" but received official disapproval and harassment. They first met secretly, but then, with remarkable vigor, pressed officialdom for recognition. According to Chan, their rapid growth forced them "to assert their position as a new type of social organization, hitherto nonexistent, as part of the local community fabric...in a traditional static society," thus generating social and political changes that may be "the beginning of a pluralistic society initiated from below" that pushes the state to obey its own laws requiring "freedom of religious belief."

Though different in sociological and political detail, similar patterns emerge in the nonregistered "dissenting community" started by Madame Yang and her brother: spontaneous, person-to-person diffusion of evangelical beliefs and resulting pressure for greater political pluralism. Even the cases of the Hebei Christian Council and the Jiangxi Bible School, which concern long-standing organizations registered with the government, exemplify a similar organizational vitality generating social and political pressure "from below." In Hebei, for example, evangelical Protestants developed working relationships with Catholics and Buddhists to lobby for changes in government regulation of religious expression, overcoming determined opposition from local Communist Party cadres.

Sushil Aaron's Study of Gujarat, India

Like most of the sixty-seven million tribal peoples, or *adivasis*, in India, *adivasis* in the forested Dangs region of the state of Gujarat are extremely poor, uneducated, and socially marginalized. Aaron recounts how Gujarat Christian Workers from southern India lived among Dangi tribals for decades and helped them overcome these handicaps, which is crucial for tribal peoples to enjoy effective democracy and political voice in India.[10]

Because he focuses on a small group of subaltern people in a remote forested area, tracing the history of both Dangis and the Gujarat Christian Workers to identify the political effects of Christian belief, Aaron produced the most detailed ethnographic account in all of the Evangelicalism and Democracy Project volumes. His chapter thus illuminates the complex interrelationship between the forces that led the Dangis to embrace evangelical Christianity, the resulting transformation in their lives as individuals, the social space Dangis occupy, and the larger local, regional, provincial, and national contexts in which these dynamics occur.

Dangi tribals have been isolated from wider Indian society for centuries, withdrawing into small forest preserves. However, those preserves steadily diminished as Britain logged the area to provide timber and later Indian authorities (in the name of conservation) and commercial logging interests continued to expropriate forest lands. Dangis have been largely illiterate, like most tribal peoples in India, and government schools are distant, poorly staffed, and taught in Gujarati, not local languages. The *adivasis* have lacked basic knowledge, such as how to dress wounds or use modern means of transport, and are impoverished and indebted. Not surprisingly under such depressed conditions, alcoholism is widespread. *Adivasis* sell produce from the forest to outsiders who exploit their poverty and limited facility with arithmetic. *Shahukars*, or moneylenders, keep them in permanent debt. Women fear sexual exploitation by outsiders. In general, *adivasis* fear a larger society that often scorns and insults them.

The people of the Dangs perceive the spiritual world as menacing and powerful, mirroring their social and material situation. They fear and seek to placate evil spirits. Local healers and power brokers accuse elderly widows and other women of witchcraft and torture and humiliate them to exorcise illnesses. The *shahukars* are believed to have supernatural powers: the moneylender is a prominent god in some places. The Dangis' spiritual world, like their social world, is one in which they are fearful, submissive, powerless, exploited, and despised.

Those Dangis who embrace Christianity experience some liberation from this subjugated status. In the process of bringing evangelical Christianity to the Dangs, Christian workers have brought literacy instruction in Dangi languages, health information, agricultural instruction, legal assistance, and access to further schooling. In so doing, they have arguably helped defend the *adivasis'* interests as well as strengthen their identity and dignity. The Christian workers also assist *adivasis* in their dealings with outside merchants, forest officials, and police officers, both incident by incident and through instruction in civil procedures such as filing appeals, requests, and reports. The Gujarat Christian Workers have well-established relationships with Dangi peoples and have gained their trust. They thus provide a pattern or example of relations with outsiders in which the Dangis are not fearful or subordinated. Typically, however, the Dangis embrace Christianity only when someone is believed to have been healed from illness because of Christians' prayers. Such "power encounters" demonstrate the power of the Christian God over evil spirits. Similarly, family and friends sometimes embrace Christianity when a man is "delivered" from alcoholism.

These healings simultaneously change Dangi religious views and transform their picture of the interrelated social, material, and spiritual worlds in which they live. Christian prayers for healing are perceived as efficacious yet are not used to extract payments, unlike the prayers of local shamans. All believers are able to speak directly to the supreme yet loving God and maker of all things. The power encounter that seems to demonstrate the reality of this God and the accompanying worldview thus results in an empowering redefinition of the self in a reimagined cosmos. In *this* cosmos, the Dangi believer, rather than being despised and powerless at the bottom of interlinked material, social, and spiritual hierarchies, is a child of God equal in dignity to any other. This revised understanding of the self and the social and spiritual cosmos is experienced as liberating at various levels.

The effects of evangelical faith in energizing and liberating individual and group life is a matter not only of building something up but also of tearing something down. For the Dangis, embracing evangelical faith involves overcoming the deadening, long-accumulated influence of oppressive, constraining, and indeed antidemocratic outlooks and customs. Evangelical Christianity here seems to generate effective resistance to certain patterns and active forms of subordination and oppression. This dynamic is profoundly democratic in its implications. First, it confers greater equality and dignity on very poor and disempowered peoples. Second, it begins to build up a culture of discussion, deliberation, and questioning that in time independently identifies and criticizes the abuses of the larger society, sometimes leading to legal challenges and increasingly to first steps toward more effective representation in the political system.

It is vital to see how changed cosmological beliefs figure in this process. Initially, apparently efficacious prayers for healing attract Dangis to Christian belief. Dangi consciousness long feared malign spiritual forces that require costly and painful propitiation, as was true also in several cases Chan studied. A God who loves ordinary people and listens to their prayers, requiring no recompense, became real to many Dangis through prayers for physical healing. These prayers are crucial in changing Dangi conceptions of their worth and place in society. This leads to a third important observation that recurs in various studies in this book: socially liberating and politically democratizing effects of evangelicalism are closely linked with its specifically religious and doctrinal content.

Aaron's study also introduces another theme that emerges in many of the Asian case studies: the relationship between groups of believers and dominant religious or national state power. This theme is picked up strongly in Fernandes's study of northeast India.

Sujatha Fernandes's Study of Northeast India

Fernandes's study of northeast India is similar to Aaron's study and some of Chan's studies in that the Christians she examines are tribal peoples. However, it is unlike any of the other studies in the Asia volume, with the exception of Chan's study of Fugong County, in that evangelical Protestants are locally a majority. Northeast India is largely remote hill country connected to the rest of India only by a narrow isthmus. Tribal peoples predominate, and various tribal groupings extend into contiguous areas of Myanmar, Thailand, and China. Many of these tribal peoples have become predominantly Christian. Some northeast Indian states also have lower plains areas, largely settled by Hindus, who are ethnically and religiously distinct from the tribal groups.

However, despite the local majority or near majority of tribal groups, and of Christians, the Northeast has serious political strife of two kinds. First, the area is riven with tribal rivalries, which antedate the arrival of the British but which have been exacerbated by British divide-and-rule strategies earlier and by the central Indian state of today. Second, armed, mutually hostile, hostage-taking liberation fronts, often proclaiming themselves Christian, contest the rule of the Indian government, seeking some independence or autonomy. (Together with absence of roads and other facilities, this makes travel in the region difficult and dangerous: Fernandes was at times unable to travel there.) The region perceives India's central government largely as a hostile outside force, in part because Delhi's policies have neglected and exploited the region, perpetuating its backwardness.

Fernandes seeks to understand how the current situation perpetuates patterns going back to the nineteenth century and asks what role the church plays in resolving conflict, particularly in overcoming disunity and violence, and also why such efforts have not succeeded. The indigenous church leaders in the Northeast have worked to reconcile estranged groups such as the Kukis and Nagas, have spoken out against violence, and have, to an extent, sought to keep the region from violent insurgencies and to keep politics honest, constructive, and well informed. Yet Fernandes also faults the churches in the northeastern states for failure to overcome the violence and division and for sometimes allowing itself to be dragged into the rhetoric of ethnic differences.

In exploring these difficulties, Fernandes touches on a topic that arises in the discussion of each of the authors: namely, that evangelicalism generates bridging as well as bonding social capital. Lim notes cooperation between Protestants and Catholics; Chan shows how Christians initiated cooperation with Buddhists to change state policy; Fernandes and Aaron note church activities generating cooperation that is otherwise rare among different tribes and villages of *adivasis*; and Hong's and Budijanto's chapters make an important point of other examples, as discussed below. Thus, although the associations formed in churches serve as schools and networks for democracy, many of the chapters in this volume also suggest that they cross ethnic and religious borders, which is important for democracy, especially in complex, plural societies. Yet Fernandes's central concern is to understand the failures and limitations of such bridging potential among the churches, for these efforts have not overcome violence and ethnic division. Why?

Fernandes identifies several reasons. Churches are, in part, fragmented into various denominations and disunited by local linguistic or tribal groupings. Historic patterns of exploitation are also a source of the problem. She traces the historical legacy of central state exploitation and neglect and of divide-and-rule policies going back over a century that created, or greatly exacerbated, tribal divisions and tensions.

In the end, however, Fernandes seems to locate the difficulties in resource shortages that arise from failures of the Indian central state to accord the region its due, marginalizing it politically, spiritually, and technically through a lack of adequate material resources. The resulting and ongoing scarcities in the region inevitably lead to harsh competition for scarce goods. Further, the rise and increasing influence of an aggressively Hindu nationalist movement alienates the Christian tribal peoples of the Northeast and contributes to hostility between insurgent groups and the central Indian state.

Although the church has played a valuable role as peacemaker, its effectiveness has been limited, Fernandes argues, partly because it has failed to confront abuses, neglects, and inequities of central Indian government policies toward tribal peoples in the area. She concludes that church will be able to overcome the violence and division and will unite tribals in the Northeast in seeking their goals more peacefully and effectively only if it speaks out more clearly against abuses of the central government. Unless the churches stand firmly as advocates for regional justice in larger terms, their effectiveness in quelling insurgencies and destructive intergroup competition will be limited at best.

The chapters on Indonesia, Korea, and the Philippines explore the more direct democratizing effects of evangelicalism in the national political context. In all these cases, the authors identify major shifts in evangelical practice and thinking, shifts to a more politically involved stance at the national level and to political involvement that is more principled and less *ad hoc*, gradually finding a grounding both in democratic ideals and in theological concepts.

Bambang Budijanto's Study of Indonesia

In the key Surakarta region of Indonesia, Budijanto shows how churches that historically had avoided the public realm have increasingly changed their thinking and practice. Churches and their leaders, especially younger leaders, in Surakarta have become more socially and politically involved, giving increasing attention to helping the needy in their communities, to building positive links with other religious groups, and to championing pluralism and human rights. Many pastors and other leaders now participate in local civic forums where local issues of concern are discussed among Islamic, Hindu, Catholic, Protestant, and other leaders. These civic forums have been effective in keeping Surakarta calm at potentially explosive moments. Although the process of evangelical involvement in politics still has far to go, it clearly seems to be moving toward more universal, principled bases, rather than a narrow pursuit of church interests. These changes were partly a response to circumstances: the economic crises starting in 1997, riots, persecution of Christians in other parts of Indonesia, and the rise of radical Islam. However, they also reflect theological reflection and maturation, the influence of worldwide evangelical movements emphasizing social justice, and the public discussions of democracy that have taken place in Indonesia in recent years.

In examining pastors in culturally and politically central Surakarta, and the reasons for their responses to the ongoing social, political, and economic upheavals of the past several years, Budijanto, like Chan and Aaron, gives a structured look at how beliefs evolve and the part religious reasoning plays in this process. After detailing the history of the region from published sources, he analyzes the reflections that pastors and senior church leaders in the Surakarta region offered on two occasions in answer to a detailed questionnaire that also encouraged open-ended responses. This method permits him to look in systematic detail at evangelical evolution in response to Indonesia's recent tumultuous political transformation, including progress toward democracy.

Indonesian Protestantism has undergone substantial change in its relation to the political sphere, not so much through any kind of direct participation in electoral politics as through the gradual development of a broader vision of social and political responsibility. Budijanto traces movement from a theology—largely inherited from the Dutch and reinforced by a long authoritarian era—that suggested churches should steer clear of civic involvement altogether to a theology that sees value in civic engagement as one way Christians live out their faith. That theological shift is played out directly in church involvements. Civic engagement does not take the form of churches actively making political endorsements or engaging in partisan activity. But there is increasing emphasis among evangelical churches on community service, on learning about civic affairs, and on forming links with leaders from other religious traditions as part of building a stronger civil society.

This shift reflects a variety of factors: the country's increasing political openness after the fall of Soeharto; the accession of younger pastors to the ministry; the widespread suffering arising from the country's long-standing economic and civic crises; the influence of theology from international evangelical groups that have highlighted the social implications of the gospel; and increasing activity by radical Islamist groups. Interestingly, these changes, linked to scriptural reflection and theology, lead pastors to consider politics and political contacts in wider social contexts: less in terms of the benefit they might bring to a local church, or even to evangelicals generally, and more in terms of a broad, principled, civic vision. That change does not represent a diminution of evangelical particularity or missionary zeal, which appear unabated in the churches Budijanto studied. Rather, it represents a maturing view of Christian civic responsibility, based on theological reasoning in the light of current experience and worldwide fellowship, which led to broader and more principled civic involvement, which in turn reinforced that growing maturity.

Similar evolutions, though in response to different sets of political circumstances, occurred over a period of about twenty years both in the Philippines, as Lim shows, and in Korea, as Hong shows. These studies are also consistent in showing increased evangelical involvement in social and political affairs. These two studies take as their primary focus politics at a national level. Each considers a transition to democracy in the mid-1980s and the role evangelicals played; each considers the role of religion in the tenure of a distinctly Protestant and arguably evangelical president; and each considers evangelical voting behavior and political endorsements, which, the authors conclude, accomplish little. As Lim considers the role of religion in People Power events, he presents a sharp debate among evangelicals, which leads, in his analysis, to greater political maturity that limits direct religious involvement in politics and gives increased attention to basic principles and fair electoral processes.

But what is most striking is that both Hong and Lim, studying countries where the direct evangelical political participation has been considerable, conclude that the most important long-term contribution of evangelicalism to democracy lies not in direct political involvement but in members' civic awareness and activity and in church teaching that strengthens moral character and shapes responsible citizens—the same mechanisms that predominate in other chapters!

Yong-gi Hong's Study of South Korea

After reviewing the history of religious involvement in Korean politics, Hong shows the wide range of evangelical involvement in the process of Korean democratization from 1987 onward. Hong interviewed former evangelical president Kim Young-Sam and studied evangelical electoral involvement. He examines the extensive involvement of Christians in the legislature and scrutinizes religious influence on voting behavior. Hong finds each of these to be important for understanding Korean evangelicalism. Nevertheless, what he finds most important and effective in recent Christian contributions to democracy is the effort to develop civic organizations that push society toward more equitable policies and fairer elections and that provide guidance on issues of public concern. Christians in Korea have often been in the forefront of organizing such movements, even when the movements have not had a specifically religious character, and have pioneered models for such involvement.

Hong particularly emphasizes the Kim Young-Sam presidency in discussing evangelical participation in democracy. Yet, he concludes that the widespread participation of evangelicals in civil society is the most significant evangelical contribution to deeper democratization in Korea. The essential weaknesses of Korean democracy are found not in any deficiency in the formal machinery of democracy but in the absence of a constructive and dynamic culture of politics and political engagement. Consequently, Korean politics tends to be organized around personalities and regional affiliations more than ideas and policies and constantly sinks into unconstructive and vicious contention. The poorly developed party system affords few resources for effectively institutionalizing any reforms that are made and often renders them ineffectual.

In this situation, Hong argues that evangelicals have been in the forefront of developing a more effective response through the creation of nongovernmental organizations (NGOs) and citizen-awareness movements. In addition, such civic initiatives, often organized by evangelicals, helped student and radical movements from the era of the struggle against authoritarian rule find moderate, constructive outlets for their energies. Some Christian NGOs have focused on improving the political awareness, good citizenship, and social responsibility of Christians in particular. However, the most prominent NGOs, though initially organized by Christians and marked by strong ongoing Christian involvement, do not have a specifically religious focus, a choice that reflects a faith-based sense of calling to serve the society at large by uniting around common civic concerns.

David Lim's Study of the Philippines

Analyzing evolving evangelical involvement in politics in the overall Philippines context, in which Fidel Ramos, a Protestant, served as an evangelically oriented and very successful Protestant president in an overwhelmingly Roman Catholic country, Lim likewise concludes that evangelical efforts to foster civil society have been evangelicalism's most important contribution to Filipino democracy and democratization. Lim includes in this category the building up of moral and social capital in the daily lives of believers and churches—the phenomenon that, in different circumstances, Chan emphasizes in China. In addition, Lim argues that the transformational impact of evangelicalism on individual and associational life depends partly on a theology that thinks through the gospel's implications for society and politics. This parallels observations made by Budijanto and Hong, who also note a similar evolution of theological reflection among evangelicals and argue for the importance of grounding coherent social and political action in sound theological reflection.

After surveying the historical role of religion in Filipino politics, Lim examines factors that provoked increasing Catholic and Protestant opposition to Marcos's kleptocratic authoritarian rule and closely analyzes the People Power events that were pivotal in toppling Marcos and initiating a democratic era. Based on impressive documentation, detailed interviews with most of the principals, and long-term personal observation, Lim compares the three major and several minor People Power events in the Philippines and the ways these exemplify distinctive strengths and weaknesses of the country's politics.

Lim assembles detailed data on voting patterns in the succeeding decades and examines how various evangelical political leaders have exercised their roles, especially considering the presidency of Fidel Ramos, an arguably evangelical Protestant. Lim interviewed Ramos and others to understand evangelical influences on the Ramos presidency, and he critically surveys a wide swath of evangelical leaders who have concerned themselves with politics over the past couple of decades. Although that involvement has not been uniformly constructive, in Lim's view, it has matured politically, evolving from a tradition of Christian indifference to politics (which was willing to take opportunistic advantage of political connections, where possible) through irresponsible policies of endorsement by individual evangelical leaders (based largely on candidates' religious views) to an increasing emphasis on careful reflection on political principles, civic concerns, and constructive discussion and evaluation of political goals.

Lim examines direct political involvement by evangelicals in detail and considers it of some importance. Nevertheless, he concludes that the role of evangelical faith in building civil society is more consequential to Philippine democracy than such direct political involvement. His characteristically thorough descriptive analysis of how evangelicalism has, in fact, fostered civil society in the Philippines suggests that evangelical contributions to civil society are in general better able to improve the quality of society and democracy.

Assessing Democratic Effects of Evangelical Christianity

Understanding whether and how evangelical Christianity strengthens or weakens democracy under various circumstances is an important task in its own right. It is also important for understanding the various roles religious beliefs and commitment can play in society, and for crafting religious freedom and civic peace on a worldwide basis.

Much contemporary evidence suggests considerable reawakening and rekindling of religion. Particularly in the global South, private religious devotion and public religious expression are on the increase (Moghadam 2003).[11] This includes the appearance of a more assertive Islam, a resurgent Hinduism, a more politically engaged Buddhism, and an expanding evangelical Christianity.

Since the seventeenth century at least, both pundits and political philosophers such as Thomas Hobbes ([1651] 1996), John Locke ([1689] 1975), and David Hume ([1741–1742] 1994) have inveighed against religious "enthusiasm," fearing the social and political consequences of unregulated, powerful, and potentially explosive religion. Academics and the popular press today decry what is often indiscriminately characterized as "fundamentalism" or "strong religion" as a potential source of intolerance and conflict worldwide (Almond, Appleby, and Sivan, 2003; Marty and Appleby, 1991, 1993a, 1993b, 1994, 1995). It is sometimes thought that resurgent religion is inherently combustible material that fuels both Western culture wars and a global clash of civilizations (Kepel 1994, Huntington 1993, 1996).

Does recrudescence of popular religious zeal necessarily cause social instability and a declining will and capacity for rational and tolerant politics? What are the logical and empirical bases for such a view?

Classic social theorists such as Tocqueville (1840) and Weber (1910), and more recent analysts such as Seymour Lipset (1994), David Martin (1999), and Michael Walzer (1965), have suggested that various forms of religiosity, and popular Protestantism in particular, have historically undergirded industry, frugality, rationality, liberty, equality, and democratization. Studies of American history suggest a close relationship between the periodic revival or "awakening" of Protestantism and democratic political activism and reform (Noll 1990; Huntington 1981, 130–166; Greene and McLoughlin 1977; Stout 1977, 519–541; Heimert 1966). Moreover, contemporary research has consistently shown a worldwide connection between Protestantism and the establishment of stable liberal democracy (Woodberry and Shah 2004, 47–61; Woodberry 2004). Is it possible that increases and awakenings of devout sentiment may, under some circumstances, help generate political societies that are more rather than less civil, tolerant, and democratic?

Chapters in this volume repeatedly identify processes and dynamics that show how evangelical Protestantism might sometimes have systematic effects—closely linked to its structure of beliefs—that promote democracy both at local and national levels. Despite variation, the separate Asian studies form a composite picture that suggests that evangelical Christianity can at times foster democratic values and practices at various social levels. Many of the themes noted here are also present in the Africa and Latin America volumes. In particular, the possibility that evangelical Christianity tends to promote equality by emphasizing the dignity of all persons and that it functions as an informal school of democracy by educating its adherents into a democratic ethos is considered in different forms in all three volumes. Of course, the impact of belief structures operates through various causal mechanisms, especially through organizational structures characteristic of evangelical churches, through the displacement or weakening of antidemocratic beliefs and practices, and generally through the strengthened efficacy of individual and associational life, particularly at a local or small scale. In the final section of this chapter, I detail further how the studies in this volume support these conclusions.

But first it is necessary to grapple with the fact that many readers will consider such contentions implausible a priori, for at least three reasons. Some might doubt that religious traditions, particularly through their religious content, could directly yield any political and economic effects at all. Others might suppose that religious conviction is the inherent or probable nemesis of tolerant, pluralistic, and democratic civic life. Yet others might express general skepticism that any ideas and ideals can effectively shape politics, arguing that power and interests, not beliefs, rule the harsh world of social and political competition. It will be useful to consider these objections to see whether the emphases and findings of this volume should bear an extra burden of proof.

Evangelical Political Effects?

The proposition that religion in general and Protestantism in particular can have important social effects is not novel. Both Weber (1910) and Tawney

(1926) argued that Protestantism has strong economic effects, making families more effective in business enterprise and capital accumulation. Weber argued that Protestantism tended to generate ways of life that were thrifty, hardworking, family-oriented, and conducive to the intergenerational accumulation of resources. Almost a century after *The Protestant Ethic and the Spirit of Capitalism*, scholars such as David Martin, Bernice Martin, Peter Berger, Lawrence Harrison, and Robert Woodberry advance neo-Weberian views that the spread of Protestantism (though today in evangelical rather than classical Calvinist form) continues to produce social effects—thrift, hard work, stronger families and communities, more male self-discipline, greater literacy and text orientation, and reduced alcoholism—that favor economic betterment.

These same social and cultural effects might also be expected to favor democratic citizenship, participation, and consolidation, both because they improve the economic lot of marginalized individuals and groups and because of directly civic and political dynamics. One could also argue that the evangelical emphasis on sacrifice (crucicentrism), on moral improvement and discipline (conversionism), on the orientation of life around a text (biblicism), and on a purposive and active life involving religious outreach (activism)—all of which Bebbington and Freston identify as central and characteristic features of evangelicalism—may provide a logical basis for expecting such effects. These effects are democratic in the sense that they help generate a class of independent persons and families with strength of conviction, purpose, and stable resources, not unlike the class of small independent farmers Jefferson thought necessary to the maintenance of democratic polity and republican self-government. Moreover, these characteristics may conduce, at least to some degree, to the establishment of networks of association and reciprocal trust starting with church networks, which provide the microstructures underlying an effective democratic polity.

They may also help explain why other cultures based on revered texts that emphasize purposiveness, sobriety, industry, family, and devotion to the texts themselves—Confucian cultures, for instance—seem to be relatively successful in establishing strong communities of prosperous and effective families and individuals. However, evangelical outreach—spreading Christian belief by means of personal persuasion and appropriation—can carry such social and cultural effects even to isolated and marginalized peoples and may therefore help make otherwise hierarchical and stratified societies more egalitarian, inclusive, and democratic.

Evangelical Protestantism has also tended to generate the kind of associational life, or "civil society," which, at least since Tocqueville, has been considered conducive to democratic politics. Tocqueville argued that a vital associational life lay at the roots of effective and enduring democracy. Later theories and empirical studies of democracy and of democratization confirm that strong associational life or civil society, including social networks of trust and cooperation, are important to a well-working democratic polity (Putnam, Leonardi, and Nanetti 1993). Other historical studies have located the genesis of democratic theory and practice in Protestant theology and ecclesiology in early modern Europe (Walzer 1965), and some contemporary studies have identified evangelical Protestant missionary activity as a crucial factor in generating democratic polities in lands of colonial settlement and in generating opposition to exploitive practices such as slavery (Woodberry 2004).

Thus, there is little basis for ruling out *a priori* the democratic possibilities of evangelical Protestantism. Of course, none of these authors are arguing that there is a necessary or universal causal relationship between evangelicalism and democracy, nor does this chapter. Rather, studies in this volume point to consistent signs that, in diverse parts of Asia, evangelical beliefs and practices *can* generate associational and individual effects of a democratizing nature.

Evangelical Protestantism is not necessarily unique in this respect. One might well suppose that in Asian contexts, other religious or cultural forms that stress family, discipline, and study may generate similar Weberian effects. Nothing here suggests that only Protestantism can yield democratic or entrepreneurial social dynamics; this book does not compare different religious traditions and could not possibly yield such conclusions. Rather, in clarifying whether and how evangelical Christianity may generate such effects under certain conditions, the volume invites wider inquiry into how various religious sources and traditions might nourish the democratic and tolerant conduct of public affairs under the proper conditions.[12]

Strong Religion and Intolerance?

A further cause of initial skepticism in many readers' minds might be the presumption that "strong" religious or metaphysical convictions as such threaten civic tolerance, pluralism, and peace (Almond, Appleby, and Sivan 2003; Marty and Appleby 1991, 1993a, 1993b, 1994, 1995). The modern journalistic tendency to suppose that religious convictions breed intolerance is bolstered by the unscholarly and indiscriminate use of the word "fundamentalism." All too commonly, the word is used, by scholars as well as journalists, in ways that carelessly conflate fanaticism, strong religious conviction, adherence to historic and orthodox doctrinal formulations, and religious nationalism. Also, the word is often used without much distinction as to which beliefs or activities are included and which excluded. With little theoretical consistency or attempt to differentiate among distinct phenomena, the idea of fundamentalism is confidently and prejudicially used in ways that lump very disparate actors such as *mujahideen* insurgents, religiously motivated terrorists, Hindu nationalists, and American antigovernment and right-wing movements together with a wide range of traditional Islamic communities and orthodox Christian churches.

Of course, the world has seen, and continues to see, important examples of ferociously intolerant and violent religious convictions. Yet, other cases of intolerance and violence in the twentieth century arose from secular or explicitly atheistic ideologies such as Nazism and communism, and these may well have been more destructive, harsh, and intolerant, whether measured by people killed, imprisoned, and tortured; by strength of state grip; by long-term damage to pluralist institutions; or by their adamant advocacy of persecution of perceived opponents and their associates (Guinness 2005). The worst cases of nineteenth-century oppression arguably arose from secular nationalisms and ideologies of Western racial and cultural superiority, which often emphasized the superiority of Western "rational" and scientific "civilization." Cases of religious oppression and intolerance by themselves prove little, as people and societies in general show pervasive tendencies to oppress and domineer. Power tends to corrupt, whether the holders of power are religious or secular. However, whether religious convictions are particularly antipluralistic, harsh, oppressive, or intolerant in the political sphere has yet to be shown. Moreover, various other studies, including those of historic waves of democratization, including the most recent "third wave" between 1974 and 1991, suggest the important contributing role of religious factors, particularly the role of Catholic and Protestant Christianity in strengthening democracy (Huntington 1991).

One cannot decide a priori whether secularism is necessarily democratic and "strong religion" necessarily divisive, violent, or authoritarian. What is needed are fresh and careful examinations of the phenomena in question. The studies in this volume attempt to contribute to such efforts.

Powerful Ideas and the Shaping of the Modern World

Many social scientists may doubt the possibility that religious belief, especially the intellectual or faith *content* of religious belief, can have pervasive political effects because they assume that the effective basis of political (and economic) life lies in material capabilities, interests, and threats rather than in beliefs or ideas. Ethical ideals and religious convictions may seem especially unlikely to affect power dynamics.

For example, scholarship in the field of international relations over the past century has been profoundly influenced by realism, which is an academic version of European realpolitik strategic thinking. As a result, international relations scholarship has emphasized that state power and interests are central to interstate behavior and are even more central to the "system" of anarchy and competition that is considered the determinative context of state action. Most challenges to this analytical framework—particularly Marxism and critical theory—have likewise emphasized material factors. These features of international relations theory reflect the preponderant thinking in economics and political science, which posits a "rational actor" or "rational choice" model of human behavior according to which materially defined power and interests provide determinative explanations of political and economic outcomes, even in domestic contexts.

Against the grain of this prevailing "realism" theory grounded in material factors alone, I argued in a previous work (Lumsdaine 1993) that a large feature of modern inter-state behavior, the massive postwar foreign aid regime, was largely constituted by humanitarian ideas and ideals and thus cannot be explained through state power and interest alone. More generally, the claim that power and interests exert exclusive and determinative influence on world politics has become increasingly implausible. (Wendt, 1999, seeks to make a similar case against privileging material explanations on general theoretical, rather than concrete historical, grounds, arguing for constructivist theory, which parallels the social construction literature in sociology and elsewhere, as applicable to politics, including international politics.) *Perhaps* the international and even domestic politics of eighteenth- and nineteenth-century Europe resembled a balance of power, a kind of chess game determined almost entirely by the players' competitive struggle for power and wealth. But does this model provide an accurate picture of the often ideologically driven domestic and international politics of the twentieth century and early years of the twenty-first century? Consider the spread of democracy in its second and third waves; the integration of Europe; the rise of Nazism; the rise and proliferation of Marxist-Leninist ideology, movements, and regimes; the rise of Third World nationalisms and decolonization; the fall of communism; the weakening of trade barriers; the rise of human rights discourse and activism; the worldwide resurgence of religion and particularly the rise of transnational Islamic, Christian, Buddhist, and Hindu movements; and the rise of religiously inspired terrorism, culminating in the 9/11 terrorist attacks. Not power and interests alone, but also beliefs, ideologies, and ideas, including deeply held hopes for a new and better world, helped motivate all these world-historical phenomena.

In many cases, these ideas provided distinct and varied normative visions of ideal persons, communities, nations, and international order: images of better people and lives, better laws and communities, and a better world. Many of the ideas led to destructive outcomes; many improved people's lot or removed invidious barriers against repressed and marginalized groups; and many had consequences that were mixed or difficult to evaluate. Whatever the consequences, though, it is now clear that ideas charged with moral, social, and often quasi-cosmic significance have played decisive roles in shaping the politics of the past hundred years.

Religious beliefs and religious affiliations have been prominent among these ideas, particularly in recent decades. Whereas sociologists of religion in the 1950s and 1960s supposed secularism to be irreversibly ascendant, many (including some who originally propounded that thesis) now concede that the modern world has become increasingly "desecularized" (Berger 1999), even as modern religion has become increasingly "deprivatized" (Casanova 1994). Indeed, since at least the 1970s there has been a highly visible and politically consequential resurgence of religion in many parts of the world. This "revenge of God" (Kepel 1994) led Huntington (1993, 1996) to consider the possibility of a "clash of civilizations" and others to study what they term "fundamentalism" (Almond, Appleby, and Sivan 2003; Marty and Appleby 1991, 1993a, 1993b, 1994, 1995). Yet, unless one is careful, such theoretical constructs can all too easily lead to the prejudicial and derogatory characterization of many or all religious movements and correspondingly a premature identification of rationality, tolerance, and civility with the "secularization" touted by academics a generation or so ago. But, as José Casanova argues, to characterize religion in this way would be to prejudge whether the public role of religion might sometimes be that of an intelligent and intelligible vision of the world capable of far-reaching influence rather than that of a merely reactive fanaticism.[13]

Rather than prejudge this question, the chapters in this volume offer a close examination of evangelical Christianity in Asia as an intelligible phenomenon with potentially powerful political effects. These political effects may arise at least in part from the content of religious beliefs and commitments. Ideas have consequences, including constructive as well as destructive transformations of human life and society.

Evangelical Roots of Democratic Pluralism?

Assorted authors have pondered how various religious and ethical traditions might contain bases for fostering democratic pluralism and humane politics. Sachedina (2001) considers how other elements of Islamic thought and practice, which include long-standing emphasis on justice, the rule of law, and concern for the poor, provide "Islamic roots of democratic pluralism." Hefner (2000) sees the roots of Indonesia's recent democratization in an indigenous "civil Islam." (Budijanto's chapter also takes note of *proletar* versions of Islam.) Varshney (2002) notes various ways in which Hindus and Muslims can succeed in building civic life together. Sen famously argued that "Asian values" were diverse and located many old indigenous Asian sources that support arguments for human rights and the rule of law, confuting those (such as Singapore's Lee Kuan Yew) who claimed such principles were un-Asian imports from the corrupt West. Confucius's *Analects* (XII, 7) speak eloquently about the importance of ordinary people's welfare and the need for government to retain "the confidence of the people." Mencius supports the rights of a misgoverned people to revolt. Numerous modern authors and not a few classic Western political theorists rooted democratic principals in Christian teachings; others sought classical republican roots. And Tocqueville (1840), Weber (1910), and Tawney (1926) and their successors find some empirical association between Protestantism and democratic practices and values and economic prosperity.

However, there is also no doubt that the causal paths by which religious beliefs and practices influence economic and political life require further analysis and clarification. Possible causal paths of that kind arise in the various chapters of this volume. They suggest a series of conceivable dynamics by which religious beliefs and social life might interact.

First, the studies by Chan and Aaron pay close attention to the adoption of Christianity by previously non-Christian peoples in circumstances where direct political expression is very difficult at best. These studies suggest ways that Christian belief and practice may have indirect effects especially on poor or marginalized individuals and groups in ways that help them attain more satisfactory circumstances and, in some cases, help them alter habitual patterns of subservience or degradation. Moreover, the studies suggest a set of causal paths by which such changes might take place. We do not know precisely how prevalent such dynamics are, but the cases surveyed here are suggestive and help us identify patterns whose prevalence we might assess in a more extensive study. These same studies suggest that the roots of these democratizing changes specifically reflect changes in outlook, worldview, and ideas.

Second, studies of more established churches, such as the chapters by Fernandes, Budijanto, Hong, and Lim, help us consider how and why direct church interventions in politics and economics have taken place and how these interventions have evolved as those churches matured in recent decades and passed beyond their missionary heritages.

Third, these studies also raise the question of whether, even in the context of established church bodies capable of political stands or electoral endorsements, direct political intervention yields as much of a democratizing effect as indirect, citizen-forming aspects of church life and involvement that are not explicitly political. We will examine each of these three phenomena in turn.

Indirect Democratic Effects Where Political Involvement Is Difficult

Where the Christian faith is new and where it faces organized opposition, evangelical faith often spreads spontaneously, as in several cases that Chan details. For people from previously non-Christian communities, the new faith may help them attain greater agency and enhance their practical skills.

As in the Dangs, literacy and other teaching programs may increase skill levels. In tribal areas in China, increased skills may arise from practices of Bible reading and hymn singing and from Bible translation into local languages. Links to other Christian groups with more detailed information may lead to further training of various sorts. This occurred when Gujarat Christian Workers linked Dangi Christians with Amos for Gujarat and in older Gujarat Christian Workers programs: hostels for Dangi children attending secondary schools or sponsorship for Dangis to pursue medical or legal training. In China, small, spontaneously arising churches seeking counsel from better-established churches nearby broadened their access to wider sources of knowledge on many subjects. Biblical orientation may promote enthusiasm and growing skill in using, comparing, and arguing from texts, which provides a basis for various kinds of other study. Thus, one important question for further research concerns how indigenous embrace of Christian faith affects skill levels, particularly among marginalized groups, either through practices that inevitably come with evangelical commitment, such as Bible study, or through church-related networks and linkages.

Based on the materials we have here it is also reasonable to ask about ways in which acceptance of Christian faith tends to give people, particularly poor and marginalized people, more control over their own lives, both vis-à-vis others and also in regard to their own habits and patterns of life. Christian faith seems to have been effective in the Dangs, in Lahu and Lisu areas, and elsewhere in helping people overcome alcoholism and drug use. Similarly, abusive behavior and infidelity seem to have declined. In the Dangs, the church support and the positive contacts with outsiders it provided seem to have given local people more resources and, as important, more confidence to question bad deals and exploitive practices that outsiders sought to impose. Aaron's account suggests several ways to explain this. Group discussion and study, including Bible study, may create a "culture of questioning": greater confidence in speaking up and in asking questions. Experience of efficacy arising from the belief in answered prayers and the changed cosmic picture that biblical cosmology introduces may help those who have adopted these views to be bolder in dealing with others. The Christian ethical framework may also help articulate a sense of just dealing, which Dangis then invoke in discussion with others. Such ethical frameworks, and an increased sense of hope, efficacy, and dignity, may also help people overcome dysfunctional and destructive behavior in their own lives through the classically Weberian virtues of work discipline and thrift and in other ways.

Weberian elements (skills diffusion, text orientation, and more stable family life as well as thrift and hard work) fit with long-hypothesized patterns and with observations of Protestantism in Latin America; they also help explain the relatively rapid diffusion of Christian faith. Chan observes that the greater prosperity of Christian villages and families in animist regions generates a good deal of interest in this faith. Decreases in alcoholism and family problems seem to be decisive influences for people, women especially. Perceived healings in response to prayer are also important. If evangelicalism brings more orderly habits or greater self-confidence and literacy, improved living standards that may result help explain its indigenous spread.

However, the observed patterns linking Christian belief and practice suggest differences from as well as overlaps with the patterns that Weber observed in European Protestantism. This would make comparative testing of patterns such as are described here even more interesting. The specifically Calvinist attempt to convince oneself of one's divine election by material success (taken as a sign of God's favor) has little to do with the lifestyle changes observed here, for instance. Weber's ethic may be too narrow to describe the mixture of new social and cosmological inputs that accompany precepts and changes in behavior in newly Christian groups. Thus, the question of how success-building characteristics are mediated by evangelicalism is important both to a better understanding of Weberian, and Weber-like, hypotheses and to their revision, refinement, and supplementation.

Presuming that such effects are taking place, as Chan and Aaron seem to demonstrate, it may be argued that these effects are democratizing ones. Raising the standard of living of relatively poor people and groups is, in itself, a move toward greater equality and thus toward a more democratic state of affairs. However, the particular activities involved do not simply raise income and savings or standards of living. They also seem to help marginalized people attain greater skills, literacy, and personal and family responsibility. In so doing, they promote greater voice, ability to question, self-confidence, and thus a greater capacity for civic engagement.

There is some reason to suppose that the intellectual, or belief, content of evangelical faith plays an important role in this process, but it would be misleading to understand this hypothesis simply in terms of *individual* outlook. The changes of life just described, and the effects of those changes as well, are not confined to or solely mediated by individuals. They arise in the context of group life, and, specifically, church activity. Thus, the potentially political indirect effects and causes of the diffusion of evangelical Christianity can include the development of a richer local associational life.

Aaron describes the existence of prayer meetings, local assemblies, and church services, as well as more social ministries such as literacy and health classes. Similarly, Chan describes how such meetings can become a focus of life activities, particularly in rural or semirural settings. These gatherings bring people together and can provide a variety of ways in which people previously unused to doing so may discuss and offer opinions, may organize smaller and larger events and learn organizational skills, and may engage in informal leadership activities. Chan notes initiation of other kinds of regular activities: publishing newsletters, organizing Bible schools, visiting the sick and elderly, and so on. Thus, the spread of faith is in some cases linked to and supports growth of a variety of voluntary, self-organized church-linked activities. The strengthening of these relatively new areas of associational life can serve as a school of democracy, training people in taking initiative, working together, discussing projects, and speaking up. Development of voluntary associational life, and the capacity for it, is thus another area where hypotheses about the indirect democratic effects of evangelical faith emerge from various chapters in this book.

In these chapters, the ways Christian belief appears to vitalize individual and associational life seem to draw not just on the acquisition of skills, virtues, or a new social context, but also on changes in outlook, worldview, or structures of belief. This distinction helps specify generally Weberian types of hypotheses and identify the *various kinds of causal links* that operate in various cases.

If certain structures of belief and religious practice can sometimes support patterns favoring more egalitarian relations, human dignity, and a measure of self-determination for all segments of society, as has been suggested, no doubt there are structures of belief that may promote the reverse. Thus, newly adopted beliefs may have social effects not only through their own characteristics, but by displacing other beliefs.

In the highly hierarchical societies common in Asia, and among marginalized people and groups, the sense of the personal care of a God who responds lovingly and personally to each believer seems to give people greater confidence and agency in their own lives. In some circumstances, this can counteract socially, hierarchically, spiritually, or ideologically mediated perceptions of inferiority or helplessness historically, which may restrict people's scope of action and keep them quiescent in response to oppressive social forces or superstitions. Thus, the need to placate potentially malevolent spirits absorbs substantial scarce resources among animist Lahu and Lisu, reinforcing cycles of poverty. In some instances that Aaron adduces, the view of a hostile and predatory spirit world seems to reflect and reinforce subservient relations with hostile and predatory outsiders, such as *shahukars*, and even to be linked directly to them.

For instance, the idea that each person can pray to the God of the universe, who is believed to care and listen, implicitly challenges at a fundamental level the sense that only hierarchically high persons or groups are important, powerful, or acceptable. As both Aaron and Chan note, such perceptions are strongly reinforced by perceptions of healings taking place in response to prayer. This process contests traditional religious views—linked to previously entrenched social practices—in which people are subordinate to malign or indifferent spiritual forces (just as they are to social forces and hierarchies) as part of an unquestioned and putatively inevitable and just social and cosmic order. Thus, it is not implausible to consider the hypothesis that in these circumstances a changed vision of cosmic order generated a changed sense of self, leading to greater confidence and agency in the context of a strong community life oriented around this new cosmic vision.

What of more explicitly *political* effects arising from such indirect democratizing changes? The (Weberian) attainment of greater confidence, prosperity, voice, literacy, and skills among relatively marginalized people—if further research bears out that under some circumstances these tend to accompany the spread of evangelicalism—in one sense constitutes *ipso facto* a democratic effect. Similarly, the (Tocquevillian) fostering of voluntary association and discussion, self-organizing activities and leadership skills, and a sense of social efficacy among ordinary participants in Church activities—if further research bears that out—constitutes a strengthening of grassroots civil society and enhancement of capacities for bottom-up voice and leadership. However, there is some evidence that even in regions where political participation is directly or indirectly discouraged, these nonpolitical "indirect democratic effects" can also push the society toward more open and democratic processes.

The associations that people form help them articulate wants and voice these wants to local authorities, even in a nondemocratic society. This then sometimes acts as a kind of pressure, which leads to social change, as Chan repeatedly shows. The broader-based articulation of wants and requests can push a society toward more open and democratic processes. It can also lead, as in Gujarat, to people contesting a subordinate status, and in some cases contesting historic patterns of subordination and abuse. This puts some pressure on society to change, but may also lead, as Aaron notes, to organized opposition from entrenched social forces.

Also, as Fernandes observes, evangelical engagement, even if initially apolitical in character, can lead to conflicts with central political authorities and can lead evangelicals to become enmeshed in existing interethnic or intercommunal conflicts. Fernandes sees the failure of churches in northeast India to stop ethnic conflicts and armed liberation movements in that area as a major problem, while also acknowledging some efforts by churches to broker intergroup and center-periphery peace. However, in other chapters, evangelicals have shown some effectiveness in fostering bridging social capital (cooperation across ethnic and religious lines) as well as bonding (within-group) social capital. Budijanto notes the effectiveness of civic forums in averting riots and in starting projects of community improvement in Solo, Indonesia, and nationwide. Chan notes how evangelical Protestants persuaded Catholics and Buddhists to cooperate in getting a less stringent religious code passed. Aaron observes the strong emphasis among Gujarat Christian Workers on building cross-tribe and cross-village cooperation in both church and civic affairs and notes its at least partial success. Fernandes reports some success in overcoming interethnic rivalries at the church level and attributes much of the remaining problem to the need to resolve resource shortages and thus to address ("prophetically") how the central Indian government sidelines its responsibilities in the Northeast.

Consideration of how these indirect effects start to spill over into public contestation or policy change leads us to examine processes by which evangelicals seek to influence policy or politics directly—or else deliberately refrain from possible direct political involvement.

Direct Efforts by Organized Church Groups to Influence Policy

There were a number of ways that churches as organized entities directly attempted to influence policy and political outcomes in the cases studied. There were struggles for democracy, and earlier for self-rule, in Korea, the Philippines, and Indonesia in which churches did or did not participate. There are regular electoral contests, which churches have sought to influence or have remained aloof from. There are particular political or social issues that churches may seek to influence. And there are ethnic or communal conflicts that churches have sought to ease or have ignored; in northeast India, there are questions of regional relations with the central Indian state and local insurgency groups.

In the main cases where authors study church involvement in regular electoral politics—Korea and the Philippines—both the authors and significant sectors in society seem to be ambivalent, at best, about the appropriateness of that involvement. As Lim notes, Melba Padilla Maggay, for instance, herself no stranger to vigorous Christian political concerns, blasts church endorsements of Filipino political candidates, particularly where these claim to have discerned God's will. Such meddling cheapens the church's voice and can even be compared to false prophecy—a *using* of the church's moral authority to promote specific temporal strategies and ends and to endorse particular persons, yet without any clear Scriptural mandate for the particular choice. Data from South Korea and the Philippines also suggest that such attempts to influence voting through religious loyalties or endorsements are singularly ineffective. The mass of citizens—and of churchgoers—seem to cast their votes unaffected by religious alignments and to regard such endorsements as poorly conceived.

The involvement of individual Christians in the political process as candidates, officials, or campaigners is quite a different matter. If those involved do not use their religious status as a basis for seeking temporal authority, few seem to object to their competing just like other candidates. However, just as with church or clerical endorsements, the authors, and apparently many church members, find problematic attempts by candidates to make their religious affiliation a basis for winning votes.

Nevertheless, it is hard to say how useful evangelical Christian involvement in politics on these terms is. Both Hong and Lim argue that the evangelical, or quasi-evangelical, presidents they study pursued effective and excellent policies. Hong presents considerable evidence that Kim Young-Sam considered himself influenced and sustained in his policies, as well as in his prior struggles for democracy, by his evangelical faith. Opinions about Kim differ widely in Korea, even among evangelicals, after the fact. Ramos, less vocal about his faith, is widely acknowledged as among the best post-Marcos presidents. Korean evangelicals in national legislative office seem, in Hong's analysis, little different from others in many of their attitudes and behavior, but the data are limited. Lim's discussion suggests that there has been a considerable crop of evangelical legislators and administrators in the Philippines whose quality was outstanding.

But both authors abstract from this detail to suggest that, in both countries, the overall problems with good governance and democratic rule are systemic and not easily remedied just by promoting better candidates for office, one by one. Hong, despite his evident admiration for Kim, sees him as having been able to accomplish but little because of the personalistic character of the Korean political system, which makes institutionalizing any reforms or advances difficult. Lim, while acknowledging the valuable part played by Ramos and others in office, likewise identifies the core problem of politics in the Philippines as located in the general corruption found in society and among venal politicians, *trapos*, and in the unresponsiveness of Filipino elites to the inegalitarian structure of society and the general unresponsiveness of the masses. In sum, both authors see the possibility of positive contributions through direct *electoral* involvement by evangelicals alone as at best limited, even under favorable conditions. What need to be addressed are problems of various sorts in the political *system*.

Direct political involvement can take another form: protests or other interventions designed to dramatically address extraordinary political troubles such as corrupt authoritarian rule. In the Philippines, the authoritarian, kleptocratic Marcos regime was brought down by an exercise of People Power evoked, in large measure, through a religious appeal from Jaime Cardinal Sin, and the maintenance of reasonable civil rule, at least arguably, sustained by a few more popular demonstrations at crucial transitional moments. In Korea, the brutal and antidemocratic *Yushin* regime, also corrupt, was also brought down by an exercise of popular protest in which the evangelical churches, despite their extremely conservative positions and general aversion to political involvement, played a pivotal role, Hong tells us. In Indonesia, the cronyistic and corrupt Soeharto regime was ended by an outpouring of popular sentiment, but one in which the churches kept their distance. Budijanto sees this detached stance as one that many Indonesians, rightly or wrongly, perceived as opportunistic and craven.

The problem of direct political involvement thus is quite different if one looks at attempts by churches or religious leaders to influence ordinary, day-to-day electoral politics or at intervention in extraordinary issues and moments of crisis. In such exceptional cases, persons and institutions that normally steer clear of political involvements—especially those which, like religious bodies and leaders, are charged with ethical guidance—may have a "prophetic" role to play, not unlike the role of a usually aloof balancer or guarantor in some political systems. Such witnessing to urgent moral and social truth may be seen as ethically incumbent upon them and understood as a matter of faithfulness to their specifically religious role. For all these reasons, in circumstances that seem to call for decisive witness, the failure to bear such witness may reasonably be seen as ethically problematic, or even culpable. By contrast, close evangelical civic involvement in the political sphere—in the day-to-day issues of politics and in ordinary political contests— may be seen, perhaps particularly by those who revere churches and their roles, as entanglement in worldly contestation, undesirable both for religious reasons, because of the church's spiritual mission, and for secular reasons, because it is an *ad hoc* meddling by religious authorities in matters not properly in their sphere.

Intervention in extraordinary situations, reflecting the church's independent and ethical voice, is quite different from direct church involvement in regular political processes. Indeed, the two are not fully compatible: To the extent the church becomes one more actor in the daily political struggle, it tends to forfeit the status that comes from ordinarily focusing on larger ethical and religious concerns, and thus loses the possibility of a distinct prophetic witness. Both considerations may have been operating in many Indonesians blaming churches for not criticizing Soeharto when democratization was in the offing. Budijanto's discussion implicitly asks whether ongoing support for current power-holders by Indonesian churches before Soeharto's ouster was both unwise and supine. Korean evangelicals may see church support for democratization in 1989 as a positive contribution to democracy, as Hong seemingly does; and many Filipinos, like Lim, might find the lack of strong evangelical support in People Power 1 a defect, and the support for the Arroyo government against mob violence in People Power 3 an improvement. Yet Hong and Lim may, without inconsistency, consider church endorsements of candidates an undesirable practice, all the more so when the endorsements reflect religious affiliation rather than principled support for policy positions. In northeast India, the circumstances are quite different, but the underlying principles are similar. Fernandes sees it as important for churches not to align themselves with ethnic differences that plague the region and inevitably find political expression. The way to democracy and to political and social health in these regions lies instead in pursuing ethnic reconciliation. Fernandes shows some ways in which churches have consistently promoted such reconciliation, while also noting that the perhaps inevitably ethnic composition of various churches in the region can be an impediment to building intergroup bonds.

Thus, she sees church involvement in the day-to-day scuffle of politics, which often reflects ethnic tensions, as unhelpful and inappropriate. But she sees a need—as yet not very well met—for the church to raise a "prophetic" voice criticizing the way the central Indian government exploits the region as a whole and plays divide-and-rule policies with the indigenous inhabitants. Such structural problems create scarcities that exacerbate ethnic divisions and keep the Northeast underdeveloped while India takes advantage of its natural resources. Unless such issues are addressed and redressed, it will be very difficult, Fernandes implies, to overcome the destructive tendencies toward local ethnic conflict and violent separatist movements. By raising these issues with a unified voice, churches are perhaps the only actors in the region able to get effective movement on them, which is essential for peace, for normal democratic functioning, and for economic development. Thus, in an entirely different context, Fernandes's arguments also suggest a crucial distinction between church entanglement in daily political and group struggles—usually unhelpful for democracy, good government, society, and the church—and use of the church's moral authority to press unaddressed issues of justice as a kind of unique prophetic witness.

Starting from this kind of analysis, what kinds of involvement in politics may help or hinder democratization?

In postwar Korea, the Philippines, and Indonesia, churches were initially reluctant to adopt an overtly political stance. The reasons for such political abstention varied. There were practical self-interested reasons, which varied from trying to avoid making waves so as to protect a relatively favored position already enjoyed, to relying on clientelistic protectors. Traditions of separation of church and state inherited from American missionaries or Dutch Christians, and sometimes from their ongoing involvement, played a role in some cases. People believed that the church should concentrate on spiritual life and the winning of souls to Christ as its spiritual mission, and concomitantly that the church should eschew distracting and unholy worldly involvements, which political action appeared to be. Theologically, Romans 13:1–7 was understood as teaching an obedience to governing authorities that (perhaps especially in nondemocratic contexts) precluded criticism or overt political involvement.

However, particularly in Indonesia and Korea, this separation coexisted with what might seem to some a kind of clientelistic relationship. In Korea, churches had a favored position, partly arising from their American denominational ties and the preponderant U.S. influence in Korea, and evangelicals were prominent and substantially overrepresented in political circles. This made their quiescence in relation to military rule something other than a clean separation from politics. In Indonesia, the churches were disfavored—at risk in a predominantly Muslim land—yet needed government protection and government approval to carry on normal activities. Thus, here a quiescent and sometimes obsequious relation to power holders again could be understood as somewhat like a tacit exchange of favors rather than a genuine principled separation from politics.

Throughout the more recent period the studies focus on, however, evangelical churches steadily moved toward a practical and theologically grounded position that saw Christians and their churches as having ethical responsibilities for society: for just rule, for the common good of society, and for a measure of social ministry and, at times, political participation to contribute to securing these things.

This evolution certainly represented, in part, a reflective response to circumstances. The sense of public outrage—not least among the educated middle classes in whose ranks evangelical Christians were heavily represented—over the torture-death of Park Chong-chul and the government's subsequent violation of its promises for reform evoked widespread protest among the churches, which led to a more robust sense of political responsibility for the welfare of society among Korean evangelicals. The evident corruption and abuse of power by Marcos led to a similar outpouring of sentiment among Filipinos, significantly sparked by Cardinal Sin's appeal to the public, which resulted in an important success for democracy. Though few Filipino evangelicals took part, this and subsequent events led them to reconsider political theology and uninvolvement. The multidimensional crisis in Indonesia and the increasing threat to churches from radical political Muslims forced evangelicals to rethink their relationship with political events and figures. And once such a process of reevaluation started, subsequent events and efforts, including what now seem to have been unwise political endorsements, became further material for reflection on the Christian's relationship to politics and the social order.

But significantly, Hong, Lim, and Budijanto each see theological rethinking as central to the churches' processes of reevaluation—in a sense, a thinking through theologically of the relations of church and society, the Christian and the social order, as if for the first time. Stances and implicit explanations often inherited from an earlier, missionary stage of Christian development were questioned, and new Scriptural models were found, not only in response to circumstances but as part of a general process of thinking through the social implications of the gospel on its own terms.

This rethinking drew on a worldwide development in evangelical thinking, which enters the accounts of the authors in this volume mainly in the influence on local churches of world evangelical movements such as the Lausanne Covenant and the work of the International Fellowship of Evangelical Students. Those developments partly reflected a reappropriation by evangelicals in England, the United States, and other countries of a much longer history of evangelical and missionary social involvement (such as Aaron recounts in the history of the Gujarat Christian Workers' forebears, typified by Bishop Azariah), temporarily in abeyance. They also reflected the shifting balance in worldwide Christianity, in which voices from the South, with their natural concern about poverty and colonialism, increasingly contributed to the overall tenor of evangelical thought.

To a considerable extent, the changes were endogenous, even if sometimes catalyzed by events. As what had been missionary churches in colonial or dependent contexts two generations back grew in numbers and confidence and coped on their own with the issues of national political life, they developed a theology, still thoroughly evangelical, that reflected a wider range of concerns about society, poverty, democracy, and justice. This responded to circumstances, of course, but it was at root a self-directed revision of one-sided missionary views or tendentious church-state clientelisms. Such changes in evangelical thinking arose mainly from within the national Christian community, but also were tied to a worldwide rethinking of the same issues arising both out of evolving biblical interpretation and the shifting demographics of worldwide Christianity.

This change was often and increasingly not simply a move toward greater political involvement, but development of consistent, theologically grounded viewpoints. These were based on understanding responsible vocation as one in which Christian concern for human life as a whole, while centered on the church's spiritual mission and cure of souls, extended to balanced involvement in people's social, economic, and political well-being in society. Such an outlook might call for direct political involvement at times, but often also for abstention from such a role. When it was seen as calling for church or pastoral input (or its absence) on important political issues and decisions, this was not simply on the basis of a single passage of Scripture (such as Romans 13) taken as a universal formula, but on a broader exegesis of basic (and often counterweighted) principles throughout Scripture. It concerned not simply the welfare of the churches themselves, or of Christians, but the welfare of the whole society, and not on the basis of religious loyalties, but based, in considerable measure, on a vision of justice and the common good.

Citizen Formation in Countries Where More Direct Political Action Is Also Possible

Hong and Lim study evangelical influences on democracy in countries that have undergone clear democratic transition and consolidation. They each find some positive contribution of Christian politicians. Each thought that the evangelically influenced presidents they studied pursued sound policies, and Lim commends evangelical legislators. Yet Hong and Lim regard these evangelical impacts on democracy as much less important than the indirect effect of church and faith formation on citizen character, including its outworking in voluntary citizen associations. The ambit of Budijanto's study does not include electoral influences or the work of Christian politicians; he sees churches as apt to strengthen democracy more through grassroots civic involvement than through direct political participation. Hong and Lim find the democratizing effects of the citizen character formation and voluntary group activity evangelicalism tend to be strong, consistent, and important.

This is particularly interesting and notable as a tentative finding for three reasons. First, it parallels Aaron's and Chan's findings in regions where direct political participation is effectively not possible to any significant degree. Similar processes of voluntary association, community building, and character formation are important in strengthening democracy across these widely differing contexts. This enhances the importance of these observations for formulating questions, hypotheses, or tentative conclusions about possible evangelical influence on democracy in the Asian context. Second, it helps us explore the way the belief structure, the intellectual or faith content, of evangelical or other religions might translate into concrete sociopolitical tendencies, which is perhaps the most theoretically challenging aspect of explaining consistent evangelical influence on small-scale economic prosperity and, especially, democracy. Demonstrating, or even theorizing, the effects of ideas on social structures, interests, or political outcomes is notoriously difficult. Observed changes in understanding and behavior by individual religious citizens can help explicate how these things may be linked. Third, these threads of inquiry line up with the classic sociological analyses of democracy and of Christian religious influence found in Tocqueville and especially Weber, as noted earlier.

Hong argues for the importance of Christian citizen formation and (consequent) voluntary association both positively and negatively. Negatively, because he sees the problems with Korean politics as systemic and rooted in attitudes toward leadership that substitute personal and regional loyalties for principled pursuit of civic ends. Positively, because he finds the Korean civic movements, and the role of evangelicals within them, a significant source of strengthening for democratic political ideals. Hong's specific observations cohere with the overall approach of democracy as rooted less in the vicissitudes of popular will and elections than in democratic values and principles. Hong finds a general strengthening of principle and institutionalization necessary to lasting political reforms, which Kim Young-Sam's presidency was largely unable to institute. This naturally leads him to list three areas in which he believes Christian participation in citizen movements can most enhance democracy in Korea: assuring fair election outcomes and good citizen information about issues and candidates, strengthening character in society (specifically among Christians), and Christian leadership in civic organizations. He also sets out a fourth concern, not linked to citizen movements: the need for churches, by fostering a more participatory structure and by de-emphasizing adulation of church leaders, to model more democratic means of participation.

Lim is perhaps more sanguine about the positive impacts of direct evangelical participation in politics in the Philippines, despite the tiny segment of the electorate that evangelicals there constitute. Nevertheless, he also argues that character formation is the most important way the church can shape a more democratic and better governed society. He helpfully distinguishes seven ways this can occur: personal civics, poverty alleviation, political advocacy, peace advocacy, community organizing, leadership development, and pluralistic structure.

Personal civics refers to the teachings on personal responsibility, care for others, and strict integrity that help form character in church members in a way that sustains the positive performance of citizen and leadership roles even on the part of ordinary people. Lim's analysis here is complementary to Aaron's account of how personal change can come out of evangelical practices and beliefs. It is in this area, he argues, that Filipino evangelicals have excelled. Whether or not one is in complete agreement, his analysis takes us forward in detailing ways that faith might strengthen citizen propensities, habits, and values to undergird a better-functioning democratic polity, and indeed a better-functioning society generally.

Lim's categories of poverty alleviation, popular education, and community organizing are roughly parallel to Hong's participation in civic organizations, and again run close to the list Aaron provides of ways that AG and Gujarat Christian Workers have, according to his informants, built up civic life in the Dangs. The categories of leadership development and pluralistic development run parallel to Hong's concern with more democratic church structure, and with the observation of both Chan and Aaron that the self-organizing character of evangelical churches equips them to function as a kind of school of democracy.

Lim's inclusion of peace advocacy brings up a final point that appears in quite a number of the essays: the extent to which the generation of social structure in evangelical churches partakes of the nature of bridging social capital. Fernandes notes the persistent efforts made by many church leaders to overcome ethnic hostilities and develop friendships across ethnic lines, even though she faults the churches' failure to accomplish more in this area. Aaron notes the efforts of Gujarat Christian Workers and AG to set up church and intervillage gatherings that involve people working together across ethnic and village lines. Chan and Budijanto both note successful efforts of Christians to work together with other religious groups. Lim discusses efforts by evangelicals in the Philippines to accord recognition to and secure more just treatment for Filipino Muslims. These efforts to reach outside one's own group clearly have roots in biblical teachings, stories, and principles and in the outreach (activism) element that Bebbington makes central to the definition of evangelicals. One might argue that in an era of church expansion in Asia, those groups good at reaching out across borders will tend to replicate groups sharing their beliefs much faster than others; however, this does not in itself account for cooperation across ethnic lines. The ways evangelical groups tend to develop bridging as well as bonding social capital may, then, be another possible link to be investigated between belief structures and social practices strengthening civic and democratic values.

Wider Implications of Democratic Political Change

It could be argued that each of the authors in this volume sees a proper role for direct political involvement at times. Certainly in cases where political involvement is possible and is deemed legitimate by society—in northeast India, in Indonesia, in the Philippines, and in Korea—a completely apolitical stance by the church under all circumstances seems problematic in light of the facts the authors present. There are times when a prophetic voice is called for—at moments of democratic protest against brutal or corrupt authoritarian rule—and in which noninvolvement is not and will not be perceived as an apolitical stance so much as an opportunistic or craven move in situations that call for bold defense of what is right. Even in more ordinary times, the authors suggest, there is a proper role for direct civic involvement by churches as corporate bodies, supporting fair play, helping weaker citizens, and so on. Yet the authors also present problems that can arise from too much direct political involvement. This can undermine the church's independence and prophetic voice, divide society, and cheapen the church's message. Strong principled involvement by individual Christians as voters, legislators, administrators, and occupants of high office in a democratic context is free from some of the problematic elements that corporate or organized church involvement in electoral politics gives rise to, and certainly is seen by the authors as a proper and necessary exercise by evangelicals of moral concern in society.

Interestingly, however, even where these kinds of involvement are readily viable, occur, and are deemed to be effective and right, the authors all conclude that these are less effective contributions to democracy than a leaven-like, *indirectly* political role that evangelicals and churches play by the gradual formation of conscience and habits of responsible citizenship and civic participation. Even where direct political involvement can do good and have significant impact, they seem to conclude, the indirect impact of evangelical religion on formation of character and society is more politically important, and certainly more important in fostering democracy.

NOTES

1. The Latin American studies appear as Paul Freston, ed., *Evangelical Christianity and Democracy in Latin America* (Oxford University Press, 2008). The African studies

appear as Terence O. Ranger, ed., *Evangelical Christianity and Democracy in Africa* (Oxford University Press, 2008). A fourth volume of studies will draw comparative conclusions based largely on the regional volumes and will appear as Timothy Samuel Shah, ed., *Evangelical Christianity and Democracy in Global Perspective* (Oxford University Press, forthcoming).

2. One major survey and synthesis is Freston's (2001), which was an earlier part of the current project; this contains many references to other literature. One thinks also of the series edited by Robert Frykenberg (2003) and Frykenberg's own work (1996, 2002, 2003) and the edited volumes by Marty and Appleby (1991, 1993, 1993a, 1994, 1995) and by Almond, Appleby, and Sivan (2003). Other recent studies of Asian politics and Protestant Christianity include those of Dunch (2001), Freston (2004), Chung-shin Park (2003), Nuh (2001), Pachauau (2002), and Ko (2000).

3. The Africa volume includes studies of Kenya, Mozambique, Nigeria, South Africa, Zambia, and Zimbabwe, with an introductory chapter by Terence Ranger and a commentary by Paul Gifford. The Latin America volume studies Brazil, Guatemala, Mexico, Nicaragua, and Peru, with an introductory chapter by Paul Freston and a concluding commentary by Daniel Levine.

4. See "Case Studies and Theory Development: The Method of Structured, Focused Comparison" by George (1979) and *Case Studies and Theory Development* by George and Bennett (2005). However, our procedures did not adhere tightly to George's and Bennett's valuable guidelines.

5. Figures for the year 2000 from Barrett, Kurian, and Johnson (2001, 12–13), combining "Anglican," "historic Protestant" (50 million), and "Independent" (155 million) churches. The last includes many newer denominations and nondenominational churches, often evangelical, charismatic, or pentecostal.

6. Figures for 2003 are from the U.S. Central Intelligence Agency's *World Factbook 2003*, available online at http://www.cia.gov/cia/publications/factbook.

7. Bebbington's terms for the last two characteristics can be confusing to some: he speaks of the need for a change of life as "conversionism" and of the emphasis on evangelistic and missionary efforts as "activism," almost the reverse of how I might have used those terms.

8. Almond and Verba's early postwar focus on the relationship of political attitudes to civic involvement was further discussed in their 1980 edited volume, *The Civic Culture Revisited: An Analytic Study*. Robert D. Putnam has redeveloped this theme in a well-known series of books in the past twelve years (see Putnam, Leonardi, and Nanetti 1993; Putnam 2000, 2002).

9. The date of the English translation of Tocqueville's second part is 1840; the French edition and the first part appeared a few years earlier.

10. Gujarat Christian Workers and Amos for Gujarat are pseudonyms.

11. The report concludes that "there is ample evidence that the argument of a 'global resurgence of religion' can largely be sustained, with the notable exception to this trend being the post-industrial countries—where the trend towards secularization itself, however, is far from consistent" (Moghadam 2003, 57).

12. For instance, various authors recently have argued that, contrary to popular opinion, there is considerable potential for civic amity and democratic pluralism in Islamic tradition and between Hindus and Muslims. See, for instance, Hefner (2000),

who argues that, in Indonesia—the largest Muslim country in the world—Islamic involvement in politics has acted, and has the potential to act, as a democratizing force. See also Varshney (2002) for an argument that personal relations among different religious communities may produce amicable working relations. For an argument that the religious and theological traditions of Islam contain plenty of material for supporting democratic and pluralist ideas, see Sachedina (2001). Of course, these theses are contested by others and fall beyond the scope of this volume; they are given simply to illustrate how arguments about bases of democratic ideals and practices in other religious traditions might be convincingly developed.

13. José Casanova's (1994) case studies of public religion in the modern world suggest that public religion may significantly contribute to democratization and the enlivening of civil society. He argues, *inter alia*, that public religion sometimes offers intelligent and intelligible critiques of secular ideologies and their failures: "The very resurgence or reassertion of religious traditions may be viewed as a sign of the failure of the Enlightenment to redeem its own promises.... Religious traditions are now confronting the differentiated secular spheres, challenging them to face their own obscurantist, ideological, and inauthentic claims. In many of these confrontations, it is religion that, as often as not, appears to be on the side of human enlightenment" (233–234).

I

The Christian Community in China: The Leaven Effect

Kim-Kwong Chan

During the second half of the twentieth century, evangelicalism grew rapidly, especially in the Third World, sometimes introducing new elements into the social fabric that had the potential to alter a country's political atmosphere. Studies of Third World evangelicals and politics yield mixed information: elitist tendencies, advocacy of marginal groups, and reinforcement of established autocracies or encouragement of democratic reforms (Freston 2001, 257–275). The common assumption that evangelicalism's cultural characteristics—including participation, pragmatism, competition, and personal discipline—foster democracy in the long run (Martin 1999, 49) must continue to be examined critically. The Christian community (Hunter A. and Chan 1993)[1] in the People's Republic of China (PRC) is an interesting test case of a rapidly growing group in an authoritarian regime slowly headed toward democracy.

Some models consider pluralism a precursor of democratic transition (Truman 1951). Does rapid expansion of Christianity—a religion that advocates justice, equality, peace, and human dignity—support growing social pluralism in China? Alternatively, do Christians—emphasizing obedience to civil authority, patriotism, and nationalism[2]—reinforce autocratic leadership? Just what kinds of political effects can be observed?

The PRC is the world's largest autocracy. According to its Constitution, one party, the Chinese Communist Party (CCP), rules China under a political system called people's democratic dictatorship. "Democracy" is applied by "the people" to "the people" and to opponents of "the people," where "the people" are those who support the regime. Opponents of the regime are not legally defined as being included among "the people" and cannot enjoy the rights enshrined in the Constitution (Morikawa n.d.). Such a "people's democracy" differs from concepts of democracy in the West, where one has the right to hold political views opposing the government. Further, in the West rights are generally regarded as innate, rights of any human being according to natural law, rather than rights dispensed by government authority. The PRC, therefore, does not currently qualify as a democratic country in the Western sense.

Despite its autocratic one-party system, for over twenty years the PRC's Reform and Open Policy has opened China to the Western world, replacing a planned economy with a market economy. Contacts with other nations have noticeably increased since accession to the World Trade Organization in November 2001. As such contacts grow, China is challenged by sociopolitical values from abroad, such as pluralism and democracy. Over the past two decades, China has experienced fundamental social transformation. Although the CCP retains its political monopoly, people have had increasing opportunities and options in life. The resulting diversity has engendered new social classes, from entrepreneurs to internal migrant laborers. Although it is called "socialism with Chinese characteristics," China's political system is actually an ambiguous, pragmatic fusion of capitalism and communism. This fusion prompts many to think that further active engagement with China will lead to democratization. Among the major arguments for the United States granting China permanent normal trade relation status in 2000 were that an increase in trade would create more U.S. influence in China and that a more prosperous, and hence more diverse, China would become more democratic. However, relationships between social diversity and democracy in China should be examined empirically.

Since the early 1980s, the Chinese government has allowed some open manifestations of religious belief—a development that was unimaginable in the 1960s and 1970s. Various religious groups have grown rapidly and become visible social communities, and their influence has been felt in society. Protestants (hereafter referred to as Christians, as distinct from Roman Catholics) are the fastest growing religious group. In 1949, there were fewer than 1 million Christians among 450 million Chinese. In 1966, just prior to the Cultural Revolution, only a few dozen churches were still open in China; all were in major cities. By the mid-1970s, the only visible sign of Protestantism was the Protestant chapel in Beijing for the diplomatic community, and many thought Christianity had ceased to exist. But as the government relaxed its policy on religion, Christians in hiding began to resurface. By 1982, the government estimated that there were approximately three million Christians, an extraordinarily large number, given the prolonged suppression. By 2000, the official figure was fifteen million Christians in a population of 1.4 billion,[3] while some unofficial estimates ranged as high as sixty million to eighty million. No one really has an accurate count, but, taking the officially recognized churches together with a fairly conservative estimate of Christians not registered with the officially recognized church apparatus, a reasonable working figure is at least thirty million (Lambert 1999, 195–203; on the methodological issue, see also Hunter and Chan 1993, 66–71).

However, China still severely restricts religion. Contacts with religious communities are closely monitored and regulated. Officially, foreign contact with church officials requires prior government approval.[4] Statistics on church membership are deemed a state secret, especially in national minority areas. Passing out church information can be considered an act that endangers state security, a rubric that applies even to internal circulars (marked Confidential) of the China Christian Council (CCC), the official national organization for registered churches. All unregistered religious groups are illegal, as is foreign contact with unregistered churches. Church visits by foreigners are expressly prohibited in many regions. Indeed, in Xinjiang Uygur Autonomous Region, to this day, the government does not allow visits, even to officially registered Christians, by Christian councils from other parts of China. China Christian Council officials who travel there must do so under false pretexts.[5] There is no unrestricted access.

Despite such limitations, informal visits can occur if a relationship of trust has been built. Official publications by the CCC and regional councils are good sources of information, if one makes allowances for the fact that official publications must be in line with the ideology and current political policies of the Chinese Communist Party. The author personally visited all but one of the seven communities studied in this chapter. They represent some of the major trends of Christian communities in China—or, at least, of those who are not in hiding—and were also selected because reliable information about them was available. Despite the difficulties in obtaining reliable data, these include two nonregistered groups. (However, their precise locations and names are not given because these groups, illegal under the law, could face persecution.)

This chapter assesses the impact of the expansion of the Christian community on current sociopolitical development in China and particularly on democratization, including development of civil society, social identity, sociopolitical influence, and political involvement of the communities studied. The conclusions drawn must be considered tentative, as the study surveys a limited range of cases.

The biblical imagery of leaven perhaps best describes the sociopolitical influence of the Christian community in China. Leaven (yeast) is a quiet agent, and yet it can transform the very nature of a lump of dough. The Christian community in China, a somewhat silent social group, together with many other newly emerging elements of civil society,[6] has been growing steadily and seems to have an increasingly significant impact on the formation of a changing China. One cannot see the yeast clearly, but we see its power in the rising dough.

This "leaven effect" is described in three stages. First, we look at the dough: the existing Chinese religious and sociopolitical realities that are the Christian community's context. This first section examines government religious policy, the governmental apparatus on religious affairs, the regime's political objectives toward Christians, and the restrictions with which the Christian community has to live. It also describes the institutional structures of the Christian community and church-state relations in China. One must bear in mind that the government-sanctioned China Christian Council portrays desired church-state relations according to the government's official line, instead of conveying the varied dynamic realities in various parts of China.

The second section examines leavening effects in seven Christian communities—some urban, some rural. Most are government-recognized; a few are nonregistered, illegal groups. Each community manifests faith differently and displays the wide range of interactions between church and society that may affect the shape of Chinese democratization.

The final section sums up and classifies the cases, relating these findings to general sociopolitical trends in China. This section, the rising dough, assesses the impact of the Chinese Christian community on the sociopolitical fiber of postreform Chinese society, which is still in the making. Reflecting on political implications of the rapid development of Christian communities in an authoritarian regime suggests that greater pluralism could be the precursor of a democratic society.

The Dough: The Sociopolitical and Religious Context of China

The Chinese Constitution states that one party, the Chinese Communist Party, rules the People's Republic of China. Marxism-Leninism, including scientific materialism (that is, atheism), is the Party's guiding ideology. This framework leaves no room for religion, which is regarded as an erroneous worldview that must be eradicated from the minds of the people. Based on this interpretation of religion, the Chinese government formulated a number of policies, from nationalizing churches to marginalization and even to forcible suppression (K. Chan 1983, 2–14). Since the early 1980s, however, the government's Reform and Open Policy has brought about a range of more liberal policies to China. One of these is the Policy of Freedom of Religious Belief.[7] For more than twenty years, this policy has been the guiding principle for Chinese religious organizations. It has two components: the status and the role of religion in Chinese socialist society and the polity of religious groups in China.

China has a long tradition of state oversight of religion, dating back almost two thousand years and rooted in the Confucian tradition that proclaimed that the current regime is divinely ordained and exercises authority on behalf of Heaven for the welfare of the people. Traditionally, civil authorities took an agnostic but respectful stance toward all religions in a multireligious society. All religious organizations, like other civil organizations, had an obligation, a sacred duty, to support the existing regime. In return, the state granted many favors, such as tax exemption on properties held and draft exemptions. However, religious organizations had to live under the supervision of the civil authority. Starting in the Tang Dynasty in the seventh century A.D., the Chinese government established a special office to oversee all religious groups (K. Chan 1992, 38–44). Any religious group that refused to acknowledge the government's rule was regarded as a cult and targeted for suppression.

Given this historical tradition of state governance of religion and the atheistic ideology of the CCP, it is not surprising that the People's Republic of China has restrictive religious policies. The Policy of Freedom of Religious Belief, as set out by the Chinese government, emphasizes that religion is a private matter and that freedom is extended to *religious belief,* not to *religion.* Individual citizens have a right to accept, to reject, and to change religious belief as desired, as a personal matter. However, there is no overall freedom of religion or for religious institutions and activities. Religious institutions must follow government-imposed restrictions and confine religious activities to recognized religious venues during a government-approved schedule. Religious activities are forbidden in all civil and government institutions, such as schools, hospitals, government offices, army barracks, jails, factories, public squares, restaurants, hotels, and social service centers. Any religious activity in a nonregistered site, such as preaching on a street corner or conducting Bible studies on a train, are illegal. Religious activities can be illegal even in business offices and individual homes, unless those places receive proper approval and registration from the relevant authorities. Therefore, there is no physical influence of religion other than religious buildings such as churches and temples. Religious activities are restricted to believers within designated religious places. This is what "freedom of religious belief" means.

Religious, moral, and social values are further restricted within one's community. Religion cannot interfere with marriage, education, and other social institutions. No religious instruction can be delivered in educational institutions. The official religious policy states that children under the age of eighteen years cannot receive religious instruction. Military, public security, and government officers (cadres) are prohibited from following or expressing religious faith. Such a religious policy permits hardly any religious influence in the public domain.

Besides forcing religion to be a totally private affair within confining social parameters, the policy also emphasizes "independence and initiative in management of religious affairs" by religious organizations (*Freedom of Religious Belief in China* 1997, 11–16). "Independence" in this context refers to freedom from any foreign control, and may be a reaction against an earlier, missionary era. As China gained its political independence after 1949, it emphasized nationalism and patriotism. Naturally, the government targeted the (then) Western-dominated Chinese Christian community for reform, transforming it from pro-Western to pro-Chinese under communist rule. The Chinese Christian community underwent more than a decade of political reform to purge itself of Western influence; otherwise, it would be regarded as unpatriotic, a political crime equivalent to treason. Religious groups, then, must be wholly independent from any foreign religious organization but not independent from Chinese political authorities. They must accept the political leadership of the government, obey the government's orders, and follow government policies. They are expected to become domesticated social groups serving the political interest of the state.

The government also established a special administrative apparatus to exercise political leadership over religious groups. The State Administration for Religious Affairs (SARA), formerly called the Religious Affairs Bureau (RAB),[8] monitors religious activities and judges their legitimacy. It has branches at various levels of government, all the way down to the township/ village level. The Chinese Communist Party's United Front Work Department (UFWD) usually formulates policy, and the Religious Affairs Bureau implements it. Together, cadres from RAB and UFWD provide guidance and supervision for religious organizations (Bureau of Democracy, Human Rights, and Labor 2000, 2–3).

It is hard to define precisely how the RAB carries out its "guidance" and "supervision" of religious groups. Theoretically, the RAB provides political direction for Christians to follow. For instance, when the national political objective was against the NATO bombing of the Chinese Embassy in Belgrade in the summer of 1999, the Christian community was supposed to issue public statements and mobilize believers for anti-NATO rallies. Similarly, the China Christian Council, guided by the government,[9] denounced the papal decision to canonize 120 martyrs who died in the Boxer Rebellion, even though it is clearly not the business of Protestants to monitor how other religious traditions conduct their internal affairs. Religious groups in China have no freedom to express political views other than as instructed by the government. The state's interest supersedes all other institutional interests.[10] Therefore, few views dissenting from government policy come from the Christian community.

Within the officially recognized Christian community, as in any religious organization in China, a hierarchical structure mirrors the government's institutional structure. There are two Protestant organizations: the China Christian Council (CCC) and the Three-Self Patriotic Movement (TSPM). In principle, the former takes care of pastoral matters, such as training of pastors and building churches, and the latter is a political association conveying the political objectives of the government to the Christian community. In practice, the same people mostly staff these two organizations, and they usually hold joint meetings to decide on various church matters. They are referred to as *Lianhui* (two associations), or as TSPM/CCC for short. The national body has headquarters in Nanjing and Shanghai. Each province has its own TSPM/CCC, and there are branches down to the parish level. Vertically, or hierarchically, each congregation should have its own TSPM/CCC under the leadership of a higher administrative level and ultimately under the national TSPM/CCC leadership. Horizontally, each TSPM/CCC is under the supervision of the local RAB. For example, a church at a municipal level would be under the leadership of the provincial TSPM/CCC and supervised by the municipal RAB (Human Rights Watch/Asia 1997, 13–16).

The Christian community in China adheres to a very strong conservative theological tradition, inherited from missionaries in the 1920s. Until it reconnected with the ecumenical community recently, it had not had access to theological developments that had taken place in the West. Like many conservative Christians, Chinese Christians have little exposure to theological thinking about politics. An emphasis on ensuring the gulf between church affairs and worldly affairs results in separating the church from temporal matters. Whether China has democracy or dictatorship is of little concern to the Christian leadership: All they want is space to operate and perhaps some freedom to expand. Their apolitical stance is ideally suited to accepting the government's leadership.

The rapid expansion of the Christian community has heightened intercommunity tensions. Because communism is the state orthodoxy, any rapid increase in the number of religious believers, especially Christians, poses ideological as well as institutional challenges. In many villages, the growth of Christian communities competes with the development of the Party branch office: Fewer and fewer people want to join the Party; more and more want to join the church.[11] China has begun holding direct elections of village administrators, replacing the system of Party-appointed village cadres. This could have significant political implications. If the Party cannot hold on to its traditional dominance, new social groups such as religious organizations could displace it. Furthermore, (Protestant) Christian groups, along with Catholics, may be the best-organized religious groups in China, as well as the fastest growing, especially in rural areas. The Christian community may well be perceived as a political threat to the Party, even apart from its message, simply because of its growth and institutional coherence.

It is no secret that the government's policies seek to curb the rapid development of the Christian community. The government demands all Christian groups, including those that simply gather at a believer's home (called "meeting point" or "family church"), to go through formal registration, and it issues regulations to limit the activities of the clergy. Some regional regulations even demand registration of preachers. Groups or individuals without registration are considered illegal and are banned or fined. Such regulations aim to dampen church growth and thus reduce the tensions it may cause.

Some leaders in the national church hierarchy, such as Bishop K. H. Ding, believe that rapid expansion of the Christian community, and the zealous evangelistic desires of Chinese Christians, are undesirable for the stability of Chinese society. Christian evangelical messages often stress the damnation of nonbelievers, as well as salvation solely by grace, through Jesus Christ. Some national leaders think that such messages offend communists, who may do many good deeds yet are without a ticket to the Christian heaven believed in by conservative Christians. Bishop Ding has launched a campaign to reconcile the conservative theology distinguishing believers and nonbelievers with his brand of process theology, which emphasizes universal salvation (see Wickeri 2000). He seeks to integrate evangelical Christianity, with its doctrinal exclusivity and institutional expansion at the expense of other communities, into a Chinese socialist society that desires a harmonious relationship among all groups under the leadership of an atheistic government. Whether the communists deeply appreciate Bishop Ding's theological efforts to provide them a ticket to the Christian heaven apart from the grace of Jesus Christ is somewhat uncertain.[12] However, any gesture de-emphasizing evangelism pleases the Party, and the Party's UFWD has promoted Ding's work.[13] Government policy prefers to maintain the status quo for religious groups in a multireligious, multiethnic society.

Government policy, and responses from government-sanctioned Christian leaders, make it clear that the church publicly endorses the regime's political leadership irrespective of what its policies are, from the one-child policy to anti-NATO bombing demonstrations. The government-sanctioned church leadership even tries to reform its religious teaching to appease the government, for instance, by de-emphasizing salvation by faith. Some see this as compromising the faith (Belz 2001, 1–4). Others consider it contextualizing faith. Clearly, the church is not an antagonistic force, nor even an independent civil organization, that can voice its conscience. Very little room is allowed for any dissenting voice in China. The mere legal survival of the Christian community is at the government's mercy. Every public expression must comply with government wishes.

Therefore, a cursory reading of church-state relations, based on the public and officially recognized Christian groups in China, suggest that the Christian community—which is actually one of the most evangelistic Christian communities in the world—steadfastly supports, and even serves, the interest of the authoritarian and atheistic regime. The Christian community lives and acts within an invisible government-shaped cage. At first glance, it appears there is no room for the Christian community, or other religious groups, to expand beyond confined parameters or to influence the society's sociopolitical domain.

The Leaven Effect: Case Studies of Christian Communities in China

Behind the official facade the Christian community in China seems to be emerging, silently yet powerfully, as an influential force in civil society. Its sociopolitical influence goes far beyond what can be published in official church magazines, such as *Tien Feng* [*Celestial Wind*]. Its impact on society, especially in rural areas, is often downplayed in official media to save face for the Party, which is not supposed to be losing ground to religious groups. The growth of the Christian community also presents a challenge to government control over religious groups. These seven cases serve to illustrate how the diverse sociopolitical interactions between Christian communities and the government affect incipient social democratization.

Case 1: Hebei Christian Council—Flexing Its Political Muscle

In 1950 there were about fifty thousand Christians in Hebei Province;[14] whereas in 2000, there were almost five hundred thousand officially registered Christians among Hebei's sixty-eight million inhabitants. But many Christians are not registered, either because they decline to do so or because the government refuses to register them. For example, Longhua County has only several hundred registered Christians, but the real figure is over twenty thousand.[15] Most Longhua Christians have joined the church since 1995. Only those who are registered are considered members of a legitimate religious organization. The county government refuses to register new converts or Christian communities, fearing that senior leadership will reprimand them for allowing Christianity to grow so rapidly. So official figures greatly underestimate the numbers of Christians in the population. Hence, the actual Christian population in Hebei is far greater than the official number suggests.[16]

Beginning in the early 1980s, Christianity was officially allowed to exist again, and many churches that had formerly existed in major cities or townships were reopened. But the province's church leadership was then in the hands of a few senior church leaders who were trusted and appointed by the government. The church in Hebei received little attention, and this community, with tens of thousands of Christians scattered around the province, had virtually no sociopolitical influence. The leadership was weak and seemed to serve government interests more than church interests. Some church leaders were appointed members of the Chinese People's Political Consultative Conference (CPPCC) at various administrative levels,[17] but these church delegates merely echoed government political directives during CPPCC meetings. Many church properties were sold off at ridiculously low prices to various government divisions and government-related units. The church grew slowly but gradually, mostly in the countryside. The church in Hebei was a typically tamed church serving the government interests.

In the early 1980s, several young Christians from Hebei applied for the newly opened Yanjin Seminary in Beijing even before Christian services were allowed in public. Most were from families with long traditions and from autonomous Christian communities (that is, unregistered Christian groups). They became the first well-trained Hebei pastors, serving in various municipal churches beginning in the late 1980s. These young pastors soon gained support from local congregations and gradually began replacing aging leaders, most of whom were in their eighties and nineties, in important church positions. In the mid-1990s, the young pastors took control at the provincial level. The government had difficulty finding trusted candidates: Those they preferred were either too old or too unpopular with the congregations. The government reluctantly had to appoint these young leaders, whose loyalty to the Party was untested, as Christian representatives in the provincial CPPCC and it was forced to allow them to assume church leadership positions.

Soon after, the young pastors established the Hebei Pastoral Training Center, a *de facto* Bible school directly under the leadership of the Hebei Christian Council. It opened in 1998 with several dozen students from all over Hebei and has since become a rallying point for young church leadership. Most of the faculty is in their late thirties and early forties and all were classmates at Beijing's Yanjin Seminary. This corps of young leaders now holds most key positions in the Hebei TSPM/CCC and in municipal TSPM/CCCs. They work well as a team that serves Christians in this province, which is critical for the development of the Christian community. They shared similar backgrounds, such as a Christian upbringing, a long Christian family tradition received at family gatherings[18] before the 1980s, a relatively good education, and similar theological training. They work well as a team that serves Christians in this province, which is critical for the development of the Christian community. They also suffered little during the Cultural Revolution, and now they are politically sophisticated and share a strong desire to serve and build the church in appreciation of the Reform and Open Policy of the Chinese government.

Not mired in animosities between TSPM and non-TSPM churches in the 1950s that still shadow many older church leaders, these young leaders can focus on the future development of the church. They are pragmatic and willing to work with the government, more from a pastoral than an ideological or theological basis. Because most of them have had experience with the autonomous Christian communities (and some are actively involved in them), they usually operate in both the registered and the nonregistered spheres. They are energetic, dynamic, and eager to incorporate new ideas.

In 1999, the general secretary of the Hebei TSPM, Rev. Jin Yun Peng, who was then in his late thirties, replaced an older pastor as the Protestant representative in the Hebei CPPCC. Soon after the appointment, Rev. Jin Yun Peng rallied Catholic and Buddhist CPPCC representatives to challenge certain clauses of the draft of the new Hebei Religious Regulations. As related in an interview with Rev. Jin Yun Peng in 2000, such independence by the religious representatives was until then unheard of. Previously, representatives had usually passed along whatever regulation was handed to them. As this religious caucus exercised its right to challenge the clauses, the government was forced to retrieve the draft for revision, and later rewrote the draft to the satisfaction of the religious representatives. Shortly thereafter, the Hebei Christian Council applied for a license to publish a weekly newspaper, arguing that this was only fair since Catholics already had such a weekly journal (interview, June 2000). In addition, the Catholic church in the province operates a printing press, along with a newspaper called *Faith Fortnightly* and a Web site (www.chinacatholic.org), and a journal, which is distributed nationwide. This is allowed because Hebei is a traditional Catholic stronghold, where one-quarter of all Chinese Catholics live. The Protestants in Hebei, on the other hand, are a tiny fraction of all Chinese Protestants. Nevertheless, the government finally acceded to the request and in 2000 the Hebei Christian Council was granted a license to publish a Protestant newspaper, called *Tien You* (Heavenly Friend), which is distributed nationally. The first issue of the Protestant newspaper in the PRC rolled off the press on June 20, 2001.

The government's eventual willingness to accommodate the Protestant groups' plans suggests that, given the right leadership, these groups could exert some influence, and successfully assert their position despite the government's opposition. It may also indicate that the government has begun to incorporate views from various sectors, providing more democratic representation.[19] Whether the government really aimed to disperse power to groups other than the CCP or had to heed these groups' views to maintain effective governance is an open question. But what is clear is that the Christian community in Hebei is no longer always subservient to the state. It flexed its political muscle and the government listened. It also rallied support from other religious groups with similar interests, illustrating the "self-enforcing" mechanism described by various political economists (Min xin Pei 1995b, 65–79). As the church in Hebei grows in unity and strength, it may amass more bargaining power to deal with the government. In this case, the yeast gradually carved out a small space within the dough despite the heavy weight of the flour.

Case 2: Jiangxi Bible School—Confrontation with the Authorities

Jiangxi, in central China, has a Christian population of 350,000 out of a total of forty-one million.[20] The Christian community there began humbly, with fewer than ten thousand Christians in the early 1980s. The Jiangxi Christian Council established a pastoral training center ten years ago, which it later upgraded to a Bible school. It moved from the balcony of the church into a country mansion as the student population grew from a couple dozen to about one hundred. In 1998, it purchased a run-down factory to refurbish this complex as a permanent site for the school. The school began full operations at the new site in 1999.

Since the early 1980s, the provincial TSPM/CCC has held province-wide meetings once every five years to elect the chief officers. These meetings provided an allegedly democratic process where delegates from various churches were free to elect the provincial officers. However, as in most elections in China, the government, in this case the provincial RAB, generally determined the candidates, and delegates voted only for those slated by the government. Candidates had to show faithfulness to the Party and loyalty to the current government leadership. In return, they enjoyed full government backing when exercising authority over the Christian community. Spirituality, Christian conduct, moral standing, and theological convictions were not the government's main criteria.

In the 1990s, the government began to look for candidates who could command respect from the congregations; therefore, popularity also became an increasingly important criterion. The government realized that leadership without popular support cannot control the community effectively. Increasingly, force and coercion are becoming outdated methods for exerting government influence as China gradually becomes more open. Since the mid-1990s a few young leaders have received leadership positions in the church hierarchy, where before then they had been a minority and had played a secondary role.

In 1999, the provincial Christian Council was searching for new leadership to replace old leaders who had passed away or were too old to function effectively. The government insisted on giving the top leadership slot to a rather incompetent younger pastor who had a track record of following government directives to the letter and of making no decision without seeking the government's opinion. Naturally, he had not been the most popular pastor among Jiangxi Christians, or the most respected colleague among the clergy. The election for church leadership was supposed to follow democratic patterns. The candidate failed to come up with sufficient votes despite being the government's unmistakable preference. This failure to vote in the government's appointee represented a clear defiance of government wishes—a cardinal political sin in the past. Because the young leaders had blocked the government's leadership plan, the government retaliated by manipulating some government ministries to close down the Bible school for violating minor ordinances. This was a classic example of "rule by laws," under which the government can selectively use numerous regulations to achieve its political objectives.

The school had to vacate the newly furnished campus but continued their classes in a rented building. Meanwhile, the confrontation over the government-approved candidate continued. The government underestimated the strength of the young leaders' objection; in the past, it had always been able to get what it wanted. Church people had generally backed down if the government applied, or threatened, pressure. Yet the government could not back down from its decision for fear of losing face. The longer this power struggle dragged on, the more the young leadership gained sympathy both from the Christians and from some liberal-minded government cadres. The government found it could not win this battle, as the young leaders stood firm. Through negotiation, a compromise was reached: The government would purchase the site of the former Bible school, the renovated factory, for more than its market value to compensate the school for the relocation expense. In turn, church leaders would accept the government-designated young pastor as second-in-command in the Christian Council. The government knew this young pastor would have little influence over the church, but at least he would provide the government critical inside information about the Christian Council. The church leadership knew they had won this battle but at a high financial cost; they had to secure another site and build a new Bible school campus. Even with the proceeds of the sale of the former site, this required raising a large sum of money, a difficult task for a church located in one of the poorest provinces in central China.[21]

Compared to neighboring provinces in southern and central China, Jiangxi Province is rather conservative politically. Control over religion has been relatively tight. Since the early 1980s, churches in neighboring provinces could invite overseas Christians to visit; Jiangxi's Religious Affairs Bureau began to permit this only in 1997.[22] Soon after the first invitation, the Jiangxi Christian Council rapidly expanded overseas contacts and collected many outside resources.[23] Having these overseas resources helped the young leadership to act more independently of government control than formerly.

These events helped many young leaders realize that they need not be as passive as their predecessors: They do not have to dance to the government's tune. The leaders have begun to take more control over the course of the Christian community from the government. The government has accepted limitations of its authority over the Christians, seeing that it had to give up some of its demands in exchange for cooperation and a harmonious relationship with the people. For the government, it is a step toward more responsible governance of a social movement that has been sweeping over the Chinese political landscape. The Religious Affairs Bureau has been one of the last government bureaus to change. In this case, the Christian community served as an agent to push for democratic representation by holding on to their position despite government pressure. Eventually, *vox populi* succeeded in speaking as *vox dei*. The yeast, again, proved to be effective in raising more democratic dough.

Case 3: Fugong County, Yunnan—A Christian County

Fugong constitutes a unique Chinese ecclesial community: a county (the basic political administrative unit) where Christians, mostly ethnic Lisu, predominate. We will first consider the sociocultural influence Christianity has had locally and then assess the current political implications.

Christianity was introduced to the Lisu people in Burma at the end of the nineteenth century and spread to China in the early 1920s.[24] Almost 60 percent of the one million Lisu in the world live in Yunnan Province in southwestern China, concentrated in the Nujiang Canyon (formerly, Selwin Valley).[25] Fugong County has the largest population among the four counties in Nujiang Prefecture, and over 90 percent of Fugong's population is Lisu. The proportion of Christians among the Lisu has grown steadily, despite the political strictures against Christianity. By 1997 there were 54,829 registered Christians among 88,498 residents: 70 percent of the county population. Almost all of the Christians are Lisu, with the exception of a few Christians from the Nu ethnic group. This is the highest concentration of Christians at the county level in China and the first primarily "Christian county."

Missionaries in Nujiang during the 1920s and 1930s were from a fundamentalist background that emphasized a dualistic worldview with strongly puritanical teachings. They were aware that the Lisu were very religious, spending vast sums on sacrifices to appease gods and spirits despite their poverty. Traditional dowry customs were also a heavy economic burden, and the Lisu often ended up in debt. The missionaries considered many customs, such as rice wine drinking, smoking, and premarital sex, incompatible with Christianity.[26] As the missionaries introduced Christianity to the Lisu, the new religion brought about social changes that affected their economy. These economic changes were noted, and praised, by the Chinese government in the 1950s, despite negative attitudes toward religion in general and missionaries especially. The popularity of Christianity among the Lisu may be partly due to economic advantages that resulted from conversion to the Christian faith and the resulting changed lifestyles. In any case, the popular embrace of Christianity has had significant political consequence in Fugong County. The following facts are all drawn from official government reports, which tend to preclude any pro-Christian bias.

Weddings were expensive events for the Lisu. The groom had to pay the bride several cows and typically ended up in debt for many years. It was not uncommon for a family to have to sell children into slavery to pay off the debt. Therefore, marriages became a trade arranged by the families instead of being decided by the prospective bride and groom. If the husband wanted a divorce, he could reclaim all he had paid. If the wife initiated divorce, she had to pay back twice what she had received from her husband. Thus, divorce led to many conflicts. Lisu men were allowed to have concubines, invariably causing complications in the family. Finally, all unmarried teens and adults could sleep in a "common house" in search of sexual partners; they were allowed to engage in sexual acts freely until they got married.[27]

A detailed study of the annual expenses of many Lisu households conducted in 1954 sheds light on the economic burden of a Lisu marriage. When a well-to-do family's son married, the wedding cost about 38 percent of the entire household's annual net income. The family became severely indebted, dramatically transformed from a well-to-do into a poor household.[28] The austere missionaries regarded these Lisu marriage customs as inappropriate and a hindrance to the spread of the gospel. Therefore, they insisted that Christians be monogamous, that they could not divorce, and that premarital sex was prohibited. Because many poor young people could not afford to marry, the missionaries insisted that both parties forgo the exchange of gifts and discouraged the wedding feast. Any consenting Christian male over the age of twenty and female over the age of eighteen could marry in a church free of charge. Christians could not marry non-Christians. Such new marriage customs attracted many people to join the church (Hanxin and Zhang 1990, 21–22). Individuals could decide whom to marry without incurring debt. Many joined the church to avoid a costly wedding. There were fewer family disputes over divorces and concubines. Forced marriages due to unwed pregnancies arising from the common house may have declined. Finally, the Christian community protected the institution of marriage.

One can argue that a Christian wedding was economically prudent for the Lisu because of its promotion of austere wedding ceremonies and reduced obligations. Having no wedding feast greatly helped newlyweds financially in this poor region and saved food that might have been wasted.[29] The money saved could be used to invest in agricultural production. Young people getting married were well aware of these benefits.

One of the few luxuries in the harsh environment of Nujiang was alcohol consumption. At the end of the first harvest, the Lisu often set up a crude brewery in the fields to make rice wine from the new grain.[30] They used a large quantity of grain to make wine and then lay drunk in the fields for several days. The grain they did produce was not even enough for basic consumption, so the Lisu went into debt long before the second harvest. In most family and community gatherings, alcohol was central; drunkenness was accepted. Alcoholism has been, and still is, an epidemic problem among the Lisu. A detailed study in 1956 suggested that an average Lisu household—excluding Christians—used 12 to 23 percent of their annual grain production to make wine. Most of these households could not produce sufficient grain to feed themselves. The average household used a lot of grain to make wine and also sold crops for cash to purchase extra wine after the harvest season.[31] Often, households ran out of food a few months after the harvest and went into debt or lived on handouts. It is hard to ignore the economic significance of wine drinking, not to mention the social consequences of alcoholism, among the Lisu. In addition, the Lisu also liked to smoke, which further consumed a substantial amount of their disposable income.

The missionaries made their teachings on drinking and smoking clear: Total abstinence was treated as a basic requirement for all Christians. The Christian community enforced this among their members and helped those addicted to alcohol withdraw from their habits. The missionaries substituted drinking local tea for the Lisu habit of smoking. Christian families saved substantially more money this way, and there were fewer crimes among the Christians due to the decline of alcoholism. In the early 1950s, even the antireligious Chinese Communist Party cadres admitted that the economic well-being of the Lisu Christians was generally better than that of non-Christians due to church teachings on alcohol and tobacco.[32]

Traditional religious customs dictate that the Lisu offer livestock or crops to various spirits regularly and at special times, such as illness and death. A 1953 survey indicated that of thirty-seven families in Chuangmedi Village, twenty-five made a total of 251 animal sacrifices to evil spirits during the year, about ten sacrifices per household. (The other families, who made no such sacrifices, were probably Christians.) In total, they offered eighty-eight pigs, 154 chickens, seven goats, and one cow, which amounted to over 11 percent of total annual village income. Allowing for the twelve households not making sacrifices, the other twenty-five households used at least 15 percent of their gross annual income for such a purpose—a very substantial proportion for this poor region. A study of a relatively well-to-do family showed that from 1929 to 1952, this family made offerings of sixteen goats, fifteen chickens, and twenty-nine pigs. Eventually, the head of the household had to sell all their land to pay for the debt incurred by these offerings. He became a hired laborer, just slightly better off than a slave.[33]

Christian teaching regarding these sacrifices was again very clear: No Christian was allowed to sacrifice to spirits after becoming a believer. This was more for theological than for economic reasons: Only God may be worshipped. Although the missionaries taught Christians to make offerings to the church, the amounts did not come near those previously offered to spirits. As an obvious side effect, those who became Christians again saved money.[34]

The missionaries' main concern was to save the lost Lisu souls from damnation, not to rescue them from their miserable economic predicament. Nevertheless, their teachings brought economic benefits. The missionaries developed a set of teachings, including three basic theological teachings and the Lisu Ten Commandments (Daoshing 1994, 1082–1083):

> One must be devoted to one God. One cannot believe in God and, at the same time, make offerings to other spirits....
> God is holy, and drinking alcohol is an unholy as well as blasphemous act.... This also applies to smoking.
> Christians are civilized; it would be uncivilized[35] and even shameful to accept wedding gifts from either party... [or] waste money on the wedding feast.[36]

There were various versions of the Lisu Ten Commandments; here are two examples:

1. No adultery.
2. No cheating and keep the Sabbath.
3. No flirting.
4. No stealing and killing.
5. No bearing false witness.
6. No smoking or drinking.
7. No traditional dancing or singing.
8. Keep close to the pastor to help evangelize others.
9. Respect your parents and abide by the law.
10. Love others as yourself, help each other, and do not envy others.

1. No smoking.
2. No drinking.
3. No gambling.
4. No killing.
5. No trading in marriage.
6. No cheating.
7. No stealing.
8. No worshipping of evil spirits.
9. Keep hygienic.
10. Stay monogamous.[37]

These teachings were practical guidelines on which Lisu Christians built and based their community. Although these teachings may sound legalistic, Lisu Christians found them easy to follow, and such guidelines helped shape a unique community based on Christian principles. These teachings were not intended to produce a sustainable economic community, but the social values of honest work and avoiding waste eventually made Christian families economically better off than their non-Christian neighbors.

In the 1920s, the missionaries also created phonetic scripts that became the predominant Lisu form of writing. Through instruction at church on hymn singing and Bible studying, Christians mastered this script and became literate despite the lack of formal education. Therefore, the Christian Lisu were, in general, more educated and literate than the non-Christians.

With superior economic, cultural, and numerical strength, and a well-organized ecclesial network, the Christian community in Fugong is naturally the most influential group in this county. There are 273 churches, one for each village in the county. The pastoral training center can house five hundred students, and the church runs a rotating training program year-round. Before 1995, the Party appointed county officers. But when the Chinese government gradually launched a program of democratic elections for county and village leaders in the mid-1990s, Fugong promptly elected a church elder as its new county governor—probably the first county-level officer in the PRC who openly professed Christian faith. He is a graduate of the Central Academy of National Minorities, a national center that trains government cadres among national minorities, but he is also a graduate of Yunnan's Theological Seminary.

Although the people's government, supervised by the local Party branch, runs the county, the influence of the Party in this county is not clearly visible. Many senior county officials are Christians or from a Christian family background. For example, the chief of the county public security is a deacon in the church. In 1997, he assured this author that there was not a single Christian being held in his jail/detention center because Christians were all law-abiding citizens. Fugong County actually has had one of the lowest crime rates among neighboring counties, which suggests Christian influences on positive social values, a feature acknowledged by the provincial government.

Christian influence is so strong that Fugong County appears to be operated simultaneously by the church and civil authorities. Surprisingly, these two seem to cooperate well. The government has been able to launch various social programs through well-established church networks. The church has conducted its pastoral affairs with virtually no restriction. In fact, the church has tried to utilize its ecclesial connections to gain overseas resources for the economic development of this county, which is one of the poorest in China and is designated by the central government for special economic assistance. In this exceptional case, the sociopolitical dynamics of the county are heavily determined by the church, rather than the Party, simply because Christians are the overwhelming majority. After all, the welfare of the county inhabitants is almost identical to the welfare of the Christians in this county. In this extreme case, the rapid expansion of Christianity creates a subtle church-over-state situation, even in a socialist-atheist country like China. The yeast has taken full advantage of shaping new dough in this remote corner of China. However, the Fugong case is unlikely to be duplicated elsewhere in China because it has sprung uniquely from a particular ethnic group apparently having adopted Christianity as its predominant cultural identity in China, northern Thailand, Burma (Myanmar), and northern India.

Case 4: The Church in Yangshan—A Newly Born Civil Group

People sometimes wonder how so many Christian communities developed recently in remote villages. In theory, if there were no Christian community before 1949, the government ordinarily would not ratify any new Christian church. Changing the status quo, especially in recognizing religious groups, is a major political decision, because it permanently changes the socioreligious dynamic in a region. The places discussed in this chapter are often "in the middle of nowhere," with no previous exposure to Christianity. They are far from cities or ports where Christians from overseas might come and they often even lack overseas contacts. Although some local Christian communities engage in evangelistic efforts, many of the new communities grew without any contact with churches in the region.

Here is a typical example of such a community, which started almost by accident (Yamamori and Chan 2000, 69–74). This community illustrates how a new group gains official recognition where no Christian group has ever existed. By receiving such recognition, the Christian community becomes a permanent social group in the local community. The local government is forced to live with such changes, making accommodations to a new religious group under its rule. The required government tolerance ushers in new social plurality, an important change indeed in any region's social and political dynamics.

The Qingyuan Prefecture lies at the northern tip of Guangdong Province. Its eight counties are among the poorest in Guangdong. Although missionaries arrived there more than a hundred years ago, Christianity made little progress among the inhabitants, who were mostly farmers. By 1949, there were several churches attended by a few hundred followers. The churches were closed when the communists took power. There was no public Christian activity until the early 1980s. Yangshan County, just north of the prefecture seat, had no record of any Christian presence at all before 1990.

In 1991, a retired primary school teacher, Chen Shaoying, visited her daughter, who was having minor surgery at the county hospital. The Chens live in a small town named Cigong, which is located about thirty kilometers from Yangshan, the county seat. In the hospital, the Chens became friends with a patient from another small town. One day, a distant relative of this person, a Christian, came to visit. The relative offered to pray for Chen's daughter. Chen had not encountered Christianity before, hearing only that it was an imperialistic attack on China. Curious, she asked the relative to explain this religion.

Hearing the gospel for the first time, Chen and her daughter accepted Jesus Christ as their Savior. A few days later, they returned to Cigong, and Chen immediately began sharing this new faith with her friends, neighbors, and relatives. The response was only modest: By the end of the year, seven people had made commitments to Christ. Chen began holding small gatherings at her home. She also traveled to Qingyuan City, the prefecture seat, looking for Christians who could help her. Making contact with the church there, Chen returned with a Bible and some booklets on basic Christian doctrine.

Most people in that region adhere to traditional Chinese folk religions, which are syncretistic mixes of Buddhism and Taoism. They will worship any god as long as it "works." People began asking Chen to pray to this new God named Jesus on their behalf. Several experienced physical healing, and word spread that Chen's God was a powerful deity able to perform miracles. Many people, attracted by the power of God, became followers of Jesus. Their ranks grew to seventy by the end of 1992, and to more than 150 in 1993. They held meetings in five homes.

Getting wind of this new "cult," the local government tried to stop it through administrative means. The man in charge of religious affairs in the county was an army veteran, a loyal Party man and former political commissar strongly opposed to religion. He told Chen to disband the groups or he would throw the Christians in jail.

Seeking help from the Qingyuan church, Chen discovered that her group could exercise its right to religious belief under the Constitution if it registered. However, when Chen spoke again with the antagonistic cadre, he said, "As there has never been Christianity in this county, we will not allow a Christian group to register here. You will get registered over my dead body. Now get out, or I'll arrest you." Such a statement followed a standing order from the government not to allow new religious groups; however, this order contradicts the national religious ordinance, which states that people have the right to change religious affiliation, for instance from atheism to Christianity. The government can tolerate already existing religious groups, but any new group means religious changes are taking place that might upset the existing sociopolitical order. Furthermore, if a new religious group registers officially, the government must recognize their political rights and share certain political authority with them. For example, these groups can claim tax-free status, and some of their leaders could eventually gain seats at the local CPPCC. They can make demands for their activities and venues. They can also invite outside groups to visit them.

Local cadres often disregard national policy. Despite the sustained intervention of the prefecture's Religious Affairs Bureau and the Christian Council, the local government refused to budge. It claimed there must be a certain number of religious believers before a church could register. The number Chen provided was not accepted, as no so-called Christians in Cigong had been baptized. When Chen suggested that the government invite an ordained minister to baptize the believers, the government replied that because there was no registered Christian group in Cigong, there was no body qualified to invite a pastor. Beyond that, there were no ordained ministers in Qingyuan anyway; all the sacraments had to be conducted by ordained ministers invited from Guangzhou, the provincial capital. The local government warned that any pastor who came there illegally would be arrested. This kind of Catch-22 situation is very common for new Christian communities in China, which are at the mercy of the government. Chen and her groups were forced into hiding for two years.

By 1994, at least 250 believers were secretly gathering in people's homes. The local government often harassed Chen and the other believers, threatening arrest. In these confrontations, Chen simply responded, "Go ahead and arrest me." In fact, she had already packed a small bag and was ready to go to jail at any time. Despite the government pressure, the Christian community continued to grow, spreading even beyond Cigong. Pastors from the Qingyuan Christian Council also paid regular visits in spite of the danger of being arrested.

That same year, Hsu Shuicun, a nurse at the Yangshan People's Hospital, visited her mother in Cigong. Hsu's marriage was in trouble, as her husband was having an affair. She had no peace and was seeking advice from fortunetellers. One day she visited her aunt, hoping to have her palms read. A neighbor, Mrs. Leung, told Hsu that there was no need to read palms because she knew of a more powerful deity who could help people. At Mrs. Leung's house, Hsu saw a calendar with a cross on it and recognized it as a symbol of Christianity. Her high school teacher had warned her that Christianity was a foreign, imperialistic religion. She found it very strange to discover this religion in a rural place like Cigong.

Mrs. Leung shared her testimony with Hsu, who immediately accepted the gospel. Hsu took a Bible, which was missing several pages, back home with her to Yangshan. She shared her new faith with her mother-in-law, who embraced this God. Soon, Hsu spent most of her spare time studying the Bible and sharing her faith. Many nurses and doctors at the hospital accepted the gospel. Hsu traveled to Cigong to seek instruction in the faith from Chen and started gatherings in her own and other believers' homes.

There are now more than five hundred Christians at Yangshan, and they are seeking registration. They use the local cement factory's hall for Sunday services and plan to build their own church. Although the gospel did not save Hsu's marriage—she and her husband divorced a year later—Hsu says she experiences peace and consolation from God. She is a very dedicated lay preacher. The gospel teachers have also traveled to towns and villages where they have Christian relatives. Meanwhile, Chen tried to get the Cigong church officially established. Together with church leaders in Qingyuan, they developed a two-pronged approach. In 1995, the Qingyuan church invited a pastor from Hong Kong to hold a baptismal service. The Christians of Cigong and Yangshan rented a bus to transport sixty Christians to the Qingyuan church.

Following the service, Cigong had forty officially initiated Christians, Yangshan twenty. The forty were now eligible to apply for registration as the Cigong Christian Temporary Gathering Point. At the same time, the Qingyuan church held a three-week lay preacher-training program. Chen and several others have completed this program and are now certified as officially recognized lay preachers, which is another criterion for registration.

Meanwhile, the prefecture Religious Affairs Bureau and the Christian Council of Qingyuan jointly issued a letter of complaint to the Qingyuan People's Congress against the cadres in charge of religious affairs of Yangshan County. The letter charged that the cadres insulted the Christian religion, created problems among the people, and refused to implement the national policy of freedom of religious belief. The leading Cigong cadre on religious affairs was forced into early retirement and replaced with more sympathetic officials. These new cadres gave oral approval for Christians in Cigong and Yangshan to hold meetings and allow them to apply for registration.

Both communities grew rapidly, with many experiencing healing after coming to believe in the gospel. By this time, Chen and her coworkers did not need to travel to nearby villages to preach because many believers brought their friends and relatives to Chen's house for prayer or discussions about the faith. Chen also organized the Christians to visit the local old people's hostel and share their resources with the poor.

Christians in Cigong and Yangshan earned respect in their communities despite their lack of formal registration. Those in Cigong rented a house for Sunday worship services, which now has several hundred people attending weekly. On December 28, 1998, the government finally granted them official registration, with the serial number 001, the first such registration in the county. By then, the church had several hundred baptized members, a team of four lay preachers, and two more applying for seminary training.

As of summer 2001, the Yangshan community of several hundred believers still lacked official registration. Registered or not, they are known by the whole community and are part of the Qingyuan Christian Council network. Both communities planned to build their own church buildings.

Ten years before, there had not been a single Christian in the county. There are now more than one thousand baptized members in two large communities and many smaller groups. It all began with a retired teacher who visited her daughter in a county hospital. As these communities grew, they had to assert their position as a new type of social organization, hitherto nonexistent, as part of the local community fabric among many existing social groups. The genesis of new social groups in a traditional static society forces changes as the society incorporates the new groups, despite the government's reluctance to make room for them. These two groups chose to claim their right through legal procedures instead of operating in secret. They studied government regulations and openly negotiated with civil authorities for years. Acting in accordance with various regulations, they complied with every legal requirement for registration. The eventual official recognition of the Christians in Yangshan marks a new era for this county: the beginning of a pluralistic society initiated by local citizenry.

This case demonstrates not only how pressure from below can create a more pluralistic society but also how government and church administrative interventions are conducted. The Religious Affairs Bureau and the prefecture Christian Council successfully intervened at the prefecture National People's Congress, with the supervision of the CPPCC, to remove an official who did not follow the government's policy. This suggests that there are channels within the government apparatus for making changes, which is in itself a departure from autocratic rule toward a more open legislative structure that can listen and respond to new voices. The church was represented at the prefecture CPPCC by a delegate who exercised his political right; the CPPCC was not a rubber-stamp apparatus, but functioned as designated by law. At least in the example of Cigong church in Qingyuan Prefecture the Christian community managed to force the local government to accept a more diverse society. Church leaders at a higher level accelerated the process by exercising their political power and proper judicial procedure. Such exercises of legal and political procedures constitute democratic progress.

The Qingyuan experience typifies the experiences of thousands of new Christian groups seeking registration in recent decades. Most groups, like these two, are in regions where there has never been a Christian church. Such Christian communities are new civil groups emerging from among average people who are then integrated into the local sociopolitical structure. Thus, the rapid development of the Christian community in itself enhances the development of a pluralistic Chinese society by forcing the government to recognize new groups as part of the social fabric.

Case 5: Opium Village Turned Christian Village—A New Sociopolitical Focus

Several years ago, China began to institute democratic elections for village chiefs; anyone can now sponsor a candidate to head a village. This social experiment met with mixed results. Some elected village heads could not function due to interference by the Party branch, which was reluctant to give up power (Li 2001, 15). In many instances, however, villages enhanced their welfare through elected village heads. Influential village subgroups, whether it is the Party branch, a clan, or a church, may significantly affect election outcomes. Where a village is predominantly Christian, Christians nominate candidates. In places like Fugong, where Christians are the majority, they change local political dynamics significantly.

The following case illustrates the political potential of a new Christian community in a few remote villages in southwestern China. Newly formed Christian churches there may soon become the predominant social institutions in many villages that in the past were the preserve of the local Party branch. The case in Yunnan Province illustrates new Christian influence not formerly found in villages there.

Ironically, this surge in Christianity has been triggered by opium use among Chinese people. Increasing numbers of drug addicts have turned to Christianity and reformed their lives. Opium and the gospel have had a peculiar relationship in recent Chinese history. Some of the earliest Protestant missionaries to China, such as Charles Gutzlaff and Robert Morrison, worked for the East India Company, which was the primary trader of opium to China.[38] The opium trade led to the First Opium War in 1839–1840 and resulted in the Nanjing Treaty, which opened China to the world and gave foreign missionaries an opportunity to proselytize. Around that time, Karl Marx and Friedrich Engels proclaimed their famous motto, "Religion is the opiate of the people," referring, however, particularly to the Orthodox Church in Russia (Engels 1878, 145).

Many missionaries responded to the problem of opium addiction in China by establishing special clinics to offer comfort and guidance to addicts by introducing them to the gospel, a venture that met with a high degree of success (Latourette 1929, 457–458). In the first three decades of the People's Republic of China, opium addiction was largely eradicated by determined government administrative efforts. At that time, religion, especially Christianity, was suppressed. The regime saw no room for ideological opiates in a socialist society. Since the 1980s, as China has pushed its new Reform and Open Policy, opium addiction has reemerged, along with other drug dependencies, especially in border areas where opium is available and relatively cheap.[39] At the same time, religiosity, especially Christianity, has grown rapidly, and in many places threatens to seriously reduce Communist Party membership.[40]

In 1998, the National Minority and Religious Affairs Bureau of the Simao Prefecture in Yunnan published a report on a new Christian community in a village in Lancang Lahu Autonomous County. Christianity was introduced to this traditionally animist and polytheistic Lahu village in 1992. By 1998, the community included approximately three hundred believers and had built a church on a prominent site next to the main highway that can hold three hundred people. The RAB report suggested that the introduction of Christianity to this village not only enhanced believers' economic prosperity but also effectively diminished crime, including opium addiction. Apparently, many former criminals—including thieves, drug addicts, and alcoholics—were transformed into lawful citizens through Christian conversion (Xu, Zhou, and Du 1998, 68–70). The report's primary focus was the relationship between economic changes and faith conversion. It neither directly explored opium addicts' rehabilitation through Christian faith nor discussed the sociopolitical influence of new Christian communities in the villages.

However, all the report's researchers spoke with the author about the positive role of Christian faith in eradicating opium addiction in this village. The government had previously invested heavily in the construction of a stone quarry, hoping to help drug addicts break their addiction through employment. That project was a complete failure. However, workers on that project noticed that Christians from other villages did not smoke opium. As a result, the government facilitated sending some ministers to preach the gospel in villages where many residents have since converted to Christianity. Since 1997, the government has employed similar ways for Christians to share their faith in villages where most residents were opium addicts. By summer 2000, each village had its own church and almost all former opium addicts were free from addiction through Christian influence (Yamamori and Chan 2000, chap. 5).

RAB researchers invited the author to visit one such village, although the author preferred to visit a new Christian village that was not a result of a government initiative giving Christianity a favorable starting point. The local authorities issued an invitation to visit a newly Christian village where Christianity arose entirely through the villagers' own initiative and was accompanied there by local officials, one of them a prominent anthropologist who specializes in Lahu culture and has published extensively in this field.[41] The following account is based on observations made during that field visit in June 2000 to the church at Baipidezai (K. Chan 2000, 4–5), a hamlet located in the Mujia Village in Shanyuan Township of the Lancang Lahu Autonomous County.

The Baipidezai Lahu hamlet comprises 207 people in fifty-four families and is located on a mountain slope near Burma (Myanmar), which is at least three days' travel from Simao City. In the past, all villagers believed in the Lahu traditional folk religion, which is centered on livestock sacrifice by a local shaman called a *muba*.[42] When someone was sick, the family invited the muba to hold a divination service. If the cause of the disease was attributed to a senior ghost or deity, the family had to slaughter a large animal, such as a cow or pig. If the cause was a minor ghost, a chicken sufficed. Sacrifices had to continue until the disease was gone.[43] This practice became one of the Lahu's main expenses and a major factor contributing to the community's poverty. In addition, most adults in the area smoked opium that is widely planted just across the border and readily available. Before 1998, the villagers had lived in extreme poverty.

Some villagers had relatives at Xiadade Village, one day's walk away. When visiting their relatives, they would notice the Christians living there. They looked healthier, cleaner, seemed to own more chickens (an indicator of prosperity), and appeared more prosperous than other villagers. They also noted that the Christians did not practice "feudal superstitions," a term used by the government to denote traditional folk religious practices, such as animal sacrifices, divinations, and worshipping of local deities. The visitors invited the Christians to explain this religion so they, too, could enjoy a similar living standard. The church at Xiadade sent a preacher to Baipedizai to teach villagers the gospel. Very soon, more than ten families became Christians and they met at home. Currently, twenty-three families—in all, eighty-five people, or 40 percent of the village population—belong to this new church at Baipidezai. The number of Christians is still growing. They recently constructed their own church building that can hold about 120 people.

The following are excerpts from this writer's interviews with the head of this Christian community in Xiadade Village. (The leader spoke Lahu; Madame Zhang Caixian, chief of the County Minority Affairs Bureau, translated between Lahu and Putonghua. The interviewer's questions are in italics.)

What are the changes that you experienced after you converted to Christianity?
I have better health. I also have a bumper harvest. I do not need to sacrifice chickens and pigs to ghosts.
Can you tell me about the teaching of Christianity?
God [Ngo Sha] will protect us. We do not work in vain. God will give us good health.
Do you see any change in social behavior among Christians?
We do not steal each other's rice. We do not commit adultery. We do not take poison (alcohol, opium, and tobacco). We lead others to labor in the field. When we are rich, we help others to become rich.
What are your religious activities?
We have a worship service on Sunday, in the evening when everyone comes back from the field. We sing hymns and listen to the sermon. The sermon encourages us to do labor and not be lazy. After the sermon, the preacher teaches us scientific agriculture methods.
Each family has a Lahu Bible and a Lahu hymnal.
Who is Jesus?
He is God (a different term for a lesser deity than *Ngo Sha*).
What is the Cross [as I pointed at the cross in the church]?
I have not learned it yet; it is a lesson for advanced Christians.
How do you join the Church?
I knelt in front of the Cross and the preacher held my hand. He prayed for me. He asked me if I want to join this religion and I said yes. He took me out to the river and baptized me. I had to burn my altar table at home, where I had worshipped other deities in the past.

Any opium addicts here?
There are twenty who are drug addicts. After we accepted Christianity, none of us take opium anymore. We dare not take it again.
Why?
There are commandments in this religion that prohibit us from smoking opium.
Can you recall these commandments?
There are twelve commandments that we have to obey. But I can't recite them from my memory. Ask the preacher; he knows.
What other changes have you noticed among the Christians after they join this new religion?
In general we have better health. The households are cleaner than before. There is no thief among us. We make our offerings by our free will.
Do you pray at home?
Yes, we have this prayer every day before we eat: "Today's food is not easy to come by. God [Ngo Sha] gives it to us. After we eat it, we will not be sick. God protects us so that we can have the next meal. He protects us so everyone is prosperous and we have peace. All our family members, from young to old, need the protection of God. After we finish this meal, we will have the next one. All our pigs will be healthy. We will have plenty of chickens and cows. God protects us so that we can live better than before. We work hard and we eat from the fruit of our labor. Our maize and grain will not be eaten by rats or cows. At harvest time, we will have a bumper harvest. The first bowl of rice is offered to God, we eat the second bowl. After we eat, our blood and flesh [Lahu expression for body] will not be sick. Lead our family members to live in peace. Amen."
What about other drug addicts who are not Christians?
The government gathered them together and rehabilitates them with medicine.
Are there any differences between Christian ex-addicts and non-Christian ones?
The Christian ex-addict does not take opium again. Many of the non-Christian addicts return to their opium habit.

In this case, the motive for seeking Christianity seems to have been economic. Villagers at Baipidezai asked the Christians at Xiadade for help. Since the Reform and Open Policy of the 1980s, some of the rural population suffers from lack of governmental support, especially in education and medical services, which previously were provided by the government. Many rural people are trapped in a vicious cycle of poverty and illness. Once they become ill, they spend many of their resources on medical services or, in this case, on religious sacrifices. They may exhaust their reserve savings or end up in debt. Often, they smoke opium to provide relief from symptoms of illness or for psychological relief. It is readily available at a relatively low cost; however, it perpetuates the negative economic cycle.

The message of Christianity, as perceived and experienced by these people, is a message of health and prosperity, both of which they desperately need. Avoiding costly religious sacrifices in times of personal calamity and illnesses improves their prosperity. The nongluttonous God of Christianity is a welcome deity to these poor Lahu peasants. Further, they are assured that the God of Christianity is the most powerful God, one who loves to protect people without asking for an impoverishing sacrifice. The other factor that can contribute to prosperity is abstention from alcohol, opium, and tobacco. This is a legacy from missionary teachings during Prohibition in the 1930s. The money saved by avoiding these expenses can be quite significant and can contribute to a family's reserve capital, giving them an economic margin in difficult times.

Health also seems to have improved as people accept this new religion. Missionaries may have contributed to better health by emphasizing the importance of wearing one's best (*clean*) clothing to church and by having a well-washed body. Many villagers had no tradition of washing either body or clothes. These new teachings introduced better hygiene as part of the new religion, thus improving general health.

The Lahu form of Christian faith is extremely contextualized and closely linked to people's daily lives, as their prayers before meals indicate. For them, faith is not abstract, but a daily experience. Their supplications reflect immediate concerns; results are visible and goals are measurable. Their positive experience reenforces confidence in their belief system.

The illiteracy rate among Lahus in Lancang County is 98.1 percent.[44] Missionaries developed a Romanized phonetic script for the Lahus in the early 1900s. Those who attend church soon learn to use that script to read the Bible and sing hymns. On average, it takes several weeks to master the script, and those who do are able to practice daily by reading the Bible or singing hymns. Those who join the church are more likely to become literate, and this elevates their social position.

There is little social or entertainment activity in these hamlets. The few television programs available elicit limited interest, as few understand the official dialect (Putonghua) in which they are broadcast. The only major social activities are festival days, when villagers sing and dance. Church activities, particularly the hymn singing during worship or evening services, draw many. Local Christians sing classic Christian hymns translated into the Lahu tongue, often, as this author observed, without fully understanding their meaning and enjoy the singing much more than the sermons or teachings, which was also observed among other minority groups, such as Lisu, Miao, Yi, and Dai.

Hymn singing, then, may serve more as a cultural binder and entertainment than as devotional expression. More established Lahu Christian communities have incorporated their traditional dances into Christian worship,[45] although this writer had no chance to observe this.

Traditionally, Lahus believed in a major deity, *Ngo Sha*, the creator of the universe who has no visible form; they also believed in a pantheon of other, lesser deities and a long list of ghosts that are believed to cause various diseases. The Lahu easily identify *Ngo Sha* with the omnipotent Christian God. They have difficulty placing Jesus or the Holy Spirit in the Lahu cosmology. Believers use another term, that of a lesser deity, to refer to Jesus, which may eventually have significant theological implications as the community encounters Christian doctrines such as the Trinity.

The villagers at Baipidezai seem to embrace Christianity out of economic desperation. They choose the Christian faith because they see the obviously superior economic conditions in Christian communities. Prohibition of opium smoking is one of many social transformations they experience during conversion. Christianity appears to be effective in rehabilitating opium addicts mainly as a result of the community support they experience in support of their new lifestyle.

The government looks very favorably on the overall social and economic impact of conversion to Christianity. Less is spent on religious sacrifices and alcohol, and decreased use of tobacco and opium also contribute to family savings. Conversion to Christianity also offers the introduction of scientific agricultural methods and makes capital available from family savings. To employ these techniques leads to improved harvests and increased income. As a result of fewer drug addicts committing fewer petty crimes, communal relationships improve. Increased literacy raises the community's educational level and individual self-esteem. A new wind of vitality seems to blow through a village as Christianity takes root. These preliminary findings contrast with the research of Qin Ning (1998), who suggested that such conservative forms of Christianity would cause negative social development among national minorities in Yunnan.[46] However, longitudinal follow-up studies are needed for a better picture of the long-term impact of Christianity.

Politically, the Party branch still plays the leading role in the community. The Party tried, without much success, to liberate Lahus from drug addiction and underdevelopment through communist ideology and medical and economic interventions. Although they are atheists, local government cadres see the transformation from polytheism (Lahu folk religion) to monotheism (Christianity) as a form of progress, a stage in religious evolution. They say the Lahus must pass through monotheism before reaching the social ideal of communism. They do not oppose Christianity but regard it as a superior form of culture that helps liberate Lahus from feudal superstitions. However, they emphasized to this writer that communist ideology is still superior to monotheism.

The church has gradually become the center of activity in this village. It has the largest building and holds meetings two or three times a week, at which almost half the village meets. It has an internal governing structure staffed by volunteers, offers what is perhaps the only regular free entertainment: hymn singing. It provides gifted people with few other opportunities to express their talents and develop leadership skills in teaching, singing, and organizing. The church fosters literacy and gives cultural identity and existential direction to its members. It introduces new skills and ways of thinking and provides connections to a wide network of Christian communities regionally and sometimes beyond. This group that emerges transformed by Christian faith has become the most influential group in the community, beginning with its economic influence and moving on to its sociocultural functions. In short, the church in this village provides a civil society that helps elevate the villager in multifaceted ways. Not surprisingly, membership has grown quickly, because for these villagers, there is everything to be gained by joining the church.

The church has no conflicts with the local village committee: The leadership of the two is almost identical. This is usually the case in national minority areas where traditional village leaders often exercise political as well as religious leadership. The government tries to pick ethnic leaders to respect local ethnic minority custom. Communist Party influence here is more administrative than ideological. Often, ethnic leaders take up leading positions in the local Party branch, but in a more traditional and ceremonial role rather than as a position based on ideological convictions. The emerging church need not cause political tensions, because often both church and village leadership positions are held by the same people. Moreover, the new lifestyle the church provides is applauded by almost everyone, including the government. It would be unsurprising if Christianity comes to predominate among Lahus in these villages, thus making the church the leading sociopolitical group.

This example illustrates how economic transformations catalyzed by Christianity can lead to political transitions in which the church becomes the main political player in a local scene in a communist country. The yeast has transformed all the dough into a radically different shape. However, one must not arrive at generalized conclusions from such an example, which took place in unique circumstances, which included widespread opium addiction and extreme poverty. Few rural communities in China are in such dire straits. In an ethnic minority region, ethnic autonomy can override ideological purity. Local leaders here have more freedom than their Han (ethnic majority) counterparts in incorporating religion in daily social and political life.

In Christian villages among Han Chinese, villages often elect a church elder as village head, less for his faith than for the respect he elicits among the villagers. In this area, there is no evidence of Christians acting as a political bloc or using their religious affiliation to support or reject candidates. Currently, the government is reevaluating the village's direct election program because of the many conflicts of interest that have occurred when villages voted out Party cadres and the two sides failed to develop a working relationship (Beech 2001, 34–35). The short-term political impact of Christian groups in rural politics is not obvious; most rural Christian communities are still in early stages and still unsure of their identity in the local sociopolitical context. But there is a growing demand in Chinese villages for more rights of self-governance, and, as this happens, the Christian community in rural areas may play a part in shaping future village politics. These rural Christian communities may, like yeast, become powerful agents in quietly shaping the village politics, given the right opportunity, by implementing their teaching skills, leadership, and by providing their guidance.

Case 6: A Dissenting Community

A large segment of the Christian community in China does not belong to the government-sanctioned TSPM/CCC organization and is, therefore, technically, illegal in Chinese society. These Christians consciously choose this status out of theological conviction, and they are willing to pay a high cost. As a result, many end up in jails and labor camps for years at a time, often without voicing any regrets. The government regards them as religious fanatics, agitators, and criminals, although the Christians regard themselves as true followers of Jesus, like St. Paul, who also suffered at the hands of civil authorities. To obey God rather than man (Holy Bible, Acts 5:29, cf. 4:19) is a traditional, underlying biblical justification. Their experiences are echoed by many communities throughout the history of the church: the early Christians in the Roman Colosseum, the Puritans who fled to the New World, and the Confessing Church persecuted by the Nazis. Such dissenting communities have been instrumental in pushing for wider religious tolerance and more participatory societies as they struggled for their survival and eventually for social legitimation. Dissenting Christian communities in China, still illegal and under government persecution, may perhaps be traveling the same route. The struggle of these communities for social acceptance often acts as a catalyst—again, like yeast—to stimulate social transformation. This case is an example of a dissenting community that eventually received *de facto* acceptance by local authorities despite ongoing *de jure* nonrecognition. (Actual names and places have been withheld.)

Madame Yang was a talented performing artist in the 1950s. The government planned to send her to the Soviet Union for further training and urged her to join the Party, a coveted honor among Chinese youth. She came from a Christian background; her grandfather was a pastor and her brother attended seminary in Shanghai in the early 1950s. She refused to join the Party. Assigned to a top Party propaganda-performing troupe, she refused to sing songs that praised atheism/communism, such as the "Internationale," with the lyric "There is no savior of the world." Soon she was arrested and sent to public trial to force her to recant her faith and embrace communism. She refused and was sent to jail and later to labor camps for education-through-labor. She spent about twenty years as a prisoner in labor camp farms. She made friends with many campmates and local peasants. (Often, prisoners were assigned to work at the local commune, especially during harvest time, when there is a shortage of labor.) Many cellmates became Christians as a result of Madame Yang's efforts, despite repeated warnings and reprimands from the authorities. During the early 1970s, in the heyday of the Cultural Revolution, there was really no effective government in China and, surprisingly, the controls were rather lax. Madame Yang introduced local peasants to Christianity and conducted Christian services at the peasants' homes. Within a few years, during which no Christian church was allowed, Yang and her followers led several thousand people to Christianity in a county where no gospel message had ever been preached in the countryside.

In the early 1980s, the government reopened a small church at the county seat for several dozen Christians who had nothing to do with Yang's group. The government-recognized TSPM/CCC church currently numbers close to a thousand people, mostly in the county seat, and is the sole official representation of Christianity there. By then, Yang's group had grown to more than twenty thousand, mostly in the countryside. To date, the government recognizes no one in Yang's group, nor are they recorded in any official documents. They still meet in households and have meeting points in almost every village of this county. They refuse to join the TSPM/CCC for theological reasons: Madame Yang taught the separation of church and state. Yang was released by the government in the late 1970s and returned to her hometown, the provincial capital. Her brother, too, was released from labor camp after more than fifteen years of hardship for refusing to cooperate with the TSPM.

This brother and sister established a well-known nonregistered church from their home in the city; it is a three-story complex with a training center for lay pastors. Together, they run theological training programs all year round. The first trainees came from village churches that Madame Yang started many years ago, and many pastors came for training from other parts of the province. They eventually built a large church and held services several times a week, including even an English service. Most in the congregation are intellectuals from local universities. Their activities have been so open that everyone in the neighborhood knows of the church; the local public security precinct is just a stone's throw away. They still refuse to join the TSPM/CCC despite constant pressure from the government and from TSPM/CCC leaders.

A TSPM/CCC church, where Yang's grandfather was pastor before 1949, just next to Yang's house, is on the grounds of the old church next door.[47]

During the 1980s and 1990s, the Public Security Bureau mounted several raids on the church because it is not officially registered, which is a crime in China. Each time the government warned them and pressed them to join the TSPM/CCC, they stood their ground, whereupon the government would mount a raid. Madame Yang was then usually arrested and charged with fines and prison sentences, ranging from a few weeks to a few months, depending on how high the fines were. The government would let the others go. This tactic was well known to Christian communities in and beyond China, and it was meant to pressure the group to submit to the government's authority. After each raid, Yang's relatives and friends donated money to pay the fine and to restore confiscated Bibles, hymnals, and pews. The church building was under the name of an overseas relative, so the government could not confiscate it. The government seemed fully aware that this group would not bend, but government cadres had orders to follow. It was a game in which neither party had illusions about the other.

It is interesting that such an illegal Christian community (often called an "underground" church in the West) is so open and public. The community does not attempt to hide its activities. The congregants do not appeal to overseas friends for help in decreasing the government's harassment. They are accustomed to police harassment and arrest, and they expect such consequences for their convictions. In fact, Madame Yang is proud of her steadfastness and regards her conviction as an honor, regardless of the cost. Likewise, her congregation regards such persecution as a mark of being true followers of Jesus. She teaches congregations and trainees to be faithful in their calling and conviction, to obey God and God alone, and to be ready to pay the cost. Her refusal to cooperate with the government has made her a symbol of strength for many dissenting groups beyond her home province.

Despite her prison record, since the mid-1990s, Madame Yang has held a personal passport, which until recently was considered a rare privilege for Chinese citizens. The government has allowed her to travel to many countries when churches overseas invite her to speak at their conferences. She has spoken to groups in Korea, Singapore, Hong Kong, and Malaysia and can travel freely to other countries. Her brother has also been allowed to travel. One may wonder how such people who resist the government so strongly can be permitted to leave China unless the government has tacitly accepted the nonregistered, illegal church as a permanent presence in local areas.

One important source of support for this dissenting group is Yang's Christian relatives overseas. They provide funding and moral support for the Yangs. When Madame Yang was arrested, overseas relatives negotiated with the authorities for the terms of release, although Yang never requested such assistance. They also help fund replacement of confiscated materials. Their ongoing support helps the Yangs sustain their ministry. Without these resources, the Yangs' ministry might not generate such widespread impact. Overseas family support is common in coastal regions, where many locals have relatives abroad. National policy directs local governments to encourage overseas compatriots to invest in and help local economic development. Yang's overseas support is not interpreted by the government as foreign mission support (which would be seen as undermining Chinese sovereignty) but as a contribution by overseas compatriots for a local cause, albeit one that is misguided by religious enthusiasm.

In this case, support from Chinese foreign compatriots is an important factor in encouraging the nonadherent political stance of Madame Yang's group vis-à-vis the government's religious policy. It is a tacit arrangement tolerated only in coastal provinces, where residents are aided by overseas compatriots and where government policy welcomes any kind of contributions from Chinese living overseas. This latitude is unheard of in interior provinces.

This dissenting Christian community seems to have forced the government to accept its *de facto* presence as a dissenting group and to tolerate its open activities in defiance of the law, albeit grudgingly. Madame Yang and her dissenting group have become well established locally. Their activities are not secret. At times, they even conduct public outreach programs for the university students and faculty nearby. After so many years of trying to force them to submit and register, the government seems resigned to putting up with the group's existence. Persistence has allowed Madame Yang and her group space in which to operate, a gray area beyond legal definition in which the government neither approves of nor tries to eradicate them. Further, this dissenting congregation exists alongside registered as well as many other clandestine, nonregistered churches. The yeast in this case raises the dough by generating a heterogeneous group within the mass, an important step toward a diverse, pluralistic society.

Case 7: A United Dissenting Voice

Some autonomous Christian communities, such as the Yangs' or Chens', are relatively small in size and have limited regional networks. But many have established extensive, nationwide links, and some such networks claim a membership of several million, although obviously none can provide concrete evidence to substantiate their claims, as they are illegal. However, the strength and influence of these groups cannot be ignored despite the obvious lack of reliable data concerning their activities.[48] Few of these groups make a major impact on the political scene, although some make headlines in Western media when Chinese authorities arrest members. Most groups concentrate on creating converts and building secret networks to sustain survival under constant government harassment and suppression. Because they are illegal, none has any formal interaction with the civil authorities or other social groups.

In 1998, several groups with extensive national networks, mostly in Henan and Anhui Provinces, issued documents[49] and made a public appeal urging the government not to misunderstand their position. Their theses were (1) they are not heretical; (2) they will neither register nor submit to the government's religious policy, obeying the Bible rather than civil authorities in these matters; (3) they are the true church in China, following biblical tradition, whereas the TSPM/CCC is erroneous because it does not follow the Bible; and (4) the government should stop all harassment of their groups, release all members who have been arrested, and allow them freedom to spread their faith.[50] The documents explain the groups' statements as well as their positions on church-state relations.

In 1999, several leaders of the groups issued two letters. The first called for the government to stop persecuting nonregistered groups and to recognize their status as legal, to accept plurality (multiple denominations) within the Protestant tradition,[51] and to revise the government's religious policy to include currently nonregistered groups.[52] The second set of appeals called for current TSPM/CCC staffs and pastors to leave the TSPM/CCC and join nonregistered churches, stating that the TSPM/CCC is no longer a true church. They implied that in the future the government should deal with them rather than the TSPM/CCC. They also appealed to overseas Christian groups to channel resources to them, the true Christian church in China, and not to support the TSPM/CCC church.[53] In short, the appeals called for replacing the TSPM/CCC with the currently nonregistered groups and recognizing them as the real Christian representation in China.

The appeal letters seem to suggest that they represent all nonregistered groups in China, but in reality, that would be impossible. Also, the negative occurrences mentioned in the letters reflect the regional situation and do not match conditions found elsewhere in China's complex religious makeup. The appeals also seem to arise from a specific region and target complaints about some local governments there.

These may be the first statements jointly issued by several influential nonregistered groups in China. The letters issued in 1998 represented groups who are somewhat influential in the four provinces in central China (Anhui, Henen, Hubei, and Hunan), which is primarily a farming region. Local government officials there are well known for their conservative attitudes and are notoriously corrupt. Governments in these provinces have generally practiced a more restrictive religious policy, and a large portion of reported cases of harassment and persecutions against Christians have taken place there. The TSPM/CCC is unpopular among Christians in these provinces, except perhaps for Hunan, due to its lack of good leadership. Thus, many Christians join nonregistered groups, which tend to offer a more authentic religious experience. Nonregistered groups are more popular, and hence more influential, in these provinces than elsewhere in China.

The government ignored the letters. Because there continues to be a standing order against all nonregistered groups, leaders continue to be arrested from time to time, but the government did not respond with a crackdown or try to target those responsible. It probably realized that these appeals came from particular groups within a readily discernible region rather than from a nationwide movement. The government's lack of response was surprising because Chinese authorities do not normally tolerate open challenges to their authority or policies. Ordinarily, the government responds to confrontation with suppression, as it did in the case of the Falungong.

Most of the nonregistered Christian groups' leaders come from rural backgrounds and are politically unsophisticated in their interactions with the government. They are most likely naïve for making confrontational political demands (for legal recognition, change of government policy, etc.) and lack a realistic appraisal of religious conditions elsewhere in China, which are eclipsed by their more negative local circumstances. Their views alienate them from many other Christian groups, including many autonomous Christian communities and some in the TSPM/CCC churches who work to build a better religious environment through existing policy and legislation and less confrontational methods. The current government, even in its apparently most liberal moments, is unlikely at this stage to accept the kinds of demands made by these letters of appeal.

Nevertheless, these attempts represent a historic landmark. They represent the first united effort by dissenting Christian groups to articulate political demands to the government. The move is courageous despite its failure to generate immediate results. These appeals reflect the political immaturity of the groups' leadership: lack of broader representation, a naïve expectation of the government's response, and an overestimation of their own bargaining power. Nevertheless, the public statements forced the government to pay attention to the widespread existence and influence of these groups in several regions of China. It also alarmed the government because of the mutual hostility and claims to exclusivity between TSPM/CCC and some nonregistered groups. Perhaps, however, these appeals will help prompt the government to seek long-term solutions that include non-TSPM/CCC churches as part of the Christian reality in China. China is currently finding ways for Christian groups to register as legitimate Christian communities without the need to join TSPM/CCC.[54] Thus, these dissenting voices bear significant political implications. They also represent yeast that is outside of the officially sanctioned realm, which can catalyze the rising of the dough: The government can be made to hear messages, even from dissenting voices. Perhaps in future, these groups can employ more politically sophisticated means to express their desires and so achieve more favorable results.

Conclusion: The Rising Dough

China is heading toward a more pluralistic society due to its economic reform policies. Nevertheless, it is still an authoritarian and a hierarchical society ruled by a single party that does not tolerate opposition voices or views. All social groups must abide by the regime's absolute authority. Within this structure, there is a legal system to control religion through various administrative measures. Groups incompatible with state ideology, such as the Christian community, are strictly supervised for fear their influence will create competition. As a result, in many official and public actions, the Christian community acts like a domesticated group subservient to the wishes of the government and in full support of the government's policy, reinforcing autocratic rule by a government opposed to democratic development.

But beneath the surface there has been tremendous social transformation. As the nation experiences rapid economic growth, attention is increasingly focused more on wealth accumulation than ideological purity. Pragmatism is the operating principle social stability for economic growth, the objective. Furthermore, there are the beginnings of social pluralism as various social sectors enjoy more autonomy and strive for their own goals. The government has allowed villagers to hold elections for their governing committees, and recently even invited capitalists to join the Party—a move that contradicts government ideology but shows a degree of pragmatism as capitalists become increasingly influential in China. As China heads toward a more pluralistic society, Christianity, too, has been making headway and carving a niche for itself.

Some Christian communities, although registered and often reported by the Western press as under direct government control, are in fact fighting for space and importance within the government's established structure. The Hebei and Jiangxi examples illustrate internal, silent gains in political power by Christian communities. They are changing the church-state relationship by forcing the government to make concessions, often within the government's own legal framework. These political power struggles may be emulated by other state-sanctioned Christian communities as they, too, begin to flex their political muscles to gain more decision-making power. This trend is growing, slowly and quietly, among most state-sanctioned Christian groups throughout China, leading to greater autonomy for groups under the government's authority and a loosening of absolute government control over religion.

Newly emergent Christian communities, such as the Lahu Village at the Sino-Burma (Myanmar) border and the one at Yangshan in Guangdong, have also broken new ground in China's local sociopolitical dynamics, as they fought to grow where no Christian groups had hitherto existed. The presence of such groups displays how China's social landscape is changing, even separately from the growth of the church. Also, the government is being forced to recognize and legitimize these social changes. As the government recognizes new groups, it signals that those groups have equal status with preexisting groups in the community. Again, this may prefigure the development of a pluralistic society where new groups can enjoy equal rights with existing groups. Sometimes, as in the Lahu Village, the Christian group has even become the most influential group in village affairs.

Fugong, the Lisu Christian county, is an even more significant example of Christian groups' strengthening influence; Christians are already the most powerful group, and occupy most important posts in the region. The Party has become a paper tiger there. The Fugong case suggests that even in autocratic China, diverse communities can exist employing their own distinctive political dynamics. The developments in Fugong County further indicate that the social strength and contribution of the church in China vitally affects its societal and political position. In today's Chinese government, pragmatism and political realism dominate.

The dissenting Christian communities also illustrate the possibility of de facto alternatives that do not compromise theological convictions. The existence of Madame Yang's church clearly indicates that there is a spacious gray legal area outside the formal legal framework; a group's legal status is not the only determinant of its success. The government may, in effect, acknowledge such groups without legitimizing them. Mere *de facto* recognition reflects an increased government tolerance toward dissenting Christian groups and a willingness to accept social groups outside the restrictive legal framework. A group can realistically fight for space and stretch beyond what present law permits. The letters of appeal exemplify the power of radical dissenting voices demanding change in government policy. Such voices may eventually push the government to legalize currently banned groups and allow diverse church-state relationships. In this sense, they may represent a pluralistic society in the making.

Although neither registered nor nonregistered churches in China have advocated sociopolitical reform or issued any statement that contests the leadership of the Party, their mere presence and struggle for existence becomes a powerful message for social liberalization. Churches also take advantage of the limited political openness to maximize their gains despite their limited power. All this contributes to an augmented social pluralism, which in turn pushes the current authoritarian regime toward a more democratic approach. It is perhaps like leaven, working silently and powerfully, changing and diversifying the whole structure of the dough from within, to make risen dough possible. The growing Christian community in China will not create democracy immediately, but, along with many other social forces, it may help produce more open government as a step toward eventual greater democracy.

NOTES

1. This study uses the term "community" instead of "church" to include all Chinese Christians in China, regardless of their ecclesial affiliation or whether they belong to registered or nonregistered churches. Many of these Christians are, in reality, living somewhere in between these two ecclesiastical dynamics. The ecclesial situation in China is far more complex and diverse than in countries where traditional terms are used to identify church heirarchy and other ecclesial terms. For example, in China there is the unofficial house church versus the official church, or underground church versus officially recognized government church. Therefore, this study uses descriptive terms such as "registered" and "nonregistered" to denote the different legal status of subgroups within the broader Chinese Christian community. Sometimes the term "autonomous Christian community" is employed to denote nonregistered groups from an ecclesial rather than a legal perspective. See A. Hunter and Chan (1993).

2. Religious organizations in China submit to the political leadership of the Chinese Communist Party, a necessary condition for their survival. Further, all social and civil organizations in China are required to implement political policies of the Chinese government regardless of their moral views on these policies. For example, Chinese Catholics must adhere to the population policy and are required to use contraceptives despite the official policy from Rome, which is against contraceptive use. Chinese Christians cannot administer pedobaptism because the government legally prohibits the instruction of religion to children.

3. Rev. Zhao Zhi-en, a senior church leader of the China Christian Council, released this latest estimate at a conference in Hong Kong (December 7–8, 2000).

4. The latest set of regulations, "Rules on Administration of Religious Activities of Aliens in China," was issued by the State Administration on Religious Affairs on September 26, 2000. Its twenty-two articles detail the religious parameters within which foreigners can operate inside China.

5. In 2000, the China Christian Council ordained a pastor, Rev. Fan Chenguang, in Xinjiang. The officiating pastors went there not as a delegation from the China Christian Council, but as part of a large delegation from the central government to visit this region. They excused themselves from the main program and made a quick visit to the local church to perform the ordination service.

6. Included here are new non-CCP groups and their representatives, who are now making their voices heard by the government and are making a political impact. They are groups such as consumers' organizations, a lawyers' union, various chambers of commerce, environmental groups, and professional organizations. See Gilley (2001, 34–36).

7. The whole policy is stated in a lengthy document called "Document Number 19" (the nineteenth Central Committee Party document issued in 1982), (translation) *The Basic Policy and Standpoint Our Country Should Have on the Religious Questions during This Period of Socialism, Zhongfa 19 (Institutional Secret)*, March 31, 1982, (mimeographed). For an English translation, see *Issues & Studies* 19 (August 1983): 72–90.

8. This study uses RAB instead of SARA because many regional offices in China still use the title RAB.

9. See the official denunciation issued by the China Christian Council on the Vatican's canonization of 120 martyrs, at http://dailynews.sina.com.cn/china/2000-9-28/131027.html.

10. For example, the RAB had issued a classified national directive on May 28, 2001, to all religious schools (seminaries, Bible schools, Islamic theological institutes, etc.) to adopt the new curriculum on politics and socialism for all these students beginning in the fall term 2001. This is a new set of government-published materials emphasizing the correctness and the scientific basis of socialism in the government of China. "Concerning the ordering and using of the teaching material for political courses in religious schools entitled: The Theory on the Building of Socialism with Chinese Characteristics," State Administration on Religious Affairs, [2001] 012, Urgent, 28 May 2001.

11. An internal government report entitled "Who Competes with the Party for the Grassroots?" quoted in *China and Gospel Monthly* (December 2000): 3.

12. Subsequent to his *Love Never Ends*, Ding published several short articles presenting a theological thesis of a merciful God that implies salvation by good deeds. See Ding (1999).

13. The UFWD officially endorsed Ding's work in 1999. However, the Party withdrew this support in spring 2001, when the government realized that such theology might cause disunity among the Christian community groups in China. See Yamamori and Chan (2000, 87–95). Since 2001, the government has neither denounced nor endorsed Ding's writings and has kept itself at a distance from his work.

14. There have been several restructurings of provincial boundaries since 1950. This is an estimate of the number of Christians inhabiting areas that belong to the current Hebei provincial jurisdiction.

15. Personal communication with Hebei Christian Council, January 2000.

16. The largest organized religious group in Hebei is Roman Catholic, estimated as at least two million and perhaps even as much as three million.

17. The government structure in China is ruled by the People's Congress, which passes legislation and appoints chief officers of the government. The CPPCC is an organ—composed of people from various walks of life—responsible for supervising the government. In the past, both the People's Congress and the CPPCC acted like a rubber stamp to legitimize the decisions of the Chinese Communist Party. This is no longer the case, especially since the early 1990s. The People's Congress and the CPPCC have been flexing their political muscles to control the course of the government, a political reform that is still in progress as China heads toward the "rule of law" governance system.

18. Also known as "house churches" in other literatures. This term can be rather misleading, for it really refers to Christian gatherings in homes in the late 1970s and into the late 1980s, when there were no church buildings to conduct services, and to new Christian communities that had no place to meet other than someone's house. This form of ecclesial existence does not mean that it is legal or illegal by the civil authority sanctions, especially since the 1990s. In 2000, more than twenty-five thousand of these home gatherings were officially registered with the government. However, many Western literatures equate the house church, an ecclesial form,

with nonregistered groups, with a legal description. Many nonregistered groups have buildings, and hold gatherings, openly.

19. This writer spoke with the deputy director of the Hebei Religious Affairs Bureau, Hu Benxun, on the inclusion of views from religious representatives in CPPCC. He suggested that it was the government's desire to have gradual openness for various views, a democratic process currently taking place in China (personal interview, June 2000).

20. Figures given by Jiangxi Christian Council as the Jiangxi Christian Delegation visited Hong Kong in April 2000.

21. Personal correspondence with the general secretary of Jiangxi TSPM/CCC, February 2, 2001.

22. The first invitation letter was issued November 1, 1997, to this writer.

23. Since 1998, the Jiangxi Christian Council has officially received several delegations and groups from overseas Christian communities. They have also visited Hong Kong by the invitation of the Hong Kong Christian Council, the first ever official visit made by Christian delegates from this province traveling outside of Mainland China.

24. Covell (1995) has written a chapter on the evangelization of the Lisu. See also Tien Ju-K'ang (1993).

25. According to the Chinese government, there were 574,800 Lisu in 1995. See Jiang (1995, 64).

26. As a historical note, the missionaries in Fugong used the term "uncivilized" to describe the traditional lifestyle of the Lisu. They were, of course, trapped in their historical context, and they regarded Christianity as being superior to the local cultures. They also taught Lisu Christians that a Christian lifestyle was more civilized than the traditional Lisu ones. The term "civilized" is used among Lisu Christians when they make reference to the traditional Lisu way of life. The Chinese authorities attacked this attitude as a form of cultural imperialism.

27. On marriage customs, see Central Government Visitation Team Second Detachment Nujiang Group (1956; 1981, 21–22). On the common house, refer to "Research Committee, National Minority Commission of the National People's Congress: The Social Situation in the Lisus," in *Lisuzu Shihui Diaocha* [Social Survey of the Lisu Tribe] (Yunnan: Yunnan People's Press, 1956), 9. These common houses have been abolished since the 1950s. However, such customs, premarital sexual practices, for instance, are still common and accepted among the Lisu.

28. See "Research Committee, National Minority Commission of the National People's Congress," 43.

29. This writer personally witnessed a Christian wedding in March 1997 and interviewed the newlyweds. Both were poor peasants and claimed that they could not afford to get married if they were not Christians and did not have the wedding in the church. Unlike most of the weddings in China (among Han and ethnic minorities alike), there was no feast or reception after the wedding service. Such austerity at a wedding is rather rare in China.

30. The common drink of the Lisu is rice wine (or grain wine), which is made by a simple distillation process of the newly fermented cooked grains. The alcoholic content is between 5 and 10 percent. Technically, this type of distilled alcoholic drink is

not considered hard liquor (which should have an alcoholic content of 25 to 40 percent). The Lisu also drink a form of hard liquor on special festival days, but it is produced by a special brewery and cannot be made at home or in the field.

31. Chinese Communist Party, Yunnan Frontier Research Office, "The Basic Situation of the Nujiang Lisu Autonomous Prefecture, 1956," in *Lisuzu Shihui Diaocha* [Social Survey of the Lisu Tribe] (Yunnan, China: Yunnan People's Press, 1956), 7–8.

32. Central Government Visitation Team, 1956, 21.

33. Ibid.

34. Chinese Communist Party, Yunnan Frontier Research Office, 1956, 7.

35. As these writers interviewed Christians in the field, similar comments were expressed: that it is cheaper to believe in Christ than in traditional gods.

36. Although this is a pejorative term, the authors wish to be faithful to the facts observed in the field. This is the original term used by the missionaries and later followed by Lisu Christians themselves in their teachings.

37. John and Isobel Kuhn were married in Kunming, and they did throw a big wedding party, as recorded in Isobel's several writings. However, it took place before they went to work among the Lisu. John and Isobel did live a very austere life, a lifestyle that was compatible with their teachings. Not all missionaries who worked among the Lisu were like the Kuhns. The Morrisons of the Assemblies of God Church in Fugong were accused of living an extravagant life. Their son was accused of raping local women, with one of them giving birth to a "mixed-race baby." This woman and the baby were well-known in the local village; they left China for Burma in 1950. See Fu (1994, 1094–1096).

38. In September and October 2000, the Chinese government published a series of articles denouncing the missionaries' anti-China activities in the nineteenth and twentieth centuries. One of the major allegations is their involvement in the opium trade. See Tong Xin (2000, 56–59).

39. The official figures on registered drug addicts in China are 148,000 in 1991; 520,000 in 1995; and 681,000 in 1999. See foreword, *White Paper on Narcotic Control* (Beijing: State Council 2000). The actual figure is far higher than the official "registered" figures. The number of addicts, even among the registered figures, is on the rise at an alarming rate.

40. This matter has been a major concern in the Party, especially in national minority areas. For a current discussion, see Mou and Zhang (1999, 374–386).

41. The bureau chief of the Simao National Minorities and Religious Affairs Bureau, Xu Yongan, is a prominent scholar who has published several volumes on cultural studies of the Lahu and other minority groups in Simao. This field research was made possible with the generous support of Mr. Xu and his staff.

42. *Muba*, or *Moba*, depending on the linguistic branch of Lahu, is the shaman or the priest of the local village. This position is handed down by family succession. There is also the *Sheba*, who is the "black" witch who can also exorcise ghosts for healing purposes. See Simao National Minorities Affairs Bureau Editing Committee (1993), 15–20.

43. There is a whole range of ghosts and deities that govern virtually every sphere of life in Lahu cosmology. See Simao Prefecture Government (1990, 352–355).

44. Personal communication with Lancang County officers, June 2000.

45. For example, the Lahu Christians at Guangbe Village, Menglian Lahu and Wa Autonomous County of Simao Prefecture, personal observation, August 1997.

46. Qin Ning suggested that the fundamentalist form of Christianity, commonly found among the Christians in Yunnan, has prevented the Christians from embracing a scientific worldview and has disconnected people from social reality—and is thus a social opium of the people. See Qin (1998, 216–221). Qin seemed to be trapped in the archaic theological controversy between the fundamentalists and the liberals at the beginning of the nineteenth century in the United States. He did not make reference to the theological development that has taken place during the past fifty years that has reoriented the Protestant conservative movement into a more integrative worldview.

47. Yang's father was the senior pastor of this church before 1949, and the Yang family has been living at the manse for many decades. This manse has now become the Yangs' property.

48. To protect the safety of these groups, some of the data cannot be published. Many claims are mere wishful thinking and exaggerated estimates. Often, the rural populations in China use descriptive numbers rather than statistical numbers to describe their strength. For example, a leader of a rural community describes a moderate size of population as several hundred, although the actual figure may be just slightly more than one hundred. He describes a medium-size community as several thousand and a big community as tens of thousands. Therefore, in his usage, the numbers are descriptive terms for the size of a community: hundreds are moderate, thousands are medium, and tens of thousands are big. However, readers often take these descriptive numbers (always in round figures) as statistical or literal, and such misinterpretation of figures often results in inaccurate and exaggerated reports. This writer has encountered many of these groups, and it is not uncommon for a local leader to claim that he has several hundred members in his Christian gathering in a village with a total village population of fewer than two hundred. Similarly, one of these nonregistered groups claims to have half a million members in a county with a total population of fewer than three hundred thousand! None of these leaders are deliberately misrepresenting things; it is just their peculiar usage of figures and numbers.

49. "Confession of Faith of House Churches in China," and "Attitude of Chinese House Churches toward the Government, Its Religious Policy, and the Three-Self Movement," November 26, 1988, by representatives from China Evangelistic Fellowship, Mother Church in Fangcheng, the church in Fuyang, and one house church in China.

50. These documents are available from http://www.cmi.org.tw, the site of China Ministry International, founded and headed by Jonathan Chao.

51. The Chinese government and the TSPM/CCC claim that the Christian community in China enters into a so-called postdenomination era where denominations no longer exist, a legacy from the missionary era. In reality, though, Christians in different regions still adhere to different traditions, such as the mode of baptism, depending on the denominational background of that region.

52. "Appeal Letter and the Current Persecutions of the House Churches In China," August 16, 1999, by China Blessed Church, China Truth Church, China Evangelistic Fellowship, and Chinese to the Lord Church. See also China Ministry International Web site for the Chinese version.

53. "Appeal Letter to Co-Workers in TSPM," August 16, 1999. See also China Ministry International Web site for the original Chinese version.

54. The imminent release of such a new regulation was reported in October 2001. See Alex Buchan, "An Olive Branch with Thorns?" Compass Direct, www.compassdirect.org. A senior official at SARA, who actually drafted it, has confirmed to this writer that the new regulation will soon be released. Personal communication, November 2001, Hong Kong.

2

Emulating Azariah: Evangelicals and Social Change in the Dangs

Sushil J. Aaron

The Democratic Impact of Evangelicalism in the Dangs

In this chapter I examine how evangelical Christianity affects Indian politics, and democracy in particular. The research focuses on one underdeveloped area of Gujarat state: the Dangs, a largely inaccessible forest area inhabited by *adivasis*, or tribal peoples, where a substantial fraction of the inhabitants have reportedly embraced evangelical Christianity to a greater or lesser degree since Christian teaching first came to the region about thirty years ago.[1] It traces the trajectory of a particular Christian organization's involvement with tribal communities since 1976.

This is not a study of participation in electoral politics. Christians constitute less than 5 percent of the population in the region of southern Gujarat, and tribals (tribal peoples) in the Dangs are *not* a significant force in electoral politics. Instead, this chapter examines how the social effects of a certain strand of Indian evangelicalism provide *adivasis* greater opportunities and create political possibility by fostering collective identity and community organization. The spread of Christianity has generated new frameworks of personal meaning, effected a measure of cultural recovery, engendered movement toward individuation, and created spaces for collective engagement through the spread of religious groups that enable tribal communities to cope with the destabilizing processes of modernity.

Dangis (inhabitants of the Dangs) generally understand Christianity in religious, not political, terms and in the context of their daily circumstances: health, livelihood, families, and local social relations. Like most of the eighty-four million other *adivasis* in India, they are illiterate and poor even in comparison to other disadvantaged Indian groups. Physically, socially, and culturally isolated, they cannot currently exert direct political leverage; they often are deprived of effective access to state agents and services and often suffer from official abuse of authority. Bereft of the power or knowledge needed to access institutions in the larger society, they do not ordinarily become involved in, or expect much from, political processes.

How, then, can we speak of the effects of evangelical Christianity in the Dangs on politics and democracy?

Christianity in India

Evangelical Christianity in India has not been much predisposed to explicit social action, despite the ameliorative impact of colonial-era missions on improvident communities in the nineteenth and early twentieth century.[2] This is evident in the recurring expansion of belief-intensive conservative Protestant groups and in the impressive growth of pentecostal churches over the past twenty years, which have come to represent popular evangelicalism (Hedlund 2000a, 2000b).

In this chapter, I discuss the activities and impact of the Gujarat Christian Workers (GCW),[3] an Indian Christian evangelical organization, on the Bhil and especially Kukna people who reside in the Dangs district in southern Gujarat and in adjoining areas in the Valsad and Surat districts. The GCW introduced Protestant Christianity to the region in 1976 and it claims there are approximately thirty-four thousand Christians in the Dangs district, roughly a fifth of the population scattered over its 311 villages. This spread of Christianity in the Dangs has alarmed Hindu militant groups such as the Rashtriya Swayamsevak Sangh (RSS)[4] and the Vishwa Hindu Parishad (VHP, World Hindu Confederation), which orchestrated well-known attacks on Christians and churches there during Christmas of 1998 and 1999 (Human Rights Watch 1999; All India Federation of Organization for Democratic Rights 1999).

The GCW originated in the mid-1960s amid evangelical revivals of congregations in southern India. It was theologically conservative and sported a corresponding animus toward liberation theology. However, GCW's leadership adopted creative social action strategies by the 1990s after encountering socioeconomic dislocation in areas where it worked. This chapter, then, recounts the story of a particular evangelical group's multilayered engagement with a target community despite limited political opportunities and a cultural illegitimacy enforced by Hindu nationalism. The study is principally based on field trips in 2000 and 2001 to the Dangs and Surat districts, from which much of the material on Christian communities is culled, as well as on published sources. Literature on the Dangs is relatively limited; David Hardiman and Ajay Skaria are the principal historical sources, Jan Breman has written on political economy, and Ghanshyam Shah has had a sustained interest in contemporary politics. One writer, E. Dasan, a Christian worker, has written on recent Protestantism in the Dangs in a valuable master's thesis discussing contextualization.

Southern Gujarat has witnessed persistent anti-Christian rioting in recent years. In March and April 2002, Gujarat also experienced unprecedented frenzied anti-Muslim rioting, which, by most accounts was a systematic pogrom orchestrated with active state government support and led by the Hindu nationalist Bharatiya Janata Party (BJP, Indian People's Party), which was then heading India's ruling national coalition. The violence elicited adverse comment from Western nations; a European Union report compared the "carnage" to "a kind of apartheid...[having] parallels with Germany of the 1930s"[5] (Gopinath 2002). Rampaging mobs appeared to target minority people and property, suggesting the kind of surveillance that Hindu militant groups exercise on religious minorities.[6] A March attack by a 250-strong mob on a Christian organization compound at a village in Panchmahal district made clear that Christians are not immune from frenzied mob violence.[7] The anti-Christian agenda in Gujarat continues. Between February 10–12, 2006, the Vanvasi Kalyan Parishad, an affiliate of the VHP, organized for the first time a massive religious pilgrimage in the Dangs called the "*Shabri Kumbh*" wherein a reported three hundred thousand pilgrims performed ritual bathing in the Purna River.[8] The event was attended by leading Hindu nationalist luminaries including Chief Minister Modi, BJP general secretary Om Mathur, RSS Chief K. Sudarshan, and a host of popular Hindu religious leaders including Morari Bapu, Asaram Bapu, and Shankaracharya Vidya Narsingh Bharati.[9] The leaders urged tribals to "return home" to Hinduism, with Modi going so far as to say that there was nothing wrong if the state government lent support to "reconversion" initiatives since the Indian Constitution expected governments to prevent forced conversions.[10]

Evidently evangelical activity falls afoul of Hindu nationalist attempts to constitute a transvalued nationalist version of Hinduism as a source of political power. Hindu nationalism stigmatizes religious minorities, emphasizing the foreign origins of Islam and Christianity, and portrays their adherents as a potential fifth column in order to fashion a Hindu vote that overcomes electoral divisiveness caused by crosscutting differentiation along caste, class, regional, and linguistic lines (Jaffrelot 1996; Basu, Dutta, Sarkar, and Sarkar 1993). In sustained Hindu nationalist denunciations in 1999 and early 2000, evangelical Christians appeared to have briefly supplanted Muslims as the object of Hindu nationalist scrutiny. The fact that Christians, a mere 2.3 percent of India's billion people, elicit an aggressive posture from national political parties that is normally reserved for more perceptible political forces shows the ease with which intercommunal relations can translate into political crises in India.

The political significance of religious politics in India underlines the importance of studying the societal effects of contemporary evangelicalism.[11] What kinds of social contexts do Christian workers involve themselves in? To what extent are they successful? What are the individual and social impacts of changed belief structures? What are their prospects as political actors? The encounter between *adivasis* and GCW Christian workers in southern Gujarat helps provide answers.

A note on methodology and sourcing is in order. For the most part, this chapter is based on five weeks of fieldwork in Gujarat in Ahmedabad, Surat, Vyara, and various villages in the Dangs in 2000 and 2001; on interviews with GCW national leaders; and on published sources. Informants included academics, Roman Catholic and left-wing activists, evangelical personnel, and *adivasi* church believers. This study depended entirely on the access provided by GCW and Amos for Gujarat (AG) to the relevant congregations. Indeed it took informal introductions to GCW leaders and a letter of introduction from headquarters to get permission to visit GCW work in south Gujarat. I also visited the Dangs in the aftermath of the attacks on Christians in 1998 and 1999.

The preponderance of interview evidence certainly came from Christians. People I interviewed ranged from village headmen (village patels, officials in charge of village security), older *adivasi* Christians involved in training activities, and younger staff or graduates. The Dangs had already been under scrutiny by the national press and by human rights organizations, breeding a certain wariness of "outsiders" among informants. In this charged atmosphere, the fact that I was a scholar,[12] an outsider from New Delhi, and a Christian worked against being able to interview others, such as government and police officials, non-Christian NGO activists, and the Hindu nationalist leadership, both for reasons of personal safety and because of the possible danger of disclosing the identity of Christian contacts in a relatively compact area such as the Dangs. To be sure, I did interview a few non-Christian activists in the Dangs who were recommended by scholars in Delhi, as well as a few dissenting evangelicals who provided insights on failures of GCW thinking and practice.

Thus, this chapter cannot assume to be a comprehensive account, given that it does not cover the entire range of villages involved and is obviously inherently fragmentary, constructed, and incomplete (Clifford and Marcus 1986). Because of the selective nature of fieldwork available at the time, I could not discern, for instance, the variations in familial,[13] spatial, or psychological patterns among different Dangis. James Clifford memorably cautioned that cultures "do not hold still for their portraits" (Clifford and Marcus 1986, 10). But this analysis, of necessity, has excluded elements of cultural and psychological fluidity that indubitably accompany any process of religious and social change while isolating some political implications of evangelical activity.

Other crucial aspects were left out as well, such as the social processes within Christian development organizations that play a role in assigning development priorities, namely, why certain development initiatives were undertaken in some locations and not in others.[14]

Notwithstanding such contingencies of representation, it is possible to demonstrate certain positive socioeconomic effects as a result of evangelical engagement with the *adivasis* of southern Gujarat. Mosse (2005, 19) has argued that developmental projects, for all their process flaws, have more to do with infusion into regional and historical processes of change: "They concern aspirations to modernity and reflect the historical reality that, for marginal tribal communities, economic [and political] survival has long depended upon forming alliances with those with better access to resources." This chapter argues, at the very least, for the existence of a similar process unfolding in the Dangs and its surrounding neighborhood.

The Context of Evangelical Involvement: Tribal India

Indian evangelicalism has been assailed in some quarters for its alleged unthinking embrace of fundamentalist values of American evangelicals that is said to foster not only a degree of financial dependence but also elements of a triumphalist illiberal religiosity.[15] Some urban evangelical movements, particularly in southern India, may perhaps fit that description, but other contemporary Indian Christian evangelicals demonstrably engage with improvident communities in rural settings, despite the absence of politically congenial circumstances that were arguably available to their colonial predecessors. Although British mission societies were known to be at cross-purposes with the East India Company and subsequently the officials of the Raj, conversions were known to occur amid an expectation of political protection afforded by the presence of British missionaries, in addition to the prospect of material benefits relating to education and health care (Wingate 1999, 2). Contemporary evangelical personnel can hardly provide such protection; they are mostly south Indians often working in northern, central, and western India, where local elites have pushed for anticonversion legislation and sometimes organized outright violence against Christians (Akkara 2000).[16]

Violent opposition to evangelical activity often occurs in isolated rural pockets and is rarely reported in the media. Informants describe attacks by local landlords, merchants, and police in Madhya Pradesh, Chattisgarh, and Gujarat, which do not assume the critical proportions that would otherwise warrant media scrutiny. Evangelicals claim that they seldom raise a fuss, for fear that seeking legal redress might provoke further attacks. A weak ecumenical network, lack of empathy from mainline churches, inadequate contact with the local media, and small numbers deprive their grievances of political significance and thus permit harassment and occasional brutality. At the same time, the geographical remoteness of *adivasi* communities and the state's inadequate developmental penetration among them provides some protective cover for evangelical personnel.

India has the largest concentration of tribal populations among the world's nation-states; its eighty-four million *adivasis* equal the total population of Germany. Their human development status is appalling even by Indian standards. According to the 1991 census, *adivasi* literacy rate is 23.63 percent, far lower than the general population (52.21) and less than that of the lower castes (30.6). The literacy rate of rural *adivasi* women is 12.74 percent. *Adivasis* are the poorest social group in the country; in 1987–1988, 52.6 percent were below the poverty line, compared to 33.4 percent for the general population (A. K. Singh and Jabbi 1996, 18). *Adivasis* are severely underrepresented in the governmental workforce. Public sector employees are classified into various categories, with Group A being bureaucrats and Group D those with low-level menial and manual jobs. The percentages of scheduled tribes in type A, B, C, and D government employment have been 2.89, 2.68, 5.69, and 6.48, respectively. Their representation in the upper grades is a mere fraction of the 8 percent of national population they constitute (Xaxa 2001).

Virginius Xaxa offers an interesting explanation as to why tribals suffer even in comparison with the *dalits*, or untouchable castes. *Dalits* were subjected to inhuman treatment as outcastes and derogated by the traditional discourse of purity and pollution, but they remained integral to the economy of the upper castes, serving them in various capacities and interacting with them daily, even if they lived in segregated areas. Therefore, sooner or later, "opportunities made available to the larger societies or the higher castes in the form of knowledge, information, technology, employment, etc., were also in sight for the scheduled castes, even though they were denied access to it" (2768). The tribes, by contrast, live in self-contained communities with restricted commerce and suffered the disadvantages of isolation. Political weakness, geographic isolation, and cultural irrelevance have made *adivasis* victims of India's developmental march. *Adivasis* constitute 40 percent of those displaced by large government infrastructure projects, especially large dams, though their share of the national population is only 8 percent – causing one scholar to comment that India's national development and tribal deprivation have become synonymous.

Land alienation is a recurring grievance among *adivasis* that dates to colonial rule. British law introduced individual land entitlements, and British forestry policy tended to erode tribal solidarity and communal control of land (Pinto 1999, 16).[17] Large parts of tribal areas remain unsurveyed after the state appropriates the land, delaying conferral of individual proprietorship.

Thus, de-recognizing corporate rights over land-based resources on which fifteen million Indian *adivasis* currently depend snatches away between 40 and 80 percent of total tribal land resources without compensation (Pathy 1998, 277).

The situation is particularly acute in Gujarat, where *adivasis* constitute 15 percent of the population. The tribal groups are distributed throughout the eastern belt and in some pockets in western and northwestern Gujarat. Eight of Gujarat's nineteen districts have sizable tribal populations. The tribal population percentages in Dangs, Valsad, Surat, Bharuch, and Panchmahal are 93.46, 54.53, 46.32, 43.88, and 38.55 percent, respectively. Clearly, they have missed Gujarat's developmental march. Literacy levels in predominantly tribal *talukas* (administrative subdivisions of a district) of Panchmahal and Baroda districts are less than 10 percent, even though government schools are established in almost all villages. The *Dangs Gazetteer* (1961) declares that the *adivasis* are by and large "illiterate and improvident" and reports that "there was practically no literate person among the Dangis before the Christian mission started its school in Ahwa in 1905."[18] School enrollment stands between 15 and 20 percent for ages six to fourteen, with a 75 percent dropout rate in primary education (Lal 1998, 67–68).

Deprivation in the Dangs

The Dangs is the smallest district in Gujarat, bordered by the Dhule and Nasik districts of Maharashtra and the Surat and Valsad districts of Gujarat, and is one of the two districts in India having around 90 percent forest cover. The Bhils are its original inhabitants. The Kuknas (or Konkanas) and Varlis (and a few Gamits and Choudhris) came later from adjoining areas to cultivate the land. Over time, all tribes have evolved a common Dangi identity of social structure, norms, customs, culture, and language. Eighty-four percent speak Dangi.

From the early nineteenth century, rapacious onslaughts on Dangi forest resources devastated cloistered tribal communities and undermined their social organization.[19] (The sections on historical conditions in the Dangs draw extensively from the research of David Hardiman, especially his publications in *Subaltern Studies*.) In 1830, the British established suzerainty, levying taxes on forest produce that *adivasis* sold to town merchants. Unable to cart timber to markets by themselves, Dangis made contacts with merchants who organized the trade. Bhil chiefs taxed the trade, receiving payment in cash or in grain, cloth, and other products unavailable in the Dangs. Dangis also sold other forest produce, including *mahua* flowers much sought by traders for liquor production. Chiefs earned levies on these and from grazing rights sought by nearby pastoral groups. Bhils lived a mostly closeted existence: contact with outsiders was limited to trader-moneylenders known as *shahukars*.[20]

British incursions set in motion a process of economic decline through their successive takeovers of the principal resource in the district—forest lands. Indian state expropriations continue to this day. The East India Company acquired monopoly rights to timber in return for measly annual compensation. The chiefs resented this but had little choice.[21] The British instituted a new arrangement in 1842 because of the Royal Navy's demand for high-quality teak. This agreement allowed the British to send peasants into the forest to cut timber and gave them sole power to cut, conserve, and plant timber in the Dangs. The Bhils had to keep out of protected areas and accept minimal remuneration for the loss of their primary resource. Toward the end of the century, forest officials representing British authority and espousing conservationist ideas undertook to "protect" the forest from the "wild" inhabitants, while taking little notice of the depletion of forests for timber. To supply wood for the burgeoning railway industry, the British gave further access to forest trees to timber contractors, who had rights to hire cutters and extract the timber. Forest officials knowingly ignored the real causes of declining forest cover, blaming the *adivasis* for violating restrictions on cultivation. The Forest Act of 1865 created "reserved" forests in which the government could ban all cultivation. The Forest Act of 1878 held that peasants living in reserved areas had no "right" to the forest (Lal 1998, 122). The chiefs repeatedly protested this habitat encroachment to no avail. Loss of livelihood drove *adivasis* into a cycle of debt to, and dependency on, nontribal merchants and moneylenders and state officials, which still continues.

The Ubiquitous Moneylender

The role of the trader-moneylender has continued since precolonial times. Hardiman's (1996b) excellent study *Feeding the Baniya* details the *shahukar*'s prominent role in Bhil societies. *Shahukars* were market intermediaries for *adivasis*, buying forest produce like *mahua* flowers in exchange for food grain that *adivasis* needed to survive the dry season and seed loans for sowing. The *shahukars* were tightfisted to protect their investment and ensure favorable terms of interest, which varied but were generally geared to create impoverishment. Such tales are not unknown even today.

Shahukars dominated the lives of the Bhils. In the long dry months before the monsoon, the Bhils depended for their survival on handouts of food grains from the *shahukars*. Marriages, funerals, and festivities were financed by *shahukars*. In return, the Bhils handed over the lion's share of the crop at harvest time (Hardiman 1996b, 2). The terms of interest were geared to sustain impoverishment. Loans were to be repaid at harvest at one and a half times with compound interest, so the balance increased. Colonial records state that half to three-fifths of the crop was seized as payment. Seizure of crops ensured that Bhils depended on the *shahukars* for food supplies, perpetuating the debt cycle. This still occurs in some places. There was no competitive interest market: normally, one *shahukar* served a village; any Bhil attempts to take government loans incurred the *shahukar's* displeasure and dried up credit. By denying market access and taking advantage of illiteracy, the *shahukars* advanced loans when the prices were high and took repayment when the worth of the goods was low (13). A total lack of liquidity prevented *adivasis* from migrating; lack of creditworthiness made loans available only in their village. Some were forced to work as slaves to pay debts. The occasional *shahukar* who was willing to forgo debts was often in a dependent relationship with big merchants and bankers.

The forest official and the *shahukar* thus functioned as twin levers of distress. An elderly tribal who worked in the 1930s in the Dangs relates work conditions:

> Prior to FCLS [see below], private contractors, mainly Parsis [a religious minority in India that practices Zoroastrianism], shahukars, and rich timber merchants of the plains area used to cut the forests. The British who were mainly interested in forest timber for ship making and railway-sleepers gave forest-cutting contracts to private contractors. These private contractors came two days in advance to our village and ordered us to start cutting. Our village Parsi used to get such contracts. After getting the contracts he came on a horse with a rifle and threw four annas (25 paise) at our doorsteps. That means we have to be ready for forest-cutting. There is no question of denying his order. If we denied it, we would have to face beating and molestation of our wives. In those days we had to go to work for 12 to 14 hours a day. In response we got only twelve annas (75 paise) as daily wage. Parsi had good contact with police and British officials. He always threatened and frightened us in case we disobeyed his order. We were like a slave. (S. Joshi 1998, 130)

Limits of Gandhian Intervention

Gandhian workers (voluntary groups inspired by Gandhi) were actively engaged in tribal societies in the region in the 1920s. They emphasized cleanliness, alcohol prohibition, and vegetarianism. For two decades prior to Independence, Gandhian workers struggled to implement a debt-relief act and a minimum wages act, and they started residential schools known as *ashram shalas* for tribal children. Gandhians also started Forest Labor Cooperative Societies (FLCS) in the 1950s. Receiving considerable support from a state government that deferred to Gandhian ideas, FLCS expanded quickly, currently numbering 140 with 67,900 members across southern Gujarat (S. Joshi 1998, 128). The FLCS sought to ameliorate the conditions of *adivasis* earlier exploited by forest contractors, negotiating fair wages and managing cooperative societies as an alternative source of credit to generate self-reliance (128).

Initially, the FLCS dealt ably with the Forest Department and contractors by negotiating coups, by bargaining collectively for a price, and by organizing auctions. These societies procured better roads, medical assistance, and potable water arrangements from the government through links with the Congress Party, which also enabled them to get state funds to establish residential schools. They have had an impact on tribal literacy in southern Gujarat—except for the Dangs, where literacy levels remained discouraging. The societies had an ameliorative, but not an egalitarian, effect on tribal communities: they simply could not ensure stable employment for the majority.

Forest cooperative societies could not succeed owing to the crippling prominence of debt in the *adivasi* economy. R. B. Lal (1998, 65) notes that the main hurdle was the non-repayment of loans given by cooperative societies. "The reason for non-repayment of loans by the *adivasis* was that they sold away their produce to local merchants [in large part to repay moneylenders]. . . . On account of non-repayment of loans, the defaulting members did not become entitled to get further loans."

What's worse, the societies had created a tribal elite that was co-opted by politicians. The popularity of the FLCS enabled them to be powerful political players, with politicians soliciting their support as conduits to deliver *adivasi* votes. By 1970, *adivasis* garnered enough political clout in the FLCS to pass a resolution that all officers in the cooperative societies—including the president, secretary, and accountant—must be tribals. But tribal leaders then brought the societies under the control of political parties and sacrificed the societies' initial objectives. The tribal leaders' intransigence also caused conflict with nontribal personnel in the societies. FLCS efficacy and popularity declined (Lal 1985, 144).

The Forest Department, meanwhile, continued to set aside increasing portions of the forest as protected and reserved areas, depriving *adivasis* of resources.[22] The complete absence of cash crops further impoverishes the Dangs. Cultivation is impossible from February to May. From March to May, the *adivasis* collect *timru patta* (the *bidi* leaf), for sale. That results in surplus labor and migration. After eight months of toil, a couple can save only 3,000 to 4,000 rupees ($85), on which the family must manage until the harvest. A 1977–1998 Gujarat government survey reveals that the Dangs has the highest unemployment rate in Gujarat.

Fifty thousand Dangis yearly migrate to work in nine sugar cooperatives in Surat and Valsad, almost like bonded laborers. Fifty thousand others come there seasonally from the adjacent area of Nandurbar in Maharashtra. One report on the plight of tribal migrants notes, "Migrant tribals are employed in construction, road laying, road repairs, digging and carrying mud, or on the farms.... Migrants do not get any housing facility and they are obliged to live either in the open, or on the footpaths, or in the slums. No notable increase was found in their incomes. Most... migrants have confessed that they would not have moved out if they had the means to earn their daily bread nearer home" (Punalekar 1998, 295).

Thus since the 1960s, tribal life has been buffeted by problems: low literacy, high unemployment, being treated by forest officials as encroachers, inadequate access to health services, and the dominant position of nontribal landowners and business people. Those staffing shops and lodgings in the highway towns are nontribal Gujarati-speaking businessmen, who have followed the Gandhians and other NGOs into the forest. With few options but poaching or cultivating in reserved forests, tribals are often arrested or harassed by Forest Department officials. Many are falsely accused. Whatever agricultural produce they raise or wood they cut fetches little due to trading cartels that peg down prices. Long-term indebtedness to nontribals creates conditions similar to bonded labor. Loss of livelihood has created a cycle of dependency on nontribal business people, who have prospered in highway towns, often through collusion with the forest officials, on the produce of the forest.

Further, many of the 311 Dangi villages are far from the highway, dispersed through a forest crisscrossed by rivers, where government officials do not bother to visit. Until recently, the postman had to walk some eighteen kilometers to deliver mail to some pockets that have no roads. State officials, mostly nontribals appointed from Ahmedabad, are reluctant to take postings in the district. Rajeev Bhargava's (1998, 117) observation about Indian democracy holds true for southern Gujarat: "The uneven spread of state power which sustains the conditions for citizenship, is one reason why, despite its formal presence, democracy is effectively non-existent in many parts of India, particularly for the marginalized groups."

Christianity in the Dangs

Christianity first appeared in southern Gujarat when missionaries from Serampore, near Calcutta, started working in Surat in 1813. Six mission organizations worked among Bhil *adivasis* by 1906 (Boyd 1971). The Marathi division of the Church of Brethren began ministry in Valsad in 1895 and operated successfully in Valsad, Vyara, Ankleshwar, and Bharuch, but insisted on conducting church services in Marathi.

Education was a priority for the missionaries; the Church of Brethren had eighty primary schools in the Dangs by 1950. Gandhian social workers were also active in education, opening additional schools, *ashram shalas*, thus bringing the total number of primary schools to 179 by 1955. All, notably, were products of voluntary organizations, highlighting state abdication of responsibility. The government, however, passed a law against private primary schools and took over mission schools in 1954, enabling it to extend the state's primary school network to about 378 schools by the 1990s and effectively scuttling overt Christian instruction in the region. Secondary education remained neglected; there was only one high school in the Dangs by 1961. In 1975, the district *panchayat* (local council) invited two Jesuits to start high schools, recognizing the inefficiency of the state-run system. There were eight secondary schools in 1980 and twenty-one in 1990. Christians run three; four are government schools; the rest are *ashram shalas* run by Gandhian and other private voluntary organizations (Shah 1999b).

The Christian schools clearly deliver the best education in the region. The Deep Darshan School in Ahwa run by the Carmelite Sisters of Charity and two Jesuit Nava Jyot boys' high schools in Subir and Pimpri had a total of eleven hundred students in 2001, 90 percent of whom were non-Christian *adivasis*.[23] Between 1988 and 1997, scores of other Dangi students averaged 36 percent on the secondary certificate examination; students from Deep Darshan School scored 93 percent. That is perceived by locals as one reason these schools have become a target of the Hindu fundamentalists. This has conceivably had an effect on higher education even though the district has a single government-run college. In 1969, there were four Dangi graduates; there are more than twelve hundred now. Among tribal *talukas* in Gujarat, the Dangs has the highest literacy: 48 percent versus 36 percent for all scheduled tribes in Gujarat (Shah 1999b). Catholics have restricted themselves to educational efforts; Protestant missions have established their presence among *adivasis*, generally living in villages of fewer than five hundred persons each, scattered across the forest.

The variety of Protestant groups in the district includes the Church of North India, the Evangelical Church of India, and pentecostal groups. Development agencies such as (the pseudonymous) Amos for Gujarat and World Vision International have projects as well.

The Gujarat Christian Workers

GCW has operated in the Dangs since 1976 and now has many adherents; dozens of congregations worship in newly constructed church buildings, or churchlike structures, which have several dozen local workers and over twenty full-time resident workers from other parts of India. GCW is a prominent, indigenously funded, Indian evangelical group which started in the late 1950s in rural southern India. It sent cross-cultural outreach workers to eighteen Indian states.[24] Its theology and practice fit Bebbington's (1989, 3) quadrilateral typology of evangelicalism: conversionism (the need for change of life), activism (evangelistic and missionary efforts), biblicism (centrality of the Bible), and crucicentrism (centrality of Christ's sacrifice on the cross). It belongs to the leading umbrella organization, the India Missions Association, and its missiological stance accords with the Lausanne Covenant.

The stated aims of GCW are to plant indigenous churches by organizing the believers as congregations and to work for the full transformation of the individual. Specifically, it endeavors:

1. To help them mature as witnessing Christians through effective pastoral care and to work with them for their welfare in the society.
2. To challenge them to take up the responsibility of reaching their own people.
3. To involve them in translation of the Bible in unwritten languages spoken in our country.
4. To involve local believers in socioeconomic uplift programs: medical programs, veterinary work, child care programs, agricultural and water development projects, and adult literacy programs.

GCW began as a fellowship of Vacation Bible School teachers who felt an urge to pray for the spread of the gospel. The teachers were part of a youth revival among a few castes, particularly the Nadars. GCW is still led principally by a group of Nadar Christians; the current executive committee and officers hail from that community, just as was the case in 1970.[25] Most funds come from prayer cells of south Indian churches composed of Nadars and other castes whose historical trajectory has served to shape GCW's evangelical strategy.

These castes experienced remarkable social transformation in the nineteenth and early twentieth centuries. Considered by Hindus to be polluting, the Nadars suffered various enforced debilities and humiliations. They were forbidden entry into Hindu temples and courts of justice, could not use public wells, and could not wear footwear, good clothes, or jewels. Milking cows and the use of scales (weight balances) or umbrellas were also prohibited. Nadar women were obliged to be uncovered from the waist up (Hardgrave 1969, 22; Jayakumar 1999, 76).

Nineteenth-century Protestant missions were perceived as transforming their society both by initiating developmental work and by advocating their cause against the upper castes and lobbying with colonial administrators. Missionaries found that though some were "very dirty, ignorant and of wild appearance," they were resolutely hardworking, with "pauperism" virtually unknown among them. They were not tempted by riches and shunned liquor (Hardgrave 1969, 39), which may explain their doctrinaire proclivity toward abstinence that is now shared by the entire Indian evangelical spectrum. Christianity made immense progress among such communities due to missionary educational and reform efforts, which uplifted non-Christians as well as Christians in these communities. Some castes lived in segregated settlements and therefore could convert as a group to Christianity without undergoing social dislocation. The resulting social mobility and eventual political power enabled them to acquire middle-caste status by the 1970s (61). Their descendants are conscious of their community's history and the transforming effects "the gospel" had on individual and group progress.[26] This is also reflected in GCW organization and strategy: the emphasis on education, biblical instruction, and character building, in a sense, re-creates their own passage out of destitution and enforced indignity.

In their missionary endeavour, the great nineteenth-century Indian, Bishop V. S. Azariah is reckoned as an inspirational figure. Azariah worked in rural Tamil Nadu and Madras, orchestrated remarkable social change in Dornakal diocese in neighboring Andhra Pradesh (then "Telugu country"), and is also the subject of an outstanding biography (S. B. Harper 2000). Almost every Christian worker I met in Gujarat knew of Azariah; the groups he founded also do Christian outreach there. Indeed, Azariah's praxis is woven into the GCW method, combining itinerant evangelism and pastoral care by indigenous Christians, contextual communication of the gospel, the church as a central agent of change, cultural recovery through translations of scripture into the languages of communities worked with, and a mediating role for Christian workers helping disadvantaged groups to cope with local authorities.

The ameliorative relief GCW seeks to provide for *adivasis* is akin to what their forebears received from missionaries over a century ago. As a European observer wrote in 1851:

> The expectation of receiving from [Christian workers] of their district, advice on difficulties, sympathy in adversity, and help in sickness, and ... of being connected with a rising, united body, guided by European intelligence [sic], and governed by principles of Christian justice; the expectation of being protected in some measure from the oppressions of their wealthy neighbors; the fact that Native Christians appear after a few years to acquire a higher standing and to enjoy more peace and prosperity than they had as heathens; the desire of advancement on the part of the lower castes, who find that they are considered by [Christian workers] as capable of advancement and taught to feel that they are men. (quoted in Hardgrave 1969, 49)

GCW Christians are also steeped in the awareness of the gospel's ability to impart a sense of freedom to the individual. Conversion accounts describe the sense of cosmic insignificance experienced by their ancestors through teachings about rebirth and karma cycles that rationalized their present deprivations as inevitable and merited. Relentlessly reminded of being impure by virtue of caste, they scarcely saw themselves as free human beings. The theological trope that Jesus identified with, and "died and rose again" for, the disparaged provided an epistemic turnaround by conferring human dignity that enabled communal progress.

Hence, GCW strongly emphasizes preaching and communication, undeterred by any anxiety about the social relevance of the message. The memory of past transformation in their own castes confers a steady stream of confidence and purposiveness to those working among impoverished communities like the Dangs.

Organizationally, GCW raises funds mostly in districts the Christian workers hail from. Hundreds of "prayer cells" of ten to twenty believers each pray for and support Christian outreach. In Gujarat, GCW has dozens of local workers at various levels, but south Indian functionaries are mostly in leadership positions. The GCW recruits workers through revivalist calls for outreach in "unreached" areas. A high school certificate is a prerequisite, and almost all the south Indian Christian workers age forty and older are graduates. Each recruit undergoes one year of training, which includes acquiring the language of the people he or she will work with. In Gujarat, most are quite adept in Gujarati and the local tribal languages.

The austere lifestyle of GCW workers is a factor in gaining the confidence of *adivasis*. GCW personnel revel in the fact that they are all underpaid, as compared with those employed in the public and private sectors. Salary gradations correspond only to experience and not to professional designations. The general secretary, the organization's CEO, receives less pay than a fieldworker with more years in the organization. An outreach worker in the field with twenty years of experience makes about 3,400 rupees (US$70) a month, including house rent (which is the same for all workers), far below what people of similar education could earn. All GCW workers send their children to a boarding school in south India, which the mission supports, as they cannot afford local school fees. In the 1970s, workers were not sure whether they would be paid from month to month, due to a financial crunch.

GCW seems to practice its "simple lifestyle" motto. The general secretary has no air-conditioning in his office (rare for any Christian organization) and travels by second-class train like his colleagues. The old headquarters building in use until 2000 (when I visited) lacked adequate lighting. GCW can barely generate funds for infrastructure, as it does not solicit foreign funds.[27] Enforced austerity helps them cope with grueling environments and helps to bridge the divide with the *adivasis*. Christian workers I met voluntarily chose to stay in poorly furnished houses in forest villages, though able to afford better, to avoid petty jealousy and to make *adivasis* "feel at home."[28] For approximately a decade, workers in southern Gujarat walked in the forest areas or rode bicycles due to lack of public transportation. Some reportedly walked eighteen to twenty kilometers through the forest daily, for many years, between two highway villages in Surat and the Dangs, to conduct night meetings. Motorcycles were provided to GCW workers only in the late 1980s.

GCW's work in *adivasi* communities shows a remarkable theological breadth and flexibility that has enabled their practice to adapt and evolve. The prayer fellowship from which GCW emerged in the 1950s aimed to conduct outreach in adjoining areas, placing near-exclusive emphasis on itinerant evangelism. It did not seek to plant indigenous churches or send workers far afield. Following an unexpectedly strong response to its evangelism, the group decided to hand over new converts to local churches for pastoral care. But such routine pastoral care reportedly proved unsatisfactory, and GCW altered course, deciding to plant indigenous churches by sending outreach workers geared to long-term involvement with communities in which they worked. Constituting worshipping communities in villages and doing sustained work in *adivasi* areas—including healing and medical work, biblical instruction, and establishment of churches—ultimately proved politically controversial, not least because it led to the community organization intiatives, as discussed below.

Adopting a developmental agenda was a radical step, because most personnel came from a background that viewed *belief* in Christ as almost the sole constituent of Christian identity. Social action was construed as a surrender to liberal theology. (Congregational belief structures in India tend to reflect a split between liberal and evangelical seminaries. Preaching about or working toward a just society is often taken to be a mark of liberal seminaries and inimical to commitment to "pure evangelism.") Also, the middle-class revival that spawned the GCW in the 1950s was "spiritual" in focus, giving prayer an overwhelmingly central role. Despite their own group's passage out of deprivation through missionary educational efforts, middle-class individuals from these castes who moved to big cities assumed a revivalist rhetoric and charismatic spirituality characteristic of migrants coping with social and economic dislocation. During the late 1970s, approximately five hundred congregations sprang up in Madras, cutting across denominational lines (Caplan 1983). Protestantism there has had a strong evangelical thrust ever since; programs of social uplift virtually disappeared from its theology.

But GCW, while remaining theologically conservative, began to view the gospel in the context of "holistic ministry" or "total transformation," which included social and economic uplift and even social activism. Certain structural features of the outreach perhaps impelled the GCW toward long-term development strategies. Outreach workers from a particular Christian organization seldom switch groups, partly out of conviction and partly because seniority-based structures of pay and respect make this difficult. Personnel also observably prefer to continue to reside in a region where they have worked. There is also no competitive job market for evangelicals in places like southern Gujarat. Such structural impediments to desertion and the fact that the mostly illiterate *adivasis* had compelling health and educational needs, rather than the anticipated purely spiritual needs nudged GCW toward community development and mobilization strategies.

The 1980s shift from evangelism alone to evangelism and developmental work also corresponded to theological evolution in the leadership. Over the past twenty-five years, GCW decision making has been in the hands of its president Dan Prabhakar, general secretary Michael Ebenezer, and field directors K. Daniel and M. Samraj.[29] The GCW executive committee is composed of two-thirds lay representatives, with a management committee to ratify administrative decisions, but these four people formulated and effected strategies. Prabhakar, a minister and former senior World Vision International executive, is the visionary who elucidated the theology of transformation through the metaphor of the Kingdom of God. Prabhakar's charisma enabled conservative GCW evangelicals to unlearn prejudices against ameliorative social initiatives and appreciate the limits of itinerant evangelism. He remains the most credible window through which the GCW cadre can access alternative theologies and strategies that aid the goal of "total transformation." C. S. Barnabas, former general director of Amos for Gujarat (AG) (described below), believes that what sets rural GCW churches apart from urban evangelical churches in India is their strong emphasis on the Kingdom of God.[30] Urban pulpit teaching revolves around cultivating personal character and themes of guilt and responsibility. Rural GCW congregations more commonly speak of the Kingdom of God—emphasizing Christ's lordship, the unity of believers, corporate holiness, and the radical effects of divine involvement in society, thus enabling communities to develop a sense of collective purpose.

Ebenezer played a crucial role in conveying these broader goals to workers. He is a revered figure within south Indian evangelicalism. His personal integrity and tireless commitment to evangelical practice displays an austerity like that of his subordinates. As general secretary, Ebenezer's leadership was characterized by a solicitude for field workers and an earnestness to accommodate their concerns. His frequent travels to visit workers on-site and regular consultations with field personnel made him a hands-on manager and ensured that headquarters kept in step with field workers' concerns.

Ebenezer's and Prabhakar's collaboration enabled them to initiate new directions in cross-cultural outreach and sustained GCW's continuity of purpose. They articulated an explicit goal that Christianized people-groups should be able, in time, to exercise political influence through individual and group empowerment. With this objective, GCW, again showing adaptability and willingness to work with other, possibly competing, organizations, approached AG in the mid-1990s to start community organizing. Cooperating with AG has helped GCW translate its hope that spiritual conversion will lead to "full transformation" of communities into substantive strategies.

Dynamics of Outreach in the Dangs and Beyond

Christian work involves evangelism in local languages, principally through night meetings held with the permission of village chiefs. GCW functionaries claim that one-third of the Dangis have embraced Christianity—a claim hard to substantiate or refute, but severely disputed by some critics and likely to surprise academics studying the region.[31] Embracing Christianity does not necessarily imply baptism. Christian workers say they refrain from the rite unless a person is nurtured for three to six months, abstaining from alcohol and renouncing idol worship. This may well be a tactical retreat from a public profession of faith to obviate needless adverse attention.

The narratives of GCW workers and tribals about response to the gospel point to the difficulty of the landscape, the prevalence of spirit worship, the nature of tribal deprivation, the effects of embrace of Christian beliefs, and the central role of healing in initiating that embrace. Stories detailing people's "backwardness" when GCW encountered them in the 1970s and 1980s preface most believers' testimony. One evangelist told me that *adivasis* did not know how to clean wounds properly or that stagnant water breeds malarial mosquitoes; they did not boil milk but made yogurt from raw milk in unwashed vessels, causing an unbearable stench.[32] Tribal believers corroborated poor levels of sanitation and stated how "improper" tribal attire had elicited ridicule from urban folks, particularly moneylenders (whom they often dealt with), prior to Christian commitment. They spoke of their enhanced self-esteem and acceptance at the marketplace due to their initiation into a measure of urban etiquette, through imitating the evangelists.[33] Christian workers claim that one can easily tell a believer from a nonbeliever in a public setting by attire alone.

The Role of Healing

Healing has been the main impetus turning people to Christianity ever since GCW's arrival in the Dangs. Interestingly, in a ministry that does not have charismatic origins, spiritual encounters are a major factor in people's embracing Christian faith. Yet this may have been inevitable among an almost entirely illiterate tribal group whose mental landscape is dominated by spirits. It again illustrates GCW's theological elasticity, especially as many workers have an Anglican background. Although GCW recruitment began in a revival with charismatic overtones dating to the 1960s in Tamil Nadu, the workers themselves generally do not indulge in glossolalia or related enthusiastic practices.[34]

But Indian evangelical theology is marked by awareness of the demonic, which features in south Indian religiosity. Caplan (1983, 35), describing the popular culture of evil in Tamil Nadu, refers to the tendency to attribute all kinds of misfortune to sorcery or capricious acts of evil spirits. Indeed, he attributes the charismatic expansion in Madras in the early 1980s to the inability of Anglican (Church of South India) churches to tackle perceived problems of sorcery and witchcraft, which plague Christians and others. Although discussion of evil spirits, and prayers against them, were familiar in the theological upbringing of GCW personnel, they never intended to draw *adivasis* to Christianity through such activities. The bulk of the GCW workforce had no experience in tackling spirits and hoped to draw converts primarily through evangelism. But 95 percent of Dangis in the 1970s were illiterate, rendering tract distribution—a foundational technique of itinerant evangelism in urban India—useless. This caused GCW members to devote themselves to prayer, and "power encounters" with spirits followed, reportedly taking them by surprise. Spiritual sessions, with extensive singing and praying, culminated in tribals being delivered from sickness or fear of spirit attacks and becoming convinced that their own alcohol abuse was wrong.

Dangis are predominantly animist in observance, worshipping spirits of animals and trees and placing considerable faith in witchcraft, demonic influence, and omens (Enthoven 1975, 164). The most popular god is the tiger (*waghdev*); they also worship snake, water, and mountain gods.[35] Dangi animism provides divine sanction for afflictions ranging from sickness to alcohol and moneylenders. The machinations of the spirit world are of immediate concern to *adivasis*, who often impute health hazards such as snakebites, ulcers, rheumatism, malaria, and diarrhea to the workings of unpropitiated spirits.

Adivasi Christians reckon that Christian belief helps unravel the complex of psychological and social disabilities that plague tribal individuals who take traditional faith seriously. They believe that Christian healing provides succor against the immobilizing effects of tribal belief systems and, further, upstages local religious hierarchies by undermining local healers. Narratives about people's religious pilgrimages indicate that fear was previously central to Dangi religious life. Lavijibhai said, "We did not know that God can be loved, we thought he was only someone to be feared." Formerly, tribals dared to engage divine beings only through *bhagats* (folk healers). Healings, following ordinary believers' prayers, undermine such religious dominance and create a social dynamic of devotion. One convert said that his previous belief system did not allow him to enter the forest freely; fear of restless spirits inhibited his spatial freedom. This changed after he became a Christian and freed him from a prior punitive religiosity.[36]

Tribal Christians, especially first-generation converts age forty-five and older, therefore take prayer seriously, and, seasoned by the Dangi traditions of *bhajan mandali* and *tamasha* (both are Dangi art forms) that extend through the night, readily endure long sessions. The GCW believes in the centrality of prayer, teaching that it plays a role in "binding" and "loosing" powers in all areas of life. *Adivasi* Christians, noticeably, make individual silent prayers before eating biscuits or sipping tea. Prayer is intimate and detailed, with believers asking God for mundane needs about traveling, conversations with people they meet, livestock, and so on. This seems to give a new individual dimension to spirituality, which is enhanced by personal devotions and supported by regular Christian instruction and practice. The switch from fear, dangers of retribution, and *bhagat* propitiation of spirits to the free practice of personal devotion seems to generate new frameworks of personal meaning.

Access to medical knowledge is also negligible. Many local healers were reportedly unaware of simple solutions to medical conditions such as administering salt and sugar for diarrhea. Traditional remedies include cauterizing ill people with hot irons, beating pregnant women's stomachs with sticks to induce labor, and pouring country liquor into newborn babies' mouths. *Adivasi* healers prescribe herbal medicines but perceive illness as dependent on the whims of the spirit world. Disease is often presumed to be the work of a witch or the aftermath of spirit possession. Often, a male exorcist is hired to exorcise the spirit or find the witch, who would then be tortured. In the case of the *dakan butali* ritual, as one GCW respondent related, "a witchdoctor is called from far away. They gather the villagers; put water in the basin and call people to put black *gram* [a variety of lentils] in the basin. Whoever's black *gram* floats is called as the culprit, who are girls mostly. The victim is blindfolded with salt and taken around the village and all the people beat her to the point of breaking hands and legs. Some commit suicide, fearing humiliation."[37] Hardiman (2002) relates that marginalized women, particularly the aged and widows, were usually singled out for this ritual, at the behest of the village leaders and patriarchs. "In this way," he says, "illness and the anxieties to which it gave rise provided means by which patriarchal elite maintained a peremptory control over the subordinate and marginal peoples of their own society" (184).

GCW evangelists declare clearly to the *adivasis* that their old deities cannot protect them. Healing prayers are offered for the sick, lame, and deaf, and people are discouraged from going to *bhagats* (S. Joshi 1999). When *adivasis* solicit prayers, they are told first to abandon idols and talismans denoting fealty to other gods. Christian conversion scuttles the "link between social control and exorcism" (2667–2675), judging by the accounts of converts who describe the failure of *adivasi* healers to cure sickness in contrast to the effect of prayer to Christ. In the late 1970s, Yamunaben, a widow and a Christian believer, was identified as a witch through the dakan butali ritual. She refused to comply with the customary demands and was supported by Ramubhai, a prominent villager who later became *sarpanch* (village headman). He refused to allow the ritual and warned the *adivasi* healer that he would go to the police instead. The *bhagat*, commonly called a "witchdoctor" by GCW personnel, backed off and instead proposed an alternative punishment: heading to a village in Maharashtra and flinging rice on an idol, predicting death would ensue. Yamunaben reportedly threw the rice on the idol and came back with no harm suffered. This act played an important part in converting Ramubhai. There are other stories of headmen who have converted because of healing in their villages. Testimony against *bhagats* and in favor of Christian healing also occurs in places where village leaders are not Christians. There are recurring reports of deliverance from alcoholism, restoration of marital tranquility, an end to polygamy, and the like. Regardless of their phenomenological status, apparent healings act as a social leveler. Cumulative political and economic dislocation of the *adivasis* and their inherited habit of subservience to nontribals has had an enervating effect on self-esteem.[38] Healing linked to belief in a personal omnipotent God who listens to all and treats rich and poor alike is felt to be an empowering experience.

One example of how perceived healings can clinch conversions is the story of Posleyabhai, a Christian believer and a migrant who worked in a landlord's house at a town called Billimoria. As Posleyabhai reports it, the landlord's son took gravely ill and was thought to be about to die "in fifteen minutes." In desperation, they asked Posleyabhai to pray. But he insisted that he would pray only after idols were removed from the house. The landlord and his wife at first refused, but eventually gave in. He prayed, citing a scripture verse (Hebrews 11:6), and the son immediately awoke. Reportedly, the next day three large cars carrying the landlord's extended family came to Halmodi, and the group sat on the ground and worshipped Jesus together with tribal believers. Obviously, such equalizing narratives bolster *adivasi* confidence and reinforce the view that Christian faith can also make social hierarchies less steep, or even level them.

There is also a material dimension to healing, for Christians attest to barren buffalo bearing calves and watermelon fields yielding unexpected produce. A typical testimony is that of Madhubbai: "My family was facing a lot of difficulties for a long time because of the evil spirits. The evil spirits were even damaging all the crops. All the efforts taken to propitiate these spirits were in vain. But after accepting Christ in our life we could experience God's deliverance from all the clutches of the evil spirits and God's blessing upon us."[39]

Healing is conducted mostly in house churches. When such an event is believed to have occurred, it generates interest among others in the village. Thereafter, testimonials from healed or converted individuals draw relatives from nearby villages, individually or as families, who then form the core of churches. House churches become the "integral and pioneering units, advance bases of action and penetration. They also bring the program of evangelization to the grassroots," says one respondent.[40] Members gather for worship, prayer, teaching, and witness, and this maintains fellowship among them, an associational life that transcends the spatial fragmentation sometimes caused by the forested areas.

The social relations generated include, in a sense, both bridging and bonding social capital (Putnam, Leonardi, and Nanetti 1993, 22). In that way, it differs from Donald McGavran's account of church growth, in which culturally homogeneous groups convert to Christianity as a group, averting social ostracism that accompanies individual conversion (in G. G. Hunter 1992, 158–162). Although the GCW sees the usefulness of contextualizing the message separately for each tribal group to realize "multi-individual, mutually interdependent conversion" (158–162), it does not encourage separate churches for different tribal groups, as McGavran envisioned. Instead, Bhils and Kuknas commonly worship together and do other activities together to a degree previously unknown. Intertribal cooperation builds social capital that *bridges* differences between groups. One respondent mentioned that a Christian Bhil *sarpanch* received help from a Gamit *taluka panchayat* member in procuring loans for buffalo, seeds, and fertilizer.[41] In the past, Kuknas have treated Bhils as inferior and did not dine with them. This sort of discrimination has reportedly lessened in Christian communities. As GCW's field director narrated, "Eating vessels were not given for the Bhil to eat in Kukna homes. We used to take people with us, including the Bhils, for pastoral visits. Since Kuknas have the habit of giving food to visitors, they started giving food to the Bhils as well."[42]

Addressing Alcohol Abuse

An end to extensive alcohol abuse as a result of prayer is another reason often cited for conversion. Historically, the Bhil's indebtedness was exacerbated by a fondness for liquor and toddy. "Bhils were great lovers of country liquor made from the flowers of the *mahua* tree. Such drink was considered by them a 'food of the gods,' an essential part of their religious and social festivities" (Hardiman 1994, 170). A Bombay University survey of eight villages of southern Gujarat in 1951 found that 72 percent of all families had one or more members who drank. "However, whereas 80 percent of the families of tribals, untouchables and other low-caste people contained one or more drinkers, only 7.5 percent of high-caste families did so" (170).

Some Bhils were known to abstain from liquor for two to three months, but serious drinking habits are well attested, with drunkenness especially during festivals and on ceremonial occasions. Liquor remains an indelible part of their culture, used to welcome guests and as a means of expressing mutual solidarity. A free flow of drinks is imperative for any social occasion, with nonavailability apt to be interpreted as an embarrassment. Toddy served as a substitute for solid food, which was often unavailable. "In all spheres of their life, drink had positive associations. It was a food of the gods, which possessed an element of divine power; it set a seal on negotiations and legitimized family ceremonies; it enhanced the pleasures of social gatherings and public festivities; it provided succor during times of scarcity. Drink, one might speculate, lubricated the whole cycle of life of the peasants" (Hardiman 1994, 177).

Deliverance from alcohol addiction ranks next to healing as a cause for allegiance to Christianity,[43] particularly among women, who readily accept Christ after their husbands give up drinking. The change yields dual benefits, bringing familial calm and freeing up savings, which in turn opens up GCW microcredit initiatives.

Evangelical presence has undercut the influence of *adivasi bhagat* exorcists, who made liquor integral to their religious ritual.[44] Converts are unanimous in blaming the *bhagats* for perpetuating ignorance and dependency. "The *bhagat* used to charge excessively each time I consulted him for sickness in the family. It would either be two chickens with three bottles of liquor, coconuts, or 50 to 200 rupees cash per visit," says Hanijbhai.[45] Surajbhai, a convert turned evangelist, and the village patel, firmly rejected the idea that some *bhagats* are beneficial and claims that after the advent of the GCW, only "illiterate people" approach the traditional *adivasi* healer.[46] Abdubhai, a former *bhagat* and a convert, reckons that *bhagats* conduct *pujas* (Hindu or indigenous worship rituals) only for money and thrive by inducing fear to get people to pay for these as means of healing.[47]

In the Dangs villages, evangelicals have successfully tapped into the existing disaffection with local healers and displaced the *bhagats*. The Christian engagement has been more long lasting than the kind that *bhagat* reformers successfully introduced in the 1920s such as vegetarianism, teetotalism, and cleanliness drives (Hardiman 1987a). Gandhian organizations established schools with government funds in the 1940s, but these, too, have declined (Hardiman 1987a), partly due to corruption and nepotistic monopoly by a few families (Hardiman 1996b, 124–125). However, over the past thirty years, GCW's theological imperatives, superior organization, and staying power have arguably sustained their relevance in the field and displaced these alternatives.

GCW relationships with tribal communities have deepened through useful contextualization of communication. They use traditional song-and-dance presentations like *tamasha* parties and *bhajan mandali*. GCW also organizes yearly market fairs, called *melas*, to preach the gospel to *adivasis*, who are attracted by the pageant atmosphere. Thus, aside from healings, GCW consistently musters many initiatives constituting a whole regime of attraction: market fairs, song and dance, scripture translation, adult education, and so on. Often, meetings are held in interior villages nightly, and these sometimes last through the night. The regular contact between GCW personnel and the worshipping groups generates an upward spiral of activity directed toward spiritual renewal or addressing social needs.

Government officials, by contrast, rarely bother to learn local languages and dialects. This exacerbates illiteracy: teachers, not knowing local dialects, communicate poorly with *adivasi* children. The state government inducts few *adivasi* teachers, has no vernacular curriculum, and insists on the use of Gujarati only in government schools. The Gandhian movement in the Dangs, dominated by Chhotubhai and Ghelubhai Nayak, also insisted on education in Gujarati only, to offset the influence of Marathi, the language of Bombay Province, to which the Dangs belonged until 1961. In the cultural clash between the Gujarati and Marathi elites, tribal languages were ignored (Hardiman 1996b, 119–120).

GCW's use of the vernacular in the process of evangelization entails a fair measure of cultural recovery for the tribals. This is particularly aided by the translation of Christian scriptures. Translated scripture portions are disseminated among literate *adivasis*. Various Protestant organizations, including GCW, cooperate in New Testament translation into tribal languages, including Vasavi, Kukni, Warli, Chowdri, Dungri Bhil, and Garasia.[48] In most languages, scripture passages are the only printed literature. Lamin Sanneh (1989, 31) argues that "mission as translation makes the bold, fundamental assertion that the recipient culture is the authentic destination of God's salvific promise and has an honored placed under the kindness of God," giving translation an equalizing function like that of healing. Vernacular translation, Sanneh notes, often resulted in the missionary losing "expert status"; translations facilitate independent moral judgment by local believers.[49] The translation endeavor in southern Gujarat would seem to make such antihierarchical judgments possible.

Resisting Entrenched Interests

Arguably, evangelicalism in the Dangs also generates a "culture of questioning," through relationships forged and maintained by consistent visits of the GCW workers. Consistent visits, regular Bible studies, and prayers for the sick build up trust in a region where organized voluntary activity barely exists. *Adivasis* live in an environment where the nontribals they mostly encounter are exploitative or indifferent Forest Department officials, police, moneylenders, liquor traders, and petty contractors. They are dubbed with demeaning names such as *kaliparaj* (a derogatory reference to dark skin). Dangi women fear sexual exploitation by outsiders. The presence of GCW and AG begins to alter threatening expectations about outsiders. Christian workers also become a countervailing source of knowledge for the *adivasis*, accessed to offset the claims of those who oppress them. They can advise *adivasis* on many issues, such as bargaining for the price of teak trees on their land and in conflicts with police or forest officials, and can petition police about nontribals who harass *adivasi* girls or get information to a nonliterate *sarpanch* about local government schemes to provide *adivasi* villages the funds they are entitled to.[50] When asked why Christians are persecuted, *adivasis* often say that moneylenders and shopkeepers, accustomed to complete deference, dislike being questioned or answered back.

The psychic hold moneylenders possessed over the tribals should not be underestimated. The Bhils believed that *shahukars* had unbeatable occult powers and thought natural forces were products of spiritual activity that could be harnessed through ritual. Hardiman (1987a, 22) writes, "In a world in which all power was seen as having magical qualities, it was hardly surprising that the Bhils believed the *shahukar*'s magic to be more powerful than theirs. By using such powers the *shahukars* were believed to be able to manipulate prices to their advantage, use the law courts to serve their interests, and keep the police and petty officials in their pockets. *Above all they possessed that seemingly most magical of all powers, the ability to read and write*" (emphasis added).[51]

The moneylender's pivotal, often dominant, role in *adivasi* communities reflected the need for liquidity. Attempts to provide loans at low interest, starting in colonial times, had failed to break their stranglehold. A 1970 survey revealed that 64 percent of agricultural borrowing in Dahod (in a neighboring district) was from local moneylenders; in 1980 it was about 31 percent (Hardiman 1987a, 51).

Although many *shahukars* have now left the area, tribals are still dependent on local shopkeepers for loans. State government budgets money for loans, but petty loans are hard to obtain; the government offers larger loans than tribals can use. Christian converts generally desist from dealing with moneylenders. This makes the evangelicals very unpopular with the local businessmen and traders. Disaffected *bhagats*, local businessmen, and some Gandhians blame GCW for attenuating their influence on the *adivasis*. Their disaffection makes them easy recruits for Hindu nationalists.

GCW's Developmental Agenda

Evangelicals have also become involved with the tribal communities through development work. One program, cooperating with World Vision India, set up hostels for tribal children attending government schools in towns, where educational standards are better. GCW created an ancillary organization, Gujarati Christi Seva (GCS; Christian Service for Gujarati), which now operates roughly twenty residential facilities hosting fifteen hundred children from various *adivasi* groups. Children from interior villages can study in semiurban public schools instead of village public schools, where attendance levels of government teachers are woeful. The GCS (a subsidiary organization of GCW) also conducts short literacy or language (Gujarati, Kukni) programs (e.g., one-month modules) for children who find government schools inaccessible. AG has facilitated many GCW projects, especially adult literacy, irrigation technology, and community mobilization. In many areas, most tribal men can speak Gujarati, though reportedly that is rarer in the interior; women usually cannot. Only Christian groups specifically address gender-linked incapacities. In March 2000 I witnessed an AG adult literacy program for women. Nineteen women paid 200 rupees each and took a week off work to learn basic Gujarati. Likewise, AG programs are the only avenues for adult literacy, as no other instruction exists in the Kukni language. Nearby, thirty-seven tribal *suvarthiks* (evangelists) and nineteen women were attending a weeklong Bible exposition training that incorporated English-language training. Such programs prove to be an important vehicle for intertribal interaction. Some Christian elders I spoke to attended a legal aid training camp organized by the AG in Delhi. Some AG personnel also arranged for small groups of *adivasis* to attend similar camps, occasionally organized by Jesuit activists, which impart the vital ability to read "first information reports" (FIRs). The ability to file an FIR, a police document that is the first official record of a plaintiff's testimony and the primary evidentiary basis for prosecution, is critical both when *adivasis* are plaintiffs and to prevent police from accepting false testimony against *adivasis*.

Development work includes medical and agricultural assistance. At the time of writing, the GCS had six rural clinics in southern Gujarat and conducted periodic medical camps that provide tribal Christians first-aid training. It conducted crash courses in lentil cultivation and introduced high-yield seed by providing seed loans to all interested tribals. In 1999, AG introduced a three-pronged plough to farmers. GCS persuaded faculty at government-run agricultural institutes to teach *adivasis* specialized pest control techniques. GCW informants say that militant Hindu groups pressure the government-funded faculty not to be involved with them and also pass on false information to *adivasis* to discourage their participation. Vested interests hostile to these programs stir up opposition by alleging that their benefits are meant only for Christians. Such allegations are used to create the impression that evangelicals bribe tribals to convert to Christianity.

GCW workers also help work through an uneasy relationship with government officials. One case illustrates the deep disaffection toward government programs. *Adivasis* stopped attending an AG lentil cultivation module when a university instructor erroneously described the event as state-funded, evidently fearful of harassment and extortion in return for receiving government favors on the basis of their experience with forest officials. They returned after receiving AG reassurances correcting the wrong information. This mediating role has also helped in efficient delivery of public services. A development worker related that a branch manager of a state bank approached the evangelicals to identify suitable individuals to start a self-help program.

Generally, the bank lacks the field experience of the GCW, which can help prevent misallocation of loans.

GCW solicited AG's help in building community organization where significant numbers have adopted Christianity. While GCW focuses on evangelism and believers' spiritual life, AG aims at capacity building for communities. It helps design programs with "core groups" formed in villages—by its report, hundreds of villages in Dangs, Valsad, and Nasik, thus far mainly among Kuknas, Bhils, and Varlis. AG helps communities strengthen their organization by mediating all development initiatives through core groups, or village development committees that are established in each village as an extension of church activity. The explicit focus is on literacy, basic health care, training in irrigation technology, and sustaining credit habits; but working through core groups also helps strengthen community organization. A core group of five elders from each local congregation interacts regularly with the development agency and is linked to core groups in other villages through representatives to area development and field development committees.

A key to strengthening community organization is training for core group members, a pared-down version of what community development officers in Christian development agencies learn before joining a field. This enables *adivasis* over time to assign priorities for village development work, whether to make irrigation or education the priority, whether to invite other villages to participate, and the like. Core group interaction between villages helps alleviate the physical isolation of village communities, which in the past impeded effective cooperation. It also produces a demonstration effect as non-Christians noticing core group initiatives start to take part also. This is especially true with the Varlis, who reportedly clamored for the initiatives after hearing about the benefits Kuknas derive from the core groups.

AG core groups mimic *panchayati raj* institutions, the constitutionally devised mechanism for village self-governance. Article 243B of the Indian Constitution mandates regular elections in each district for administration at district, *taluka*, and village *panchayat* levels. The idea was to let power flow upward from five elected village representatives operating as mini parliaments with power to allocate development expenditure and exercise authority over the police and bureaucrats. Lower functionaries in the police, excise, forest, and revenue departments were to have minimal responsibility and were held accountable to the *panchayats*. This system was designed to make local elected bodies the locus of authority instead of concentrating power in the hands of the district collector (bureaucrat) and elected representatives in larger units like the State Legislative Assembly. The 73rd Amendment Act of 1992 instructed each state to enact legislation suitable to its context, reviving *panchayati raj* institutions. The panchayat was to have power to levy, collect, and appropriate taxes, tolls, and fees. State governments were to provide the *panchayat* with grants-in-aid for implementing its plans. In addition, the state finance commission in every state was to review the financial position of *panchayats* and make recommendations to the governor for allocating funds to them (Sheth 2000, 101–104).

But implementation has been tardy in Gujarat, and elsewhere, and does not address tribal concerns. For instance, the amended Gujarat Panchayat Act of 1998 does not give village *panchayats* power to grant proprietary or mining licenses or concessions for exploitation of forest resources, which is important in a district like Dangs. Gujarat's *panchayats* are constituted in a way that makes the *taluka panchayat* (a larger territorial unit), rather than the elected village council, or *gram sabha*, the center of power. There has been no implementation of the central government's Bhuria Committee recommendations for extending provisions of the 73rd Amendment to scheduled areas like tribal lands with the provision that customary law should take primacy in administration and that the *gram sabha* be given charge of forest management, taking precedence over the Forest Department (S. K. Singh 2000, 31). Politicians and bureaucrats across the country have inhibited *panchayati raj* to clip the emergence of local autonomy that could produce competing elites. Legislative Assembly members and district officials continue to handle discretionary funds that perpetuate patron-client relationships at the expense of elected village representatives.

In the Dangs, the *panchayats* have limited leverage, restricted to rudimentary road construction, water supply, and electrification, and devote most of their energies to mediating law-and-order disputes. The GCW initiative in fostering core groups and in routing development money through them, by contrast, gives Dangis a credible, parallel experience of village self-administration, albeit on a very limited scale.

These core groups also serve as a potential buttress against Hindu militant incursions. Asheemanand, a VHP activist who orchestrated attacks on Christians in December 1998 and 1999 and organized the Shabari Kumbh *mela* in February 2005, cultivated disgruntled tribals and local *bhagats* who allegedly pinpointed the location of Christian churches and congregations. Armed with this knowledge, Asheemanand mobilized a horde of VHP activists from outside to go on a demolishing spree in the Dangs; many GCW churches were destroyed.[52] However, local VHP influence has not been able to enlarge its influence dramatically, notwithstanding the resources that (as the 2006 Shabari Kumbh event showed) it has at its disposal. Locals attribute this to VHP's inability to inhabit the forest recesses and also the loyalty of south Indian evangelicals who did not desert them following the 1998–1999 attacks. By contrast, Hinduized tribals felt that the VHP abandoned them after state-level BJP leadership directed the VHP to stop the attacks.

Christian commitment has created separation between Christian and non-Christian *adivasis* in some instances. This may reflect ideas of the church as a sanctified community expressed through moral regimes dealing with sexual conduct and alcohol. The very habit of regular churchgoing tends to create an enclave culture to some degree. Some non-Christian *adivasis* complain that Christians do not participate in festivals and tribal customs. Christian *adivasis* do participate in many tribal customs, but avoid those perceived as having idolatrous elements. But development work and core group activity tend to offset, in some instances, the effect of any Christian exclusivism and cultivate goodwill that undermines the social appeal of Hindu militancy.

Community organization is of recent vintage, starting in the mid-1990s. GCW changed course, apparently seeking to accelerate community empowerment to accompany individual and family efforts to prosper. This strategy involves communities more broadly, thus reducing reliance on individual success stories. Community development promotes individual embrace of modernity, but without commensurate corporate advancement the latter risks developing mutual alienation.

However, community organization that was initiated by AG should not be construed as a sudden development in which GCW personnel played little part. GCW has long actively assisted tribal Christians' interaction with the government, providing advocacy for tribals and assurance and support in the public sphere. For instance, they financially supported a young man named Anil to pursue a law degree in faraway Ahmedabad. Anil, now a thirty-one-year old lawyer and first-generation convert, runs a legal aid center in southern Gujarat affiliated with a well-reputed human rights group in Ahmedabad. The center represents tribals, who have cases constantly filed against them for allegedly violating forest laws. Anil has won village-level elections in the past and is assisted by two Christian women lawyers. They had a standing caseload of about 150 lawsuits by 2001.

Blind Spots and Future Challenges

GCW's failings include (1) difficulties in effectively handling issues related to cultural pluralism, (2) difficulty in delegating authority, and (3) some disinclination to be involved with local nonevangelical resistance movements.

One source of disaffection toward evangelicalism has been the sometimes divisive impact of Christian belief among closeknit tribal communities. This is played out in practice by a reported refusal by Christian *adivasis* to take part in social rituals (S. Joshi 1999, 2670). Though GCW has incorporated some rituals into church conventions, they risk alienating fellow *adivasis* and undermining tribal unity because of an exaggerated emphasis on doctrinal correctness and a conviction that other faiths are inferior.[53] Doctrinaire certainty about the superiority of Christian belief predisposes evangelicals toward an instrumentalist view of other cultures, despite their undertaking genuine cultural recovery initiatives.

This has implications for the cohesiveness of its congregations as well. The moralizing (and exclusivist) rigor of GCW's theology is fast losing appeal among educated youth. The theological instruction their parents embraced, which propelled them to literacy and conscientization, does not resonate as much today. GCW's call to a "sacrificial lifestyle," now taken as an organizational standard, receives somewhat erratic consent from the urbanizing youth. There is a possible tension here between the aims of GCW and AG, even though relations are observably harmonious between their local personnel, as the latter's community programs are more appealing to the youth. GCW most wants to make new believers and sustain their spiritual life in church communities, and it sets annual evangelistic targets. GCW is committed to raising new indigenous evangelists (*suvarthiks*) to spread the gospel throughout tribal Gujarat, a goal that requires their ongoing presence. AG, however, may be sowing the seeds for GCW's irrelevance through self-help initiatives that involve *suvarthiks* and educated youth. Core group activities are so popular that some converts look for guidance more from development practitioners than resident evangelicals. Thus, when a small section split with GCW in 1999, even senior GCW evangelists relied on youthful AG staff, who had worked in the Dangs less than five years, to convince church elders which faction to choose.

GCW also struggles with ceding positions of authority in local church congregations. GCW's plan ultimately to hand over local *adivasi* churches to the Church of North India is still unrealized fifteen years after conversion momentum began. Two reasons given are that congregations are not spiritually mature, and that the Church of North India liturgy is too staid to accommodate tribals' enthusiastic worship. However, GCW's failure to delegate authority might be a cause for future concern. Commitment to evangelistic targets could undermine devotion to "total transformation" and provide rationales for deferring indigenous church autonomy. True, salaried tribal *suvarthiks* do most of the evangelistic work, but as yet there are no plans for tribal leaders beyond the pastor and evangelist levels. GCW argues that education levels among tribal elders prevent tribal accession to ecclesiastical authority. But young people who are educated at the seminary level are expected to embrace the sacrificial lifestyle of GCW personnel first. This sacrificial lifestyle criterion as a prelude to devolving authority is and will be a cause of resentment. This is so partly because renouncing authority would entail professional redundancy for GCW functionaries who have lived for most of their lives outside the provinces they hailed from. Most have struggled with a poor pay structure and have virtually no career to resume if they leave places like southern Gujarat, an anxiety that breeds an inflexible hold on power.

Organizational divisions further threaten moves toward autonomy. Clan-like divisions exist in the GCW, according to informants. Subtle turf wars hinder coordination among different program departments, leaving some vital needs neglected. Printing and distribution of Christian literature in the vernacular lags behind congregational demand in Gujarat. Also, headquarters uses finance, in an already cash-strapped mission, to ensure that field workers toe their line,[54] and workers who are popular in field areas frustrate top-down directives. Field staff have the potential to be sovereign in their own domains; that led to the split in which a few senior leaders tried to separate Gujarat as its own diocese, under the rubric of autonomy. Prabhakar and Ebenezer's leadership contained tensions for many years but there could well be additional challenges in managing the organization's divisions after Ebenezer's recent retirement and with Prabhakar's reduced involvement.

Given all that, a grand strategy to increase autonomy is unlikely, especially when tribal deprivation is perceived to be an urgent concern. If there is no genuine delegation of authority in the years to come, that might well cause palpable friction between *adivasis* and "outsiders." Continuing non-*adivasi* leadership suggests a limitation of current south Indian–led evangelicalism, despite its enviable tenacity and motivating heritage: a possible inability to delegate. Is there warrant for wondering if GCW can be effective only in dispossessed contexts?

Evangelicals have also had a mixed record in cooperating with organized resistance spearheaded by non-Christian actors. Activists accuse evangelical groups of not pulling their weight in movements protesting enforced land dispossession by Forest Department strictures through the 1980s and early 1990s. One popular movement in the late 1980s came together under the banner of Adivasi Bhoomiheen Kisan Hakk Sanrakshan Samiti (Association to Restore Land Rights of Adivasi Peasants). Its demands included regularization of plots of forest land to *adivasis*, provision of land for landless *adivasis*, reasonable prices for forest produce, proper wages for daily labor, and acknowledgment of *adivasi* ownership of trees on their land. In 1991, the movement was brutally put down: a Christian woman called Taraben was killed in police firing, houses and grain were set ablaze, and more than three hundred people were booked for offenses using the notorious Terrorists and Disruptive Activities Act (All India Federation of Organization for Democratic Rights 1999, 13). Evangelical groups seem to have played no role in this movement; one activist accused them of being police informants at the time. The tenuous local position of the GCW functionary, by virtue of being an outsider from south India, might explain the tendency to desist from participating in organized resistance. It might also entail the unraveling of the entire evangelical project in the wake of relentless state scrutiny that normally follows a repressive phase. This has probably changed due to the outright Hindu nationalist aggression in the late 1990s. The activist also remarked that by the late 1990s, evangelicals were willing to work together with civil liberties groups and undertake common programs like advocacy training but still shied away from open association with resistance struggles.

Situating Evangelicalism in the Dangs in Contemporary Indian Political Context

We are now in a position to answer the question with which we started the chapter: In what sense, then, is evangelical Christianity in the Dangs pertinent to politics, and to democracy?

It is argued here that evangelicalism has acted as a favorable attritive agent for democracy: evangelical growth in tribal areas has challenged regnant structures of power despite aggressive Hindu nationalism, historical structures of oppression and disparagement, and the indifferent prevalence of the rule of law, although the scale of change is limited. Whether that will continue is still an open question, given issues that GCW struggles with, relating to pluralism and autonomy, and other extraneous factors that might emerge.

But there is an immediacy of evangelicalism's impact on life in southern Gujarat that is notable. It is enabling Dangi *adivasis* greater access to opportunities, resources, and equality, particularly in overcoming hindrances to respect and fair treatment. It also provides ways for them to engage the increasing incursions of modernizing and globalizing India without simply being increasingly marginalized and displaced.

To summarize, the democratizing effect of *adivasi* Christianity lies in undermining the debilitating effects of elements of *adivasi* religious beliefs. Embrace of Christianity has helped many overcome paralyzing fears, as they begin to see themselves as free moral and social agents rather than as receptacles of spirit world machinations. Freedom from alcohol abuse has also been transformative, freeing up money and time and strengthening self-confidence and family life. People's belief in the equality of all in the sight of God (reinforced by healing events) refurbishes an autonomous identity that gradually reconceptualizes their social sphere and undercuts the authority of exploitive ritual, medical, and commercial practices and their agents. The program-intensive, socializing mode of evangelicalism helps overcome the spatial isolation of communities which obstructs associational life. Segregation in the forest blocks *adivasi* mobilization while correspondingly enabling gradual ingress by business interests. A range of church activities has helped scale down intertribal taboos and internal Dangi discrimination, particularly among the Kuknas and the Bhils, though intermarriage is still rare.

Christian development activity took the form of joining religious teaching with medical improvement, education, assistance in dealing with exploitive outsiders, and ultimately community development efforts. Very notably, it fostered adult female education, introducing regular literacy modules in villages. These reportedly are the only voluntary educational activities specifically focused on women. Evangelical translation endeavors undergird this, as most Dangi women would have trouble becoming literate in a non-Dangi tongue.

Evangelicalism thus plays a role in cultural recovery by imparting literacy in the tribals' native language and translating portions of scripture into those languages.

Explicit democratizing or empowering effects occur through advocacy work whereby GCW workers assist *adivasis* in handling court disputes, in countering moneylenders' schemes, and in guiding village headmen to draft petitions to the government, which generates some modest situational governmental accountability. These multipronged interventions have helped in coping with financial, medical, and legal trickery, manipulation, and harassment, initially on an *ad hoc* basis, but increasingly through training and capacity building among the *adivasis*. Active church life provides a vital information resource, and the south Indian Christian workers serve as advisors on the move, displacing traditional forms of social control that include inequitable client networks.

On a broader plane, advocacy work is crucial for political empowerment. Over the past decade, all this has enabled younger, educated tribals to practice law or run for office and has built up village and intervillage community institutions. This is particularly helpful in a region marked by irregular intervention by poorly motivated NGOs and an indifferent state administration. The Dangs heretofore has typified a situation characterized by poor institutional performance and the prevalence of "traditional forms of social control," where "economic relations are to a great extent reproduced through social and political forms of domination" (Heller 2000, 490). In sum, GCW involvement has had democratizing influences both because of the greater equality and rights that Dangis have begun to get, crucial to any meaningful sense of democracy as equality or as self-governance, and also because of the potential for further equality and for explicit political organization in the future.

But anything that works to free Dangis from outside predatory forces necessarily poses a challenge to those who have benefited in the past from the Dangis' vulnerability and exploitability. This was reflected by the widespread attacks on Christian *adivasis* in Christmas week 1998 and 1999, principally by riotous mobs mobilized from outside the Dangs by Hindu nationalist figures. Thus, these developments in south Gujarat are significant not only for their local properties: status changes and material improvement wrought among the *adivasis*, or the way evangelicalism transmutes itself to pursue novel social action strategies, defying any straitjacketing as an unreflective project aimed exclusively at Christian conversion. They also are significant for the way they position evangelicalism vis-à-vis the Indian political elite, particularly that of Hindu nationalism. In the Dangs, Swami Asheemanand, associated with the Vanvasi Kalyan Parishad, part of the Rashtriya Swayamsevak Sangh (RSS) family, orchestrated the attacks in 1998 and 1999.[55] That the rioters knew the exact location of forest village churches suggests collusion by local business people, particularly moneylenders and alcohol traders, and perhaps by some disgruntled non-Christian *adivasis*.[56]

Therefore, evangelicalism poses a threat to those who profit by exploiting tribals, both by raising awareness among dispossessed groups and by its potential to strengthen links with other dissenting actors. For instance, the Maharashtra-based *dalit* Republican Party of India (RPI) gave support in early 1999 to evangelicals who were beaten by the Hindu nationalist Shiv Sena in Nasik district, bordering the Dangs. RPI representatives from Mumbai sought out the evangelists who work among the Varlis to convey their support, carried the news of the attacks in their party organ, and organized a strike and silent march in the city of Nasik. Extreme Hindu nationalism is wary of just such convergence among subordinate castes and groups.

Evangelical success in tribal areas has evidently disturbed holders and structures of power, albeit on a very limited scale, and as a result, becomes a focus of controversy. For this reason, what is happening in southern Gujarat bears crucially on the conflicts currently determining the very future of Indian democracy. It helps chart Indian political currents by showing the strong reaction to seemingly small democratizing influences and religious choices among Dangis. This section of the chapter examines that set of issues.

Christianity draws attention in India to various overtly political issues. The bounds of religious freedom have provoked heated debate. Article 25 of the Constitution states that "subject to public order, morality and health, and to the other provisions of the Part, all persons are equally entitled to freedom of conscience and the right freely to profess, practice and propagate religion." There have been regular attempts to use the public order proviso to regulate conversions through parliamentary legislation.[57]

Another contentious issue is the impasse over granting affirmative action in jobs and education (known as "reservations" in India) to *dalit* Christians just as to other *dalits*, people from the former "untouchable" castes. *Dalits* who have adopted Christianity (45 percent of the Indian Christian community) were deemed, per a 1950 presidential order, to lose their status as low-caste individuals after conversion. Reservations *are* granted to low-caste Buddhist and Sikh converts.[58] Christians' national electoral irrelevance and inadequate ecumenical strategy, complicity of non-Christian *dalit* leaders in northern India, and the church's failure to give the *dalits* leadership commensurate with their numbers all contribute to the stalemate. Similarly, the official form for the 2001 census, controversially, did not allow scheduled tribes or castes to list Christianity as their religion. Christianity also provokes national security fears among Hindu nationalist groups owing to its majority status in the northeastern states that border China and Bangladesh. Christian majority states such as Mizoram, Nagaland, and Manipur have had militant rebels who claim evangelical identity. Lutheran Church's support for a separate state in Jharkhand, which achieved fruition in November 2000, also displayed significant evangelical engagement with politics.

Christian evangelicalism *per se* shaped recent political conversation in India in ways unimaginable a decade ago. Events related to evangelicals since 1997–1998, principally in Gujarat and Orissa, provoked animated discussion in India during 1998–2000 unlike any other topic, eclipsing even the 1998 nuclear tests. Attacks by Hindu nationalist cadres on Christian individuals and on churches there led to much political acrimony, partly fueled by Prime Minister Atal Behari Vajpayee's call for a "national debate on conversions"—a victim-blaming justification of the violence. This peaked when John Paul II expressed his hope for "a harvest of faith" in Asia in the new millennium, during a November 2000 papal visit, incensing his official hosts. Violence against evangelicals also provoked international media coverage, special reports by human rights organizations and others, and diplomatic attention, such as the U.S. State Department's Report on Religious Freedom (Human Rights Watch 1999; U.S. Department of State 2000). Attacks against Christians gained international attention after Hindu militants burned alive Australian missionary Graham Staines and his two young sons in 1999, a gruesome murder arguably orchestrated by an activist from Bajrang Dal, an affiliate of the RSS, which is the vanguard of the ruling BJP.

Evangelical Christianity's political significance is revealed by its prominence in India's nationalist soliloquies since the mid-nineteenth century, in efforts to find a cultural basis to shore up the authority of the nation-state in a splintered sociopolitical landscape. The majority Hindu community has perceived Christianity as a religious vestige of British colonialism. Christians, often classified as primarily low-caste adherents of a foreign faith, are castigated for an evangelical fervor deemed unpatriotic and "un-Indian" owing to the "foreign" origins of the faith.

Christianity retains a cultural salience inconsistent with its demographic status, despite Hindu nationalist attempts to undermine it through its cultural agenda during its tenure in power between 1999 and 2004. Such attempts include introducing Vedic astrology as a course in select Indian universities and adding illiberal antiminority content and Hindu tradition to school textbooks (Bidwai 1999, 108–110; Safdar Hashmi Memorial Trust 2001). Substantial Sangh Parivar (the Hindu nationalist family of organizations) energies are devoted to Christian missions. Indeed, the VHP was formed in 1964 expressly to oppose Christian missionaries.[59] Of course, "Hindu nationalism" as discussed in this chapter refers only to the aggressive RSS version so prominent in India today. An intolerant, dominating, violent, or abusive Hindu nationalism no more represents Hinduism than Muslim suicide bombers or terrorists represent Islam, or than racist southern sheriffs represent American Christians.

This study suggests that militant Hindu nationalism is set to collide with evangelicalism as the RSS, hitherto largely limited to towns and cities, increasingly penetrates into rural areas to expand the BJP electoral base. Understanding RSS efforts is pertinent to studying the evangelical role in social change because Hindu nationalism is now trying to gain the loyalty of the disempowered sections of society and to displace Christian evangelicalism. Potential conflicts reflect the groups' sociological composition and bases of support. The Sangh Parivar mainly derives its support from the upper castes, principally Brahmins and trading castes.[60] Many Indian evangelicals come from disempowered backgrounds. Also, the evangelicals studied here work among marginalized groups and thus may threaten the ideological and mercantile dominance of upper castes, increasingly aligned with Hindu nationalist groups.[61] Hence, evangelicalism becomes not only an ideological rival, but a movement aiding subalterns that antedates Hindu nationalist engagement with rural India, especially tribals. Thus, it must be thwarted to achieve that hegemony of nationalized Hinduism called *Hindutva* that the RSS seeks.

The escalating scale of attacks, and the evident unwillingness of the BJP government to enforce the rule of law when attacks occurred, provoked fears that the BJP might give Christians a political scapegoat-function similar to that assigned to Muslims. This issue touches the whole fabric of Indian political life. India is a mosaic of different languages, ethnic groups, castes, and religions. If the attempt to create a single-valenced India continues, it would be an unparalleled disaster for human rights and will undermine the foundations of the secular Indian state, which has allowed the Indian mix—Sikhs, Hindus, Muslims, south and north Indians, *adivasis*, and speakers of Hindi, Tamil, Kannada, English, Bengali, and so on—to live together as a single country. The results are hard to predict, but the systematic massacre of thousands of Muslims and the lasting displacement of hundreds of thousands into refugee camps in Gujarat during spring 2002 is one indicator.[62] This pogrom, carefully planned and countenanced, or even abetted by the BJP-run Gujarat state government, suggests that the issues raised by resistance to a Christian presence in the Dangs go far beyond the Dangs, or Gujarat, or Christianity. Thus, any effectiveness with which evangelicalism can assist tribal peoples and foster a measure of independence, self-governance, and ability to resist exploitation will surely continue to create conflict. In this sense, evangelicalism's democratizing impact among tribals is intensely political in its meaning and effects and is centrally related to whether India's polity retains its balance or traverses a path to illiberal and authoritarian cultural nationalism.

This represents a continuity in the kind of impact that evangelical Christianity has had on various improvident or subaltern communities since the nineteenth century. It provokes the same opposing interests in Indian society that resist that kind of change. It addresses the needs of disempowered communities neglected by dominant political interests and a partisan state.

The situation in southern Gujarat also indicates that much of Indian politics continues to be a clash of two sociologies: a politics defined by the domination of the upper caste and middle and lower-middle classes, with significant support from business interests (Heller 2000, 495),[63] occasioned by a sectarian agenda for the Indian state, but resisted by all shades of protest movements attempting to free social space for communities and individuals to develop and cope with widespread inequities. As Corbridge and Harriss (2000, xix) write, "The designs of the Hindu nationalists and of the economic reformers are opposed by a diversity of social and political movements which are part of another long history, that of resistance to the established order by those who have been the objects of oppression."

In this context, a certain strand of Indian evangelicalism, including agencies such as GCW and AG, proves to be an agent of resistance to domination and a harbinger of democracy for its target communities. Indian evangelicalism has been assailed for endorsing a supposedly foreign faith, for diluting its Indian identity, and for peddling an otherworldly spirituality that ignores local impoverishment. But the wholly Indian and Indian-funded GCW demonstrably contests that stereotype. Little wonder that it elicits much resistance from a Hindu nationalism that is only the latest political vehicle of India's dominant interests.

NOTES

1. See section on "Dynamics of Outreach in the Dangs and Beyond," below.

2. That Christian mission, not colonialism, altered Indian social practice has come to receive a measure of acceptance. Copley (1998, 6) writes, "At no stage did the Empire ever challenge Indian religions and social institutions, and above all, caste, in the way Mission did. There was a fierceness and wide scope to the challenge posed by Mission which compels its discussion as a distinctive ideology." Historian Sumit Sarkar (1999) writes:

> Missionary complicity with colonialism in India has also been much exaggerated and simplified. Early Company rulers like Hastings and Cornwallis, far from encouraging missionaries, often developed close collaborative relations with orthodox Brahman literati, and the Baptist mission had to set up its first outpost in Serampur, then outside British Bengal. Later, too, there have been many missionary critics of colonial policies. Above all, at the other end of the social scale, recent historical research is increasingly highlighting the extent to which sustained Christian philanthropic and educational work have had an empowering impact on significant sections of *adivasis*, dalits and poor and subordinated groups in general.

3. The organizations and people referred to are given pseudonyms, as requested, to protect their physical safety.

4. The RSS, which translates benignly as "National Volunteer Service," has been a Hindu militia masquerading as a movement for cultural revival from

its inception in 1925. Its founders barely disguised their admiration for Italian fascism and Nazism. M. S. Golwalkar (1938a; cf. Noorani, 2000, 20), its most supreme director, wrote in 1938 in the aftermath of the Nuremberg Laws, "Germany has also shown how well-nigh impossible it is for races and cultures, having differences going to the root, to be assimilated into one united whole, a good lesson for us... to learn and profit by." Later that year, Golwalkar (1938b) declared, "If we Hindus grow stronger in time Moslem friends... will have to play the part of German Jews." The RSS controls the ruling BJP's executive committee. Its one million–strong volunteer force, modeled after the Hitler Youth, and its affiliate body, the Vishwa Hindu Parishad (World Hindu Confederation), plus a plethora of organizations that it has established to culturally engage India, make it indispensable in Hindu nationalist electoral mobilization. For an ideological and organizational overview, see Embree (1994, 617–652).

5. *Indian Express*, April 22, 2002; *Hindustan Times*, April 24, 2002.

6. More than two thousand people, principally Muslims, were killed, with virtually no attempt by the BJP state government to quell the violence. Gujarat Chief Minister Narendra Modi of the BJP later called the pogrom a "natural reaction" against the February 27 fire on the Sabarmati Express at Godhra where fifty-seven, mostly VHP activists were burned alive. The fire was allegedly set by Muslims; later official investigation showed it to have arisen from natural causes. In the following three weeks, Gujarat witnessed a total vitiation of civil liberties, with the systematic targeting of the Muslim community by the state administration. A resolution passed by the Rashtriya Swayamsevak Sangh (RSS), Hindu nationalism's vanguard organization, at its national meeting in Bangalore *after* the riots, which asked the Muslims to earn the goodwill of the majority Hindu community, was particularly portentous for the Indian polity at large. "Let the Muslims understand that their real safety lies in the goodwill of the majority community," the resolution read. *Indian Express*, March 18, 2002.

7. The mob first attacked Muslim people and property, and then turned its attention to the compound. Some sixty schoolchildren in the hostel were chased out and the property looted while resident missionaries were away. An informant expressed concern to this writer about the prospect of this event garnering media coverage immediately as the Hindu militants were expectedly looking for a provocation to attack Christians as well, which might have been imminent given that they are well informed about the exact location of minorities.

8. The Kumbh was designed as an effective show of force by bringing in huge numbers into a small district with a population of 150,000. Christian groups alleged harassment prior to the event while some drew attention to the ecological impact of clearing eight square kilometers of land. Also, inducting the *Shabri Kumbh* into the regular Hindu religious calendar involved the construction of a new tradition. The VHP "hit upon the figure of Shabari" in the Ramayana epic and announced that Shabari offered the fruit to Ram in the Dangs at a place called Subir and went on to construct a "grand Shabari Mata Mandir" in 2004. See Manini Chatterjee, "Sangh's New Kumbh to Take Hindutva Offensive to the Dangs,' *Indian Express* (New Delhi), September 21, 2005; Manas Dasgupta, "All Set for 'Shabri Kumbh' amid Reconversion Fears," *The Hindu* (Delhi), February 11, 2006.

9. In fact, the organ of the RSS, *Organiser*, reports that Morari Bapu "conceptualised the event" and led its inauguration. See Tarun Vijay, "The Grand Mingling in the Shabri Kumbh," *Organiser* (Delhi), February 26, 2006, p. 14.

10. Manas Dasgupta, "Tribals Urged to 'Return Home.'" *The Hindu* (Delhi), February 12, 2006.

11. A considerable part of Sangh Parivar (the Hindu nationalist "family of organizations") energies are devoted to the Christian missionary enterprise; indeed, the VHP was created in 1964 with the express purpose of opposing Christian evangelical activity.

12. At that time, I was an independent researcher not professionally affiliated with a university.

13. There are, for instance, cases of lone individuals converting to Christianity unaccompanied by families, as S. Joshi (1999, 2670) reports, as distinct from other accounts of entire families becoming Christian following a healing event or deliverance from alcohol.

14. David Mosse (2005) presents an excellent account of social processes in development agencies, focusing in part on how information is used in such settings "to secure reputation, conceal poor performance or to negotiate position in the organization or with outsiders." On the basis of studying Britain's Department for International Development projects in *adivasi* communities in the 1990s, he argues that the effects of development rarely proceed in a linear fashion from development design to implementation. In fact, in many cases, it is the contingencies of social practice that actually produce policy after duly frustrating it. This chapter has clearly not tackled those dynamics.

15. An extended exposé-type piece, titled "George Bush Has a Big Conversion Agenda in India," *Tehelka*, February 7, 2004, is representative of the outrage caused (in liberal circles) by the interest of American evangelicals in converting India.

16. For instance, in November 1999, the Orissa government amended the existing Orissa Freedom of Religion Rules of 1989, declaring that "any person intending to convert his religion shall give a declaration" to a magistrate that "he intends to convert his religion on his own will." The amendments also lay down that "the concerned religious priest shall intimate the date, time and place of the conversion ceremony" to the district magistrate fifteen days before it takes place. Violation of the provisions is punishable by imprisonment up to two years and a fine if the person who has converted is a minor, woman, tribal, or member of a low caste (Akkara 2000).

17. Colonial legal policy on common property land based itself on the principle of *res nullius*, which held that if property is not legally owned by an individual it must be nobody's property. "The establishment of individual property rights in land, the creation of a land market, stringent forest laws, and an exploitative excise policy had all worked to impoverish the tribals, pushing them into the clutches of landlords, moneylenders and liquor contractors" (Akkara 2000).

18. *Gujarat State Gazetteers: Dangs District* (Ahmedabad: Government Printing, Stationery and Publications, 1971), i, 447. Colonial records describe Bhils and Gamits as "thin, without an ounce of spare flesh, and short in stature" (Hardiman 1994, 101), with poor health. They suffered from badly enlarged spleens and, like many people who developed resistance to malaria, from associated blood disorders.

19. Until 1830, the Dangs were ruled by Bhil chiefs who exercised authority over other tribes without being distinguishable in appearance from their subjects, living in huts like fellow Bhils. Though treated with great deference by their subjects, Bhil chiefs enjoyed no material superiority over them. Not uncommonly, Bhil chiefs depended on Gamits for food stocks and in return laboured for them. Their hierarchy was based on power and status, not material wealth. Tribal rulers found accumulating wealth distasteful: all a Bhil chief's belongings, including his gun and the furniture in his hut, were burned on his funeral pyre (Hardiman 1994, 101).

20. But the Bhils were also known for their martial potential and were feared by the adjoining princely states for being expert raiders.

21. The British were careful to be deferential to the chief in the annual durbar ritual where chiefs were felicitated. This practice, too, continues today at the behest of the district administration; observers find it a humiliating spectacle, reminding the chiefs of their lack of substantive power.

22. "Reserved" forests in the Dangs increased from 22,280 hectares in 1961 to 91,200 hectares in 1990; "protected" forest increased from 77,973 hectares in 1955 to 85,500 in 1990. In the late nineteenth century, around 66 percent of the Dangs area was available for cultivation. Today, the Forest Department controls 53.11 percent of cultivable land, and 87 percent of the population make do with 32 percent (Shah 1999b).

23. Interview with Fr. Raphael, Pimpri, August 2000.

24. Interview with GCW senior representative, June 2001.

25. A significant share of Indian missionary enterprise is led by the Nadar community, with renowned figures Samuel Kamaleson of World Vision, Theodore Williams, formerly of the Indian Evangelical Mission, Emil Jeba Singh of Good Samaritans, and, arguably the most famous Christian healer in the country, D. G. S. Dhinakaran, to name a few.

26. This is sustained by elements of the evangelical subculture such as witnessing, public prayer, and preaching that simultaneously reinforce the awareness of caste heritage while impelling evangelical ambition.

27. There are some departures from group norms: some workers solicit prayer groups for additional needs even though gifts, including cash, are supposed to be handed over to the organization after a worker's salary level is met.

28. Interview with Kalpabhai, September 2001.

29. Both field directors left the organization in 1999 to form the splinter Gujarat Christian Mandate.

30. Interview with C. S. Barnabas, November 2001.

31. I was not in a position to confirm whether this was true, as explained in the discussion of methodology given above. Writers who have traveled extensively in the Dangs have differing figures as well. Activist-writer Irfan Engineer (1999), who worked in the Dangs between 1989 and 1993, says the majority "did not accept Christianity" while availing themselves of the educational, health, and other services offered by Christian groups. Satyakam Joshi (1999, 2670) notes the "major increase" in the past twenty years and puts his estimate between fifteen thousand and twenty thousand Christians.

32. A left wing Jesuit who decries the evangelical tendency to belittle tribal traditions related that he was witness to tribals jumping in and out of a bus's windows, not understanding the use of the bus's door. Another observer related tribals' lack of familiarity with soap for washing.

33. Christian workers do not suggest that *adivasis* change their attire; this is something *adivasis* undertake on their own, perhaps as a way of moving toward entry into the larger society. Christian tribal women in villages noticeably shook hands with outsiders, which is probably quite rare in rural India.

34. This is evident in their reserved worship and prayer patterns. Prayer sessions are conducted in a very subdued fashion, even if the sessions last through the night. The worship sessions of the all-India conference for all the GCW staff that I attended in June 2001 was marked by no more than reluctant hallelujahs and the hesitant raising of hands.

35. *Dangs Gazetteer 1961*. However, Hindu deities like Hanuman are a part of the Dangi pantheon, probably as an import through Kukna migration from the coastal area, though GCW workers say instead that Hindu businessmen introduced Hanuman to the Dangs.

36. S. Joshi (1999, 2670) writes of the perceived inadequacy of existing *adivasi* belief systems to cope with their various disabilities: "There is a desperate yearning for protection from a more effective cosmological force, and they have therefore turned to a deity who they feel is more efficacious in this day and age."

37. Interview with GCW field director, June 2001.

38. For untouchable castes, who interacted daily with Hindu society, this was enhanced by the discourse of purity and impurity, which drilled into untouchables that they were worthless and impure. Because *adivasi* animist beliefs do not involve concepts of purity and pollution so prominently, there was less ideological sanction behind *adivasi* deprivation.

39. Interview with Mahdubhai, September 2001.

40. Interview with Philip, GCW worker, August 2000.

41. Interview with Ramubhai, GCW churchgoer, September 2001.

42. Interview with GCW field director, June 2001.

43. For one left-wing activist, reduction in alcohol abuse was the biggest success of evangelicalism.

44. The Dangi *bhagats* are not to be confused with the Bhagats of northern Gujarat, who embraced Vaishnavism or Shaivism and appropriated the Brahmanical aversion to meat and liquor.

45. Interview with Hanijbhai, September 2001.

46. Interview with Mohanbhai, GCW churchgoer and evangelist, September 2001.

47. Interview with Abdubhai, GCW churchgoer, September 2001.

48. The India Missions Association supports translation. Orient Bible Translation has nearly finished translating the Bible into the Dangi Kukna language. The progress in Chowdri is more typical, with twenty-four New Testament books and five "good news" booklets.

49. Sanneh (1989, 5, 28) demonstrates this with African translations, which were sometimes used against colonial authorities: "For example, the Luo tribesman

Matthew Ajuoga... helping missionaries translate the Bible... discovered that the missionaries translated the Greek word *philadelphia*, 'brotherly love,' into Luo as *hera*, and this experience caused him to protest, saying that 'love' as the Bible explained it was absent from the missionaries' treatment of Africans." See Sanneh (1987, 331–334).

50. Christian workers are known to alert *adivasis* to unfair price tactics of cartel contractors or business people who are known to buy *adivasi* products at inordinately low prices.

51. Ranajit Guha (1985b, 21) records that the *dalit* Rathwa caste had a patron deity who was a moneylender: "Reduced to a state of near servitude by the moneylender [they] pay him the ultimate tribute of making a moneylender of their own patron deity. The apotheosization of the usurer could hardly go further." Cf. Hardiman 1987a, 22.

52. A resolution of a conservative Hindu convention in adjoining Nasik district in January 1999 warned Christians not to take advantage of poor *adivasis* and issued a deadline to stop conversion activity by March 31, 1999. "Sammelan Warning to Missionaries," *The Tribune* (Chandigarh), January 7, 1999.

53. A left-wing activist said the difference between Christianity and Hindu nationalism is that the former seeks to assimilate *adivasi* cultural practices, but the latter seeks to decimate them.

54. Administrative headquarters reportedly expects staff to adhere to their recommendation on what model of motorcycle to use; all GCW workers, noticeably, drive the same brand!

55. A list of news reports at http://in.rediff.com/news/dang.htm provides overall coverage of attacks in the Dangs.

56. Most significantly, the state BJP government provided support to the anti-Christian activists. The most senior bureaucrat in the Dangs, District Collector B. N. Joshi, was present at the December 25 meeting at Ahwa organized by the Hindu Jagran Manch that led the rioting. Moreover, a confidential circular issued three weeks earlier, on December 3, 1998, by the deputy superintendent of police of Dangs directed that "facts regarding Christian priests and Christian religion" be collected in the district as suggested by state minister Mangubhai Patel. See National Alliance of Women (1999, 6).

57. Most prominently, a contentious private member's bill in the 1950s, titled "Indian Converts (Regulation and Registration) Bill," instituted a Niyogi Commission, whose controversial findings are considered uncontroverted evidence to this day by Hindu nationalists. The commission, set up in 1954 by the Madhya Pradesh state government to look into political activity by missionaries, dealt extensively with conversions and blamed foreign missionaries for political instability. Pointedly, Jawaharlal Nehru, India's first prime minister and a doctrinaire secularist, opposed "regulations of Religious Conversions," saying that "such curbs will only lead to other evils." Lok Sabha address, December 3, 1955, quoted in Wingate (1999, 34).

58. For a historical treatment of Indian Christianity and caste dynamics, see Forrester (1980) and Webster (1992).

59. For a fairly comprehensive evaluation of its ideology, see Van der Veer (1994).

60. For a sociological analysis of the BJP's electoral base, see Ghosh (1998). One study found that in central Uttar Pradesh, RSS volunteers working in villages candidly explained that their organization depended on upper castes. One *shakha* (branch) member openly stated that the *shakha* members were drawn mainly from traders, and an ex-president of the BJP unit in Khurja described the party as a "middle class upper caste party" (Basu et al. 1993, 88).

61. One estimate reports that the number of indigenous Indian missionaries grew from 543 in 1972 to twelve thousand by 1994, and fifteen thousand cross-cultural missionaries and five thousand local missionaries by 1997. Patrick Johnstone refers to 198 mission agencies, and the Evangelical Church of India counts three hundred mission agencies (cited in Rajendran 1998, 13, 55).

62. See http://www.sabrang.com/cc/archive/2002/marapril/index.html for an extended account of the Gujarat massacres in 2002.

63. Increasingly, some argue that India's postcolonial political passage can be characterized as reluctant relinquishing of dominant castes' control of state institutions in the face of persistent struggle, largely due to the instrument of elections. For a literary variant of the same perspective on postcolonial India, see Pandian (2002). Aloysius (1998), in his sociological analysis of the national movement, interestingly interprets the entire nationalist phase, under Mahatma Gandhi's leadership, as an elaborate effort to clinch upper-caste control of state institutions. Upper-caste predominance in the Gujarat state legislature indicates their political control: upper castes comprising Brahmins, Vanias, and Rajputs, who collectively amount to 12 percent of the population, held 41 percent and 35 percent of the seats for their respective parties, the BJP and Congress, in the 1995 and 1998 Assembly elections (Desai and Shah 2002, 15). Upper castes comprised nearly 50 percent of legislators for the Congress and BJP in the 1991 Uttar Pradesh election. They made up 65 percent of the BJP state executive in 1998–1999 and on average amounted to 49 percent of the Congress state executive in 1990–1999 (Zerinini-Brotel 2002).

3

Ethnicity, Civil Society, and the Church: The Politics of Evangelical Christianity in Northeast India

Sujatha Fernandes

In the main prayer room of the mission headquarters in Ukhrul, a small hill town in the northeast Indian state of Manipur, is the figure of a Naga tribal warrior with a club in his right hand and a crucifix in his left, which bears the inscription "Christ, the Hope of Ages." Christian religious discourse has framed the ways tribals of the northeastern states interact with each other, creating a moral universe through which tribals evaluate their peripheral relationship to an increasingly Hindu-identified central state. Evangelical activity in the Northeast has provided the means for the development of a civil society through local organizations and networks that provide the possibility for northeastern tribals to articulate and advance their particular political goals in the Indian federalist system. However, in practice, this process has been impeded by the fragmentation of politics in the Northeast to the point that the individual northeastern states, let alone the region as a whole, have been unable to unite their concerns. Although individual groups have achieved certain goals in relation to the center, such as the recognition of statehood and the right to political representation, they are still far from formulating and presenting their demands to the center in a sustained manner. In the post-Independence context, the northeast region has been torn apart by violent intraethnic conflict that further reduces the ability of groups to put forward a unified political agenda. Given the success of evangelical activity in nearly all parts of the region and its contributions toward building a strong civil society, why does the region continue to be fragmented politically? Can the conditions for democratic political practice in the region develop despite social fragmentation?

Conventionally, civil society has been understood in elite models of democracy as a set of associations, such as family, religious groupings, and private clubs, that promote a stable democratic polity by bringing group interests to bear on political decision making. In the work of theorists such as Robert Putnam (Putnam, Leonardi, and Nanetti 1993), civil society is seen as "cultural cement" that teaches citizens about their roles and obligations in society. However, such formulations are inadequate in the context of multiethnic, dependent states such as the northeastern states of India, where the church has played an important role in promoting civic consciousness and stability. Yet the region remains fragmented and politically powerless in relation to the center. The case of northeast India suggests that in contexts of economic vulnerability and tensions between marginalized ethnic groups, political goals of stability and citizen obligation may not be as important as demands for justice and autonomy. In such a context, perhaps we can look to the more dynamic concept suggested by Jean Cohen and Andrew Arato (1997, 19) of a differentiated model of civil society based on "social movements for the expansion of rights, for the defense of the autonomy of civil society, and for its further democratization." In cases of ethnic fragmentation and regional underdevelopment, civil society is faced with the task of articulating local political demands for justice and inclusion, which is a more contestatory role than is accorded to elite models of democracy. The case study explored in this chapter forces us to rethink conventional notions of civil society and broaden the role accorded to religious associations and social movements in the context of multiethnic, underdeveloped societies.

The central argument of this chapter is that, despite the efforts of evangelical leaders to create strong, self-sufficient tribal polities, they have been hampered in their goals by internal features of evangelical organization, external conflicts between hostile tribal groups, and the integration of Christianity into various dominant structures of power. Evangelical organizations are forced to make certain trade-offs between the preservation of culture and language in its diversity, and the goals of political unity that modify tribal diversity to promote the shared concerns of tribals. At times, the decentralized nature of Protestant evangelical churches means that larger denominations are split into several smaller organizations, usually along tribal or ethnic lines, bringing strong localisms into play. The cost of such decentralization is usually broader political unity. Church leaders are ineffective in a context of tribal warfare and conflict, which was fanned by British colonial policies of divide and rule and worsened by conditions of structural inequality and migration into the region. Finally, evangelical leaders themselves have cooperated with dominant groups to promote political stability and hegemony in ways that have detracted from their ability to represent the agenda of the subaltern groups. This chapter explores the ways these three themes are played out throughout the history of the Northeast, in both the colonial and post-Independence contexts. The continuities between the historical and the contemporary periods convey certain insights about the nature of evangelical organization in multiethnic societies, as well as the complex and contradictory relationship between evangelicals and political power.

This chapter addresses the contemporary relationship between politics and evangelical activity through a study that is historical and comparative. Focusing on the northeast Indian state of Manipur, the study makes comparisons with Mizoram, Nagaland, and Meghalaya and draws out the implications of the historical data for the contemporary political climate. The first section explores the interaction among Christian missionaries, tribals, and the British state in the colonial context, showing how the attempt of missionaries to build an autonomous tribal leadership was hampered by the diversity of tribal groupings and the ties of the missionaries to the colonial state. The second section focuses on the first two themes in the present: how evangelical practices of congregationalism have given expression to diversity, but also how, in a context of ethnic violence and rivalry, this decentralized organization leaves the church unable to overcome fragmentation. In the final section, I explore the third theme, suggesting that the evangelicals' desire for stability in the region has impeded their ability to foster social movements for justice and equality, leaving the space open for insurgent and terrorist organizations. In the multiethnic context of a dependent region such as northeast India, an expanded notion of civil society can suggest some paths toward achieving democratic political practice.

Christianity and Civil Society in the Colonial Context

Christian missions in the nineteenth century were not able to establish a stronghold in mainland India due to the strength of established religions such as Hinduism and Islam; they had much greater success in their attempts at conversion in the area today known as northeast India, an area that lies to the north and east of Bangladesh and is linked to India through the northern part of western Bengal. Northeast India consists of the seven states of Arunachal Pradesh, Assam, Manipur, Meghalaya, Mizoram, Nagaland, and Tripura. These states contain an immense diversity of language and culture, including about two hundred different hill and plains tribes speaking about 175 different languages (Verghese 1996, 2–3). Presbyterians and the Baptists were the earliest Protestant denominations to evangelize in the area; Presbyterians gained a stronghold in Mizoram and among the Khasis and Jaintias of Meghalaya, and Baptists were mainly involved with the tribals of Manipur, Nagaland, and in the Garo Hills of Meghalaya (Downs 1992). Missionaries were unable to win over

TABLE 3.1. Overview of Christian Population in Northeast States over Time (%)

	Assam	Arunachal Pradesh	Tripura	Nagaland	Mizoram	Meghalaya	Manipur
1961	6.4	—	0.9	53.0	—	—	19.5
1991	3.3	10.3	1.7	87.4	85.7	64.9	34.11

Source: Joseph E. Schwartzberg, *A Historical Atlas of South Asia* (New York: Oxford University Press, 1978; second edition, 1992).

substantial parts of the population in Assam, Arunachal Pradesh, or Tripura for a variety of reasons, including the difficulty of entering some of these areas and the greater Hindu populations of areas such as Assam. However, they succeeded in converting large numbers of the predominantly tribal populations of Nagaland, Mizoram, Meghalaya, and the hill tribals of Manipur. Table 3.1 provides an overview of Christian populations in these states over time.

As can be seen from Table 3.1, between 1961 and 1991 there was only a small growth in the Christian population of Tripura, and even a decline in the state of Assam, whereas Arunachal Pradesh shows a more substantial population of 10.3 percent. However, significant growth in Christianity occurred in the states of Nagaland, Mizoram, and Meghalaya, where large numbers of tribals converted. In the state of Manipur, the overall percentage of Christians tends to be smaller because the majority of the settled population living in the plains is Hindu, although nearly the entire tribal population in the hill areas has converted to Christianity.

In this section, I explore the role of the church in building cohesive structures and organizations of civil society among tribals in the colonial period. I also show how the attempts of missionaries to promote the independence and self-sufficiency of tribal communities were constrained by mission ties to the colonial government. The northern hill tribals of Manipur are taken as a case study, as some of the most intractable ethnic problems have emerged in this region.[1] In some aspects, Manipur is a unique case in the Northeast as the hill tribals came from a vast diversity of different language groups, as compared with tribal groups in Mizoram, Nagaland, and Meghalaya, which tended to be more homogeneous (Downs 1992, 76). The information presented here is limited in that I deal mainly with Naga conversions by American Baptist missionaries. However, the case study presented in this historical section also contains several features generalizable to other states, tribal groups, and evangelicals in the Northeast, including the creation by missionaries of self-propagating independent institutions that gave tribals the tools to emerge as a semiautonomous realm through which they could assert their distinct concerns against the British rulers. The missionary involvement in the British policies of divide and rule in Manipur was also a feature in other regions, such as Nagaland and Meghalaya.

The early evangelical missionaries to northeast India entered this region at approximately the same time as the area was being brought under colonial administration. The first American Baptist missionaries arrived in Manipur in 1896, only five years after it had been brought under British control. It was the British political agent Colonel Maxwell who facilitated the entry of the missionaries into the tribal areas, establishing the first links between the American Baptists and the British state. The British government wanted to develop a layer of tribal intermediaries known as *lambus*, both to collect revenue from the tribal populations and to maintain British control over them. This required the education of a layer of young tribal males, a task that the missionaries were recruited to do. In 1896, the first American Baptist missionary, William Pettigrew, was given permission by Colonel Maxwell to begin work among the Tangkhul Nagas in the northeastern district of Ukhrul. Maxwell was quick to support Pettigrew because of the educational work he planned to carry out among the tribals. Pettigrew (1922a, 5) believed that "if there was to be built up and trained a number of these young hill boys for future service to the Mission as well as to the State, some sort of education was necessary." In certain respects, the American evangelical missionaries and the British state coincided in their aims. The *lambus* acted both as future evangelical leaders and as native informants for the British state. However, there were certain tensions between the missionaries and the British, as the missionaries refused to be what Pettigrew (1910, 80) refers to as "paid subordinate officer[s] of the State" and "prisoners of the great 'shorkar.'" Although they complied with the orders of the British state, the American Baptists were resentful of being under their jurisdiction.

While the missionaries were crucial to the British government's tasks of administration, they also had their own agenda, which involved reshaping tribal life and culture in their own image. The task of religious conversion could not be, as Pettigrew (1910, 75) recognized, "a mere moral conversion." Implanting Christianity meant supplanting traditional practices and introducing the tribals to all the conventions of European education and civilization that accompanied Christian doctrine. Channeling the Tangkhul Nagas into a Christian moral universe was not only about educating the tribals in Christian doctrine, but also about surveillance of every aspect of tribal life, the criminalization of traditional customs, and the disciplining of tribals through strict timetables of school and church. Before Christianity could be adopted, tribal religions had to be destroyed. In 1910, it came to the attention of Pettigrew that some of the converts had participated in the *Kathi Kasham* tribal feast. Upon making a detailed study of this feast, Pettigrew decided that it was anti-Christian because it "included the offering of sacrifices to evil spirits" (74). Pettigrew recognized that the incorporation of tribal religion into every aspect of tribal existence meant that it had a strong hold over people, and after the feast, he reports, "We fully expected all to lapse back into heathenism owing to the powerful influence of tribal custom" (74). Pettigrew drew sharp boundaries between Christian faith and traditional practices, arguing that the new church must adopt "a covenant which takes a strong stand against this evil, and most of the evils found on this field" (74). The missionaries recognized that the Tangkhul world was saturated with religion; it informed every aspect of tribal life. The American Baptists associated all the customary feasts, traditional music, dances, and even clothing with heathenism and therefore labeled them as anti-Christian.

The British authorities found these activities of the missionaries highly disturbing. Beyond educating a certain layer of tribals and subduing tribal rebellion to British rule, the British government opposed any further intervention into tribal culture. British administrators had pragmatic concerns about the effects of missionary activity. The British administrator J. P. Mills (1941, 349), who oversaw missionaries' activities in Manipur in the early part of the century, argued that by changing the cultural practices and customs of the tribals, the missionaries were bringing disease and ruining "tribal culture." Furthermore, he recognized the symbolic power of Christianity and its destabilizing effect on local authority, arguing against the ethos of individualism that he saw the missionaries bringing into the tribal world: "Not only is this individualism wrapped up with the strong emphasis on personal salvation; it is also the direct and natural reaction against the destruction of all the old things that mattered in village life" (351). By outlawing the communal feast, the Kathi Kasham, and dislodging the privileged brotherhood, or *morungs*, from their central position as the regulator of tribal social life, the missionaries were destroying the system by which "young Animists learn to be useful citizens" (351). This point was crucial for Mills. The British government maintained control over the hill areas by operating through the traditional institutions of tribal society. By creating alternative institutions and practices to traditional tribal society, the missionaries provided a framework for Nagas to question local authority and assert their independence. Mills addressed this issue explicitly: "A 'Civilized' Naga is apt to call customary discipline restraint, and many of them are eager to leave their villages and live free of all control" (351). Although the rejection of tribal culture was part of the defeat of a way of life, it was also a way out of the stifling orthodoxies and hierarchies of traditional society. At times, the questioning of local authority led to the questioning of British authority. In 1928, Laurie Hammond, the governor of Assam, then a province of British colonial rule, reported that the Christian Kuki tribals of the eastern district of Manipur had refused to carry out forced labor in construction, declaring that they were no longer subjects of the British state, but had become Christians.[2] Evangelical missionary activity provided the basis on which oppositional identities could be constructed.

Missionaries were aware of the destabilizing impact of Christianity on tribal society. As Pettigrew (1922a, 25) stated, "The chiefs and elders know what it will mean if there is a mass movement of the tribe. Although they all know that their legitimate privileges will stand and not be interfered with, they also know and fear that their illegitimate privileges will not be agreed to by those who give up the old customs and habits." Through the alternative religious institutions of the Baptist missionaries, the new converts came into contact with British legal and institutional norms and concepts such as "legitimate" and "illegitimate" privileges. Challenging the illegitimate privileges of the chiefs and elders meant making them accountable to their subjects, a practice that was not a part of precolonial tribal politics. Although the missionaries were concerned with building local institutions in order to propagate the Christian message, they contributed to the development of an indigenous civil society that was able to make political demands on the colonial state. Evangelical churches became a vehicle through which precolonial political structures adapted to a new colonial context. As Jean Comaroff and John Comaroff (1997, 94) argue in their study of Christian missionary activity among the southern Tswana in South Africa, "In many places, the mission hierarchy was iconic of local political hierarchies—and therefore, opened up a symbolic space for their renegotiation." American Baptist missionaries provided a language and a moral universe in which Nagas could recuperate a desire for autonomy and self-sufficiency outside the increasingly redundant tribal institutions.

The simultaneous participation of young tribal men in both the colonial bureaucracy and the church hierarchy gave rise to a civil society that was outside the control of the British colonial government. By virtue of their multiple positions as pastors, teachers, evangelists, interpreters, and head clerks, they stood at the nexus of the colonial bureaucracy and the church organization. Although these two structures often worked together, they were also in contradiction. Whereas participation in the colonial bureaucracy was intended to train a layer of natives subservient to British rule and authority, the aim of the church was to train evangelists who could eventually carry on the teachings of the mission independent of the foreign missionaries. In a 1926 report, Pettigrew (1926, 53) describes the twenty-four organized churches and thirteen branch churches that now existed in the northeast and Sadar areas of Manipur state: "The organized as well as the branch churches are practically self-supporting. Their buildings, and their local expenses are all the time supported by the church members." By encouraging self-supporting, self-propagating religious institutions among the tribals, the missionaries indirectly generated an indigenous civil society from within which tribals could assert their own political agenda against the colonial state.

In many aspects, Christian missionary activities provided the basis for the formation of a collegial society that could promote unity among tribes. In addition to giving tribals a voice through semiautonomous religious institutions and advancing a civic consciousness, Christian missionaries carried out the work of Bible translation, which reduced the vast diversity of tribal languages and facilitated communication among different subtribal groups based on a shared written language. This language often corresponded somewhat to the language spoken in the area where the missionaries worked, and it was then imposed on other tribes. For instance, the Tangkhul Naga script was developed according to the language spoken by Tangkhul Nagas in the Ukhrul area, where Pettigrew began his work, and it was then taught to Tangkhul Nagas in other areas. Prior to the missionaries' arrival these groups would have been unintelligible to one another; the creation of a common language gave them a means of communication. As Adrian Hastings (1997, 179) argues, by bringing "a reduction in the number of ethnicities and vernaculars," Christian missionaries promoted the development of larger cultural, economic, religious, and political communities. By organizing multiple tribal groups together in mission structures, Christianity laid the basis for cooperation among them. For instance, Thadou Kukis, a group that had migrated into Manipur from the south, were taught in the mission school alongside Tangkhul Nagas and participated alongside their Naga counterparts in mission structures.

However, the downside of the aggregation of several ethnic identities under larger rubrics was that it stabilized and fixed identities that had previously been fluid, thereby laying the foundation for future conflict. The potential contradictions and difficulties of forging political unity in a context of linguistic and cultural diversity has been noted by the Comaroffs (1997, 400–401): "Ethnicity everywhere at once constructs people, placing them definitively in space and time, and effaces them, submerging their individuality and opening them up to the stigmatization of otherness. In some circumstances, it also affords them a basis to protest the contours of the world as they find it—but often, in doing so, confines them to an ethnicized Tower of Babel, a universe of competing identities." Even as evangelical Christianity served to strengthen tribal autonomy and the unity of individual tribes or aggregations of tribes, it simultaneously set in place identifications that made a greater regional assertion difficult. Partly related to the specific organizational features of evangelical Christianity, this situation is also related to the larger trade-offs between unity and diversity in a situation where several tribes or ethnicities coexist. However, it was the political value associated with these ethnic differences that generated the potential for violent communal conflict that followed in the decades to come. It is not unusual that tribals would adopt the same communal identifications attributed to them by the British during their divide-and-rule campaigns, to later rebel against what they perceived as a cultural colonization by the Hindu central government.

The divide-and-rule policies of the British began much prior to the entry of the Christian missionaries into the Northeast. Although it was not until the late nineteenth century that the British established colonial rule in the Northeast, they had entered this area many decades before and had undertaken fairly aggressive policies before they succeeded in bringing these areas under administrative control. Nagas were concentrated in the districts of Chandel, Ukhrul, Senepati, and Tamenglong, and Kukis were scattered throughout the region of Manipur. Lal Dena (1996, 3) argues that the initial aims of colonial policy were to insulate British territory from any Burmese threat, and in 1840 Political Agent McCulloch adopted the policy of settlement of Kukis along the front line and in Naga villages. As Dena argues, "The double purpose of the Kuki settlement in and on the frontiers of Manipur was that the warlike Kukis had to act as a buffer, first against the Burmese, and secondly, against the recalcitrant Nagas and Lushai tribes" (3). The colonial administrators also used the Nagas against the Burmese in a similar manner. The Thadou Kukis were a migratory clan who had entered Manipur around the eighteenth century and began living among the Nagas. The Nagas and Old Kukis who had migrated before the Thadou Kukis lived together in stable villages with marked boundaries and fixed settlements, but the houses and settlements of the Thadou Kukis were more temporary. Although this had led to some intertribal warfare and clashes in the precolonial period, it was not until the colonial period, and the deliberate policies of the British to pit tribes against one another, that these differences took on the larger political meaning of Kuki versus Naga.

In the second decade of the twentieth century, the newly established mission churches were employed in the British divide-and-rule policy, a policy that was to be replayed again and again in the ethnic violence and conflicts that beset postcolonial northeast India. In 1917, when Thadou Kuki chiefs in the south of Manipur launched an insurgency movement against the British government, the Christian missionaries and Christian converts, both Kuki and Naga, played an important role in the suppression of this insurgency. The Kuki rebellion lasted from May 1917 to September 1919, and a military operation, known as the Kuki Punitive Measures (KPM), was launched against the rebellious chiefs. Pettigrew was given a commission in the India Army Reserve during this war, and another Baptist missionary doctor, Dr. Crozier, was assigned as a special medical officer for the KPM (Pettigrew 1922a, 93). It was the Christian converts, as native informants, however, who played a crucial role in the KPM. In his tour diary, J. C. Higgins records, "We have about 180 fighting men, including officers, orderlies, signalers etc., a 71b ML gun, and 608 coolies, controlled by some 28 *lambus*, interpreters, headmen etc."[3] As interpreters, headmen, and *lambus*, the mainly Christian native informants provided intelligence to the British side and helped to round up the rebellious Thadou Kuki chiefs. During the Zeliangrong Naga movement in the 1940s, the colonial officials recruited Kukis to suppress the movement. The consolidation of colonial control over different tribal groups led to a deepening of ethnic divisions, and the participation of the church in this process implicated it in the violent ethnic conflict that ensued.

A historical analysis of early evangelical activity in Manipur highlights two main points about the relationship between Christianity and politics. First, it shows how Christian education and involvement in Christian mission structures developed a layer of tribal leaders who were able to voice their concerns and agendas against that of the colonial state. Second, it shows how the missionaries and converts were constrained in their support for tribal autonomy by their ties to the colonial state, whether as "prisoners," as some missionaries understood it, employed to train a layer of tribal leadership loyal to the colonial state, or as participants in the divide-and-rule policies of the British colonial state, through which the British sought to use certain tribal groups against others to maintain their control over these groups. The following sections explore the ways these themes have reemerged in the contemporary context.

Disunity, Ethnic Conflict, and the Church in Contemporary Northeast India

Prior to Independence and particularly in the lead-up to the independence movement, Christianity played an important role in developing the organizational and leadership abilities of tribals in the Northeast through its mission structures and educational endeavors. It politicized communities and provided symbolism for latent opposition to the colonial regime and more generally to injustice and inequality. However, in the post-Independence period, the church has been ineffective against the numerous splits that have characterized post-Independence tribal society, along with the turbulent and often violent political conflicts that mark this period. Christianity has been unable to bridge the chasms between different tribal groups, and its own sectarian differences have often compounded tribal differences. In the post-Independence period, class, tribal, and ethnic differences have reemerged with a vengeance. The Northeast has become a hotbed of insurgency movements, with demands ranging from secession to autonomy within the framework of the Indian state. Dialogue across differences has been replaced by intolerance, violence, and communalism. Drawing on interviews carried out in Manipur, Mizoram, Meghalaya, and Nagaland, I explore the relationship between the church and politics in northeast India today.[4]

In contemporary northeast India, the church has continued to foster civic engagement, particularly in those states with majority Christian populations, such as Mizoram, Nagaland, and Meghalaya. Putnam (Putnam et al. 1993, 183) has argued that religious institutions can be "the cultural cement of the civil community" by providing "a conception of one's role and obligations as a citizen, coupled with a commitment to political equality." Church and political leaders confirmed the church as the cultural cement of society in northeast India and that it seeks to encourage political participation based on an understanding of Christian principles and theological ideals. Although churches do not field candidates in the elections, they do carry out a range of political activities. As Rev. Zaihmingthanga, ex-secretary of the Mizoram Presbyterian Church, stated, "We normally issue pamphlets on the eve of the elections encouraging our members to cast their votes and utilize their franchise responsibly." The church does not mention the names of particular political candidates, but "highlight what kind of people are trustworthy, and have a good reputation in church and society," therefore giving citizens a guide as to selection of responsible leaders. This process involves bodies as high as the executive committee of the Mizo Synod, which, as Rev. Lungmuana of the Mizoram Presbyterian Church, states, personally appeal to people to reflect on the kind of candidate they should vote for.

By encouraging discussion and debate over questions of good governance, citizenship, and responsibility, church leaders provide a means for ordinary citizens to engage in democratic politics, making informed decisions about their political leaders. According to Lungmuana, the church in Mizoram presents its view of politics to the population, encouraging them to participate actively: "We do outreach to all the villages, also in towns, telling them what we mean by politics and how we form the government, that we are important in forming the government, and we encourage our people to participate in the forming of the government by voting." Rev. Ngurhnema, a pastor in the Baptist Church of Mizoram, states that church bodies such as the Mizoram Kohran Hruaitute Committee (MKHC, Committee of Church Leaders in Mizoram) become involved in elections by formulating the qualifications that should be expected of members of the Legislative Assembly and members of Parliament. Ngurhnema stated that these prescriptions play a very important role in determining which candidates are selected in Mizoram.

Churches also play important political roles outside of election time. As Ngurhnema stated, the church creates lobbies on social and moral questions such as the sale of alcohol; the church in Mizoram successfully lobbied the state government to pass a bill for prohibition of liquor. When the Australian Christian missionary Dr. Graham Staines and his sons were burned alive by Hindu extremists in Orissa, church groups in Mizoram organized processions and submitted a memorandum to the prime minister registering their concern about the persecution of Christians around the country. Bodies such as the MKHC are also invited by the state government to send representatives to various committees, especially when matters relating to the public interest are slated for discussion. Rev. Zaihmingthanga talked about the ways the church can act as a watchdog, particularly on issues of corruption: "We also came to know that there is corruption in high places, and we preach against this in the pulpits and this has become a slogan all over." As C. Apok, a Nagaland Christian MP, states, churches "are playing a very vital role, shaping the social fabric of the state." Others suggested that the intervention of the church both during and outside of elections could ensure that the state is accountable to its citizens. In states such as Manipur, where Christians are a minority, Pastor James Dhale, a church leader in Manipur, argues that the church has less of an influence at the level of state government but can have a greater influence at the village and district levels. Despite the smaller population of Christians in Manipur as compared with Mizoram, Meghalaya, and Nagaland, Dino L. Touthang of the Evangelical Fellowship of India Commission on Relief (EFICOR) states that the district of Churachandpur in southern Manipur still produces the largest number of civil servants who are key lay evangelicals serving as top bureaucrats in different departments of the Indian government.

However, despite the attempts of the church to create a unified civic community based on the broad tenets of Christian belief and practice, the post-Independence period has been marked by the splintering of the evangelical movement and tribal society more generally into several different, sometimes competing units. Christianity in the Northeast is represented by a few denominations, such as Baptists, and although this may be a force of unity, the Baptists practice a congregational polity that allows strong localisms full play in church politics. For instance, the history of the American Baptist movement in Manipur is one of fragmentation and division of the association into more than twenty-five separate associations. Tensions between Kukis and Nagas in the immediate aftermath of Independence were so high that even the Standard Committee of the Associations was unable to resolve the differences within the North West Baptist Association that arose between these two groups, and in 1948, they were organized into two separate associations (Manipur Baptist Convention Literature Committee 1997). The fragmentation of the evangelical movement was also based on linguistic and cultural differences within larger tribal groups, and so the Naga Baptist Association split again into sixteen smaller associations. The Zeliangrong Nagas split from the Naga Baptists to form their own association, but because the organization covered the three smaller tribal groups of Zemei, Liangmai, and Rongmai, finding a common language in which to conduct worship and publish literature was difficult. Consequently, they split again into three groups (90).

Fragmentation is not only linked to the congregational polity, as practiced by the Baptists, but is a more general feature of evangelical churches. Hastings (1997, 202) has shown that as Christianity splits into a diversity of ecclesiastical streams, attention is drawn to the "dualism implicit within its political agenda—nation-forming on the one side, universalist on the other." Although evangelical Christianity promoted unity and brotherhood, its practical organization encouraged decentralization and supported the autonomy of individual tribal identities and cultures. As Frederick Downs (1992, 129) has argued, "The several ecclesiastical structures developed by the Protestant missions were decentralized in nature, with the basic authority resting in units that corresponded by and large to a single tribe." David Martin (1999, 41) has also argued that the creation of an autonomous social space as a result of the evangelical upsurge leads to the multiplication of enclaves, particularly in the absence of the kind of hierarchical structures imposed by the Catholic Church: "Divine validation loosens their tongues, and they engage in a free communication with one another within the constraints of vigorous pastoral authority." In the postcolonial context, the establishment of indigenous evangelical churches encouraged the growth and development of tribal consciousness. Particularly because evangelicals find their broadest base of support among "those who count for little or nothing in the wider world" (41), the opportunity for tribals to express their voices and develop their political consciousness gives rise to the multiplication of groups, a process that, given the vast diversity among tribal groups in the Northeast, could continue indefinitely.

The division of the evangelical movement into several separate organizations may lead to fragmentation, but it does not have to perpetuate sharp divisions regarding values and interests, particularly in cases where the overarching denomination is the same. However, in the case of the Northeast, divisions in the church have mirrored the communal tensions and ethnic and tribal differences that have plagued these states. For instance, in Manipur, where ethnic infighting has been strongest and most intractable, the church has been unable to overcome the serious ethnic violence that has consumed the state. Kuki leaders have aspired for a territory of their own, comprising the districts of Churachandpur, Chandel, Senapati, Tamenglong, parts of Ukhrul in Manipur, and parts of Nagaland, Assam, and Burma (Joshua 1996). They envision their own territory along the lines of the Naga territory of Nagaland, which was established in 1963. Kuki militant organizations such as the Kuki National Army (KNA), the Kuki National Organization, and the Kuki National Front have come into conflict over these demands with the National Socialist Council of Nagaland (NSCN). Violence escalated between the military organizations and the NSCN in 1993, and since then there have been serious ethnic conflicts between them, including the killing of innocent civilians and extortion.

If the church acts as a form of cultural cement, why has it been unable to bring together warring parties in service of a larger Christian vision? Political leaders and church leaders who were interviewed suggested that the church's engagement in tribal and community politics reduces its ability to overcome ethnic and political conflict and divisions. Valley Rose Hungkyo, a social worker in Manipur, stated that the church has been unable to overcome ethnic conflicts because church leaders are part of their communities and "have their own inclination towards their own community." They are handicapped by their allegiance to their community, and if they tried to stand against the conflict, they would lose the support of their communities. That is, in certain cases, what Paul Freston (2001) refers to as "local subversion" comes into play, where local interests subvert the values of the worldwide church. However, Freston's notion conveys a sense of grassroots rebellion, whereas in this case, local subversion plays into tribal divisions and conflicts. Rev. Lungmuana stated, "People cannot come out of the tribal ghetto, and are rather exclusive from other communities." Others also saw the problem as one of a crisis in leadership and the importance of tribal political and ethnic identity over Christian principles of brotherhood and equality. Apok stated, "Unfortunately in Christianity we have so many denominations, and the leaders of different denominations are busy pointing to the differences between each other rather than the common factor, which is their belief in Jesus Christ." Vice Chairman Laltlanmawii of the Mizoram Presbyterian Church argued that "there is no unity among the different denominations, and as such the church is unable to overcome ethnic fragmentation."

In some extreme cases, church leaders even play a role in fanning communal tensions and ethnic rivalries by resurrecting age-old myths about tribal difference and the wrongs done to one tribe by another. Hastings (1997, 206) argues that church leaders can be extremely nationalistic, continuing "to reinforce myths and practices which produce the alienation between communities upon which rival nationalisms inevitably feed." During the Kuki-Naga conflict in Manipur, several church leaders on both sides became engaged in the politics of ethnic conflict. For instance, in a statement entitled "Facts about the Naga Conflict," the Manipur Naga Baptist Church Leaders' Forum (1994, 1) stated, "While as Naga church leaders we deplore violence, especially killing of innocent people both by the Kukis and the Nagas, it is important that one should also look at this sad development from its proper historical perspective. And when one examines dispassionately the historical perspective both at present and the past, one indisputable fact emerges, and that is, the Kukis are the aggressors and the Nagas have reacted to protect their land, which is inseparable with their identity." This so-called fact sheet makes several claims about Naga and Kuki history, such as "I. Naga as the indigenous race and the Kukis as the nomadic people in Manipur and Nagaland" and "II. Kukis as the aggressive invaders of the indigenous Nagas" (1, 2). Rather than encourage dialogue, tolerance, and understanding among different tribal groups, statements such as these add to tensions and conflict by reaching into a mythical past for justification of essential differences between tribes.

Some interviewees suggested that the church can move beyond fragmentation and disunity by uniting all denominations under a single name or organization, yet it seems that such organizations would neither be useful nor possible in the current context of the Northeast. Separate congregations allow tribal groups to keep alive their distinct languages, cultures, and customs and to come together in solidarity with other members of their group. Further, as this section has argued, it is not the division of the church into separate denominations and associations that engenders discord and conflict, but rather the political significance that is given to those differences. The evidence presented here suggests that in a context of multiethnic conflict, despite its civic activities, the church may not be able to provide the unifying and cohesive fabric required of a coherent civil society unless it takes on further demands of justice and human rights. The next section explores the limitations of peace initiatives without further political demands of justice for the oppressed hill tribes and looks at how some sections of the evangelical movement are looking for a way beyond the current impasse.

Taking a Stance: The Church as Peacemaker

Undoubtedly, evangelical organization was crippled by the vast diversity of tribal groups. The awakening of tribal identity and political consciousness in the aftermath of the independence movement militated against the attempts of the church to represent all tribals in a unified Christian movement. In some ways, the church has tried to bridge the gaps between tribal communities and halt the process of fragmentation. In the insurgency movements of the Nagas and ethnic conflicts between Nagas and Kukis, the church has tried to play a brokerage role. Rev. Kashung, a Naga church leader in Manipur, talked about Christians' active role in mediating disputes between Kukis and Nagas. Kashung states that he personally visited all sixteen villages where there was conflict and called together the village chiefs, pastors, and student and women leaders and tried to initiate talks. He invited all of these groups to participate in a reconciliation festival. Unfortunately, the Kuki church leaders could not attend because they were warned by the Kuki underground insurgents not to participate. But the reconciliation festival went ahead without their participation. Kashung also described the conflict resolution workshops held by the Manipur Baptist Convention (MBC) in Gauhati, Kohima, and Imphal.

Kuki church leaders also gave examples of the ways they participated in processes of reconciliation between Kukis and Nagas. Touthang describes the closing session of the Conflict Resolution Seminar organized by the Evangelical Fellowship of India and MBC in Imphal in January 1996, which key church leaders from Kuki and Naga tribes attended:

> Having spoken for three days from God's word the call of the church to the ministry of reconciliation, I initiated a ceremony of a tribal custom/ritual of *zolpa* [best friend] during which I embraced Reverend S. Hockey and chose him as my *zolpa*. The institution of *zolpa* is carried out between two people who decide to establish a strong bond between them and thereby vowing to each other that they would stand for each other at all times. Reverend Hockey was the then executive secretary of the MBC from a Mao Naga tribe and I from a

Kuki tribe. As a token and a sign of our acceptance of each other as *zolpas* we exchanged tribal shawls, embraced each other and prayed for one another. We then challenged the others to do the same thing. It was a very moving experience to witness many of the Kuki and Naga church leaders pairing off two by two (a Kuki with a Naga) accepting each other as *zolpas* and then praying for each other.... Till today my family and Reverend Hockey's family maintain strong ties as *zolpas*.

Attempts at symbolic unity by church leaders play a very important role in promoting acceptance and reconciliation between the tribes. Rev. Hawlngam Haokip of the Kuki Baptist Convention said that Christianity was important in affirming tribal values, even though "if I belong to Jesus there is no difference between Naga and Kuki." He argued that it was important to retain a sense of tribal identity while realizing unity through the practice of religion. The use of a tribal tradition of *zolpa* to express solidarity between different tribes is perhaps an example of this.

Nonintervention or neutral arbitration has been the main strategy employed by the church in relation to conflict in the Northeast. Rev. Zaihmingthana stated, "Our church never takes sides.... We try to pacify the warring parties, and we try to negotiate meetings between both the parties and pray with them, telling them Christ will convince them." The church has attempted to play the role of neutral arbitrator, particularly in mediating ethnic disputes. Still, although they have had notable successes in this arena, they have been unable to end the cycles of political and ethnic violence that continue around them. Niketan Iralu, an international resource speaker in Nagaland, claims that by taking on the role of neutral arbitrator, the church evades crucial social and political questions that it actually needs to take a stance on. He locates this evasion in the lack of preparation of the church for such a political role: "Our church is still very young, and is finding itself called upon to play a role in the conflict in Nagaland and they do not know what to say because the church considers its primary responsibility as preparing Christians to go to heaven after death. They have done very little thinking as to what they are to do while they are here on earth." According to Iralu, unless the deep political and social causes of the violence and conflict in the Northeast can be analyzed and dealt with, peace accords are a "superficial exercise," which only "puts an ointment and a plaster" on the problem. Nonintervention on the part of the church may make it ineffective in dealing with the burning political questions—tribal, ethnic, and regional—that concern the Northeast today.

Different social groups and different ethnic groups emphasize demands and needs that are very specific to their social class, their tribe, or their ethnic group. The demand for the rights of particular tribes and subtribes in relation to others, the antagonisms between different social and economic groupings, and the tensions between ethnic groups have been created in a post-Independence context of large-scale migration, differing social and economic opportunities for various groups, and a new relationship with the Indian state. The last, in particular, has provided much cause for tension, as Hastings (1997, 165) explains: "The multi-ethnic state in which one ethnicity, without necessarily constituting a majority, is yet far larger than any other and in a position to dominate, is a situation in which other ethnicities, instead of accepting a larger national identity, are likely to produce conflict and even a desire to secede." The stark sociocultural differences between the tribes of the Northeast and the populations of the rest of India fuel the desire for self-government. Demands for autonomy are reinforced by the lack of infrastructure, lack of capital, and lack of basic facilities such as education, primary health, sanitation, and electricity, combined with pervasive corruption in the bureaucracy and the stalling of development projects in the region as a whole (Madhab 1999). There are certainly similarities and grievances that face the population as a whole, and there are parallels between the independence movement against the British and the regionalist assertion of autonomy in the context of the Indian federalist system.

In what seems to many to be a vacuum of church leadership, political demands have been taken up by insurgency groups and terrorist organizations. Insurgency groups all over the Northeast such as the NSCN and the Mizo National Front (MNF) claim that they are the true defenders of Christianity. The rallying cry of the NSCN, "Nagaland for Christ," has inscribed their vision of Christianity into the heart of their political project, which includes the integration of all Naga inhabited areas. Similarly, the MNF makes the suppression of Christianity one of the key points of its declaration of independence, claiming that the Indian government has "been pursuing a policy of exploitative measures in their attempt to wipe out Christianity" (quoted in Hluna 1985, 184). Since 1946, the KNA has sought to uphold the "unity and territorial integrity" of Kuki tribes in Manipur (Dena 1996, 4). In the 1960s, the KNA again raised the demand for a Kuki state within the Union of India, which was toned down to a demand for a full-fledged revenue district within Manipur. The lack of church leadership and direction in crucial social and political questions has led to the proliferation of political and terrorist organizations, which claim Christianity as their moral basis and demand autonomy as a way of dealing with grievances and problems.

Insurgency groups, terrorist organizations, and separatist movements taking the idiom of Christianity as a way of defining their political project have at times come up against the church, which tends to be more moderate politically and more conciliatory toward the Indian government and the Indian security forces. The Church Peace Council was a major player in the negotiations between the Indian government and the Naga insurgents in the

1970s, convincing the underground to give up their arms and accept without condition the Constitution of India (Verghese 1996, 94). In return, security force operations ceased, the curfew was lifted, and up to six hundred political prisoners were released (94). The signing of the Shillong Accord on November 11, 1975, was a major turning point for the movement toward peace. However, in their manifesto of 1980, the NSCN denounced the Shillong Accord as "the most ignominious sell-out in history" by "downright, reactionary traitors" (quoted in Verghese 1996, 97). They condemned the Naga church leaders for agreeing to join the Indian Union (98). Similarly, during the insurgency crisis in Mizoram, the president of the MNF, in a meeting between church leaders and leaders of his underground outfit in 1966, requested that the church maintain opposition to the abuses of the Indian Armed Forces against the Mizo population, particularly when it involved desecration of church buildings and disruption of worship (cited in Hluna 1985, 114). The willingness of insurgent groups to fight for certain basic rights of tribal Christians gives them the moral high ground against church leaders who may be unwilling or unable to speak out about abuses and injustice.

Militant organizations tend to make more radical demands for change than church leaders do, and they often resort to violence and tactics of coercion, alienating fellow tribals. In states such as Mizoram, when insurgency movements grew in 1966, there was a pronounced conflict between church leaders and insurgents over strategy and particularly over the role of violence. As Rev. Zaihmingthanga reported, the church and the underground were at war with insurgents who kidnap church leaders. These tactics by insurgent groups isolate them from the population rather than building a participatory, democratic movement for large-scale change; they encourage what Rev. Wungnaoshung of the Missionary Training Center in Manipur referred to as a "gun culture" rather than "peoples' politics." Wungnaoshung argues that given its leadership role and centrality in the lives of tribal people, the church seems best situated to promote a democratic movement that makes radical demands on the state, thereby marginalizing the politics of violence. However, this would mean the church's abandoning a policy of neutrality and taking an active role and stance on important political issues.

Some church leaders seek to emphasize their neutrality in political issues; others act as spokespersons for the region, criticizing the role of the Indian state in the affairs of the Northeast and making demands on the central government. Rev. Kashung argues that the constant turmoil of the Northeast cannot all be blamed on ethnic and tribal differences, but is linked to exploitation of the region by the central government: "If you look around at Imphal, or Ukhrul or Senepati or Gauhati or Shillong, you just see, who controls the market, who controls the trade, and where does the money go? Even the administration, who controls the administration? We are just puppets, we have a puppet government, we have a puppet administration and we are not permitted to grow in our own customs and lifestyles." According to Kashung, peace accords and cease-fires can only be very limited unless these questions are addressed and unless the church takes a stand on these issues. He argues, "If we are given the right, the opportunity, then we can live in our own customs, in our own law and ruled by our own people, then this [fragmentation] would never happen." Rev. Lungmuana also argued that problems of underdevelopment and isolation were important causes of unrest in the Northeast, and unless these questions were addressed by the central government, it could never hope for peace. According to Lungmuana, if there was development in the Northeast, and if more representatives from the Northeast had permanent positions in the government, then people of the Northeast would not feel so antagonistic toward India: "If they feel they are neglected they cannot be good citizens." Ultimately, as these leaders argue, the church's attempts at building civic community and promoting peace in the region will be futile unless it can engage with deeper issues of resource control, political power, and underdevelopment.

The Northeast has suffered deleterious consequences as a result of the divide-and-rule policies of the British colonial powers in the early twentieth century, and church leaders are only beginning to come to terms with the historical consequences of Christianity's involvement in such policies and the ways the divide-and-rule policies of the Indian government are achieving the same effects. Ringkahoa Horam, a lay evangelical leader in Manipur, stated that Kuki and Naga ethnic rivalry can be linked to the divide-and-rule policy of the British that has been inherited by the Indian government, and that to subordinate the Northeast to central control, the Indian government is trying to play the same game of divide and rule. Dr. D. Singson, principal of the Trulock Theological Seminary, points to "Western imperialism" and the general buildup of arms and war materials, as contributing to the violence.

Dr. Thomas Joshua (1996, 495) points to even more disturbing links to underground smuggling networks and drug rackets, suggesting that the Kuki-Naga conflict may have been linked to the attempts of Naga underground forces to take over lucrative smuggling opportunities from Burma into Manipur and Nagaland. He argues that ethnic violence between insurgent groups in Manipur began when Kuki militants asked Naga insurgents to leave Moreh, a town on the Burmese border that has a sizable Kuki population and is a known center of heroin smuggling. Control over Moreh was a point of bitter confrontation between the two groups, as such control facilitated easy access to Burma and the rest of Southeast Asia, and the extortion of taxes and commissions from the smugglers was the easiest way for militant groups to earn money to buy arms (495). Iralu asks questions about the role of the Indian security forces, suggesting that their desire to become involved with such rackets may have given them reason to enter the fray, stirring up tensions even further. If the connections among underground insurgency groups, paramilitary groups, and smuggling rings really extend as deep as Joshua and Iralu suggest they do, then church leaders pursuing peace accords and negotiations become irrelevant. As Iralu suggests, it will be impossible to move forward unless the truth is revealed: "Both sides need the truth and the church will be the best body to do this." The potential for violence and conflict to erupt again and again can be stemmed only by an analysis of the causes of the conflict and the willingness of the church to take action to address it.

Problems in the Northeast have taken on an urgency in the past few years, with the increased power of the Bharatiya Janata Party (BJP, Indian People's Party), a right-wing Hindu fundamentalist national government from 1998 to 2004, and increased attacks on Christians and other religious minorities in mainland India. Rev. Kashung said that the armed militant wing of the BJP, the Rashtriya Swayamsevak Sangh (RSS, National Volunteers Organization), has been making attempts to penetrate into Manipur, Shillong, and Nagaland and that one hundred RSS militants were trained by the BJP in Manipur in 2000. He said that Christian MPs have been converting to the BJP in Manipur and Nagaland. Pastor Dhale said that since the coming to power of the BJP, the Home Ministry has begun auditing the accounts of Christian leaders in Manipur to see who is financing them. Hindu organizations like the Ramakrishna Mission receive millions of dollars from abroad, and Dhale claims that they have not been under the surveillance of the Home Ministry, showing a clear religious bias on the part of an allegedly secular government. Hungkyo said that in states such as Arunachal, which are predominantly animist, more temples are being constructed in an attempt to convert the people to Hinduism. All of these interviewees foresaw increasing tensions and clashes between Christians in the Northeast and the central BJP government over these issues and called on the church to play a role in defending the people against attacks and violence by Hindu fundamentalists and extremists.

Conclusion

The evangelical church in northeast India has been unable to overcome the violence and ethnic conflict that has beset the region since independence from the British due to a number of complex, interrelated factors. The practical organization of the church and the tendency of evangelical movements to facilitate the expression of a multiplicity of voices rather than suppressing them under hierarchical structures contributes to the fragmentation of society in the contemporary period. Factors of underdevelopment, deprivation of resources from the center, and the failures of political representation in India's federalist system have given rise to cycles of crime and violence that generate conflict out of disunity and chaos out of fragmentation. Further, like the cooperation of *lambus* as native informers in the colonial state apparatus, the interest of contemporary church leaders in stability, which suits the interests of the Indian government, reduces their ability to promote the values of liberation and autonomy that are promised by evangelical theology. Such a scenario reveals the inadequacy of elite models of civil society as simply a form of cultural cement, suggesting the need for a more expansive, participatory concept that sees civil society as a movement for the rights of subaltern groups and for greater democratization.

The church has provided the possibilities for organization, education, and politicization of communities. It has shown that it can be a "voluntary" organ of civil society and that it can play a peacemaker role, without aligning itself with insurgency groups or the repressive state apparatus. In a situation where traditional tribal institutions have been dramatically weakened, evangelical Christianity has provided a forum through which tribals can express their political concerns and an idiom through which to frame their demands and concerns. Whether the region can move beyond the divisions that render it impotent—from tribal conflicts to cultural and economic divisions—and have a unified voice in the federal arena depends more broadly on the ability of evangelical Christianity to facilitate healthy and vigorous debate in the Northeast on the problems that it faces. This would involve the multiplicity of evangelical Christian groups, as well as non-Christian tribals in the Northeast, engaging in a dialogue that brings out in the open the numerous issues facing tribal communities.

NOTES

1. The study focuses mainly on the Tangkhul Nagas of northern Manipur.

2. Assam State Archives (hereafter ASA), Governor's Secretariat (Confidential)—Political A, June 1928, Nos. 1–13: Note Regarding Missions in Manipur State, Laurie Hammond, February 20, 1928, 9.

3. ASA, Governor's Secretariat (Confidential)—Political B, March 1919, Nos. 1–397: Tour Diary of J. C. Higgins Esq. I.C.S. Political Officer, March 1918.

4. This section is based on interviews coordinated by Dino L. Touthang of the Evangelical Fellowship of India Commission on Relief in February and March 2001. There were eight interviews with church leaders and political leaders in Mizoram, seven interviews with Naga church leaders and political leaders in Manipur, four interviews with church leaders in Meghalaya, one interview with a political leader in Nagaland, and interviews with Rajya Sabha and Lok Sabha MPs in Mizoram, Manipur, Nagaland, and Mizoram. The author personally carried out three interviews with Kuki church leaders in August 1999. See the bibliography for more details. It is extremely difficult to carry out field research in northeast India, mainly due to Indian government restrictions. Although the author did spend two months in Assam, Manipur, and Meghalaya in 1999 carrying out research, it was necessary to rely on the help of

EFICOR to carry out the remainder of the field research. The difficulties entailed by such long-distance research have prohibited a more comprehensive survey of the region, and the range of interviewees is fairly narrow. The hope is that from the initial concerns put forth in this study, others can follow up and provide more detailed regional studies.

Interviews

Personal interviews were carried out during a trip to Imphal in August 1999:

Y. K. Shimray, earliest living Tangkhul Naga convert, Imphal.
Rev. Hawlngam Haokip, general secretary of the Kuki Baptist Convention, Imphal.
D. Singson, principal of Trulock Theological Seminary, Imphal.
Rev. Siekholet Singson, first ordained reverend, Kangpokpi, Manipur.
Yangkahao Liukham, early convert, Ukhrul, Manipur.

Interviews coordinated by Dino L. Touthang of the Evangelical Fellowship of India Commission on Relief in February and March 2001:

Lungmuana, former executive secretary, Mizoram Presbyterian Church.
Dr. C. Silvera, former union minister, 1994–1996, Health and Industry, Mizoram.
Rev. Zaihmingthana, former secretary, Mizoram Presbyterian Church.
Pastor K. James, church leader, Manipur.
Rev. Wungnaoshung, director, Missionary Training Centre, Manipur.
Ringkahao Horam, academic and lay evangelical leader, Manipur.
Valley Rose Hungyo, social worker and journalist, Manipur.
Rev. Woleng, pastor, Tangkhul Baptist Church, Manipur.
Dr. Horam, professor, Manipur.
Rev. Kashung, Tangkhul community church leader, Manipur.
Niketan Iralu, conflict resolution/international resource speaker, Nagaland.
Hiphei, MP, Rajya Sabha, Mizoram.
O. L. Nongtdu, MP, Rajya Sabha, Meghalaya.
Holkhomang Haokip, MP, Lok Sabha, Manipur.
C. Apokg, MP, Rajya Sabha, Nagaland.
Vanlalzawma, MP, Lok Sabha, Mizoram.

Written questionnaires coordinated by Dino L. Touthang of the Evangelical Fellowship of India Commission on Relief in February and March 2001:

Elder Rokanlova, Dawrpai Church, Mizoram.
Laltlanmawii, vice chairman, Mizoram Presbyterian Church.
Rev. Vanlalchhuanawma, registrar, Aizawl Theological College, Mizoram.
Prof. R. L. Hauni, principal, Academy of Integrated Christian Studies, Mizoram.
Rev. C. Ngurhnema, pastor, Baptist Church of Mizoram.
Dr. G. H. Khonlah, church social worker, Meghalaya.

Documentary Sources

Government Printed Sources

National Archives of India, New Delhi
> Foreign and Political Department–Internal A, October 1919, Nos. 191–196.
> Foreign Department—McCullough, W. Account of the Tribes of the Valley of Munnipore and of the Hill Tribes, Selections from the Records of the Government of India, No. XXVII, 1859.

Assam State Archives, Gauhati
> Governor's Secretariat (Confidential)—Political B, March 1919, Nos. 1–397.
> Governor's Secretariat (Confidential)—Political A, June 1928, Nos. 1–13.
> Governor's Secretariat (Confidential)—A, December 1930, Nos. 1–11.
> Governor's Secretariat (Confidential)—B, December 1933, Nos. 580–604.

4

Evangelicals and Politics in Indonesia: The Case of Surakarta

Bambang Budijanto

This chapter examines how socioeconomic and political instability affected Indonesian evangelical perspectives and engagement in politics from the early 1990s onward, focusing on the Surakarta region. This region was selected because it is considered the political barometer of Indonesia[1] and is, together with Yogyakarta, the capital of Javanese culture and etiquette. About 60 percent of Indonesians are Javanese.

The study employs in-depth interviews with key academics, historians, and NGO activists and with thirty-five evangelical leaders and pastors, who constitute approximately 40 percent of religious leaders in Surakarta. Interviews were conducted in January 2001, during the Wahid government, and in July 2001, just after Wahid's fall, as Megawati formed a new government.

Historical Background

Sociopolitical Background

In 1963, Indonesia was one of the poorest countries in the world (Dirkse, Husken, and Rutten 1993; World Bank 1990). Over 60 percent of the population was in absolute poverty. Ruinous inflation, sharp falls in rice production, and other domestic production declines in the 1960s caused the fall of the Soekarno regime and the rise of the New Order government under Major General Soeharto in 1965.[2]

There was constant struggle to establish national unity during Soekarno's regime (1945–1965) despite various religious and regional revolts and fractious political parties.[3] The parliamentary government (1950–1957) that followed the struggle against Dutch rule (1945–1949) had had no fewer than six coalition governments, lasting from six months to two years (Ricklefs 1981, 225–244). Economic growth concerns, the dominant issue in the early post-Independence period (1945–1953), were neglected under growing pressure from the three political factions, the Communist Party (PKI), the modernist Muslims (Masyumi), and the armed forces groups.

Soekarno hoped the 1955 parliamentary election would provide a "political panacea." But no party obtained more than 23 percent of the votes (Kahin 1995, 50).[4] Instead, the election produced ever-increasing factionalism within parliament. Kahin identifies this as the key factor behind Soekarno's political shift to "Guided Democracy" (1957–1965), by which Soekarno tried to contain the uneasy tension between the army and the PKI while using both for his own ends (51; Crouch 1979, 186–188). Growing tensions culminated in the September 30th Movement's "aborted coup," followed by arguably the worst massacre in postwar history. Some five hundred thousand alleged communist supporters were killed (Crouch 1979, 192; Ricklefs 1981, 274) in late 1965 and early 1966. The origins of the coup remain unclear,[5] but its consequences are apparent. The armed forces, spuriously claiming legitimacy, became the unchallenged power after 1965.

The Guided Democracy period had ruinous impact on plans for economic development. National resources and energies were diverted to campaigns to recover West Irian (1961–1963) and in confrontation with Malaysia (1963–1966). By late 1965, the nation's social, political, and economic structures were close to collapse. Massive student demonstrations in Jakarta during the first ten weeks of 1966 produced a state of near anarchy (Crouch 1979, 192). The consumer price index rose from 100 in 1954 to 600 in 1961 and 61,000 by 1965; at its peak, the price of rice rose 900 percent annually (Arndt 1971, 373; Ricklefs 1981, 268). The rupiah fell to 1 percent of its previous value on the black market (Ricklefs 1981, 192; Anderson 1990, 108).

General Soeharto's New Order government immediately set a different course. Soekarno's economic self-reliance policies were replaced by an open market economy with massive influxes of Western aid (Anderson 1990, 112–113; Crouch 1979, 196; Dirkse et al. 1993, 5). Hyperinflation was perceived as one key in destroying Guided Democracy (Anderson 1990); the new government made controlling inflation a high priority and succeeded within three years (Mortimer 1973, 54). By 1972, GNP growth was estimated at over 6 percent, inflation was down, and exports showed spectacular rates of increase (Mortimer 1974, 54).

But Indonesia's impressive economic growth was not accompanied by comparable political development. Sajogyo's (1972) authoritative study, *Mod-*

ernization without Development in Rural Java began to pinpoint the social effects of the Indonesian growth model. As often noted, significant increases in overall food production were achieved by rural "depoliticization" (Mubyarto and Soetrisno 1985; Hardjono 1983; Hart 1986; Sjahrir 1986). The government considered involvement in politics by the rural poor an impediment to development (Mubyarto 1988, 47) and regarded intense political party competition prior to 1965 as the source of rural conflicts. To concentrate on economic development and protect peasants from the "bad influence" of political parties, the government's "floating mass" policy prohibited political parties from operating or carrying on any activities in villages except for a few weeks' campaign prior to general elections (Mubyarto and Soetrisno 1985, 37).

In the early 1990s, many considered Indonesian development under Soeharto an economic miracle. Yet, academic and NGO communities became increasingly concerned about worsening corruption, collusion, and nepotism, despite the presumed economic success (Schwarz 1994). The New Order's centralized, totally controlled security approach allowed Soeharto to retain power for thirty-two years, until May 1998, when bloody riots in Jakarta and Surakarta forced him to step down.

Soeharto's "disciple," Vice President Habibie, became Indonesia's third president. Habibie fully understood that his presidency was only transitional. His association with Soeharto, and his primary support base, the Ikatan Cendekiawan Muslim Indonesia (Indonesia Association of Muslim Intellectuals), which had made him "crown prince," ultimately worked against him during his seventeen-month presidency. East Timor separated to become an independent nation, and there was a new freedom of press and the most democratic general election since 1955. In October 1999, the New Order election machine, Golkar,[6] refused to nominate Habibie for president, ending his twenty-five-year political career.

The Indonesia Democratic Party of Struggle (PDIP) won the 1999 general election with a 35 percent plurality. People expected party chair Megawati, the daughter of founding president Soekarno, to become president, replacing Habibie. To her supporters' amazement, a coalition between Golkar and the Central Axe (Political Islam) factions blocked her, making Islamic teaching against women's leadership and the strong Christian presence in PDIP leadership their prominent objections. They engineered the election of Abdurrahman Wahid, a Muslim cleric who was chairman of the largest Muslim mass organization, Nadahdatul Ulama (forty million members), as Indonesia's fourth president. When the news of Megawati's defeat reached supporters in Surakarta, the town erupted in chaos as angry, frustrated PDIP supporters rampaged. The next day, Megawati accepted Wahid's conciliatory request to become vice president.

Constant cabinet reshufflings marked Wahid's twenty-month rule. The Central Axe parliamentary faction that had first nominated Wahid was disappointed by his weak support for them. The PDIP faction remained bitter. Wahid had always supported Megawati, and many in the PDIP regarded his accepting the nomination and displacing her as president in 1999 as treachery and betrayal of a close friend. Wahid's attempts to reform the armed forces were unsuccessful, and the army and police generals challenged him on various issues in return. In the end, the cross-party forum, facilitated by PDIP, Central Axe, and Golkar parliamentary factions, with armed forces and police support, succeeded in calling a special session in July 2001 to investigate presidential accountability. They impeached Wahid and installed Megawati as president. Wahid was accused of involvement in two monetary scandals: of failing to resolve the economic crisis and ethnoreligious conflicts, and of abetting the disintegration of the nation.

Indonesian Society and Religion

Geertz's (1959) *aliran*[7] thesis describing the religiopolitical layout of post-Independence Indonesia was given much credence until the 1980s. An *aliran* was more than merely a political party or viewpoint: *alirans*, or "streams," were a "transformation of long-standing *santri, abangan*, and *priyayi* traditions into modern universalistic ideologies" (Geertz 1965, 127–128).[8] The Partai Nasional Indonesia (PNI, Nationalist Party) and the PKI were composed of both the *priyayi* adherents to Hindu elements in Javanese syncretism, who tended to be white-collar employees, and the *abangan* followers of animistic syncretic elements, mostly poorer peasants. Opposing these nominal Muslims were the devout *santri*, predominantly business people and richer peasants. The more orthodox of these were associated with the Nahdlatul Ulama (NU, Revival of Ulama, a Muslim scholars' organization), the modernists with the Masyumi Party (127–129). Critics argue that Geertz's *aliran* thesis oversimplified the complexity of Islam in Indonesia (as in his *Religion of Java*, 1960) and stereotyped Islamic sociopolitical groupings (Hefner 2000), but the political regrouping of post-Soeharto parties along *aliran* lines to some extent confirmed the *aliran* thesis.

Hefner's (2000) book, *Civil Islam*, presents Indonesia's recent democratic transition as a challenge to the common view that Islam is incompatible with democracy (see Lawrence 1998; Huntington 1991; Gasiorowski and Power 1998, 740–71). Over 80 percent of Indonesia's 212 million people officially profess Islam. Hefner's thorough description of the complexity of Indonesian Islam traces the roles of Muslim intellectuals, leaders, and youth from the various sociopolitical groupings and finds that both "cultural" and "political" Muslims enhance civility and promote democratization in Indonesian society.

This chapter, correspondingly, investigates how and to what extent Christian churches, especially evangelicals, contributed to the process of democratization in Indonesia in the 1990s. The study examines events and currents that informed evangelicals' political involvement and also considers how democratization, rapid sociopolitical changes, and the recent multidimensional crisis shaped how the church relates to the society.

Church and Society

Christianity came to Indonesia in the mid-sixteenth century (End 1987), with the Dutch facilitating the early spread of Protestantism.[9] As often happens, Indonesian Protestantism copied Dutch Christianity in form and content (Cooley 1981, 309); Christianity became known as the Dutch, or the colonial, religion (Ngelow 1996, 13–14; Guillot 1985, 24) and alienated Indonesian Christians from their culture and society. Several efforts to develop local/indigenous expression of "Indonesian or even Javanese Christianity" were considered heretical (Akkeren 1994; Sutarman 1988; Hoekema 1997).[10] Christians' alienation from Indonesian culture and society in colonial times produced a "sterile Christianity," cut off from social and political life outside the church (Sumartana 1982, 17).[11] As a result, Christians were powerless and unable to respond to challenges in that era. Although the introduction of "ethical politics" (see Van Neil 1984; Verkuyl 1990; Baudet and Brugmans 1987; Ngelow 1996; Shiraishi 1997) by the Dutch in 1917 made Christians generally aware of a need to engage actively in sociopolitical activities, Christian leaders, struggling to establish the Christian presence in Indonesia, gave insufficient attention to progressive aspirations (Ngelow 1996). The absence of Protestant representation on "the Sutardjo Petition" in 1936,[12] in which other religious leaders participated (including J. Kasimo, representing Catholics), indicated a lack of concern for human rights issues and national dignity (Suwondo 1999, 5).

As the Japanese occupation began in 1942, there were several incidents in various cities in central Java's north coast of attacks on and harassment of European, Chinese, and Christian communities by Muslims.[13] These incidents brought about church solidarity in affected areas and other parts of Java. At about the same time, Dutch Christians, the Zendings, were changing their structures and approaches to accelerate the development of autonomous Indonesian churches. This also increased nationalist feelings within the Christian communities (Hoekema 1997, 228).

From 1945 to 1959, the young government faced enormous challenges, including a war of independence and regional revolts. The church again failed to respond to these national challenges, showing a lack of theological reflection on the church's engagement with the state and society. Several factors contributed to this unpreparedness. First was the Zendings' ambivalent theological approach, as has been elaborated by Mastra (1970) and Sumarthana (1982). The missionaries were citizens of the Netherlands as well as loyal to their religion, and the easiest way to address the conflict resulting from these different identities was to avoid any interaction between the church, which was the agent of the Kingdom of God, and the colonial government, which was the agent of the Dutch. This ambivalence continued long after Independence. Second, a pietistic theology put all the church's energy into spiritual life and neglected other aspects. Third, as a minority group and the repeated target of ethnic and religious riots, Christians felt insecure and tended to attach themselves to the ruler as patron: to the Dutch during colonial times and to the government following Independence (Sumartana 1982).[14] This survival strategy produced an opportunist mentality that impeded the church from functioning as a prophetic voice to the government and society. The church's dependency on the government, adopted in fear of fundamentalist Muslims, affected the whole mentality of the church during the New Order regime.[15]

In the 1960s, the churches were necessarily involved in political life. President Soekarno proclaimed a "neverending revolution," requiring all elements of society to support nation-building programs (Simatupang 1982, 26). Toward the end of Soekarno's leadership, as his government became very authoritarian and most Indonesian political and religious elements supported creation of a new regime, Christian communities affirmed Soekarno's dictatorial rule instead of condemning it. Muslim leaders regarded this as opportunistic (Suwondo 1999, 5).

By the 1970s, Protestant churches tried to articulate a theology that gave the church a role in Indonesia's sociopolitical life (Nababan 1971), but this effort proved too late to be effective. By then, Soeharto had become very influenced by the Indonesian chapter of the Center for Strategic and International Studies (CSIS), leaving little room for other religious groups to influence public policy from within the center of power (Hefner 2000, 156).[16] By the end of the 1970s, Soeharto had established himself as the sole power and center of all the public institutions in the country, including the legislature and judiciary, political parties, the armed forces, and major recognized religious groups.[17] Given such presidential power, there was only one safe option for the Protestant churches: to seek his protection and favor.

Thus, until recently, most Christians tried to be insiders, siding with any ruling party or government. The church's relationship to power changed little: a patron-client relationship with the Dutch colonial government, a feudalistic relationship with Soekarno, and opportunism practiced the New Order era. The reasons varied—theological pietism, sociocultural patterns, survival strategy—but the basic attitude remained constant.

The Setting: Surakarta

Surakarta in central Java, popularly known as Solo, is low ground at the junction of three rivers: the Pepe, the Bengawan Solo, and the Jenes. Seen as an Indonesian political barometer, Solo is a land of many contrasts. Thought of as the capital of Javanese culture—known for its tolerance and refinement—and as the epitome of Javanese etiquette (Shiraishi 1997, 51), Surakarta has often been the center of major radical movements and social unrest. Capital of the strongly feudalistic Mataram Kingdom (after 1743), surprisingly, the community's egalitarian nature has been very apparent from time to time.

Senapati (ca. 1584–1601) is considered the founder of Mataram, although it remains unclear whether Senapati conquered Mataram (present-day Kartasura, eight kilometers north of Solo) or whether Jaka Tingkir of Pajang gave it to his father (Ricklefs 1981, 46–48). Mataram reached its peak under Sultan Agung (1613–1646), Senapati's grandson, establishing sovereignty over the Javanese heartland by 1625. In 1740, a war between the Dutch and the Chinese in Batavia sparked a rebellion against the ruler of Mataram, Pakubuwana II, whom the Dutch supported (Ricklefs 1981, 87–92; Hadiwijaya 1990, 15). The rebels conquered Kartasura, the Mataram capital, in 1742. Six months later, after defeating the rebel army, the Dutch reinstalled Pakubuwana, who had sought their protection. In 1743, he abandoned the court at Kartasura; six months of occupation by the rebels and the Chinese made the court "unclean," no longer able to serve as the center of the Mataram kingdom (Kusumodilaga 1990, 263). Pakubuwana built a new court at the nearby village of Solo, the junction of rivers linking eastern Java (Kusumodilaga 1990, 268). The formal move took place in 1746, and Pakubuwana renamed the place Surakarta Hadiningrat. The court remained unstable, with one rebellion after another. The treaty of Giyanti (1755) took away half the kingdom, as the Dutch recognized Mangkubumi as Sultan Hamengkubuwana I, who then established his court in Yogyakarta (1756). The 1757 Salatiga Treaty further reduced the kingdom (Shiraishi 1997, 2; see also Pringgodigdo 1938; Tjitrohoepojo 1939), which progressively lost sovereignty under successive government treaties (Filet 1895; Larson 1987), while Mangkunegaran enjoyed greater economic freedom (Suhartono 1991, 23). Apart from the Java War (1825–1930), the Vorstenlanden (land covered by the Surakarta and Yogykarta kingdoms) (Rouffaer 1931) enjoyed considerable political stability throughout the nineteenth century. But as the twentieth century began, Surakarta regained its importance as the idea of nationalism emerged in many parts of the archipelago.

The Serikat Islam (SI, Islamic League), founded in Surakarta, was one of Indonesia's first modern organizations. A fast-developing grassroots organization, SI was never intended as a political organization. Rather, it recast a local amateur security organization called Rekso Roemekso in Surakarta, mainly to compete with the Chinese Kong Si (business cooperation) association (Suhartono 1991, 81; Shiraishi 1997, 55). It had an estimated thirty-five thousand members in Surakarta by 1912, almost every adult resident except Chinese, Indo, Dutch, and *Priyayi* (Kartodirdjo 1973, 333; Shiraishi 1997, 64).

But SI became increasingly leftist and militant, expanding rapidly in rural and poor areas among farmers and laborers. A radical movement began in 1915 and culminated between 1918 and 1920, started by a mass strike of SI members against a Chinese firm called Sie Dhian Ho. Numerous acts of defiance followed against local Dutch and Bumiputera officers. A prominent leader of religious background, H. Misbach, who had been editor of the *Medan Muslimin* and *Rakyat Bergerak* newspapers, was elected as the leader of Insulinde in Surakarta. Insulinde, a radical Indo-European party, began agitating and, in May 1918, advocated refusal to pay government taxes in many villages, such as Banyudono, Ponggok, Delanggu, and Kartosuro. Shortly afterward, Insulinde campaigned for rejection of "compulsory working" until the government increased wages. Misbach was arrested by colonial police in May 1920 and jailed for two years. Communism began expanding in Surakarta in August 1922, when Misbach was released. Although communist expansion diminished after a failed rebellion in 1926, Surakarta has always been fertile ground for leftist, egalitarian, socialist, and communist movements (Shiraishi 1997, 464–468). The birth of the Sarekat Rakyat (Populace League) also illustrates how receptive Kartasura was to the idea of socialism.[18]

After Independence, growing conflict in 1947 and 1948 between the communist-linked Barisan Tani Indonesia (Indonesia Farmers Front) and the Sarekat Tani Islam Indonesia (Indonesia Muslim Farmers Front), a rightwing organization related to Masyumi, culminated in the 1948 destruction of the PKI base in Madiun, an incident often considered a second communist rebellion. Surakarta then became the main headquarters of the Communist Party in central and east Java. The mayor of Surakarta was the one high-ranking government officer in central Java who publicly supported the 1965 "aborted coup." In the 1955 general election there were four main parties: PNI, PKI, Masyumi, and NU. Of 123,653 votes cast in Surakarta, the PKI got the most, 57 percent, followed by PNI (30 percent). Masyumi got 11 percent and NU only 1.6 percent (1,998 votes). Voting in the first general election under the New Order government in 1971 showed that Surakarta's ideological composition remained the same, with the PKI's votes going to Golkar (the ruling party). With the PKI banned, Golkar won, with 58 percent of the 102,246 votes in Surakarta, and obtained eighteen seats, followed by PNI with 21 percent and Parmusi with 10 percent.[19] The Catholic Party, the Christian Party, and NU obtained one seat each. The severe defeat of Islamic parties in Surakarta was not surprising. The immediate impact of the 1965–1966 massacres of PKI members and sympathizers, as elsewhere in central and east Java, turned people away from Islam and Islamic parties. Hefner (1990) correctly observes that Ansor (NU's youth organization) and other Islamic groups were in the forefront of these killings, which took some five hundred thousand lives in three months. Many people converted to Hinduism, Christianity, Buddhism, and Kebatinan (Javanese mystical "inwardness" groups; Ricklefs 1981, 273). Islam remained the majority religion in Surakarta, but the Islam of Surakarta is neither a "modernist political Islam" that aims at establishing an Islamic state, nor a "traditionalist pietistic Islam" that seeks to develop their followers through *da'wah* (a kind of Islamic preaching).[20] Islam in Surakarta is mostly a *"proletar"* Islam that seeks social justice.

Sustained by Golkar's overwhelming (63 percent) victory in 1971, the government reformulated the political structure. Apart from Golkar, the parties were to realign themselves into two new parties. The first, the Partai Persatuan Pembangunan (PPP, United Development Party), consisted of the Muslim parties: NU, Parmusi, Partai Serikat Islam Indonesia (Indonesian Islamic League Party), and Perti (Pergerakan Tarbijah Islamijah, or Islamic Educational Movement). The second, Partai Demokrasi Indonesia (PDI, Indonesian Democratic Party), consisted of PNI, Parkindo (Christian Party), Catholic Party, Murba (left-nationalist party), and Ikatan Pendukung Kemerdekaan Indonesia (The League of the Upholders of Indonesia's Independence). In the 1977 general election in Surakarta, Golkar maintained its victory with 51 percent of the votes; PDI obtained 32 percent and PPP 17 percent. Surakarta's voting pattern continued similarly in the next four general elections (1982, 1987, 1992, and 1997). In the first post-Soeharto election in 1999, PDIP, a nationalist party led by Megawati Soekarnoputri, received some 60 percent of the votes in Surakarta. PDIP's slogan, "the party of Wong Cilik" (socioeconomically "small people"), expresses what made it attractive to the people of Surakarta.

Christian Political Involvement in the 1990s

By the late 1980s, Soeharto, recognizing the army's diminishing support,[21] turned his attention to the modernist (political) Muslims, who had been marginalized from the late 1960s on (Schwarz 1994, 37, 274–289). Modernist Muslim figures moved into Soeharto's inner circle very quickly, and within a few years dominated the ruling party (Golkar), the parliament, the armed forces, and the cabinet. The modernist Muslims feared they would miss the chance to take over the strategic role as Soeharto's political advisor, and consequently pushed too hard, marginalizing and frightening traditionalist (moderate) Muslims, nationalists, other religious groups, and secular and nationalist armed forces personnel, which then formed a coalition.

During the New Order regime, Soeharto and the army were the two most powerful political players (Budijanto 1997). Through the 1980s, "often targeted" minority groups, such as Christians and Chinese, saw them as protectors from the political Muslims of the extreme right. In the early 1990s, when Soeharto courted the political Muslims, Christian politicians were left with very little space and limited choices. Meanwhile, hostility toward the church and Christianity escalated very rapidly. The Indonesian Christian Communication Forum (1997), or FKKI, which came into existence as a response to this hostility, reported that 452 church buildings were destroyed or burned in five years.[22]

While the Catholics (CSIS) continued to search for ways to regain their strategic role under Soeharto,[23] Protestant politicians began to see an alternative for the future of Indonesia. They and other nationalist activists within the PDI thought Megawati might boost the party's popularity and eventually challenge Soeharto. In the early 1990s, Christian politicians worked in two sectors. First, as early Megawati supporters, they mobilized mass support.[24] Second, they helped develop a coalition among nationalists, traditionalist Muslims, other religious groups, and armed forces personnel. In 1995, people representing these different groups established a forum called Yayasan Kerukunan Persaudaraan Kebangsaan (The Harmonious Brotherhood Nationhood Foundation). The forum itself was not mass-based, but it represented large, powerful, and diverse groups, such as NU, Christians (Protestants), nationalists, nationalist armed forces personnel, and NGO communities.

The courtship between Soeharto and the political Muslims, and accelerating hostility against the church, produced what Hefner (2000) calls a "red-white and green" (nationalist and cultural Muslim) coalition. It also transformed church-state relations. The courtship and hostility created common ground between Christian politicians and the churches (Christian masses), giving the politicians broader and stronger mass support, and united churches from different theological streams—ecumenical, evangelical, and pentecostal—to work together more closely. Hostility against the church also accelerated evangelicals' political involvement.

The FKKI was a major breakthrough in evangelical sociopolitical involvement, born in direct response to Black Sunday (June 9, 1996), when ten churches in Surabaya were brutally attacked. Neither a political party nor a political advocate in the strict sense, the FKKI is sharply focused on solidarity and advocacy for victims of religious harassments, who are mostly Christians. The way they presented their cases was political. FKKI helped churches to rebuild buildings burned or destroyed, but it was also very active in doing advocacy work for victims, speaking out and writing protest letters to the president, parliament, the United Nations, and other institutions, which put political pressure on the government.[25]

The increasing willingness of evangelical and mainline "ecumenical" churches to work together stemmed from other factors, too. One was the growth of new, charismatic megachurches in the big cities of Indonesia, which began in the early 1990s. Unlike traditional pentecostal churches in rural or poorer urban areas, the new charismatic churches expanded among the middle and upper-middle class in Jakarta, Surabaya, and other big cities. In Indonesia, as elsewhere, economic strength entails connectedness to government officials and to power, and this fostered political involvement, especially as the more established mainline churches that had always had access to the government rapidly lost that ground.

Another factor was a growing media presence. The socioeconomic strength of charismatic churches gave them better access to media such as television. Television had always been fully controlled by the government, with a weekly one-hour slot for a Christian program, given to mainline churches only. But when the government began privatization in the late 1980s, several private television stations came into being. Although the stations were established and owned by Soeharto's family and cronies, they were mainly businesses, not politically oriented. The charismatic churches understood the power of media and used their economic resources to acquire increased access. They bought airtime or were invited to fill out weekly Christian programs that the station allocated for one to three hours per week on four major private stations.[26]

Third, the numerical expansion of evangelical churches was significant. As I have argued elsewhere (Budijanto 1997, 278–279), the growth of Christianity in the 1970s was much smaller than what some Christians publicly declared, and less extensive than what the Muslims feared (Willis 1977; Hefner 2000, 107). The growth of evangelical churches was in part at the expense of mainline churches, although there are no official data to prove this in detail. Nevertheless, evangelical churches, particularly pentecostal and charismatic churches, did experience substantial and very rapid growth in the 1980s and 1990s.

Fourth, the emergence of holistic evangelical leaders in the late 1980s and especially the early 1990s also contributed to the increasing collaboration between mainline and evangelical churches. Iman Santoso (1986, 1988), a member of a reformed church in Jakarta and former leader of Indonesia Intervarsity Fellowship, pioneered major strategic and functional collaborations, networks, and partnerships across theological boundaries. In January 1991, a National Prayer Network (NPN) was formed with Iman Santoso as chair. His background in the reformed church, evangelical commitment, academic excellence, and spirituality enabled him to gain respect from a variety of church groups. Unlike other prayer movements, the NPN-sponsored prayer movement focused on sociopolitical issues. The emphasis on prayer, fasting, and spiritual warfare and great expectations for God's intervention, attracted evangelical, pentecostal, and charismatic churches; the substance of the prayer—sociopolitical and spiritual transformation—attracted mainline churches.

Of course, not all Christian groups were in accord politically. Some factions in both mainline and evangelical churches retained an unconditional submissiveness to the government. As students, intellectuals, and other groups demanded Soeharto's resignation and his dictatorship ended, a number of leaders from the Indonesia Council of Churches offered *bulu bekti* (a gift or act of appreciation showing loyalty to the ruler) to Soeharto. Similarly, when most people demanded complete reform—and a new government free of corruption, collusion, and nepotism—some evangelical-charismatic leaders prayed, prophesied, and affirmed Habibie's continued presidency.[27]

Until the late 1980s, (Protestant) Christian churches held one of two main attitudes toward political involvement. Mainline churches tended to side with the government, a stand originally based on theological grounds and later valued as a survival strategy. Evangelical churches tended to distance themselves from political involvement, finding a theological basis for their position in a pietistic interpretation of Romans 13 and a view that regards politics as dirty.

Thus, political alienation, pressures by Soeharto and the political Muslims, and hostility and harassment against churches in the early 1990s shaped a new evangelical involvement in politics. Phenomenal growth among the big urban charismatic churches, privatization of media, and the emergence of the holistic evangelical leaders who facilitated the collaboration with the mainline churches, all contributed to the growth of evangelical political involvement, though the shape and degree of involvement varied from place to place and denomination to denomination.

Social turmoil preceding the 1998 "reformation" in Indonesian politics not only shaped evangelicals' political involvement; it also changed evangelical perspectives on what mission meant in the Indonesian context. Evangelicals, who previously had considered interfaith forums useless and unnecessary, became active in civic friendship activities aimed at preventing further societal chaos. In many cities, evangelicals established interreligious forums that brought together Protestant pastors, Muslim leaders, Hindu priests, Buddhist monks, Catholic priests, Chinese business people, NGO activists, academics, and others. The Samaria Forum in Surakarta, Intervide in Yogyakarta, and the Gedangan Forum in Salatiga (fifty-two kilometers north of Surakarta) are examples of civic forums that emerged in many Javanese cities and served as a short-term practical course on religion and politics.

Christianity in Surakarta

The Zendings (Dutch Christians) apparently did not plan strategically for early Christian expansion in Java and disregarded Surakarta's strategic role in Java's history. As Guillot (1985) observes, early Javanese conversions to Christianity were largely the fruits of local evangelists like Sadrach and Tunggul Wulung, and early Javanese congregations developed around the work of laypeople, such as Mrs. Philips and Mrs. Le Jolle. The minimal attention Zendings gave to sending missionaries to the Vorstenlanden, center of the Mataram (Javanese) kingdom, was surprising. Of the sixty-nine missionaries sent to Java between 1813 and 1900, only three worked at any time in Solo. Milne arrived in Batavia in 1818 to work among the Chinese. In later years, he moved to Surakarta, but his primary work there was translating the Bible into Javanese. Gericke also worked as a Bible translator in Surakarta between 1827 and 1857. Finally, P. Jansz, a Mennonite missionary, arrived in Semarang in 1851 but then worked for many years in Jepara. Later, he, too, moved to Surakarta to do Bible translation (6–17). There was little or no intentional evangelistic work in Surakarta before the twentieth century.

In 1910, however, Dr. H. A. Van Andel began running Christian schools and hospitals in Surakarta and distributing Christian books. In 1911, he pioneered the Margoyudan church, which built a church in 1919–1920 and inaugurated it in 1920. In 1925, several Javanese parishes of a Christian church in Surakarta separated from the ethnic Chinese churches they had developed and built an Indonesian Christian church in Lojiwetan, Sangkrah. The church has made significant contributions in the life of the residents of Surakarta for the past ninety years through education and health services. Christian schools and hospitals made people more receptive to Christianity. In colonial times, higher education was the only path for a change of life from an ordinary peasant into a new *priyayi* (educated or office employee class). Earlier in the century, higher education was usually available only for relatives of existing *priyayi*. Christian higher education in Surakarta provided ordinary people and peasants one of their first opportunities to advance.

Before 1965, Christianity in Surakarta grew rather slowly, and mainly through the church's social work. But following the 1965 "aborted coup," the massacre, and the banning of the PKI in 1966, many PKI supporters and suspected supporters, in Surakarta and many parts of Java, turned to Christianity for political protection.[28] From 1966 to 1968, the number of Christians increased significantly. Toward the end of the 1960s, the Christian population in Surakarta had come to represent approximately 17 percent of the population, up from around 2 percent in the 1950s. Several evangelical Bible and theological schools established around Surakarta in the 1970s laid foundations for a second phase of church growth in the 1980s and early 1990s. Official statistics from the mid-1990s listed 27 percent of the population as Christian.[29] The number of local church buildings grew from sixty-four in the late 1970s to 144 in 1995. A third phase of growth in the mid-1990s was accelerated by the May 1998 riots.

Religious differences never caused serious contention in Surakarta. Social unrest, riots, and radical movements sometimes occurred but not for religious reasons. Unlike other regions of Indonesia, Surakarta's upheavals always had socioeconomic and political, not religious, causes. The Indonesian Council of Churches report to the December 1998 World Synod VIII of the World Council of Churches in Harare, Zimbabwe, listed approximately five hundred churches that had been recently destroyed in Indonesia, but none in Surakarta. May 1998 and October 1999 riots devastated cities in Surakarta, destroying several hundred buildings; no churches were harmed.

Evangelicals, Civility, and Democratization in Surakarta

Evangelical Groupings in Surakarta

There are three major groups of evangelical churches in Surakarta: (1) classical pentecostal churches such as the Assemblies of God, Four Square, and Church of God; (2) charismatic churches, including some pentecostal churches that have experienced charismatic renewal and other churches newly established from house prayer groups; and (3) conventional evangelical churches, such as the Southern Baptist, Christian and Missionary Alliance, Nazarene, Mennonite, and Seventh Day Adventist churches.

Pentecostal churches were first established in Indonesia in the early 1920s (Sumual 1981). In Surakarta, and typically in Indonesia, their congregations mostly live in slum and rural areas. In interviews, pastors spoke of their "initial calling" or "initial vision," listing several motivations for working in poor areas. Some believed they had a divine calling to serve the poor. One prominent pastor received a prophecy in his youth from an American evangelist: "He prayed for me. At that time he said that 'there will come to you a lot of people who are filled with sorrow, a lot of people who are filled with heaviness, poor people'" (interview, July 26, 2001).

Most pentecostal pastors, however, cited the receptiveness of poor and socially marginalized groups as their main motivation. A high percentage of the poorer residents of Surakarta supported the PKI. Leftist movements that began in 1912 culminated in the early 1960s, when PKI became Surakarta's most powerful political institution. When Soeharto banned PKI and massacred supporters in 1966, many former PKI supporters became Christians (Ricklefs 1979).[30] The churches then saw a great need for Christian workers in Surakarta. This need, arising from people's "receptiveness," motivated most of these pentecostal pastors to minister among the poor there. Their choices apparently were neither strategically driven nor theologically motivated. Even the pastor quoted above said he was reminded of this prophecy only after he had already worked among his poor congregation for a few years.

The way these churches ministered reflects this. Pentecostal churches focused on their congregations' spiritual nourishment and well-being and on making them firm and committed Christians despite any economic difficulties or political pressures they encountered. Pastors did not engage in sociopolitical advocacy for these marginalized people, nor did they address their members' poverty strategically and theologically or generate programs to improve members' economic well-being. They focused on deepening people's spiritual commitment to help them remain faithful to God amid poverty and suffering. The pastors' interpretation of the 1965 "aborted coup" and massacre influenced how churches developed programs for these new converts. As several pastors put it during interviews, "God had allowed the 1965–1966 incidents to bring millions into salvation."

The more recent charismatic churches have a significantly different sociotheological approach. Most charismatic churches evolved from house prayer meetings, which sprang up in the mid-1980s; some were classic pentecostal churches that experienced charismatic renewal and then adopted the charismatic sociotheological approach to ministry. Where classic pentecostalism sought to escape the world and its pleasures—scorning all that modernization offers, such as technology, modern management, wealth, media—charismatic churches deliberately use those means to pursue their mission. This shift from traditional pietism to an approach receptive to modern capitalism is reflected in liturgy, church administration, building layout and decoration, and the maximum use of technology, including in the sermons.

Charismatic churches in Surakarta, and nationwide, have increasingly gained greater sociopolitical influence through members' economic status and political connections. The Christian business community serves as a bridge between the church and other sociopolitical players in the city. When businesspeople joined charismatic churches, they brought with them links to government officials, military personnel, and community leaders. For instance, when the situation in Surakarta was very tense in late 1999, many churches expected to be targets of a riot planned by some radical Muslims. Mainline and (non-charismatic) evangelical churches sought to protect church buildings by making intensive use of the interfaith forum, which proved to be effective. Charismatic churches used connections established by their business people to seek protection by contacting leaders of the Satgas PDIP, the ruling party's security force.

The pastors of charismatic churches are mainly Chinese with some business background. Most were businesspeople who left their businesses to become pastors and have little or no seminary training. Instead, they bring professional and business skills—marketing, communication, technologies, management, and business strategy—into the ministry. Their congregations, principally Chinese businesspeople and shop owners, consider the sermons' pragmatic business approach "down to earth." Classic pentecostal churches serve the lower strata of society; charismatic churches attract middle and upper-middle classes. The cell group system has provided a main impetus for their phenomenal growth.[31]

It is hard to say how much growth came from new converts and how much from former members of other churches. But many pastors who lost church members to charismatic churches were bitter. On the surface, this bitterness seems to have been resolved through the interchurch forum. On several occasions, charismatic churches have stated that they never intended to attract members from other churches. In public statements and from the pulpit, they repeatedly discouraged members of other churches from joining their congregations. Yet, some charismatic pastors explained, changing church membership is a delicate pastoral issue. Pastors felt torn and were reluctant to close their doors completely to members of other churches who expressed strongly felt needs.

Some subcutaneous bitterness remained among non-charismatic pastors toward their charismatic counterparts. In interviews, pastors recounted how hurt and bitterness had occupied them for years and negatively impacted their ministry. Some initially attacked the charismatic churches, but later their unhappiness produced more reflective responses. Reflections focused on evolving attitudes toward ministry and congregational growth rather than on their practices. Their main aim was not to compete with charismatic churches, spruce up their own churches in areas where charismatic churches had attracted former members, or emulate successful new strategies. Instead, they wanted to avoid hurting other pastors as they had been deeply hurt when key members left their congregations. They resolved to grow, not by following the charismatic churches' path, but by "new conversion" only. This eventually increased their evangelistic activities. Interestingly, this reflection finally contributed significantly to the growth of Christianity over the past few years.

Conventional evangelical churches—such as Baptist, Christian Alliance, Nazarene, Mennonite, and Seventh Day Adventist—form a third group. Most of these serve middle- and lower-middle-class people, small-scale merchants, and the *pegawai* (employee) class. Despite some theological variations, their approach is somewhat uniform: the world, wealth, and modern technologies are seen neither as necessarily evil nor as particularly useful for their mission. They neither seek to exploit these things nor try to escape from them.

Indonesian Evangelical Interpretation of Romans 13:1–2

Christians with passive or submissive attitudes toward politics and government often found theological justification in Romans 13:1–2: "Authorities are instituted by God. Consequently, he who rebels against authority rebels against what God has established." Indonesian evangelicals—pentecostal, charismatic, or conventional evangelical—interpret the text somewhat similarly.

Evangelical pastors in Surakarta expressed two major viewpoints when asked to apply this passage to Indonesia's presidents since Independence. Older pastors (age forty-five and older) in all three groups tended to interpret the passage literally, saying that God established or ordained each of the five presidents and brought down each president, and that God had a certain task or purpose for each president to accomplish. Asked to identify those tasks and purposes, most conventional evangelical pastors were reluctant to comment, simply saying that God knows best for Indonesia. Pastors from pentecostal and charismatic churches were usually willing to try to explain why God chose each president and to identify the tasks that God gave each. One pentecostal pastor described God's agenda for the five presidents as follows:

> Soekarno was ordained as the first president to guard Indonesia from becoming an Islamic state; his fall in 1966 was also ordained by God to bring millions to Christ. Soeharto was ordained to guard Indonesia against communist infiltration; his fall was ... God's judgment upon him ... as hundreds of churches were burned and destroyed during the last ten years of his leadership. Habibie was president of Indonesia for a short period of time.... During his leadership East Timor gained its independence from Indonesia. In the sixties and seventies ... communist expansion ... threatened the stability of the Southeast Asian region.... The United States established its military base in Subic, South Philippines, to halt the communist aggression. Nowadays, the threat comes from the radical Islamic world with their petro-dollars. The Islamic fundamentalist movement ... could disturb the balance of power ... in [this] region. East Timor, as a Roman Catholic country, is an ideal location of a United States military base, which would halt the aggressive expansion of the fundamentalist Muslim groups.... So God ordained Habibie for that purpose.... Wahid was ordained by God to protect the minority groups, including the Christians. Lastly, Megawati was ordained by God to replace Wahid, because significant numbers of Christian politicians belong to her party. (Interview, July 26, 2001)

Another elderly pentecostal pastor referred to Genesis 3 to interpret the rise and fall of Indonesian presidents:

> In Genesis chapter 3, Man fell into sin and was cursed by God. It was the Woman that had caused Man to fall. The same principle applied to Indonesian presidents. The first president, Soekarno, fell from power because of his womanizing lifestyle. The second president, Soeharto, was dominated by a woman, his wife. Soon after his wife died, he fell from the throne. The third president, Habibie, "like a woman," could not make up his mind on many issues. Wahid, the fourth president, was toppled by a woman, Megawati. With Megawati, a woman, as the fifth president, the curse has ended and Indonesia is entering into a new prosperous era. (Interview, July 28, 2001)

Younger pastors (under age forty-five) across all three groups of evangelicals tended to interpret Romans 13 differently. They saw God's role in presidential elections as less directive than did their older counterparts. They thought God did not determine who would become the president of Indonesia but "allowed" a particular person to become president. They often quoted two Old Testament passages to support their argument. One was the choosing of Saul as Israel's first king (1 Samuel 8). The passage states that God did not want Israel to have a human king, but God allowed them to have a king as they wished. The second, 1 Samuel 19:9, says, "But an *evil spirit from the Lord* came upon Saul as he was sitting in his house with his spear in his hand, while David was playing the harp" (emphasis added). The younger evangelical leaders said, "The Lord withdrew His protection over Saul and thus allowed the evil spirit to disturb him," not at all that the Lord sent an evil spirit to Saul. Similarly, Romans 13:1, saying that "there is no authority except *from God*" (New American Standard Bible, emphasis added), need not mean that God chose and established each president, only that God "allowed" them to become president.

Where older pastors saw God as the only and ultimate determinant of presidential elections, and thus put all the responsibility on God, younger pastors believed that God does not usually intervene directly in presidential elections. Anyone elected president must have God's permission, but that person is not necessarily God's choice for president. Younger evangelical leaders' altered perspective on Romans 13 marks an important change, which could have a vast impact on evangelical churches' involvement in politics.

The Domain of Social Identity

The fundamental difference between older and younger pastors went far beyond hermeneutical approaches to Romans 13. The underlying difference seemed to be in the domain of their social identity. The older pastors' domain of social identity was the Christian community in Indonesia, or Surakarta, and especially the evangelical churches. In interpreting and assessing sociopolitical issues, older pastors mainly considered the evangelicals. Many older pastors repeatedly referred to Romans 8:28 as pronouncing their underlying belief: "We know that in all things God works for the good of those who love him, who have been called according to his purpose." Based on this verse, they thought that when God ordained someone to become president of Indonesia, he did so "for the benefit of the evangelical churches in Indonesia." God's agenda for the Indonesian church determined his choice of presidents. Further, as God alone knows his agenda for the church and loves the church greatly, the church need not worry about who is elected. Whoever is elected will eventually serve God's purpose for the Indonesian church. The church's task is to discern God's mind in ordaining a person president and respond accordingly.

Sociopolitical instability and changes of presidents three times in just over three years (1998–2001) led the younger evangelical leaders to reconsider the domain of their social identity. The reality of politics, involving complex tensions and conflicts locally and negotiations and compromises at higher levels in recent years, was not easily explained by older Indonesians' evangelical theology. Human rights and the need for a larger public space for the minority groups—especially Chinese and Christians badly mistreated during Soeharto's last decade—were among the major issues that ended Soeharto's rule. Most younger Christian leaders were willing to occupy this larger public space. As their access to public space significantly increased, unavoidably their social identity also expanded. The younger pastors thought much more broadly. The frame of reference for these younger pastors was not the evangelical community alone but Surakarta or Indonesia as a whole. The criterion of a good president was not just how he or she served the evangelical community, but how well he or she served the whole nation. The rise and fall of presidents might have to do with much more than the needs and interests of evangelicals.

Civic and Political Engagement

Several older pentecostal pastors interviewed had been active members of Golkar (the ruling party) before Soeharto fell. They did this mainly as a strategy to secure government permission to build a church or to obtain more space for religious activities, such as house church fellowships. Under constant pressure from some Muslim groups, the New Order government developed rules that made constructing church buildings very difficult. These pastors used Golkar connections to get permission to construct church buildings. In the final years of Soeharto's regime, their involvement in Golkar decreased and then almost completely disappeared, probably due to the "Islamization" within Golkar.

Churches led by younger evangelicals instead increased their awareness and engagement in politics after Soeharto fell. A few were local board members of various political parties. Although the reason for their involvement was not always clear, these younger leaders, in striking contrast to older pastors, did not view political involvement as a means to gain privileges for church building or other pastoral tasks.

Two issues were systematically brought into Indonesian public discourse toward the end of Soeharto's regime: democracy, which implies political openness, and human rights, with special emphasis on mistreatment of minority groups. New political parties that emerged after Soeharto's fall tried, accordingly, to portray themselves as open, pluralistic parties.[32] In such an atmosphere, it was not uncommon for newly founded parties' leaders to ask younger Chinese and Christian leaders to join. Pastors' initial involvement was mainly a response to these invitations.

However, they were not merely passive in this process. They certainly had concerns and newly developed convictions about sociopolitical life in

Indonesia and Surakarta. Most who accepted these invitations were motivated by the multidimensional crisis, which greatly disturbed life in Surakarta and throughout Indonesia. Although uncertain how their political involvement would address their concerns, the pastors hoped that it could help prevent chaotic social unrest, like the May 1998 and October 1999 riots, from recurring.

The percentage of young evangelical leaders directly involved in political parties is still small. Others expressed their concerns by attending or sending other church leaders to attend seminars, discussions, and workshops on sociopolitical issues. Accompanying the rapid changes and new openness in post-Soeharto political life, seminars, talk shows, and discussions on sociopolitical issues became novel and attractive activities in major Indonesian cities. In Surakarta, the academic community, study centers, and the interfaith forum organized most such seminars and discussions. Organizers were mostly nonpartisan and primarily sought to develop greater political awareness.

Some younger leaders have intentionally encouraged, helped, and trained their congregations to increase their civic and political participation. At least three pastors encouraged their members to seek greater roles in voluntary local governance and public services. There were two main goals: influencing local public policy and gaining acceptance by the community. Of course, this greater emphasis on civic and political participation did not mean that civic and political education displaced these churches' main function of fostering spiritual growth. But civic and political awareness was incorporated into the church's program: these churches were preparing themselves to participate more fully in their communities' civic and political life.

Civic Friendship: The Interfaith Forum

Generally, NGO and academic communities think intergroup conflicts in the 1990s were encouraged by Soeharto as part of his strategy to prevent the consolidation of moderate Muslims (NU) and the nationalist fronts. Attacks on churches in Surabaya (June 1996), Situbondo (October 1996), and Tasikmalaya (December 1996) and murders of a couple dozen local NU leaders in east and central Java, together with the 1997 economic crisis, set the stage for the formation of interfaith forums in many cities. Local NGO activists and academics brought together leaders from different faiths to form these forums. The term "interfaith" (instead of "interreligious") was selected to include faiths the New Order government did not recognize as religions, such as Confucianism and Kebatinan.

In Surakarta, an interfaith forum was created immediately after devastating May 1998 riots, which demolished hundreds of buildings and took several lives. Like interfaith forums in other cities, it did not aim to discuss or resolve theological differences. The forums aimed to develop closer relationships, effective lines of communication, and regular exchanges of information among religious leaders. This helped religious leaders understand one another's contexts better and thus helped them prevent intergroup ethnic or religious conflicts. Although some concern remains that the forums are elite gatherings, they nevertheless succeeded in defusing several potential religious conflicts in Surakarta.

Evangelical leaders from all three groups expressed strong support for the interfaith forum. Although the degree of involvement varied, most have gained greater awareness of Surakarta's sociopolitical realities through forum discussions and seminars they attended. The forum developed what they called "action dialogue," discussing how people from different faiths look at a common issue from their distinctive perspectives, and then trying to solve a problem together. Discussion topics ranged from the "New Indonesia" to cultural analysis of various past conflicts in Surakarta. Concrete results of these dialogues ranged from working together on food distribution and on seminars to making joint public statements, organizing public prayer together, or simply disseminating information to followers.

Some large charismatic churches approached security more pragmatically. Instead of participating actively in the interfaith forum work on the common welfare issues, they worked with nonreligious groups to protect themselves. Knowing PDIP had dominant grassroots support, they tried to resolve security and welfare issues in Surakarta by working with PDIP leadership.

The interfaith forum is a positive outcome of the multidimensional crisis and the May 1998 riot. Recent threats and riots caused a sense of insecurity that led most evangelical churches to become more open to others. They began seeing the value of civic friendship with other religious groups. No one religious group is dominant in Surakarta, and none by itself can control conflicts or guard the city from riots, but forum participants together were able to avert various potential interreligious conflicts and thus secured peace in the city. As participants developed more mutual understanding, they also started to exchange perceptions on other matters affecting the welfare of Surakarta residents. After three years, the interfaith forum remained a place where leaders of different religious groups developed friendship and discussed issues. Civic friendship at the interfaith forum has yet to involve people at grassroots levels. But taking part in an interfaith forum was new territory for most of the evangelical churches, and they are in an initial learning phase.

Evangelicals' involvement in the interfaith forum was driven mainly by perceived needs, not theological rationales. Ongoing economic crisis and political instability give evangelical leaders little space to reflect theologically on involvement in the interfaith forum. Most kept evangelism and discipleship, on one hand, and civic involvement, on the other, in separate boxes. The former constitute the spiritual domain; the latter are considered a mere supplement to spiritual concerns. Some younger leaders, however, gave indications that they may soon supersede this dualism and work toward a more comprehensive approach.

New Civic Vocabularies

The openness after the May 1998 riot introduced evangelical leaders to new vocabularies of human rights, pluralism, democracy, public policy, and justice, which the Internet, mass media, and the interfaith forum have helped promote. Throughout their interviews, evangelical leaders repeatedly referred to human rights, pluralism, and democracy. Most seemed familiar with the terms, yet each term carried different connotations.

Evangelical leaders spoke of democracy less than human rights and pluralism in the interviews. They often found the concept of democracy unclear and considered the term vague. Some older pastors from the conventional evangelical groups saw the endless economic crisis as a result of ongoing daily street demonstrations, which they understood as the manifestation of democracy. They did not know whether Indonesia presently needs or wants such democracy and were also unsure whether democracy is compatible with the church structure.

But the term "human rights" resonated. They felt their right to exercise their faith had been badly violated by the government. The right to construct a church building, the right to share the gospel, and the right to convert people to Christianity were not granted. They could also easily appreciate the idea of pluralism. They considered the government to have denied Christians the right to freely exercise their faith, referring to human rights in these terms. They also had experienced threats, harassments, and persecution from the Muslim hard-liners; referring to these hard-liners, they noted the importance of pluralism. Evangelicals quickly adopted new terms with which they could identify their experiences.

Initially, they considered human rights and pluralism to refer to aspirations for freedom in evangelistic activities, to change religion (conversion), and to construct church buildings. Thus, most evangelical pastors used these terms in regard to their own spiritual goals and free exercise of their faith, without necessarily considering what those terms meant for other religious groups. But as they began to participate in interfaith forums their understanding of the terms became broader. Some evangelical leaders expressed the need to protect all minority groups, whatever their religious or ethnic affiliations. This shift of understanding was still in its very early stages and did not occur across the board.

A few younger leaders used the terms more comprehensively and inclusively, referring to the protection of ethnic minorities, to maturity in dealing with differences in society, and to the importance of law enforcement. Just as with the interfaith forum, they have not had the chance to reflect theologically on these terms. We must wait to see how these younger leaders will deal with the paradoxes of evangelism and pluralism, and of conversion and human rights, in the next few years.

Evangelicals' Interpretation of the Multidimensional Crisis

People in Surakarta generally associate the multidimensional crisis that has continued since 1997 with the devastating May 1998 riots, which took over a dozen lives and destroyed hundreds of buildings and thousands of jobs. The pastors had no consensus opinion about the causes of the crisis, but generally believed that the Lord allowed it to happen for the benefit of the Indonesian church. The benefits they saw included God's discipline, which purifies the church, God's judgment on those who hate the church, God's opening the eyes of the church to be holistic in its ministry, and God's reminding His people to go on evangelistic missions (Acts 8:1–4).

However, the most common view emphasized the many converted to Christianity in recent years, using the term *Panen Raya* (great harvest). There were several explanations of why and how conversions took place. First, people learned from the May 1998 riots that wealth acquired over twenty years disappeared in a matter of hours. Chinese businesspeople felt that there is no real security in this world. It was suspected that quite a few *abangan* and secular Muslims opened their hearts to the Christian message out of sympathy and admiration. For ordinary *abangan* people, that Christians did not retaliate when their holy places were burned and destroyed was noble.

Interestingly, pastors originally from outside Java in all three evangelical groups perceived the crisis—including religious and ethnic conflicts since the mid-1990s, particularly the 1998 and 1999 riots in Surakarta—as the work of the devil. The reality of a spiritual world and spiritual battles is much more salient in some tribal contexts outside Java, for instance in Kalimantan, Sumba, and Toraja. Other explanations of the crisis and riots included socioeconomic pressures, government policies and poor governance, value clashes (traditional and modern), and radical Muslim movements. Perspectives on the crisis have shaped how evangelical churches in Surakarta respond, develop ministry strategies, and will present themselves in the future.

The multidimensional crisis and the riots stimulated evangelical churches in Surakarta to develop more holistic ministries. Few evangelical churches in Surakarta previously had programs specifically caring for the poor. Health, education, and other programs were administered mostly by Roman Catholic and mainline Protestant churches. But nowadays, almost every evangelical church in Surakarta has some program of caring for the poor. It remains unclear whether the motivation is firm Christian conviction or averting social unrest.

Evangelicals and Pluralism

All evangelical pastors interviewed clearly stated that they wanted to evangelize as many people as possible; few, however, thought that the ideal was for all Indonesians to become Christians. A significant number of key respondents saw the ideal framework for Indonesia as pluralism, understood as acknowledging the existence of every ethnic and religious group in the country. Each must respect others' distinctiveness and freedom to exercise his or her faith and culture. Such pluralism was not seen as conflicting with their evangelistic activities, as they considered evangelism part of their spiritual practice. As they respect the *da'wah* (proclamation of the Qur'an), they also expect the Muslims to respect evangelistic activities.

Some respondents thought the key to establishing a plural Indonesia lay in *Pancasila*, the national ideology, which implicitly affirms Indonesia as a plural country. Others referred to the national motto: *Bhineka Tunggal Eka* (Diversity but One). Thus, many evangelical pastors see the ideal for Indonesia as that proclaimed by the founding fathers in 1945. They conclude that the root of disintegration, ethnoreligious conflicts, and social unrest has been the unfaithfulness of current leaders and some radicals to Pancasila and Bhineka Tunggal Eka. The key to economic recovery, political stability, and a conflict-free Indonesia lies in rediscovering the foundational pluralism expressed in Pancasila. Esteeming human rights, including freedom of speech, religious freedom, and protection for minorities, is seen as a consequence of pluralism.

A number of pastors add economic aspects and popular well-being as part of their ideal for Indonesia, by referring to a Javanese saying: *"Gemah Ripah Loh Jinawi, Kerto Raharjo,"* that is, "Prosperous, fertile, peaceful and orderly." (*Raharjo*, "orderly," suggests either "well organized" or law enforcement.) Some younger pastors include social justice and liberal democracy as important ideals. Older pastors are concerned about protection and argue their case from the value of pluralism within Pancasila; younger evangelical leaders seek to engage both theologically and practically with universal concepts, such as human rights, pluralism, and social justice, and to develop a comprehensive and inclusive approach for the church in Indonesia.

Conclusion

Evangelical churches in Indonesia learned things the hard way. The enormous threat that came from Soeharto's courtship with the political Muslims produced deeper church involvement in politics. The socioeconomic crisis taught them more holistic approaches to ministry. The May 1998 riots led the church toward active civic friendship with other religious groups. The unending crisis and ever changing national leadership spurred evangelicals to reflect on their theology and hermeneutical approaches.

Evangelicals' contribution to enhanced civility and democratization in Surakarta, and throughout Indonesia, has increased significantly in the past few years. Formation of interfaith forums in many cities and active clergy involvement in them indicate that Indonesian evangelicals have begun a new journey of civic friendship with other groups. Younger leaders' participation in sociopolitical discussions, workshops, and seminars shows that evangelical churches in Surakarta, and elsewhere, have begun to take a new role in shaping the future of Indonesian civility. These leaders are beginning to develop new vocabularies, using terms such as democracy, civil society, pluralism, and the public sphere, that were foreign to evangelical pastors a few years ago.

Pastors expressed eagerness to see the church grow in numbers as well as in its societal function. While committed to evangelization as their primary calling and vision, the evangelical leaders in Surakarta spoke of a plural Indonesia as their ideal for the nation. Younger evangelical pastors held that God did not specifically choose presidents (but allowed election of presidents). However, once a president was elected, it is the church's obligation to submit to the government. These and other paradoxes have begun to emerge into the evangelical praxis.

Although evangelical churches in Surakarta do somewhat resemble those in other cities in Java, one must be cautious about generalizing. In the past five years, evangelical churches in many other cities have undergone a significant transformation in their understanding, roles, and place in Indonesian society. But it is too early to assess the long-term impact on civility and democratization in Indonesia.

In Surakarta, surprisingly, it appears that sociotheological groupings have much less influence on evangelical political involvement than was previously supposed. Leaders from the three sociotheological groups had quite similar perspectives and civic engagement. The research, however, shows that younger evangelical leaders from all three groups differ from older leaders and are changing their political perspectives more. Although it is too early to assess the impact on civility in Surakarta, impacts within the church are already evident.

NOTES

1. The riots that forced Soeharto to resign in May 1998 centered in Jakarta and Surakarta. Again, when the Assembly failed to elect Megawati the fourth presi-

dent in October 1999, upheaval was concentrated in Surakarta. Similarly, reactions against the U.S. attack on Afghanistan (October 2001) also started here.

2. Arndt (1971, 359–395), Mortimer (1974), Crouch (1978), and Cribb (1990) provide extensive treatment of Indonesia's economic turmoil and political conflicts of the mid-1960s.

3. Insurgents included Darul Islam (West Java, 1948–1962), PKI (Madiun, 1948), the South Malucu Republic (1951), Kahar Muzakar (South Sulawesi, 1950–1951), the All-Aceh Union of Ulamas (1953), Permesta (North Sulawesi, 1957–1961), and the Revolutionary Government of the Indonesian Republic (Bukittinggi, 1958–1961). Ricklefs (1981, 225–271) details civilian parties' struggles to gain greater control over the government.

4. Twenty-eight parties won seats, but only four had more than eight seats: PNI, Masyumi, NU, and PKI. Many smaller parties made forming a governing coalition difficult. See Kahin (1995, 50); Ricklefs (1981, 238).

5. Crouch (1979, 188–192) briefly reviews attempts to explain the origins of the September 30th Movement. Notable is Benedict Anderson and Ruth McVey's (1971) preliminary analysis, widely known as the Cornell Paper, which interprets it as a movement of air force officers and dissident junior army officers from central Java against army leaders in Jakarta.

6. Army officers established Sekber-Golkar (Sekretariat Bersama Golongan Karya, Joint Secretariat of Functional Groups) in October 1964 to coordinate anti-PKI organizations within the National Front. This federation, composed of 146 organizations in 1966, swelled to include 210 organizations in 1967, and 249 in 1968. Soeharto used it as the government party, through which his supporters competed in elections. Although most affiliated bodies were civilian, the most influential were led by army officers. Six out of seven *Kino* (Kesatuan Induk Organisasi, Basic Organization Units) were led by army officers, including Brigadier General Suhardiman and Major General Sughandi. See Ward (1974, 25–26); Crouch (1978, 266).

7. *Aliran* (stream) usually denotes the political alignments of a variety of village-level organizations—women's clubs, youth groups, Boy Scouts, private schools, peasants unions, art groups, and trade organizations—which form the primary bond linking the village to the national political system. In the *aliran* system, people were grouped politically not by class or ideology but according to religious beliefs and sociocultural values that found expression in the post-Independence Indonesia political party system.

8. Geertz's (1960) study of Java distinguished three categories of Javanese Muslims. The *santri* are Muslims who strictly observe Islamic ritual and ethical prescriptions. The *abangan* are less rigorous in performing orthodox duties and are influenced by aesthetic and ritual styles related to Java's pre-Islamic past. The *priyayi* are the upper class, somewhat influenced by Indic religious practices. The *priyayi* are, as Kodiran (1971, 342) has argued, more a social than a religious group, but Geertz rightly noticed that the *priyayi* belief orientation in Mojokuto significantly differs from the *santri* (Arab-oriented) and the *abangan* (traditional Javanese-oriented). Geertz (1984) disagrees with his critics' understanding of religion (Suparlan 1981, x–xi), taking religion as an anthropological system. See also Jay (1963); Bachtiar (1973, 85–115).

9. The early evangelization in Java was mostly done by Javanese evangelists or Indonesian Christians from other islands (Eastern Indonesia), such as Kyai Sadrach and Kyai Tunggul Wulung. Dutch missionaries were mostly "maintainers" and "instructors." When people were persuaded to become Christian through the preaching of local evangelists, they were sent to the missionaries for baptism and further Christian instruction (Guillot 1985, 3–30; Muller-Kruger 1959, 58).

10. A statement by Frans Lion Chachet (1835–1899), a Reformed clergyman who opposed a Javanese Christian leader, Sadrach, illustrates this. Chachet said that Indonesian Christianity had to be clearly segregated from Sadrach, "the liar," who had poisoned Christians and had led to the birth of Javanese Christianity, which did not place Jesus Christ at the right position (quoted in Steenbrink 1993, 106). Guillot (1985, 84–90) further discusses tensions between Dutch clergy and Sadrach followers.

11. Sumartana (1997) argues that the spread of Christianity in the colonial age was, to some extent, a strategy to tame Indonesians. A patron-client relationship was developed between Dutch and Indonesian Christians, which developed into a patron-client mentality characterizing much Indonesian-Christian relations with postwar governments.

12. In July 1936, Soetardjo, a Javanese member of the Volksraad, submitted a petition to the Volksraad, passed in September 1936, which called for greater Indonesian autonomy.

13. These were by no means the first or the most brutal attacks against Chinese and Christians in Indonesia. Chinese and Christians have been targeted in almost every social unrest since 1740, when the Chinese community in Batavia was massacred, until the latest, May 1998 Jakarta riots. In the 1990s alone, more than four hundred churches were burned or destroyed (Hefner 2000, 190–193).

14. Adherents of Protestant churches outside Java are mostly indigenous and tribal peoples in the interiors of Sumatera, Borneo, Sulawesi, and West Papua or small islands in West Sumatera, North Sulawesi, and Maluku. They are economically, educationally, and socially far behind Javanese Muslims. Javanese and Sundanese Christians are not better off than their Muslim counterparts. Chinese Protestants in Java are economically and educationally more advantaged than others in the country, but during the New Order regime, they were constantly intimidated and given no space for political involvement (Schwarz 1994). Unlike their Catholic counterparts, Protestants had no strong national institutions, let alone firm international support.

15. Soeharto's New Order government intentionally made minority groups dependent on him through intimidation and violence (Hefner 2000). They were used both as scapegoats and milk cows.

16. Recent articles by Muslim leaders on the New Order in the 1970s and 1980s openly blame Ali Moertopo and CSIS for creating an antagonistic relationship between the army and the *santri* community. See especially "Akhirnya Naro Melakukan Kudeta" (1995); Nasution (1995); A. M. Fatwa, interview, *Tiras*, November 9, 1995, 52; Sayidiman Suryohadiprojo, interview, *Forum*, Jakarta November 6, 1995, 80–84.

17. For Soeharto's systematic strategy to control parliament, see Ward (1974); for New Order strategy to control the armed forces, see Schwarz (1994); for Soeharto's strategy to control political parties, see Crouch (1978, 234–252) and Utrecht (1974); and on control of major religious institutions, see Hefner (2000).

18. "Insulinde" is the Indies Archipelago but was also a radical Indo-European party founded in 1907.

19. Populace League was the new name given by the Communist Party to the Red Islamic League. See McVey (1965).

20. Soekarno banned Masyumi, the Muslim Modernist Party, in 1960. Masyumi leaders were very active in supporting Soeharto's overthrow of Soekarno, expecting that Soeharto would lift that ban. Instead, Soeharto established a new Muslim party, Parmusi (Partai Muslimin Indonesia, Muslim Party of Indonesia). None of the charismatic Masyumi's former leaders were allowed in the party's new leadership (see Crouch (1978, 259–263); Salam (1970, 269–270).

21. Recently, new vocabularies distinguish political Muslims from cultural Muslims. Political Muslims are those whose aim is to establish an Islamic state out of the present Indonesia, largely but not exclusively represented by the modernist Muslim groups, such as Muhammadiyah and Masyumi. Cultural Muslims are those Muslims who believe one must not use or manipulate religion for political gain, largely, but not exclusively, represented by the traditionalist Muslim groups (the NahdlatulUlama) and the neomodernist Muslims.

22. The armed forces were led by General Benny Moerdani, a Javanese Catholic of the CSIS circle. Reportedly, he chided Soeharto over his children's bad behavior (Schwarz 1994; Hefner 2000).

23. Whether these hostilities and harassments were religiously, socioeconomically, or politically motivated remains unclear.

24. There are strong indications that CSIS used internal PDI conflict to regain its favored position in Soeharto's inner circle (Hefner 2000).

25. From the PDI congress in Surabaya (1994) and the difficult years that followed, when Soeharto tried to isolate and alienate Megawati, these PDI Protestant politicians proved their loyalty and demonstrated fierce support for Megawati.

26. FKKI gave President Soeharto a comprehensive statement reacting to the church destructions (see Indonesian Christian Communication Forum [FKKI], 1997).

27. Christmas season 2000 was another major breakthrough for evangelical churches, when *The Jesus Film* was aired for the first time by a national television station.

28. Habibie and his cabinet members were integral to the New Order regime. Annete Jeff and Ruth Hammond report a two-hour meeting with President Habibie on June 10, 1998, in which some evangelical leaders prayed for, affirmed, and prophesied concerning Habibie's presidency, saying, "President Habibie is under Divine Protection, has been appointed by God...as President of a transitional government but that if he would humbly and righteously walk before the Lord, God would establish him as the elected President, and...the nation would prosper under his leadership."People not registered as members of one of the five official religions (Islam, Protestantism, Roman Catholicism, Hinduism, and Buddhism) were often accused of being PKI supporters. Because the Muslims, especially members of the Ansor (NU youth organization), were behind the massacre of the PKI supporters in rural Java, alleged communist supporters mostly turned to religions other than Islam for protection. Ricklefs (1979, 100–128), Lyon (1980), and Geertz (1972, 62–84) dis-

cuss the growth of Christianity and Hinduism in the aftermath of the 1965–1966 bloodshed.

29. An inside source at the Surakarta Biro Pusat Statistik (Central Statistics Bureau) unofficially indicated that the percentage of Christians in Surakarta neared 40 percent by the mid-1990s.

30. These new Christians were economically poor and politically marginalized. They and their children were usually denied political rights and were not allowed to join political parties or become government officers. They lived under constant government suspicion. From 1965 until 1999, the government appointed military officers as mayors of Surakarta.

31. One charismatic church, for example, had 273 cell groups in 1999; two years later, the number had grown to 1,324, with a total membership of around fifteen thousand.

32. This was especially true with the National Mandate Party chaired by Amin Rais although it was known for exclusiveness, and its main base was Muhammadiyah (the second-largest Indonesian Muslim group). The party called for Chinese and Christians to sit on the board, both nationally and locally. Similarly, the Nation Reawakening Party, founded by Nahdlatul Ulama, endeavored to make itself an open and inclusive modern political party.

5

Evangelicals and the Democratization of South Korea Since 1987

Rev. Dr. Joshua Young-gi Hong

Scholarly interest in religion and political socialization (D. E. Smith 1974) resurfaced in recent studies of religious influence in public affairs (Yamane 1997), well before religiously linked conflict reached the headlines. Religion helps shape political culture and political behavior, often providing comprehensive norms that generate action. Cross-national research shows a strong positive association between the percentage of Protestants in a society and the level of democratization (Woodberry 1999, 1).

In this chapter I examine how evangelicals affected South Korean democratization.[1] After two-and-a-half decades of military-dominated authoritarianism, Korea had a rapidly growing economy but no democracy, until mass protests led to electoral democracy and civil and political rights in 1987 (Diamond and Kim 1998, 2). What role did the churches play? Scholars have given scant attention to the role of the evangelicals in Korea's democratization and democratic consolidation. In this chapter I review the useful though sparse scholarly literature, but I rely principally on observation, interviews, documents,[2] and the writings of pastors, theologians, and civil-society activists.

I argue that Korean Christians have significantly boosted democratization. Progressive Christians contributed most before the 1987 transition. Since then, evangelicals have been pivotal in democratic consolidation through political leadership and civil associations. I explore church involvement before 1987, then analyze the role of evangelicals in the 1987 People's Uprising. I also discuss evangelicals' subsequent electoral behavior, role in political society, and civil society activities. Finally, I assess evangelical contributions to democratic consolidation and the possibilities for strengthening Korean democracy.

Paving the Way: History and Theology of Christian Democratic Movements Until 1987

The trajectory of Korean Protestantism is unique in Asia. Protestantism arrived in turbulent times. Since its inception, it has been linked with values of modernity, including education, knowledge, equality, and freedom. Under Japanese rule (1910–1945), Korean Christianity forged a strong link with Korean nationalism. From early on, an unusually high percentage of intellectuals were Protestants. The Japanese government refused to hire Protestant intellectuals, a decision that fostered nationalism. The church was very active in the 1919 Independence movement. Although the two hundred thousand Korean Christians were a mere 1.3 percent of the population, fifteen of thirty-three signatories of the Declaration of Independence were Christians, and 2,087 of the 9,458 people imprisoned for demonstrating were Christians (M. Yi 1991, 349).

From the early 1930s, the Japanese attempted to impose emperor worship to help bind together their intended empire. In 1935, all educational establishments, including Christian schools, were ordered to participate in Shinto shrine ceremonies. After strong resistance, the two largest denominations, Presbyterian and Methodist, involuntarily complied. The Japanese tried to undermine other denominations by removing foreign missionaries from authority. In 1937, they warned Koreans to have no contact with foreigners. By the mid-1940s, 90 percent of missionaries had left; those remaining were harassed incessantly (A. E. Kim 1995, 34–53).

The political and social roles of theological conservatives and liberals alike involved inconsistencies and ambiguities under Japanese rule. Conservatives took an apolitical stance, but toward the end resisted Japanese rule on the basis of faith concerns. Liberal Christians participated in political and social affairs but often cooperated with the Japanese, for example, sharing an anticommunist bent with pro-Japanese groups. Many Christian leaders protested against oppressive policies and were arrested, tortured, and killed. Many others stayed away from the nationalist movement. Some church leaders were closely involved with the Japanese, which caused conflict within Protestant churches after 1945. The passive stance some churches took toward Japanese rule extended later to their acceptance of military rule and lack of sympathy with democratic protests.

Korean Christianity after the Liberation (1945)

After the 1945 liberation, and especially after the Korean War, the church faced three ongoing tasks: removing vestigial Japanese influence (*Minjok Chonggi*, or National Spirit), promoting democratization (*Minju*), and supporting unification (*Tongil*). The missionary and colonial inheritance dichotomized religion and politics and fostered denominationalism and fundamentalism. Most Korean churches axiomatically assumed that they should concentrate on worship, Bible study, evangelism, and spiritual life and stay away from politics.

Syngman Rhee used anticommunism as an ideology to control politics, religion, culture, and economic activities. He showed little interest in democratization. After Independence, many elites helped the Japanese. The Korean church felt comfortable with its privileges and freedom. It depended on the United States and felt no need for autonomy from U.S. governance. Rhee, a Methodist elder, was ordained in 1956. Many Protestants participated in Rhee's Liberty Party, some because he was a Christian (see Table 5.1). Most churches took conservative political and social roles, and many Christian leaders continued to support Rhee, even when the regime became increasingly corrupt, arrogant, and aloof.

There were several reasons for this conservatism. Missionary theology had emphasized separation of church and state, and the ongoing U.S. missions' support fostered pro-Americanism and anticommunism. Christian refugees from North Korea were understandably strongly anticommunist. Korean churches had many middle-class and elite members, and thus benefited from government policies. The church was also ethically naïve, approving of Rhee simply because he was a Christian. Internal church structure was dominated by conservative leaders and sometimes by pro-Japanese groups, such as pastor Chun Pil-sun, the president of Presbyterian Tong-hap. Many political leaders were conservative Christians who wanted the church to stay out of politics. Church growth (and intrachurch politics) also absorbed attention, leaving churches little time to think about the country's social realities. The authoritarian orientation of the church leaders within the church's own organization also negatively influenced Korean politics (S. Yi 1995). In

TABLE 5.1. Religious Composition of Political Parties, 1952–1962 (%)

Party in Power	Protestant	Catholic	Buddhist	Confucianist	No Religion
Liberty Party	39.2	7.4	16.2	17.6	18.9
Democracy Party	19.8	11.9	7.0	22.1	39.5
Republic Party	27.7	4.3	19.1	8.5	40.0

Source: I. Kang (1996, 178).

sum, failure to transcend missionary and colonial heritages caused divisions among Korean churches and robbed the church of a prophetic voice about sociopolitical reality.

Theological Streams' Views about Social Involvement

The ideology of the Park regime, which began in 1960, focused on economic growth. The government sought economic growth through rapid industrialization and urbanization—an urgent practical task, to be sure—but it behaved undemocratically, ignoring human rights and exploiting and suppressing labor. Korean society sought material affluence apart from spiritual values. These materialist, growth-oriented priorities affected the thinking in the churches. Pastors concentrated on numerical growth as the criterion of success, neglecting economic and political implications of the gospel because of their difficulty and lack of obvious rewards, as well as because of a conservative theological legacy.

The church could either conform, by emphasizing church growth while neglecting social concerns, or resist social injustices. From the 1960s on, three divergent political stances emerged: a cooperative position toward the government (conservative churches, e.g., Presbyterian Hap-tong), a middle position (Methodist and Presbyterian Tong-hap), and opposition to military government (e.g., Presbyterian Kijang, which developed *Minjung*, people's theology).[3] Most churches remained silent about military autocracy, but starting in the early 1970s, churches and politics experienced the "creative tension" Bellah (1965) describes, as democratic activists, Christian students, and some progressive churches initiated an intense democratization movement, resisting the autocratic government. Despite the contrasting theological positions, seeing the Korean church as neatly divided into fixed progressive and conservative camps vastly oversimplifies the dynamics. Churches with differing positions influenced each other, and, in the end, worked together to promote democratic consolidation.

The Role of the Korean Church in the Democratization Movement

Repressive rule suppressed and stunted civil society in the 1960s and 1970s (Yu and Park 1992). Voicing normal demands for political democratization or economic equity could even be a source of grave personal danger. Because few stable civic groups existed to undergird a regime transition, the prime mover of political change was movement politics, which alienated most people and lacked regular or sanctioned channels for voicing demands to the state. Protest was possible only in universities and churches, which retained some open space for protest because of the great respect professors and pastors command in Korean society. The church's moral prestige also added weight to its critiques. So students, professors, and clergy organized protests (D. Cho 1999, 129), campaigning against the authoritarian regime through prayer meetings, fasting, and mass demonstrations.

An organized democratization movement began in the 1970s (H. Cho 1990). Starting in 1974, the Democratic Recovery People's Committee (Minju Hoibok Kukmin Hoi'ui), composed of Christian pastors, professors, and political activists, became a center of anti-autocracy and *Chaeya* (dissident: literally, "out in the fields") movements, forming a Democratic People's Coalition (Minjuju'ui Kukmin Yonhap) in 1978 and a People's Coalition for Democracy and National Unification in 1979.

This democratization movement focused on human rights, labor, and implementation of a new democratic constitution. Religious groups provided a core organizational structure. Criticism of the government was illegal under the repressive *Yushin* system, so church organizations, being legal entities and therefore very difficult for the regime to assail, were important for the democratic movement. Some churches and cathedrals were frequent sites for meetings, prayers, and demonstrations, as police hesitated to break up even antigovernment activities taking place on sanctified ground (Y. Chang 1998, 42). The National Council of Churches Hall and Myongdong Cathedral, the seat of Cardinal Kim Su-han, were famed democracy movement sites. Dissident church leaders organized antigovernment groups. Many activists and students participated in the Federation of Christian Youth for the Defense of Democracy (Minju Suho Kidok Chongnyon hyop'uihoi), the Catholic Labor Youth Coalition (Katolic Nodong Chongnyonhoi), the Industrial Mission Committee (Sanup Sonkyohoi), and the Christian Academy.

As Chung Chol-hui (1995) argues, the social origins of Korean democratization lay in micromobilization and in frameworks of meaning (such as *Minjung* theology) pioneered in the church and the university. Korean Christian involvement was quite unlike that in Western and Latin American countries (C. Choi 1992). Western and Latin American counterparts (such as the Christian Socialist Movement, the Social Gospel Movement, and Catholic Action) arose after and against strong preexisting social movements, sometimes to keep Christians from forsaking religion for radical labor and socialist movements. Severe military government repression and restrictions on open communication in Korea generally precluded formation of mass movements. Christian social movements in Korea were thus forerunners to other resistance movements and helped "promote their growth" (I. Kang 2000b, 226).

Although politically and theologically liberal Protestants and Catholics constituted a small percentage of Korean Christians, many scholars agree that the churches offered a haven for the oppressed and an outspoken voice when others were silenced (Brouwer, Gifford, and Rose 1996), keeping the democratic spirit alive. Churches were cradles in which other protest movements were formed and nurtured.

Gradual Change in Evangelicals' Political Consciousness

Most evangelical Christians initially did not support the democratic movement, seeing protests against military rule as tied to communist influence and intent on radical social reform. In the 1970s and the early 1980s, evangelical churches considered progressive church and Christian student democratization movements sectarian, one-sided, and too closely linked to radicals. Korean Protestants typically viewed citizens' political activities negatively. In one 1982 survey, only 5.5 percent thought the church should organize against social wrongs and human rights violations (Institute for Modern Society 1982, 153–155). In a Gallup survey (1984, 178–180), only 19.1 percent of Protestants approved of Christian participation in political, economic, and social demonstrations.

But by the early 1980s, theological self-examination by evangelical churches gradually led to more concern about sociopolitical responsibilities. For one thing, the 1974 Lausanne Covenant, and the 1982 follow-up Grand Rapids Report, emphasized social justice as part of the biblical mandate. These worldwide evangelical voices began to influence Korean churches and key evangelical leaders, such as Kim Myung-hyuk and Chun Ho-jin, especially in the mid-1980s.

Second, the aftermath of the 1979 democratic movement in Kwangju galvanized many students, intellectuals, and religious groups: the National Council of Churches, YMCA and YWCA, Catholic Farmers Federation, the Catholic Committee for Justice and Peace, and the like. Brutal repression of the Kwangju Uprising (or Massacre) left evangelical consciences burdened. The repression was a turning point, providing impetus for the democratic movement of the 1980s, and became an emotional rallying cry, sparking anti-Americanism because of the U.S. connivance with it. Participants "in the democratic movement of the 1980s continued to look back on what had happened there and their sense of shame was converted into hatred for the dictators" (D. Kim 1997, 99). The June 1987 climax of the democratic movement was, in effect, "the nationalization of Kwangju."

Third, evangelical churches began to resent some government actions. Like anyone charged with care of a valued institution, religious leaders give priority to institutional interests (O, Kyong-hwan 1990, 322–324). The government held national examinations qualifying people for prestigious civil service jobs on Sundays, which seemed to evangelicals to infringe on their freedom of Sabbath observance. Government plans to build shrines to Dangun (the mythic ancestor of Koreans) throughout the country seemed idolatrous. Such strongly felt issues predisposed evangelical churches to participate in democracy demonstrations in 1987.

Evangelicals' participation was indirect and contrasted with that of progressive churches. Evangelical church participation typically consisted of holding a special prayer meeting or issuing a statement (which such churches do with any issue they take seriously). One 1987 church declaration stated, "We believe that it is wrong for the churches to become political groups which have direct involvement in politics.... This is not the inherent role of the church.... [But] we, evangelical churches, confess that we have not played a role of the salt and the light in Korean society" (quoted in M. Kim 1998, 20–21).

By the 1980s, political awakening began to sprout among evangelical churches generally. The umbrella Korean Evangelical Fellowship (KEF) issued a 1986 statement on human rights that noted the need for its moral inspiration, suggested church involvement, and pressed the government for political democratization, freedom of the press, and extension of human rights. The KEF had issued statements only six times previously; from 1987 to 1999, it published fifty-five such statements (M. Kim 1998).

Evangelical Christians and the 1987 Popular Uprising in Support of Democratic Transition

There was significant democratization worldwide in the 1980s and 1990s (Remmer 1995). South Korea's democratic transition was successful by many criteria (Burton and Ryu 1997, 1), comprising all elements of procedural democracy or polyarchy (Dahl 1971). Evangelicals played an important role.

The Democratic Struggle in 1987

On January 14, 1987, Seoul National University student Park Chong-chul died after being tortured by the National Police in the Seoul police station. Police claimed Park drowned while he was held under water during interrogation, but the autopsy showed that Park died from blood clots induced by electric torture. Catholic churches held a mass for Park on January 26. Afterward, 150 priests held a demonstration that drew two thousand participants (W. Kang 1997, 124). Park Chong-chul's death mobilized massive nationwide demonstrations against the military government that spring. Demonstrators demanded democratization, reform, and sweeping constitutional amendments to the 1972 *Yushin* constitution, with its strict prohibition of political criticism and its easily manipulated system of indirect presidential elections. For months, while demonstrators battled riot police, President Chun seemed amenable. But on April 13, 1987, Chun reversed his public pledge to allow direct, popular election of his successor. Chun and his henchmen clearly intended to prolong the military regime by avoiding elections.

Park's death by torture and the April 13 declaration retaining the *Yushin* constitution allowed diverse pro-democratic groups—conservative institutional political opposition parties, moderate religious groups, and radical activists—to unite on the most moderate goal: revision of the constitution. The Popular Movement Headquarters for the Attainment of a Democratic Constitution (Minju Honbop Jaengchyi Kukmin Undong Bonpu) formed on June 19, 1987, and included many Christian leaders, with Protestant pastor In Myung-jin and Catholic priest Kim Sung-hun as spokespersons. A wide coalition of opposition and civil society groups, the People's Movement to Win a Democratic Constitution, began the "6.10 Struggle," demanding direct presidential elections and other democratic reforms.

The scale and nature of demonstrations in the summer of 1987 were unprecedented (Oh 1999, 91). Focusing on direct presidential elections was the key. Previous democratic activists had marginalized themselves since the 1970s, advocating anti-American and anticapitalist revolution (interview 10). However, people interpreted the 1987 *Chaeya* movement as a moderate attempt at political democracy (D. Cho 1999, 125). Antigovernment demonstrations exploded simultaneously in Seoul and some twenty other cities and quickly spread to thirty-seven urban centers.

The Role of Christians in the 1987 Democratic Struggle

The Korean National Council of Churches (KNCC) and the National Pastors' Federation for Justice and Peace Practice issued a statement against Chun's April 13 declaration, demanding democratic revision of the constitution. Catholic priests began protest fasts and prayer meetings on April 21, and many laypeople and Protestant pastors joined the fast. A "prayer meeting for the nation" was called as a visible protest action. KNCC-affiliated denominations held a series of prayer meetings for the nation (Korean Methodists on June 21, Presbyterian Tong-hap on June 22, Salvation Army on June 28, Presbyterian Ki-jang on July 7, and so on).

Religious meetings turned into street demonstrations. After fifteen hundred clergy and laity attended its June 21 "prayer meeting for saving the country," the Methodist Church issued statements on democracy and unification and decided to continue prayer meetings until democracy was achieved. Participants with pickets and placards demonstrated for forty minutes after the meeting, directly behind government offices. Two young Christians were injured by a police tear-gas bomb.

During the Presbyterian Tong-hap prayer meeting in Saemunan Church, with twenty-five hundred pastors and Christians from all over the country, Rev. Kim Hyung-tae, echoing Acts 5:29 and 4:18–19, said, "We are here today in decision even for martyrdom. The Church obeys only God, not the [dictates of] the unjust state." They marched up Chongno Street in downtown Seoul, with candles and placards "against military autocracy, for democratic government." Police injured thirty-one demonstrators; twenty-one pastors were arrested.

Conservative churches actively joined the democratic struggle, holding prayer meetings in many cities and regions (Christian Institute for the Study of Justice and Development [CISJD] 1987b, 269–270). The council of churches in Chonnam Sinangun decided to hold prayer meetings until the April 13 declaration was retracted. In Taegu, a conservative area where many public officials come from, Presbyterian churches had a prayer meeting for two hours in the Taegu Cheil Church with fifteen hundred pastors and church members. After the prayer meeting there was a candlelit Cross March for Attaining a Democratic Constitution (a procession behind a raised cross) displaying denominational district flags. Demonstrators sang hymns and shouted "Overthrow military autocracy" and "Presidency with my votes." Street protests by Taegu Presbyterian Tong-hap churches, renowned for their conservatism, were unprecedented.

The conservative Holiness Church sent out a May 19, 1987, letter saying, "We repent of our sins of not having carried out the role of watchman for the country [referencing Ezekiel 33:1–9] and ask all the congregations to pray for the nation." On June 23, it held a prayer meeting in Holiness Hall and demonstrated on the street. Six pastors were arrested.

The Presbyterian Hap-tong denomination set aside five days, June 22 to 27, as a prayer week for the nation, requiring every local congregation to hold a fast or a decision prayer meeting daily. Its president's official letter declared, "The present political reality causes anxieties to the people and national development. This hinders the development of democracy. That is why we are starting a prayer gathering." The letter suggested "democratic political development," "conducting local autonomy elections," "preventing violations of human rights," and "abolition of torture" as prayer topics.

A major prayer meeting held in Kwangju showed conspicuous participation by conservative churches. The Kwangju Christian Committee for Mission Freedom (pastor Kim Chae-hyun, Presbyterian Kaehyuk, president) planned the meeting in the Kwangju YMCA gymnasium hall. When police prevented them from entering the hall, people began to demonstrate in the street. When the police fired a tear-gas bomb, old men, women, and children lay on the ground and began to pray. Those who ran from the tear gas regrouped, and suddenly a crowd of twenty thousand had gathered. The astonished police allowed a one-hour prayer meeting. Afterward, some fifty thousand people marched five hundred meters. Statements were issued rejecting the April 13 declaration and asking for freedom of the press, with 534 signatures representing fourteen Protestant denominations (interview 14).

People Power: The June 29 Declaration

Thus, church demonstrations were prominent in the June struggle. Although evangelicals formed only a part of the democratic struggle, they played an important role. Large demonstrations involving respectable citizens recalled People Power in the Philippines, which had swept Marcos out of office a year before. Roh Tae-woo, President Chun's anointed successor, disappeared from public view for several days. While he stayed in touch with Chun, Roh Tae-woo and a few confidants drafted a decidedly conciliatory declaration. This famed June 29 Declaration of Democratization and Reforms accepted direct presidential elections under a drastically amended, basically democratic constitution. This well-timed move adroitly defused explosive popular demands, at the very last moment averting humiliating political defeat—and possibly a huge bloodbath. Roh's lengthy reform declaration listed eight items: (1) direct presidential elections, (2) revision of the election law, (3) amnesty for dissidents and restoration of civil rights, (4) a new constitution strengthening all basic rights, (5) a new press law promoting press freedom, (6) local autonomy going ahead as scheduled, (7) a new political climate of dialogue, and (8) bold social reforms to build a clean society. The June 29 Declaration was a key victory for democratic transition.

How to Explain the Democratic Transition

Which model best explains the 1987 democratic transition? What factors were connected to the Korean churches? Several relevant models of distribution of power can be invoked to explain changing allocations of values and resources. A popular rule model (Mitchell 1970) suggests that each citizen participates in deliberations, with more or less equal voice. A pluralist interest-group model (Truman 1951) suggests that, as most individual citizens cannot participate directly, organized groups and associations serve as surrogates. A power elite model (Mosca 1939; Dye and Zeigler 1981, 3) suggests that the key political, economic, and social decisions are made by tiny minorities, the power elites.

Following Fritschler (1969), who emphasized the multiplicity of political arenas and agents, Pae (1992, 274) contends that no one model uniformly and consistently explains who has power and propounds a "political satellites" model to explain Korean democratization. Various groups in society revolved around the centers of power of two distinct camps, "for" and "against" democratization. Which coalition prevailed depended on the extensiveness and intensiveness of participation and commitment in each coalition. As those favoring democratization garnered heftier satellites, democratic transition became possible. Thus, as the pro-democracy coalition gained extensive support and intensive commitment, its resources finally overwhelmed and paralyzed the antidemocratic, pro-government patron-client coalition (277). Pae identifies key leaders and the opposition national assemblymen as an inner orbit; pro-democracy intellectuals, professors, students, and religious leaders are identified as a middle orbit; and pro-democracy workers and voters are classified as a distant, outer orbit of support.

In sum, Korean evangelicals had great impact because of their large and increasing numbers, their education, status, and connections in Korea, and their connection with the West. Korean evangelical contributions to democratization drew on churches' numerical strength, organizational capacities, international connections, and economic and financial resources. The way in which actors were networked within Korea and linked outside to Western actors was key to successful democratic transitions. Therefore, we now turn to a discussion of these networks, in which the Korean church was prominent.

The Korean Church's International Network

Protestant influences on democratization, as Huntington (1991) and others note, prominently include links with churches and other actors abroad. Korean church links with outside actors were crucial, both in influencing Korean churches and in giving those churches additional security and influence.

Woodberry (1999) argues that Protestant societies are particularly closely linked in networks of religious organizations, trade, political alliances, and so forth. Protestant nondemocracies link to older, solidly democratic, Protestant countries, exposing people to democratic ideals. Kang In-Chul (1996) argues that missionaries exerted decisive influence on the sociopolitical character of Korean Protestant churches, both by their support and by exerting control. Kang also argues that, from early on, the Korean state gave Protestant churches considerable autonomy and many privileges, while strongly controlling every other social sphere, because of Korea's structural dependency on the United States. But societies in which states intervene heavily in the religious sphere and in which civil society is relatively immature, churches, even in internal matters of doctrine and organizational structure, face a very different challenge than in the West. What role, then, was played in church contributions to the 1987 democratic transition by religious doctrine and by the Korean church's external links, especially with North America?

Huntington (1991) hypothesized that a growing Korean Christian population offered solid doctrinal and institutional bases for opposition to political oppression because Christianity promoted ideas of equality and respect for authority independent of the state. However, empirical evidence provides at best weak support for the thesis that Christian belief contributed to democratic sentiments among the mass of Korean Christians. One regression analysis based on a 1987 survey (K. Yi and Moon, 1994, 4) found age and level of education significant in explaining democratic orientation, whereas variables such as income, occupation, gender, and religious background had no independent predictive power. It may be impossible to parse out the mutual intercausation, and leaders may be different from the general population, but Yi and Moon concluded that the higher democratic orientation scores of most Christians were attributable not to their Christianity, but to their younger ages and higher educational levels.

Without rejecting Huntington's (1991) view that in the West Christianity promoted respect for authority independent of the state and provided a doctrinal and institutional basis for opposing political repression, one must recall East Asia's unique historical legacy. In the West, the principle of separation between church and state emerged from indigenous struggles for religious freedom; in Asia, that principle was often introduced under pressure from the West. Religious autonomy, resulting not from Christian doctrines, struggles or local consensus, was extended because of outside pressure and was often accorded to Christianity but not to traditional Eastern religions. On the other hand, Koreans do tend to associate Christianity with modernization, Westernization, and rapid industrialization, which made it easier for the church to resist political oppression.

The growth of Christianity helped build both international and national networks of support. The rapid growth of conservative churches in the 1970s and 1980s owed little to international support, but Western ties did help Korean Christians to protest the authoritarian regime. Pae (1992) argues that the Chun regime considered using military power to quell the popular uprising of 1987 but refrained from doing so because of U.S. pressure. Although its membership was a numerical minority, Christianity had a very secure place in the public arena. Being recognized as Christians helped dissidents avoid being branded pro-communist, and overseas religious organizations protected Christian dissidents. Non-Christian dissidents had less protective support. Military repression of Christians would have provoked international outcry and strong U.S. pressure. Churches' links with the outside world helped them retain a degree of immunity from government interference.

Networks among Churches and with Other Groups in Korean Society

Churches also had domestic organizations and networks, reinforced through the patterns of regular Sunday worship and interchurch links. Since the 1970s, progressive churches have contributed greatly to building civil society making public declarations about political issues, mobilizing Christian support, and forming coalitions among churches and with other groups. The mass of evangelical Christians, through church linkages, in effect supported progressive churches. When pastors and Christian students were jailed at a 1973 Easter service, the KNCC reacted strongly, mobilizing Christians of all stripes against the regime. In 1974, a group of Christian professors made a declaration about the national state, and the KNCC organized its

Committee for Human Rights. In 1976, a notable gathering of one hundred pro-democracy leaders—especially priests, university professors, and civic leaders—at a special Mass at Myongdong Cathedral commemorated the March 1 National Independence movement.

Christian leaders, students, and professors were key participants in the antimilitary, anti-Yushin coalition that issued a Democratic Peoples Charter in 1975, a Democratic Declaration to Save the Nation in 1976, and a March First Democratic Declaration in 1978. These declarations encouraged increasing numbers of citizens to join voluntary organizations, thus enlarging and energizing civil society. Sectors that had previously been indifferent to political problems, including professionals, technicians, independent business people, and even low-ranking public bureaucrats, began to identify with the goals of political democratization (Oh 1999, 90). This again illustrates the interaction between more and less evangelical parts of the Korean Church.

Similarly, during the 1970s, progressive churches indirectly contributed to the growth of conservative churches as their resistance to autocratic governance gave churches greater social credibility (interview 16). The actions and arguments of progressive churches also influenced conservative churches. In the 1970s, Christians could not bridge the chasms among different theological positions, but in the 1980s, the democratic movement widened beyond the KNCC and progressive churches (Chae 1995, 100). Stronger coalitions emerged as the KNCC, KEF, Christian students, Catholics, and others joined together. Many evangelicals also participated in democratization movements as individuals. An umbrella Korean Association of Protestant Churches began in 1987 and soon took an interest in social and political issues.

Extensive mobilization of civil society brought crucial pressure for democratic change (Diamond 1994, 5). A 1987 grand alliance exerted strong "people power" pressure on Chun's regime, reflecting an energized, autonomous, voluntary, and self-supporting civil society bound by shared values in which evangelical participation was crucial. Political dissidents, pastors, professors, and students, including members of conservative churches, supported the opposition party, the New Korean Democratic Party, which became the largest opposition bloc in the National Assembly following the February 1985 elections. This bloc was led by the two best-known opposition leaders, Kim Dae-Jung and Kim Young-Sam, both Christian and both long-time democratic reformers.

Middle-Class Participation, Economic Factors, and Democratization

Huntington (1991, 65–66) suggests several reasons economic development is conducive to democracy. Development fosters feelings of interpersonal trust, life satisfaction, and competence, all of which correlate strongly with the existence of democratic institutions. Development raises education levels and provides more resources for distribution among social groups, facilitating accommodation and compromise. Economic development also promotes the opening of societies to foreign trade, investment, technology, communications, and a growing middle class, conditions that many scholars have long suggested are conducive to democratization (Lipset 1959, 1994).

Empirical evidence from East Asia lends additional support to the view that democratization is facilitated, though not caused, by economic growth (Curtis 1997, 141). A growing middle class, a more diverse society, and development of civil forces were concomitants of Korea's very rapid economic growth. In the 1987 democratic transition, journalists reported an important new phenomenon: Many demonstrators were solid middle-class citizens (Oh 1999, 92). The middle class had previously kept its distance from street clashes. But after the torture-death of Park Chong-Chol, a Seoul National University (SNU) survey reported that 85.7 percent of the middle class wanted to protect human rights even at the cost of economic growth (*Hankook Ilbo*, June 9, 1987).

Cleavages between institutionalized politics and civil society help explain the Korean democratic transition. As Im Hyung-Baeg (1996) points out, a "crisis of economic success" plagued military rule, illustrating what Haggard and Kaufman (1995) call "authoritarian withdrawal in good times." Economic failures in Latin America forced some dictators to relinquish power. But even as economic success and industrialization in Korea led the military to include the rapidly expanding middle class in the political process (Shin 1999, 249), the middle class became fed up with the authoritarian state and its excesses. Middle-class civil dissidents supplied the prime energy for democratic change (Han 1995, 12). Countries experiencing a "crisis of success" are often better prepared for democratic consolidation than those in a "crisis of failure."

Korean Christianity grew rapidly during the postwar period, especially during the 1960s and 1970s. There were three hundred thousand Protestants (and a few Catholics) in the entire peninsula in 1945. By 1960, the Protestant population of South Korea was six hundred thousand. But by 1974 there were 3.5 million Protestants and eight hundred thousand Catholics, roughly 13 percent of the population. Protestants plateaued at almost 8.9 million by 1983 (8.76 million is the figure given for 1995; see Table 5.2).

A large proportion of the Korean educated middle class came from Christian backgrounds. Women, young people, urban dwellers (especially in metropolitan cities), and the educated have higher percentages of Protestants than other religious groups in Korea (Gallup 1984, 1988, 1990). The middle class grew from 19.6 percent in 1960 to 39.6 percent in 1990, taking education and average household income as criteria (Hong 1992), and Protestants had the highest percentage of middle-class people. A 1992 SNU Institute for Population and Development survey of religion and social class found 57.6

TABLE 5.2. The Growth of the Korean Protestant Church, 1970–1983

Year	Protestant Population	Growth Rate per Year	Number of Churches	Growth Rate per Year	Protestant Share in the Population
1960	623,072	—	5,011	—	—
1965	812,254	6%	6,581	6.3%	6.1%
1970	3,192,621	59%	12,866	19.1%	18.6%
1975	4,019,303	5%	16,089	5.0%	15.9%
1976	4,658,700	16%	17,846	10.9%	17.8%
1977	5,001,491	7%	19,457	9.0%	18.3%
1978	5,293,844	6%	20,109	3.4%	13.8%
1979	5,986,609	13%	21,205	5.5%	20.2%
1980	7,180,627	20%	21,243	0.2%	23.5%
1981	7,637,010	6%	23,346	9.9%	25.6%
1982	8,676,699	14%	24,031	2.9%	—
1983	8,889,194	3%	25,746	7.1%	—

Source: J. Chung (1987).

percent middle class among Protestants, compared to 38.7 percent among Buddhists and 44.5 percent among those without religious affiliation. Church growth may not have been an independent source of Korean democratization, but the development of a Protestant middle class propelled evangelical churches into the public sphere (interview 7).

In sum, networks of "people power," encompassing political parties, and civil society effected democratic transition, and it is hard to discuss those networks without including the Korean church. Christians, especially those belonging to progressive churches, led in the democratization movement during the 1970s (interview 3). In the 1980s, the churches played a role in the growth of a middle class and of improving education levels. Especially in the June 1987 struggle, evangelical Christianity seems to have played a significant role as an organizing and mediating force during the military regime's crisis of legitimacy (interviews 1, 2, and 7). Christian students and members of progressive churches, neither of which was numerically large, exercised significant influence on politics and society during most of the democratization struggle. In addition, the more numerous evangelicals were an influential force in the People's Uprising of 1987.

Evangelical Christians and Electoral Behavior Since 1987

What has characterized evangelical Christians' electoral behavior since 1987? Evangelical voters are not a unified bloc, and the voting patterns are complex, but politicians pay attention because many voters are evangelicals (Martin 1999, 39).

After Roh's June 29, 1987, democratic declaration, street demonstrations decreased strikingly. As the December presidential elections approached, serious friction developed between Kim Young-Sam and Kim Dae-Jung. Policy differences played a role—D. J. Kim was more progressive and Y. S. Kim more conservative—and although the two would not say so publicly, much of the disagreement was over who should be the opposition party candidate.

The KEF and many other conservative churches insisted that churches should not become involved in partisan politics by supporting any particular candidate. Movement groups and the progressive wing of Korean Protestantism initially split into three camps, each advocating a different electoral strategy.

One camp supported Kim Dae-Jung as the more progressive candidate. This included the famed Korean Students Christian Fellowship, other student groups, some *Minjung* theologians, and some evangelical pastors who formed a People's Movement Coalition for Democracy and Reunification (PMCDR). Ham Suk-Hon and Moon Ik-Hwan became the PMCDR's advisors; fifty-nine Protestant pastors, such as Kim Yong-bok, Kang Ku-Chul, and Yi Man-Sin, and twelve Catholic priests, such as Ki Chun and Che Jung-Ku, served on the executive committee (CISJD 1988). Ahn Byung-Moo, a famous *Minjung* theologian, Democratic activists, and many prominent figures actively supported Kim Dae-Jung: 5,639 people lent their names to the PMCDR effort. Kim Dae-Jung was also endorsed by fifteen groups affiliated with the PMCDR: twenty-one groups (seven of them specifically Protestant) in the Korean Women's Groups Coalition, seven labor movement groups, the National University Students Federation, serving as an umbrella group for other student groups, 223 Buddhist monks, and 202 Catholic priests.

A second camp argued that the "electability," not the progressiveness, of a candidate was crucial; the most essential goal was to defeat Roh Tae-Woo. They insisted that the two Kims settle on a single candidate through negotiations (Kim Sun-Hyuk 2000, 97). Many people, including professors, pastors, monks, social activists, journalists, writers, lawyers, and some student groups (the Seoul Labor Movement Coalition and the Fellowship of Christian Youth) took this position. Twenty Protestant pastors, including many key leaders in the KNCC (e.g., Park Hyung-Kyu, Oh Chung-Il, Kim Dong-Wan, In Myung-Jin), and eighteen Catholic priests, such as Chung Ho-Kyung, Park Chang-Sin, and Ham Se-Ung, actively participated. A smaller, third camp that included many radical student groups and labor unions deeply distrusted political society and wanted to have an independent "people's candidate." But the second and third camps later merged and pushed for a grand compromise.

As Table 5.3 shows, if either had run and the other supported him, Roh would have been decisively defeated. But the two Kims did not come to terms; both ran, splitting the large opposition vote. Roh Tae-Woo won with 36.6 percent of the total votes cast! The grand coalition that brought about democratic transition fell apart in the presidential elections.

TABLE 5.3. Popular Vote in the 1987 Presidential Election (%)

Roh, Tae-Woo	Kim, Young-Sam	Kim, Dae-Jung	Kim, Jong-Phil
36.6	28	27.1	8.1

Religion and Electoral Behavior in 1987 and 1992

We do not have the empirical data to sort out clearly how religion affected voting in these presidential elections. Oddly, virtually all mass-sample election surveys failed to include a religion variable. But we get some insight from interviews and elite surveys.

In the 1987 presidential election, So Ui-Hyun, the general president of Chogyechong, the largest Korean Buddhist sect, publicly supported Roh Tae-Woo, a Buddhist. The Catholic Priests' Association for Justice, which had played a key role in the democratization movement and had exposed the torture death of Park Chong-Chul and the regime's cover-up, openly supported Kim Dae-jung, a devout Catholic.

What about evangelicals? In a 1988 nationwide random sample of 452 Protestants by Om Sung-Chul (1989), most rated Kim Young-Sam higher than other presidential candidates. Pastors and elders were even more likely to prefer Kim Young-Sam. Overall, 76.2 percent of respondents said they would prefer to have a Christian president. A separate survey by the CISJD (1987a) showed a triumphalist orientation: 75.2 percent of Christian (Protestant) pastors (n=787) and 89.6 percent of laity (n=1,783) thought that Korea should be a Christian nation.

Table 5.4 displays an Institute for Modern Society poll of the party preferences of clergy and persons with religious vocations, both in 1990 and retrospectively for 1988. Protestant pastors said they favored Kim Young-Sam's Democratic Party (55.7 percent) in 1988; Buddhist monks, Roh Tae-Woo's Democracy and Justice Party (58.2 percent). A marked plurality of Catholic priests favored Kim Dae-Jung's Peace Democracy Party (43.8 percent). After a three-party merger in 1990, Protestant pastors favored the newly reconstituted (merged) ruling party (Ryu 1990, 57–59), perhaps because Kim Young-Sam had joined it.

There were no military and no Buddhist presidential candidates in 1992. Buddhist voters that year generally fell into two camps: some objected to supporting a Christian as president; others thought there was no alternative to Kim Young-Sam, the ruling party candidate (I. Kang 2000a, 165). Historically, Korean Buddhists' formal organizations have tended to support the ruling party.

In 1992, most progressive Christians supported Kim Dae-Jung, although a few favored Kim Young-Sam. For many progressive Christians, what

TABLE 5.4. Support of Religious Groups for Various Candidates, 1988 and 1990

			Group Expressing Preference		
Party Name	Candidate	Religion of Candidate	Buddhist Monks	Protestant Pastors	Catholic Priests
1988: Election for National Assembly					
Democratic Justice	Roh Tae-Woo	Buddhist	58.2%	14.8%	10.2%
Democracy	Kim Young-Sam	Protestant	7.5	55.7	23.4
Peace and Democracy	Kim Dae-Jung	Catholic	9.0	27.3	43.8
Republic	Kim Jong-Phil	Protestant	14.2	1.7	1.6
Others			2.9	0	6.2
No Answer			8.2	0.6	14.1
Total			100.0%	100.0%	100.0%
1990: After the Three-Party Merger					
Democratic Liberty	(three candidates)		41.0%	34.1%	8.6%
	Roh Tae-Woo	Buddhist			
	Kim Young-Sam	Protestant			
	Kim Jong-Phil	Protestant			
Peace and Democracy	Kim Dae-Jung	Catholic	7.8	21.0	25.0
Democratic			10.1	9.7	18.0
No Preference			41.1	35.2	48.4
Total			100.0%	100.0%	100.0%

Source: Institute for Modern Society, "Research on Party Preferences of Clergy and Persons with Religious Vocations" (1990).

mattered was not the candidate's religion but his ideology and political commitments. Key members in the KNCC, such as Oh Chung-Il, Kim Dong-Wan, and Kim Sang-Kun, and the progressive Protestant churches organized a Christian Coalition for Producing Democratic Government (CCPDG), which wanted a regime change in the presidential election and saw the ruling Democratic Liberal Party as an extension of the military regime; they did not support Kim Young-Sam, its candidate. The CCPDG also criticized the People's Party (whose candidate, Chung Ju-Young, was chairman of Hyundai). By implication, the CCPDG supported Kim Dae-Jung.

An analysis of numerous interviews (e.g., interviews 1 and 6) suggests that many influential church members actively supported Kim Young-Sam. Most evangelical leaders spoke in favor of Kim Young-Sam, largely because he was a Protestant elder (in the Chung Hyun Church, a Presbyterian Hap-tong megachurch). Chung Hyun's founder, Rev. Kim Chang-In, did not officially support Kim Young-Sam, but some elders did (evidently with Rev. Kim's blessing; interview 9). The National Association of Protestant Elders supported Kim Young-Sam (interview 3). Some evangelical and progressive pastors and elders, such as In Myung-Jin and Han Yong-Sang, organized an election movement for him (interview 4). When Paik Hwa-Jong, editor in chief of the *Kookmin* daily newspaper, wrote an editorial column criticizing Kim Young-Sam, many Protestants called him up to protest (interview 2).

Rev. Cho Yong-Gi, senior pastor of the largest megachurch, the Yoido Full Gospel Church (now with 750,000 members), told the Christian Revival Association that Christianity should rise high in Korean politics. Christians should be in Congress and an elder should be president (Cho's speech, October 18, 2000). A number of National Assembly candidates visited the church. Cho sometimes signaled his preference for particular candidates who were evangelical Christians, usually those who attended the Yoido Full Gospel Church. He did not explicitly support Kim Young-Sam in 1992, but Yoido church members were in no doubt about whom he supported.

Korean political leaders tend to use religion to market themselves. Some scholars think that during the 1992 campaign, Kim Young-Sam politicized his religion (interview 5). Kim would say, "I will let Christian hymns to be sung instead of Buddhist hymns if I get into the Blue House." This appeal to Christians manifested a kind of corporatism (interview 5), which other religious groups naturally disliked. Some conservative Christians liked it; others strongly disapproved.

Politicians court evangelicals because of their numerical strength, which is nearly 20 percent of the population. The Yoido Full Gospel Church staged a prayer rally for the world in crisis in Chamsil Stadium on October 19, 2001 (a month after the September 11 attacks), which some 120,000 members and one hundred major church leaders attended. Many politicians, including almost all major political leaders, attended, conscious perhaps of parliamentary by-elections slated for October 25 in three districts. Participants included Han Kwang-Ok, representative of the Millennium Democratic Party (MDP), Lee Hoi-Chang, president of the historically dominant Grand National Party (GNP), Kim Jong-Phil, the president of the United Liberal Democrat Party (ULDP), Nam Kung-Jin, government minister for Culture and Tourism, and more than twenty other MPs. President Kim Dae-Jung, at an Asia-Pacific Economic Cooperation summit at the time, sent a video message asking for intercessory prayer.

The proper norm for political participation by evangelical churches is to establish a voice that, while articulating legitimate, appropriate institutional interests, also has as its main focus raising concern for justice and for moral principles. But political elites try to cultivate religious groups, and some church leaders are influenced by religious loyalties. Local autonomy and election of local officials may well have strengthened this political use of religion. This is unfortunate, as trying to mobilize religious groups for political ends generates fruitless conflict, just as Korean regional rivalries have done in the past.

Regionalism and Korean Elections

Korean politics has been dominated by parties that attract strong regional support, which affects voting far more than religion does. Although we have no empirical survey data to prove that evangelical Christians' voting responds more to regional than religious affiliations, some data strongly suggest it. Interviews during the 1992 presidential election show that most evangelicals—like people of every kind—supported the candidate from their region: voters in the Honam, or Cholla, region supported Kim Dae-Jung, who is from that region. For instance, members of the Presbyterian Kaehyuk (Reform) churches based in Honam Province voted for Kim Dae-Jung (interview 11); he took 95 percent of the vote in South Cholla. A similar pattern affected support in other regions and for other candidates in elections for MPs in 1988, 1992, and 1996 (Moon 1996). Regional affiliation, rather than class, gender, religion, or even ideology, has been the strongest basis on which political parties attracted votes.

There are various explanations for this preference. Some scholars (e.g., Park Chan-Wook 1996) note that politicians' election strategies purposely exploited regional conflict. The competition between two ideologically similar parties (Kim Young-Sam's Unification Democracy Party and Kim Dae-Jung's Peace Democracy Party) may also have contributed to regionalism's substantial importance.

Until the June 29, 1987, declaration, diverse forces from the middle class to industrial laborers participated in pro-democracy protests. However, after the declaration, moderate political elites conducted negotiations with the old regime. Activists' attempts to participate were unsuccessful, and the discussion of democracy was narrowly focused, confined to steps toward (incomplete) procedural democracy, and securing some rights of political assembly (e.g., an end to the banning of political activities by labor unions). Attempts to develop progressive political parties were blocked.

Opposition and ruling (military) parties competed by exploiting regional loyalties. Chang Hun (1997, 265–267) has evidence tracing this process since 1987. Some (Kim Yong-Hak 1989) argue that the state's growth strategy during rapid industrialization created uneven development and fostered regional conflicts; others argue that such structural factors don't sufficiently explain how regions became linked to particular political parties. People from Cholla certainly believe that over the past forty years, the Kyungsan region was strongly favored in industrial projects and that Cholla was neglected or even deliberately discriminated against. All the presidents and most high-level leaders in Korea prior to Kim Dae-Jung's election came from the Kyungsan region—and indeed, from a particular high school in that region! But the Cholla (Honam)-Kyungsan rivalry is very old and very deep, dating perhaps as far back as the unification of the peninsula in the seventh century. At work, especially in government offices, there are typically mutual support and social associations based on family provincial origin. Parents from Cholla, or Kyungsan, are often opposed to their children's marrying the children of people from the rival region, or even associating too much with them at university, although both families may have lived in Seoul for years, or even generations.

Table 5.5 shows the strong regional influence in the 1987 and 1992 presidential elections. Kim Young-Sam's origins in Kyungnam Province made him the local favorite in both Kyungbuk (North Kyungsan) and Kyungnam (South Kyungsan) provinces, except when Roh, who was from Kyungbuk, ran. In the 1997 presidential election, Kim Dae-Jung took 95 percent of the vote in his home province. Arguably, the percentage for Kim Young-Sam was at least as high in his home province, allowing for people from other regions who

TABLE 5.5. Regional Vote in 1987 and 1992 Presidential Elections (%)

Thirteenth Presidential Election (1987)

Candidates (Candidates' Provinces)	Roh Tae-Woo (Kyungbuk)	Kim Young-Sam (Kyungnam)	Kim Dae-Jung (Honam [Cholla])	Kim Jong-Phil (Chungchong)
Nationally (All Korea)	36.6	28.0	27.0	8.1
Seoul and Kyong-Ki	33.7	28.2	28.0	8.2
Chungchong	32.2	19.5	11.6	**33.7**
Kwangwon	57.9	25.5	8.6	5.3
Honam (Cholla)	9.6	1.2	**86.2**	0.5
Kyungbuk	**66.8**	26.1	2.4	2.3
Kyungnam	35.9	**52.8**	6.8	2.6

Fourteenth Presidential Election (1992)

Candidates (Candidates' Provinces)	Chung Ju-Young (Kangwon)	Kim Young-Sam (Kyungnam)	Kim Dae-Jung (Honam [Cholla])	Others
Nationally (All Korea)	16.3	42.0	33.8	7.9
Seoul and Kyong-Ki	19.8	36.0	34.8	9.4
Chungchong	23.8	36.2	27.3	12.7
Kwangwon	**33.5**	40.8	15.2	10.5
Honam (Cholla)	2.3	4.2	**90.9**	2.6
Kyungbuk	17.0	**61.6**	8.7	12.7
Kyungnam	8.8	**72.1**	10.8	8.3

Source: National Central Committee for Election (1994)

Note: Percentages for provincial favorites (local sons) are shown in boldface have settled there recently for economic reasons. Clearly, regional rivalries are a significant impediment to Korean democratization.

Predominant Evangelical Political Orientation

Most evangelical Christians take a cautious, moderate political stance, as Paik's 1994 survey of Protestant Christians' political and social consciousness shows (n = 2,000). Paik called this "critical conservatism," a dissatisfaction with existing political realities, coupled with dislike of radical political change. Paik showed also that the level of political participation by Korean Christians was very low. Some evangelical Christians have actively worked for fair elections (see below), but many, like other Koreans, vote based on personalities. That tendency was pervasive and nationwide, but stronger among men than among women and stronger among those with higher education (Paik 1994). In Korea, parties are often little more than symbols around which candidates rally their supporters. The parties remain the weakest link in the democratic process, standing for little beyond their leaders' *ex cathedra* pronouncements (Steinberg 1998, 80). As a consequence, rather than choosing candidates on the basis of policy differences or their effectiveness in securing real and useful results, Koreans are vulnerable to demagoguery and swayed by religious or regional loyalties.

Some evangelical groups see prayer as a means to reform political culture. Christian Embassy, a mission organization founded by some evangelical leaders in 1999 for political and economic leaders, started an intercessory prayer movement for MPs (*Kookmin*, daily newspaper, July 17, 2001). These evangelicals believe that praying for political leaders is one significant way for them to participate in democratization if sincere prayers are directed toward national unity and the fostering of just, democratic institutions.

Evangelical Christians and Political Society: Kim Young-Sam and Other Evangelical Politicians

Political parties in Korea characteristically have been personality-driven and ephemeral. Parties have been tied to a single leader, existing largely to promote his or her victory. But top-down imposition of policies is often unsuccessful. Effective presidential influence depends on bureaucratic actors who have considerable autonomy, and on public opinion. Many principal opposition movement leaders, such as Kim Young-Sam and Kim Dae-Jung, have been Christians who championed democracy for decades, becoming symbols of the democratic movement and exercising symbolic and practical leadership.

TABLE 5.6. Percentage of Votes Received in Presidential Election (1992)

Candidates	Kim Young-Sam	Kim Dae-Jung	Chung Ju-Young	Park Chong-Chan
Votes Received	42	33.8	16.3	6.4
Candidates	Paek Wan-Gi	Kim Ok-Son	Yi Byung-Sung	
Votes Received	1	0.4	0.1	

The president's religious affiliation has sometimes affected church-state relations inappropriately. This may reflect Korea's long history of state control of intellectual and religious doctrine. Various long-lasting dynasties promoted Buddhism, or Confucianism, as Korea's official philosophy, often suppressing rival schools of thought, and Japanese colonialism made an official cult of Shinto. North Korea has also made a cult of sorts out of veneration for "Great Leader" Kim Il-Sung and his son, the "Dear Leader" Kim Jong-Il. In postwar South Korea, the first republic accepted a separation between politics and religion in principle, but in practice, this was constantly marred by one-sided support given to Christianity and a repressive policy toward other religions. The second republic was also pro-Christian. The third to sixth republics were pro-Buddhist. The Kim Young-Sam government was evaluated by some as pro-Protestant.

Kim Young-Sam was the first fairly elected civilian president after thirty-two years of military domination, receiving 42 percent of the popular vote; his democratic reforms as president strengthened Korean democracy. Kim Dae-Jung finished second, with 33.8 percent, trailed by Chung Ju-Young, with 16.3 percent (see Table 5.6). Until the year before the election, Kim was an important leader of the democratic political opposition. His thirty-year career of defying the authoritarian state was facilitated by the relative safety afforded by operating within the structures of the Protestant churches (Brouwer, Gifford, and Rose 1996, 109). How Kim Young-Sam's faith influenced his actions and democratic reforms as president merits detailed examination.

Kim Young-Sam's Evangelical Commitments and Roots

Did Kim Young-Sam's Christian faith affect political reforms and the democratization of Korea during his presidency? Kim Young-Sam says his democratic vision was influenced by his religious beliefs and his suffering. Christian faith appears to have been significant in his life and political career. Many people I interviewed did not know whether Kim's democratic beliefs and struggle were directly affected by his Christian convictions, but generally found his democratic reforms consonant with Christian values (interview 4).

Kim has a devout family background. His paralyzed grandfather was healed upon receiving prayers and later founded the Sin Myong Church (interview 14; Kim Young-Sam 2000, 94). Kim's wedding took place in a church, which was highly unusual in Korea at the time. His wife, Son Myung-Sun, was a dedicated Christian from her earliest years. In the course of two special interviews with him, spanning more than four hours in August 2001, I asked Kim who influenced his Christian faith most. He replied, "It was my mother. She was illiterate, but was able to memorize and read the verses of hymns. She liked to hear the Bible. I put her favorite Bible in her tomb, as her will directed." Kim became an elder in a Korean megachurch, the Chung Hyun Church, Presbyterian Hap-tong, in 1978, and there was schooled in a Calvinist theology of society.

Kim held prayer services for the smooth start of the civilian government on the first Sunday after his inauguration as president (Kim Young-Sam 2001a, 65). Every Sunday, he invited Protestant pastors to hold a service in the Blue House.[4] He told me that he had never skipped Sunday services during his presidency, even on overseas visits. "I visited Czech Republic... [as president, in March 1995]. Many Korean residents there warmly welcomed me... [at] the Prague airport.... The next day a Korean pastor studying there led a Sunday service in my lodging place" (Kim Young-Sam 2001b, 42).

Kim often asked various prominent evangelical pastors to pray for him and the nation. He says in his autobiography, "I am still thankful to those pastors for their helping me to lead the country with courage by prayer and wisdom from God's words during my presidency. I endeavored continuously to lead a life of abstinence and moderation as a Christian.... In particular I am most grateful to Rev. Cho Yong-Gi and Kim Chang-Hwan. Those two pastors gave me great help with prayer when the country was at stake.... I used to receive prayer on the phone before important meetings or statements usually by pastor Cho Yong-Gi and Kim Chang-Hwan" (2001b, 387).

Kim's Christian Faith and His Struggle for Democracy in Korea

Faith played a role not just in Kim Young-Sam's five-year presidency but also in his thirty-year struggle in the democracy movement, in which faith motivated and sustained his struggle:

> During the early stages of my life as a politician, many conservative Christians and pastors, including the senior pastor of the church I was attending persecuted me, saying that Christians should not participate in politics.... There were many pains during my democratic struggle; however, the power by which I was able to stand against those pains and persecutions was my Christian faith. During my house arrest for nearly 3 years, I read the Bible over and over. I could not help reading the Bible. The Bible gave me power and

comfort. Christian faith gave me conviction and courage that there was nothing to be afraid of. (interview 14)

Kim identified democracy as the most important value in building a healthy society, and he emphasized that his courage and conviction for democratic struggle were inspired by Christian values. Individual conviction exerted more influence on his democratic struggle than opportunities or organizational context. The most difficult period for him was the period of house arrest (1979–1982). The military government prevented him from meeting with people, and faith sustained him in his loneliness and troubles. One verse, Isaiah 41:10, encouraged him most: "Do not fear, for I am with you; do not be dismayed, for I am your God. I will strengthen you and help you; I will uphold you with my righteous right hand" (interview 14).

Kim Young-Sam's Democratic Vision and Reforms as President

President Kim's inaugural address on February 25, 1993, outlined his aims for democratic consolidation, envisioning "a New Korea." The New Korea he sketched was a sharing community, working and living together in harmony, in which justice would flow like a river (referring to Amos 5:24). Kim told me that this concept stemmed from his faith: "The New Korea aimed for 'clean government' and 'clean nation,' and I think it was closely related to my Christian faith. The core idea of the New Korea was to restore the spirit of Puritan Christian faith. For example, I did not allow any politicians to receive political funds. And I am still proud of that" (interview 14).

Kim's notion of democracy went beyond a minimalist definition of democracy that many scholars use, following Dahl (1971). Kim Young-Sam thought that democratic consolidation required building a true moral community and the removal of every vestige or enclave of authoritarianism. Purification and purgation were central to his thinking, suggesting that attaining democratic ideals proceeded from individual ethical values and practices. Elite convergence and institutionalization, conversely, did not figure prominently in his discourse.

In *Polyarchy*, Dahl (1971, 128–188) argues that the beliefs of political activists are a key element in regime change, and much subsequent research supports this. How was Kim's vision translated into concrete reforms? Hahn Bae-Ho (1997, 2–7) summarizes six changes of Kim Young-Sam's democratization reforms: (1) depoliticization of the military, (2) replacing political unrest with political stability, (3) moving from centralized rule to regional autonomy, (4) moving from coercion to compromise, (5) moving from surveillance to respect for public opinion, and (6) moving from an all-powerful executive branch to party politics. Kim's own view was that his greatest achievements during the presidency were reform of the military, his policy on Real Name accounts, and moral cleanliness in not receiving political funds (interview 14). However, I classify his major accomplishments under four headings: Real Name reform, local autonomy, election reform, and reform of the military:

> Real Name Reform: Korean inheritance tax was often evaded by the very wealthy using a technically legal process of registering assets under fictitious names. The Reform of Real Names was a law abolishing this common practice, which had facilitated political corruption as well as tax evasion.
>
> Local Autonomy: Kim actively supported enactment of local autonomy legislation. Under authoritarian rule, local government at the state, city, or town level was in effect merely a local administrative arm of the central government. It was generally unresponsive to the local people it governed and often oblivious to essential local planning and economic needs. Local autonomy legislation provided for election of key local officials, previously appointed by the central government, and placed much more decision-making power in local hands.
>
> Election Reform: Kim's election campaign, "the campaign to rectify the past," began in October 1995, with investigations of political slush funds amassed by former president Roh Tae-Woo and later those of Chun Doo Hwan. Chun was sentenced to life in prison and Roh to seventeen years in prison. These reforms were steps toward making public officials, even at the highest level, accountable to serve the public interest and obey the law.
>
> Reduction of Military Interference in Politics: President Kim Young-Sam's reform of the military was among the most important achievements of his presidency. Many new democracies are threatened, explicitly or implicitly, by a military establishment that considers itself the guardian and arbiter of the national interest (Diamond, Linz, and Martin 1995, 46). Transition to democracy from a military regime depends on whether civilian control of the military succeeds. Some Latin American countries have been plagued by military interventions in politics even after a democratic transition. Kim realized the importance of eliminating military power from politics and writes in his autobiography that he knew his thorough plan to defuse the power of the military was risky (Kim Young-Sam 2001a, 125). As soon as Kim became president, he dismantled the *Hanahwoe* (the "One Association"), a private, secret organization within the army that had great influence. Doing so was important for averting military subversion and coups, and therefore also enabled civilian authority to operate more independently of military views and demands.

Progress in these four concrete issue areas had lasting impact and translated Kim's vision into practice. However, his desire to build the moral community of a New Korea also had problems and encountered setbacks, and he was involved in significant failures, mistakes, and discouragements in the course of his presidency.

Mistakes, Failures, Disappointments, and Limitations in Kim Young-Sam's Presidency and Democratic Reforms

Kim's moral vision has not, in fact, been very effective in consolidating democratic institutions and legitimating democratic values. His political party had ties with previous conservative authoritarian rulers. The Democratic Liberal Party emerged from a coalition with a previous ruling party controlled by military leaders. Kim Young-Sam shrewdly joined with that ruling party to extend his power base. With this coalition of political powers, he won the election, but his alliance with the former foes of democracy necessarily compromised his stands, which limited his policies and reforms (Kang Wi-Jo 1997, 144). Kim himself noted these difficulties: "I felt that reform was more difficult than revolution. Many people supported Real Name reform, but once I began the policy, many opposing forces emerged. They thought that the policy would not bring them benefit. I began to know that many people objected to policies when their vested interests were threatened. The most difficult people were conservative forces and forces of vested interests" (interview 14).

The grand alliance of conservative and progressive groups that ushered in the Kim Young-Sam government circumscribed how reforms proceeded. They were "reforms from above" in a situation in which the very problem was top-down governance. Kim acknowledges that his attempts to build a New Korea tended to revolve around his personal decisions—again, a top-down and unaccountable method—rather than becoming institutionalized. He argues that this was unintended and beyond his control (interview 14). In a passage that recalls Lázaro Cárdenas's ironic defense of his having included the military as one of the four leading sectors of the PRI (Cárdenas reminded critics that it had been the one and only effective political force in Mexico before his reforms). Kim complains:

> Some scholars may not understand the reality of politics. For example, in regard to military reform, I could not say anything about it before I became the president. During the Chun regime, one general called all the congressmen who belonged to the National Security Committee to the party. There, all the congressmen were beaten up by military soldiers and nobody could reveal the event at that time. The military power was absolute. Also, in regard to the Real Name

Reform, if the reform was known beforehand, it was impossible to execute the reform. So I had to make major decisions alone.

One can argue that Kim carried out democratic reforms by personal fiat because Korean political society was dominated by conservatism. In addition, his ruling party was deeply divided, one group moving toward reforms, while another group was moving toward conservatism (Choi Jang-jip 1996, 251). When "reforms from above" were implemented, these heterogeneous coexisting elements hindered the reforms. By making himself the personal center of rule and retaining power by direct appeals to the people, Kim Young-Sam ignored the mediating process rather than working through the political system, transforming his political reforms into mere populism (Kim Se-Jung 1999, 128).

Lee Jeong-Jin (2000) argues that institutional democracy is closely related to popular support rather than personal ability. Public support became a crucial resource of power for President Kim Young-Sam. In the early part of his term, he drew on strong popular support to carry out reform. But as public support gradually declined after 1994, Kim's influence within the ruling group weakened, and he frequently shifted his position in making important decisions, following public opinion. This weakening support arose, in part, from scandals in his administration, including one (linked to the failure of Hanbo Steel, Inc.) involving bribery and tax evasion by Kim's son. Public approval declined markedly, as Table 5.7 shows. When the South Korean economy went into crisis in 1997, Kim lost almost all his presidential authority.

Kim Young-Sam's uncompleted attempt at democratic consolidation suggests that democratic procedures will not be effectively institutionalized unless the particularistic political habits and corrupt practices of the authoritarian past are transformed into community-oriented and universalistic ones (Han 1995, 203). In acknowledging that he failed to inculcate people with democratic consciousness—for instance, low-ranking government officials were still willing to receive bribes—Kim says that many Korean people seem

TABLE 5.7. Polls Evaluating Kim Young-Sam's Performance as President (%)

Date of Survey	Good	Normal	Bad	Don't Know
May 1993	84.2	9.8	3.4	2.6
Sept. 1993	82.7	7.6	5.9	3.8
Nov. 1994	42.7	25.6	25.9	5.8
Apr. 1995	44.9	9.0	41.7	4.5
Sept. 1995	33.3	16.2	45.2	5.3
Nov. 1996	27.4	27.7	36.7	8.2
Mar. 1997	8.8	8.8	73.2	9.2

Source: Gallup Korea, "Polls Evaluating Kim Young-Sam's Performance as President" (1997).

to be still conforming to the old legacies of bad habits (interview 14). Kim complains that he had great difficulty meeting people's high expectations for democratic reforms. Despite those high expectations, he continues, people failed to support him when his reforms jeopardized their own vested interests. Yet Kim's democratic attempt was also hindered by particularistic interests of his own, including his son's improper actions and his imprisonment of his two immediate predecessors. Kim's rule was also compromised by the inclusion of long-time antidemocratic forces, and it can be argued that this arose from Kim's willingness to relax his principles and democratic commitments to ensure he would gain power (interview 14).

Kim Young-Sam's democratic reforms were like the "delegative democracy" O'Donnell (1994) describes. They were based on the leader's personal decisions, without much involvement from political parties and institutionalized systems. Whether or not there is a core group supporting reform is an essential factor in determining its ultimate success or failure (Hahn 1997, 10). Neither the apparatus of Kim's ruling party nor the bureaucrats were committed supporters of Kim's reforms. The president was his own key supporter; he had to generate support anew for each new issue. In sum, Kim Young-Sam failed to build a broad alliance that could have undergirded his democratic reforms.

Kim's institutional reforms have failed to bring about substantive democratization. As his successes thoroughly infuriated many authoritarians, his failures disenchanted many democrats. The Kim Young-Sam government ended up immensely unpopular. Kim felt anguished when he resigned his presidency, although his Christian faith helped him overcome those difficult periods (interview 14).

Kim states that the concept of democracy he had before becoming president changed as a result of holding office: he learned that direct election of the president and the freedom of the press were not sufficient for democracy; a mature democratic consciousness in the population was important as well (interview 14). Some critics insist that Kim Young-Sam's personality structure was authoritarian, that in the course of strife against military dictators, he had developed a nonliberal character, in effect picking up the ways of his foes (Kim Se-Jung 1999). A person's general democratic convictions are one thing; capacity and willingness to effect democratic reforms is another. A shadow falls between the dream and the reality. Democratic realities and practices are hard to realize out of one's hoped-for democratic ideals.

A new democracy normally faces great challenges because of the legacy of the past regime (Rose, Shin, and Munro 1998, 3). The experience of Kim's democratic reforms shows how hard it is to consolidate democracy, and how difficult it is to break with an authoritarian past and destructive cultural values. Balancing self-interests with the common good in its details can be even more difficult than installing democratic mechanisms initially. After democratic procedures are in place, popular dissatisfaction with public performance and public officials may remain, and developing adequate ways to respond to public concerns remains a daunting challenge. Both Kim Young-Sam's democratic reforms and his failures highlight the importance of a democratic culture of political parties and a mature democratic consciousness in a country's population. Seung characterizes the democratic reforms of the Kim regime as "the delayed consolidation of democracy." Kim Young-Sam's Christian faith influenced his democratic convictions, but it could not guarantee his democratic practice as president.

The Role of Religion in Evangelical Politicians' Thoughts and Actions

How do religious beliefs function in politicians' thinking and action more generally? In this section I examine evangelical Protestants in Korean politics. First, consider the weight of the evangelical presence in Korean political society. In the 1992 elections for the National Assembly, some ninety Protestants were elected out of 299 members of Parliament (MPs) (*Korean Torch*, July–September 1993, 22). The number of Protestants in the National Assembly gradually increased (interview 3). The number of Christian politicians was particularly large in the 16th National Assembly, which opened in 2000 (see Table 5.8).

Evidently, many key political leaders are evangelical Christians. In the 16th National Assembly, 75.9 percent expressed having some religious affiliation. Christians (Protestant and Catholic) constituted 177 members, almost 65 percent of all MPs, as contrasted with 26 percent in Korea's population. Of 112 Protestant MPs, sixty-eight hold important church positions (e.g., deacon or elder), mostly in evangelical churches, and there is one Anglican priest (Lee Jae-Jung). Five MPs attend the Yoido Full Gospel Church, which has seven hundred and fifty thousand members, and five attend Somang Church.

TABLE 5.8. Religious Affiliation of Members of Congress, 2000

Religion	Number of MPs	Percentage of MPs	Percentage in 1995, Korean Population
Protestant	108	39.6	19.7
Catholic	69	25.3	6.6
Buddhist	30	11.0	23.1
No Religion	66	24.1	49.3
Total	273	100	100

Source: Kim Sung-Woong (2000).

Conflicts between personal convictions and party loyalties are one index of religious influence. A survey of "congressmen and religion" (Kim Sung-Woong 2000) found that 84 percent of Protestant MPs (forty-three out of fifty-one responding) and 93 percent of Catholic MPs (fourteen out of fifteen responding) said their religious faith contributed to their political activities and, in particular, influenced their decision-making and policy views, a higher percentage than for Buddhist MPs (62 percent) or those without religious affiliation (33 percent). Asked what they would do if the views of their political party conflicted with their religious convictions, Protestant MPs divided evenly between saying they would follow their party's line (36 percent) and saying they would follow their religious convictions (36 percent); 27 percent said it would depend on circumstances.

Evangelical influence is seen not only in the number of evangelical MPs and the weight of their convictions but also in organizational activities. As early as 1968, Protestant MPs organized the Breakfast Prayer Meeting of the National Assembly (BPMNA, Kukka Chochan Kidohoi). This sparked the organization of a Buddhist Breakfast Prayer Meeting from 1980 on. Kim Young-Jin (2000), the BPMNA president, thinks that religion is above politics and that it provides meaning and guidance on how to go forward. He believes that politics has influenced even the deepest areas of human life and that religion can contribute to making a good and happy community. The BPMNA is the best-organized group of Christian MPs and definitely influences politics. Former MDP representative Kim Jung-Kwon (a devout evangelical), former ULDP president Kim Jong-Phil, and former GNP president Lee Hoi-Chang are all BPMNA advisors.

The evangelical and Protestant presence in politics is far greater than the Protestant percentage of the general population. Protestants may have provided an initial basis for political society in a historically traumatized country where political society was lacking (Freston 2001, 68), which makes evangelicalism potentially crucial for democratic consolidation. However, the development of Christian vision in politics is very weak (interviews 3 and 16). Evangelical congressman Hwang Woo-Yea makes a point of this. He initiated the Christian Institute for Politics in 1998, seeking to help Christian politicians do politics with a Christian mind. The Institute has held several seminars, including a March 2002 international symposium on "Korean Christianity and Politics," but as yet has no well-defined institutional shape (interview 12). Some Christian politicians who participated noted various structural barriers to political reforms. MDP assemblyman Cho Bae-Suk emphasized that Christian politicians need a Christian mind to collaborate for political reforms (interview 17).

Political vision for reform is often hampered by the weak institutionalization of political parties and divided political interests.[5] A consolidated, well-functioning party system has yet to be developed in Korea, and evangelical politicians could contribute powerfully to this. But various Christian MPs say there is no systematic effort among evangelical politicians to better institutionalize party politics. As Kim Young-Sam's democratic reforms illustrate, a personal Christian vision of democracy is not sufficient to bring about substantial democratic changes. But a more broad-based and systematic effort by evangelical Christians could improve the political system.

Evangelical Christians and Civil Society

In the third wave of democratization, no phenomenon more vividly captures the imagination of democratic scholars, observers, and activists than civil society. Diamond (1994, 4–5) defines civil society as the realm of organized social life that is voluntary, self-generating, largely self-supporting, autonomous from the state, and bound by a legal order or set of shared values. Without a strong civil society, democracy is unstable. Underdeveloped media and weak citizen participation allow a democratic regime to become nondemocratic.

Korean civil society arose in the context of millennia of strong state dominance, the harsh Japanese colonial state, state-controlled dirigiste economic development, and disunity in Korean society based on regional discrimination. The military government (with U.S. connivance) justified oppressive authoritarian rule as a struggle against communism during the tense and dangerous standoff between South and North Korea. All this reinforced strong tendencies in Korean culture to not rock any boats, and political expression became locked and frozen (Kim Ho-Gi 1997, 234). Korean civil society itself partook of a deep-rooted conservatism, rather than being a potentially free space in which to generate a struggle against state dominance. To view the state as the sole source of autocracy and think of civil society as a reservoir of pure democratic sentiment is oversimplified and ignores this deep-rooted conservatism (Son Ho-Chol 1995, 45). Some civil society movements were opposed to democracy and worked against it.

Civil society started to become dynamic only in the 1980s. State authoritarianism restricted political parties, through which diverse forces in civil society otherwise might have naturally channeled their energies. Thus, these forces concentrated their work *outside*: The celebrated Korean word *Chaeya*—indicating "out of power, in opposition"—was coined to refer to democratic activists and the social space in which they operated. *Chaeya* was a loose assemblage of dissident groups, which included activists, politicians, writers, youth groups, journalists, and church leaders. They formed in the early 1970s and grew much stronger in the late 1980s, leading the democratic struggle. Before 1987, there was no clear distinction between *Minjung* and civil society movements, or between radicals and moderates, because of the shared goal of democratic struggle against authoritarian rule. Since the introduction of a more limited procedural democracy, divergence on issues and methods has created rifts.

As the struggle against autocracy rapidly receded after 1987, democratic issues diversified. Radical social movements eroded and lost their dynamism; people turned away from groups that persisted in their old, radical methods of struggle (interview 10). People's movement groups (*minjung undong tanch'e*), pivotal in democratic transition, sought a new identity and role. The student movement retained its radical movement style and its Marxist, pro–North Korean overtones even into the 1990s. Student and radical social movements therefore became isolated (Cho Dae-Yop 1999, 133–136) as a shared ideology disappeared.

Two other factors contributed to a less activist, more conservative stance among the middle class after 1987. First, numerous radical labor strikes between 1987 and 1988 alienated the urban middle class, reducing support for social change (Kang Mun-Gu 1992, 329) and even for democratic reforms, as they perceived threats to economic and political stability. Thus, the middle class acted as a quiet balancer between the conservative authoritarian ruling groups and forces favoring all-out democratization of Korean politics and economy (Oh 1999, 115). Second, the collapse of socialism in the Eastern bloc in 1989 and the decline of a worldwide socialist movement undermined the typically radical, or even pro-socialist, ideological basis that once underlaid the Korean civil society movement.

Evangelicals' Leading Role in Citizens' Movement Groups Starting in the 1990s

Civil society now challenges government practices in diverse ways (Kim Ho-Gi 1995, 328) that provide wider social bases for democratic participation. After the June 1987 victory, visible state persecution of dissent disappeared, opening up legal space for various popular movements (interview 10). In the early 1990s, older, more radical democratic movement groups were at a standstill. Evangelical response to this changed context was increasingly manifested in their civil society movements. Citizens generally agreed that social movements had been a valuable social resource in democratization. But the May 29 declaration and the events surrounding it influenced evangelicals deeply, leaving a strong positive attitude. As radical social movements waned, evangelical social concern awoke over issues such as unification of North and South Korea, economic justice, and the environment. Religion-related groups, already organized and tightly knit, were well-equipped and ready to take a leading role initiating new social movements and issues.[6]

Citizens' movement groups (*siminundong tanch'e*) proliferated after 1988. One study counted forty-seven groups created between 1988 and 1993 (Kim Sun-Hyuk 2000, 106); by 2000 there were an estimated 1,150 Korean nongovernmental organizations (NGOs). Various NGOs feature religious groups, women, environment, labor, farmers, human rights, local autonomy, poor people, politics and administration, unification, international affairs, the handicapped, welfare, social service, youth, teenagers, education, media, health, and consumers. This explosion of citizens' associations was particularly salient in the areas of social issues and women's and youth organizations.

Christians played a major role in this expansion. Evangelical Protestants were most active in new civic groups, followed by progressive Protestants, and then by Catholics (interview 6). Buddhist citizen NGOs, such as the Federation of National Buddhist Movements, were very few. By some estimates, Christian-based groups constitute nearly 70 percent of all the NGOs and related groups (interview 13). Evangelicals began numerous civil movements on a wide variety of social issues in the early 1990s (interview 11). The detailed discussion here focuses on three prominent groups founded by evangelical Christians: the Christian Committee for Fair Elections (CCFE), the Christian Ethics Movement (CEM), and the Citizens' Coalition for Economic Justice (CCEJ).

Evangelicals and the Campaign for Fair Elections

The Catholic Church launched a committee for fair elections for the 1987 elections; Protestants organized a similar committee. However, what disunited the election monitoring movement were differences between these Christian groups and the old National Democracy movement, whose activists concentrated on strategies for getting approved candidates elected president, sidelining election supervision. The evangelicals' campaign for fair elections was unsystematic and not very energetic; people supervising this election were given only superficial training (CISJD 1988, 38).

But in 1990, a cluster of evangelicals, headed by Yi Man-yol, an evangelical professor in Sung Myung Women's University, organized a Christian Committee for Fair Elections; Son Bong-ho, previously codirector of the CEM, became its president. An evangelical pastor, Soh Kyung-suk, who founded the CCEJ, gathered all kinds of civic groups that wanted fair election campaigning and organized the CCFE on January 17, 1991, for the first local elections, the 1992 presidential election, and subsequent elections.

The CCFE analyzed candidates' public promises and presented them to voters in an impartial way. CCFE activities were generally regarded as a landmark success and gave impetus to building a broader network of civic activists. The CCFE started with nine groups, but by 1995 it included about five hundred groups. The CCFE has demanded revision of unfair election laws and has run centers for reporting unethical conduct, held hearings, sponsored policy debates, published reports comparing candidates' promises, distributed selection criteria for choosing good candidates, and developed ties with other groups to enhance voter participation.

The CCFE has become a prestigious nationwide organization encompassing all classes and religious groups, including Protestant, Buddhist, Catholic, and Confucianist. Evangelicals have continued to play a major role. The activities of the CCFE have helped change the election culture enormously, contributing significantly to democratic consolidation.

The Christian Ethics Movement

Whereas the CCFE and the CCEJ are general citizens' movements, the CEM is an explicitly Protestant movement and *theologically based*. The CEM was initiated in December 1987 by thirty-eight evangelical Christians, including Yi Man-yol, Son Bong-ho, Chang Ki-ryo, Yi Myung-soo, and Kim In-soo. The idea was initially conceived by Christian professors at Seoul National University (SNU) who were doing Bible studies together. Son Bong-ho (1997, 21), a professor at SNU and a CEM cofounder, describes the background as follows:

> At that time, there were three positions in Korean Christianity about Korean society.... Progressive Christians struggled for democracy and social structural reform. [Some] conservative Christians strictly separated church from the world and did not regard democratization and economic equity as their duties, by concentrating on personal evangelism and mission. However, a number of evangelical Christians stood between the two positions. They believed that social inequality and anti-democracy of the government were not valid, but they were suspicious of the radical methods to achieve that goal.... We thought that there must be diverse ways to achieve the social ideal of democratization and equality. However, we thought... the moral life and ethical example of Christians [was needed].

The CEM has focused on ethical commitment by Christians, hoping to set an example. If Christians serve society and demonstrate sacrifice and love, this alone would give the church an important role in society and politics. The CEM has twin functions: It is a Christian civil movement group, and it also seeks to be relevant to Korean society generally. The CEM promotes individual character (ethics and thinking) in ways specifically addressed to Christians and also in ways useful for all citizens regardless of religious beliefs (interview 8).[7] However, this activity is not based on individuals' actions alone; the CEM manifesto emphasizes Christian responsibility for politics, economics, and society and calls for community organization, including action by local congregations. Personal conscience and social institutions are both important. Social reform occurs as individuals' thinking changes and also through institutional reform. Both are necessary, and each supports the other.

CEM membership grew from twenty-four hundred after two years to more than ten thousand today. Its activities are so numerous they are hard to summarize. The CEM urges Christians to practice an honest, simple, moderate, and sharing lifestyle. It labored for reform in the church, including concern for pastors' ethics, and it rejected the common practice of pastors' sons being their successors in large congregations. CEM campaigns against corruption and dishonesty. It has also monitored the consumer culture and government policies; its campaigns against a consumer culture are well-known. It tries also to curb a culture of lasciviousness in society, pinpointing and opposing unnecessarily lascivious content in weekly periodicals and sports dailies. In 1991, it convinced each newspaper to pledge to produce a "wholesome" first section of its newspaper. It has organized Christian forums along occupational lines, for example, a CEM lawyers' association and a CEM teachers' association.

In this context, I focus on how the CEM contributed to the consolidation of political democracy. First, the CEM has been actively involved in the Fair Election Campaign. Its core slogan for fair elections was "From Personality-Centered Votes to Policy-Centered Votes." It sent all candidates questionnaires about their policies and made a comparison list. The CEM participated actively in CCFE, believing that institutional reform was important. But in keeping with its primary mission of making the individual Christian voter more ethical and informed, it also addressed Korean Christians specifically.

Second, the CEM strove to improve democratic citizenship through civic education. Tocqueville argued that the source of American democracy lay in the voluntary and autonomous groups and organizations of civil society. Concerned by lack of participation and undemocratic views and attitudes, CEM tried to strengthen Korean democracy by running an Academy for Democratic Citizens, which prepares people to participate in civic movements.

Third, the CEM inaugurated the Justice Politics Forum (JPF) in 2000. The Forum aimed to foster future leaders who would promote justice and to develop dialogues and policy programs to nurture such leadership. The CEM does not support particular politicians or seek a Christian political party, and the JPF addressed timely, relevant topics. Table 5.9 gives examples of seminar topics held in 2000.

TABLE 5.9. Seminar Topics of the Justice Politics Forum of CEM in 2000

Seminar Topics	Time
Suffering and Politics	July 2000
Is Justice Politics Possible in Korean Society?	August 2000
The Reality of Evil and the Way of Solution: The Connection between Politics and Economics	September 2000
Is Democracy Possible within Korean Political Parties?	October 2000
Reform of Local Autonomy	November 2000

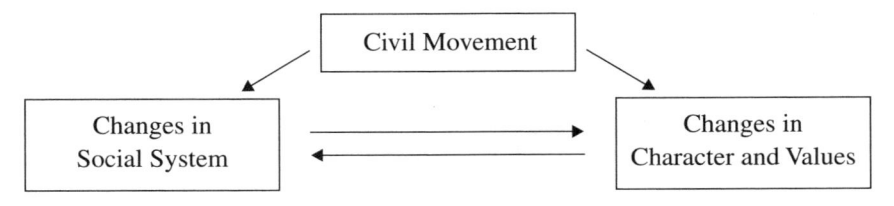

```
                        ┌──────────────────┐
                        │  Civil Movement  │
                        └──────────────────┘
                       ╱                    ╲
                      ╱                      ╲
                     ▼                        ▼
    ┌──────────────┐  ─────────────────▶  ┌──────────────────────┐
    │  Changes in  │                      │      Changes in      │
    │Social System │  ◀─────────────────  │ Character and Values │
    └──────────────┘                      └──────────────────────┘
```

FIGURE 5.1. Dynamics of the CEM Spirit

A key goal of CEM in changing social structure is to alleviate people's sufferings (see figure 5.1). Cofounder Son Bong-ho argues that because the whole universe is under God's sovereignty, extending to both secular and sacred areas, Christians cannot ignore politics, which are critical in protecting religious freedom, establishing justice, and above all in protecting the weak. Participation in politics can be a ministry for Christians. However, evangelicals' political consciousness, he argues, is immature, like that of other voters generally. The complexity of thinking among Christian politicians is also low. Thus, a more Christian politics requires Christian civil movements to raise consciousness.

The CEM is aware of its theological underpinnings. Min Chong-gi (2000, 100–102), a former professor of the Westminster Graduate College who directs its education committee, sees the civil society movement as a mission movement. Min suggests several reasons for this: "First, the church enjoys freedom of ministry in the age of civil society. The Christians' ministry is unlimitedly open in the space of civil society. Second, the church and Christian citizens are given the possibility of finding the holism of prophetic messages in all the arenas, including politics, economics, culture and art. Third, the church in civil society is awakened now that it exists not only for individual salvation but also for the recovery of the church community and for social transformation."

Seeing Christian civil movements only from political and economic perspectives misses the point. The church—the body of Christ—should respond to the calling of God, whose character is just and loving; civil movements are part of this holistic mission. Min notes that the extremely high proportion of Christians and Christian groups in the Korean Federation of Civil Society Groups also, incidentally, opens opportunities for mission and evangelism, because of the respect Christians have gained through civic-minded efforts.

Park Duk-hun (2000, 136) argues, "True meanings and theological truths about God, human beings, salvation, and the church are inviting us to the politics of civil society that seeks God's justice" and demands "forceful action" (Matthew 11:12). If united, Christians can be a sling and stone that triumph over Goliath, a tool that successfully resists powerful, arrogant political and economic forces (Min Chong-gi 2000, 102). By reforming Christians' mindset and ethical way of life, a traditional evangelical goal, the CEM hopes to magnify Christians' social influence. Yi Chung-sok (1997), professor at Reformed Theological Seminary and a member of CEM's theological committee, evaluates CEM as very effective. He thinks no Christian movement or group in Korean church history with such a small number of Christians has had so great an influence on politics, economics, society, and culture.

CEM, and the CCEJ to which we now turn, illustrate how evangelical leaders' theological convictions influence their social and political activity. The organizational strength of the CCEJ and CEM and evangelicals' active role in strengthening Korean democracy derive in part from the specifically theological convictions of evangelical leaders such as their founders, Prof. Son (CEM) and Rev. Soh (CCEJ).

Rev. Soh's Evangelical Faith: Citizens Committee for Economic Justice

Many movements bear the stamp of a founding leader's ideas and vision. The founder of the Citizens' Committee for Economic Justice, Pastor Soh Kyung-suk, was once a notable radical student activist. He was jailed three times during the 1970s for his energetic participation in democratic struggle and played a leading role in the Korea Student Christian Federation, the womb of progressive Christian students' movements. He says, "During my youth, *Minjung* theology was a living theology that moved me and made a great contribution toward my total dedication to the Christian *Minjung* movement. It was a sort of guide that made me give up my major studies [in engineering] and dedicate myself to the progressive Christian movement" (interview 10).

However, while studying in the United States (1982–1986), Rev. Soh, brought up within the evangelical faith tradition,[8] began to recover that evangelical faith and realize its dynamic social implications. He saw *Minjung* theology as limiting, because it tended to absolutize the *Minjung* movement and identify *minjung* (people) with Jesus (Soh 2001). Soh (2001) began to argue that although we lead a movement for good against evil (Romans 12:21), we should not fail to recognize that we are sinners. As Soh states: "While I was in Korea [before 1982], I was not able to make my religious experience my own. The theological background around me was all *Minjung* theology. I had no room to theologize my evangelical faith experience [in an environment where] the resurrection of Jesus was being understood as the resurrection of the *minjung* [people]" (interview 10).

When Soh returned from the United States, he observed that many student Christian social movements and progressive churches were steeped in socialist ideology. He argued that Christian social movements should be based on Christian evangelical faith instead. Because of his views, Soh was not well received in progressive church circles. He was also unwelcome among conservatives because of his image as "a pastor of the social movement camp."

He saw that the KNCC and progressive Christian groups were losing their influence. In anguish, he started a new movement for economic reforms for social justice, the CCEJ.

Rev. Soh founded the CCEJ in 1989 together with five hundred people representing various walks of life—economics professors and other specialists, lawyers, housewives, students, young adults, and business people—to respond to what participants perceived as the extremely unjust structure of Korean economic life. Numerous evangelical Christians took part in its inauguration. The movement aimed at economic development and social equity. Its slogan, "Let's Achieve Economic Justice Through Citizens' Power," emphasized that deep-rooted economic injustices could not be cured by government alone, but ultimately must be solved by the organized power of citizens.

Rev. Soh also started a new "Korean Sharing Movement" in 1999. He told me that his main interest was once justice, but now it is sharing (interview 16). His new movement aims at helping refugees from North Korea and the Korean Chinese in Korea, but ultimately works toward the unification of Korea as a mature, developed country.

Rev. Soh thought that the fruits of economic development should be shared by all the common people, not just the small group of "haves"; he designed a broadly based movement that could raise issues of justice and champion the needy, while including all citizens, not only radicals, activists, or *minjung* (poor and oppressed people). The group proposed gradual but thorough reform of the economic system. The CCEJ was defined as a movement (1) led by ordinary citizens, (2) using legal and nonviolent methods, (3) seeking workable alternatives, (4) voicing the interests of all people, regardless of economic standing, and (5) working to overcome greed and egoism to build a sharing society. From its inception he made this plain: "The force we are trying to gather includes not only marginalized *minjung* but also every citizen who has goodwill for a democratic society of welfare, regardless of social class. A movement based on the agreement of citizens in general will be a shortcut to democracy and unification, although it may appear slow" (interview 10).

Within a few months the membership grew to three thousand, and the CCEJ was generally recognized and commended as the most broadly representative civil society group in Korea. People holding every kind of religious and nonreligious view joined. However, evangelical and conservative Christians, including students from the conservative evangelical group Campus Crusade for Christ, were particularly energetic participants.

IMPACT OF THE CCEJ AND ITS ACTIVITIES

The CCEJ has assumed a commanding position as the voice of middle-class Koreans interested in reform. Before the CCEJ came into being, no organization was pointing out the structural injustices in the Korean economy or engaging citizens for economic reform. The CCEJ achieved several important successes early, most notably the "real name system" for registering property and all financial transactions. Its forums, seminars, and public discussions raised awareness about economic issues, especially equity and just distribution of benefits in society. It also supported a central bank independent of government control, revision of tax laws to discourage land speculation, and regulation of the rental system on behalf of poorer citizens. Its Economic Injustice Complaint Center, Legislature Watch, and Research Institute for Economic Justice have received widespread public attention. The CCEJ conducts research into dozens of policy sectors, covering almost every aspect of social, economic, and political life, and publishes a bimonthly English-language newsletter, *Civil Society*, and a Korean monthly magazine, *Wolgan Kyongsillyn* (CCEJ Monthly), which combines academic and more journalistic articles on economic reform issues.

Since 1989, CCEJ concerns have expanded to include environmental protection, democratic development, and national reunification. It uses a variety of methods: lobbying government officials for policy changes, pressing for legislation, issuing statements, demonstrating, and holding press conferences. Many activities are carried out in cooperation with other citizens' organizations. For example, in 1993–1994, CCEJ helped to form the People's Coalition to Protect Korean Agriculture, a network of 190 organizations that pressured the government to protect Korean farmers and the Korean food system from the possible negative effects of opening up of agricultural markets, as had been agreed upon in the GATT Uruguay Round. Following the initial local elections and enhanced local autonomy in 1995, the nationwide network of CCEJ branch organizations helped educate local political leaders and citizens about effective political participation and sustainable local development. The CCEJ also participates in the Fair Election Campaign.

The CCEJ now has a very solid status among civil movement groups. Tilly (1978, 125) distinguishes two main types of social movement based on their relationship with the government: the polity member type and the challenger type. The latter has a conflicting or confrontational relationship with the government. Lo (1992) distinguishes two types of civil movement groups based on members' characteristics, management system, key resources, and mode of participation and behavior: the market type and the communal type. CCEJ is a market-type and polity member social-movement group. The CCEJ has a diverse membership of individuals and a professional management system, and it relies on indirect participation. Its resources depend not on government funding but on membership fees. Rather than using confrontational, anti-establishment methods such as demonstrations and mass meetings, it uses conventional and respected techniques, such as public hearings, discussion meetings, workshops, campaigns, and presentation of policy alternatives. CCEJ activities attracted media attention from early on, in part because the organization differed from social movements of a challenging and communal type, which have been more common in Korea. This attention has contributed to the widening scope of CCEJ activities (Cho Dae-yop 1999, 267).

The CCEJ's contribution lies not only in its own activities but also in its influence on other groups. As the first major movement of its type, it has also provided a fresh model for social movements in the new context after democratization. Curtis (1997) presents the need for economic equity as one of the main lessons from the East Asian experience of democratization. By focusing on economic equity, the CCEJ furthers Korean democratization by adding economic justice and social democracy to the democratic agenda. Soh's (2001) approach has also had great influence on the thinking of many evangelical leaders, who have come to see social action and citizen participation as a biblical approach. Soh notes the importance of churches in civil society and suggests that, for balance, and to enlist many evangelicals, small churches should form the core of Christian social movements. If megachurches alone lead a movement, this could compromise its democratic structure.

Soh's contribution to the Korean civil society movement can be marked as a highly successful case of evangelical participation in politics, and one that is firmly grounded in the evangelical faith. He believes Christian social action must seek the kingdom of God. He says evangelicals must avoid two great perils: One is to seek only the heavenly world, neglecting social transformation in this world; the other is to seek the kingdom of God only in this world, without eschatological hope. *Minjung* theology exemplifies the latter problem. Christian political action finds its basis in the incarnation of Jesus, which implies the salvation of body as well as spirit. Because Christians are *in* the world, but not *of* the world, Christians cannot ignore politics, which greatly affects people's concrete daily lives. Soh argues, therefore, that evangelicals' social action must proceed in the light of Christian faith. Evangelicals need to participate in social movements on a theologically informed basis, acknowledging that they themselves are sinners and must therefore shed any self-righteous attitudes (interview 19).

Other Evangelical Contributions to Civil Society

Woodberry (1999) suggests three ways that religious traditions may foster civil society: (1) religious organization develops habits of behavior and institutional models that people apply to other areas of life; (2) religious organizations staunchly resist oppression; and (3) religious organizations influence the number of participants and character of nonreligious civil society.

Associations within the church generate space for trust, and the churches teach their members civic skills (Putnam, Leonardi, and Nanetti 1993). Rapidly growing evangelical churches among Korea's educated citizens, which fostered participation and self-organizing groups within the church as members, formed home-cell groups and committees and overcame dilemmas of collective action. This may have led to participation and institutional success in the broader community. In addition, the churches taught responsible citizenship as part of their teachings about Christian life. Evangelical churches giving members explicit training for democracy, for instance, also taught about human rights and decision making (interview 6).

Evangelical participation strengthened civil society by its relative popularity. One survey by CEM and the Institute for Korean Christian Church in 1992 found that evangelical groups like CEM and CCFE were better known to Korean Christians than progressive ones such as the Human Rights Committee of the KNCC or the Christian Federation of Social Movements. Progressive social movements stagnated and got less recognition partly because they were often elite-based movements, without a wide base in churches, and partly because most Korean Protestants were critical conservatives who preferred moderate to more radical groups.

Evangelical leaders have become more positive toward civil society movements and are awakening to their role in the larger society. The Korean National Association of Christian Pastors (KACP) was inaugurated in 1998 by fourteen associations of evangelical pastors from major Korean denominations (e.g., Tong-hap, Hap-tong, Kijang, Methodist, Holiness, Assemblies of God, Anglican) to renew the divided Korean churches and play a role in Korean society. The KACP organized a major conference in March 2000 on Civil Movements for Social Reform and Christians' Participation, the first such conference ever. The KACP invited major Korean civil movement groups, mostly Christian, such as Networks for Green Transport, Asian Institute for Civil Society Movements, Christian Ethics Movement, Green Consumers Network in Korea, the Political Watch, and the Citizen's Coalition for Economic Justice.

By joining voluntary associations, evangelical Christians, as individuals, enlarged their hearts and cultivated a commitment to leading a humane and civilized life. By aggregating and representing their concerns in the political arena, in groups, they helped check any tendencies toward authoritarianism, enlarging autonomous spheres of social power within which citizens can seek changes, protect themselves from tyranny, and democratize from below.

Evangelicals and Democratization:
Contributions and Challenges

The democratic ideal is a paradox: An inevitable gap exists "between democratic ideals and democratic realities" (Dahl 1997, 74). Some scholars (B. Kim 1998) take fair, free, and competitive elections as sufficient criteria for democracy. Others (Im Hyug-baeg 2000) consider Korean democracy as still unconsolidated, emphasizing (Diamond and B. Kim 2000, 4) that consolidation involves establishing a responsive, accountable, civilian political regime that has full control over the military, guarantees civil rights, and also presides over a Tocquevillian social democratization. It is true that Korea has consistently improved civil liberties and political democracy after a democratic transition. But by any measure, Korea is still on the road to full consolidation. Gallup Korea surveys reveal that, although general support for democracy is widely shared, that support has not broadened, deepened, and stabilized (Shin 1998, 28).

Further democratization in Korea now will proceed amid turbulent times, and evangelical input may be important. There is little evidence that religion is losing its grip in Korea, or indeed, in the United States or in the non-Western world. Predictions of increasing secularization and declining religious influence in politics find little confirmation (Scott 1995, 31). Religiously inspired cultural change remains a lively option in many parts of the world (Fukuyama 1999). Responsible, faith-inspired political participation will remain an unavoidable issue for Korean evangelicals with their weighty political resources.

Various factors awakened evangelicals' political consciousness. Progressive Christians' active democratic movements revitalized theology through contact with evangelicals internationally (e.g., the Lausanne Covenant), a sense of institutional threat, and growth of middle-class church members. Curtis (1997) concluded from examining the experiences of the Philippines, Japan, Singapore, South Korea, and Taiwan that external and internal networks, economic growth, political leadership, and civil society were important factors in raising political consciousness.

So far, evangelicals have contributed to Korean democratization in a variety of ways. The greatest contribution was their involvement in civil society, which will become increasingly important. Many evangelicals are critical of electoral politics and political parties but are more favorably disposed toward Christian social movements, especially favoring moderate movements compatible with Koreans' critical conservatism (Paik 1994, 77). Evangelical Christians, especially after 1987, helped build effective networks and civil associations. The political vision of some Christian politicians, such as Kim Young-Sam, also contributed. Arguably, evangelical churches helped build the middle class. But evangelicals have yet to widen the basis of democratic involvement and to increase the scope of participation, involving ordinary people from all walks of life.

What tasks face evangelicals in helping develop Korean democracy? First, building networks and coalitions are among the most effective methods to develop democracy. Networks, among Christians and with other groups, were central in the democratic transition. It follows that evangelicals' internal schisms could impede their contributions to the democratization of Korea and may weaken civil society. Differences between the progressive and evangelical churches have narrowed since 1987, and discussion of unity among Protestant churches has increased (*Choson Ilbo*, November 11, 1994). Yet evangelicals are themselves fragmented and may find it hard to unite on social and political issues. Some evangelical leaders, dismayed by splits and disagreements among churches, worry that evangelical Christian bodies may become more polarized and lose influence on future Korean social and political development (interview 2).

Greater church unity could benefit the entire society. Rev. Soh Kyung-suk (2001) argues that with close cooperation among Christian civic groups, denominations, and institutions, Christian social movements would flourish, strengthening evangelicals' positive social influence (and the effectiveness of evangelism). Yi Man-yol (1989) concludes that convergence between conservative and progressive Christians, and among evangelical churches, could create new ways to address Korean social, national problems, if evangelicals can avoid letting institutional interests or "group egotisms" blur a clear vision of a democratic society (interview 2; cf. O, Kyong-hwan 1990). Factionalism leads to fruitless power contests,[9] but respect and cooperation among evangelicals that promote a shared moral and religious vision can benefit the whole of society.

Second, civil society movements provide effective ways for Korean evangelicals to participate in politics, and evangelicals provided important leadership in the 1990s. Prof. Son Bong-ho (2002) regards Christian participation in civil society groups as most appropriate for Korea's religiously pluralistic society. This participation becomes effective as people see evangelicals working for justice and for the common good.

However, some (including even civil society activists) have recently expressed cautious doubts about the overall impact of Korean civil movements, some of which can be politicized, avoiding financial transparency, intent on vested particularistic interests, or tending toward a demagogic populism (interview 16). Civil society can play a negative role in democracy as well as a positive one (Rudolph 2000a). Koreans' participation in civil society is mainly confined to fraternal and religious associations (Steinberg 1997). Diamond (1994, 13–15) raises similar caveats, arguing a need for limits on civil groups' autonomy. Civil society must be autonomous from the state, but not alienated from it; watchful, but respectful of state authority. Reviving old themes, Huntington (1997b, 7) likewise cautions that weakening state authority could become a problem in democratization: "By weakening state authority ... democratization also brings into question authority in general and can promote an amoral, laissez-faire, or 'anything goes' atmosphere." Civil society must learn to encompass pluralism and diversity (Diamond 1994, 6).

A healthy evangelical civil society movement and evangelical institutions committed to the expansion of democracy require Korean evangelicals to understand the most effective ways to conduct civil society activities (interview

18). Pluralism goes far beyond mere "social differentiation," the existence of groups with diverse characters and goals. A multitude of groups does not, by itself, ensure a pluralistic approach. Social pluralism requires understanding and appreciation of dissent, tolerance, and reciprocity (Sartori 1997). Many Korean evangelicals have not properly assimilated ideas of social pluralism (perhaps confused by theological advocates of a "religious pluralism" as weakening or abandoning Christianity's truth claims, which is, of course, a very different matter).

Third, solidifying democratic values is critically important to democratic consolidation. That requires reform not just in national politics: Individuals and groups must unlearn age-old norms and practices of authoritarianism and particularism in daily life, both of which impede democratization (Shin 1999, 254). Yet most Koreans are still neither deeply committed to the fundamentals of democratic rule nor fully disengaged from authoritarian habits (Shin 1998, 30). Korean political culture seems to lack what Lipset (1994) calls "the effectiveness domain of democratic culture." According to a survey in 1997 among the national and local communities, a large majority (70 percent) still identifies more closely with the latter, and many evangelicals have not transcended such regionalism.

Although Christians show a strong democratic orientation (Om 1989), negative cultural and historical legacies still impede translating that orientation into democratic practice. Evangelicals' democratic consciousness needs to mature. One way for Korean evangelicals to further the democratization of political culture would be to build healthy Christian institutions in accordance with democratic norms and values (Han 1995), for instance, by making churches themselves more democratic. Reform of undemocratic internal church structures lags: Many evangelical leaders maintain a strongly authoritarian church leadership structure (interview 15). Democracy depends on socialization in a civic culture as well as on institutional change: values of pluralism and equality, public spirit that subordinates private egotisms, orderly self-restraint, and positive participation. Democracy lies in people's hearts, in learning democratic culture, not in legal documents alone (Pae 1992, 167). In Korea, family egotism and conservative authoritarianism erode civic culture (Kim Ho-gi 1997, 243), and that conservative authoritarianism still operates in evangelical churches. Developing democratic civic culture that is in line with the spirit of evangelical Christian faith also requires recognition that our best values are subject to corruption: Faith, by itself, does not guarantee civility. Institutional safeguards are needed to secure trustworthy performance in public arenas (Wuthnow 1996, 70). Christian participation in politics, like that of other groups, therefore needs appropriate safeguards.

Fourth, reform of political culture and strengthening civil society depends on strengthening institutions. In understanding civil society in democracy, Foley and Edwards (1996, 47) argue, political associations as well as prevailing political understandings are crucial. Democratic development occurs when political leaders believe they have an interest in promoting it or a duty to achieve it (Huntington 1997a, 10). Korean institution-building, especially the institutionalization of party politics, has been tardy. Many scholars see the culture of political parties as a great problem in Korean democratization (Kim Byung-kook 1998). Political parties have not been transformed into adequate institutions of representative democracy. They remain regionally based and hierarchically organized. I argued that Kim Young-Sam's political reforms failed to consolidate democracy because of a failure to institutionalize party politics to support them. For a new democracy like Korea's to mature and endure, citizens and officials must be freed from the particularistic identities inconsistent with the obligations of democratic citizenship (March and Olsen 1995, 39). But Koreans generally remain tightly bound by particularistic loyalties and networks of "specific reciprocity" in ways inconsistent with the public good (Shin 1999, 257). Overcoming regionalism is one critical example (interview 10).

This is a duty especially for Christians, as the Bible teaches that one should "love one's neighbor as oneself" (Matthew 22:39; Mark 12:31; Luke 10:27; Romans 13:9; Galatians 5:14; James 2:8), treating them justly and caring for their welfare "without partiality" (Romans 2:11; Ephesians 6:9; James 2:1–9; I Peter 1:17; etc.), and that one should, like Jesus, "seek not only one's own interests, but also the interests of others" (Philippians 2:4). For evangelicals, social and political commitment is a matter of theological identity, not just of miscellaneous political predilections. The critical political issue for Korean evangelical churches, then, is how they mobilize their immense resources in accord with a well-worked-out theology of politics and social change.

Finally, developing political theology is vital to evangelical contributions to building democracy. Theology is foundational for Christian thinking. Articulating theological reasons for commitment to democratic ideals provides a powerful democratic impetus, as Christian political initiatives find a unique basis in sound theological understanding, shaped and motivated by Christian faith, prophetically applied in specific sociopolitical contexts (Kim Nyung 1996, 104–107) to establish a good and just political order. This chapter showed how evangelical faith and reasoning motivated evangelical leaders to support democracy. But Korean evangelical political theology is currently weak (interview 8). To escape from the iron cage of a religious mentality without social vision, evangelicals must develop a theoretical framework for understanding democracy in fundamental and substantive ways, not superficially or procedurally (interview 7; cf. Kim Byung-kook 1998). The mode and quality of democratic participation matter greatly (interview 5). Korean evangelical democratic politics and social action need more developed and coherent theological foundations so that religious conviction supports freedom, justice, and peace, not political preconceptions or particularistic interests.

Minjung theology fortified progressive Christians' thinking under Korea's military regimes and contributed in some ways to evangelicals' support for democracy as well. However, *Minjung* theology was an elite project esteemed in rarified progressive church circles; it never fit the orthodox belief and "critically conservative" political thinking of the vast evangelical majority of Korean Christians. It also lacks the flexibility to be applicable in Korea's new post-transition democracy (interview 10). When introduced in the mid-1980s, the Lausanne Covenant helped ground political thinking biblically and theologically. CEM and CCEJ applied such ideas in the Korean context. Prof. Son based Christian contributions to social reform in the ethics of Christians' daily lives, and Rev. Soh applied biblical principles of economic justice concretely to Korean society. But only a few key Korean evangelicals have developed a theologically based social and political vision. Most lack the religious vision to support consolidation of democracy. Despite efforts to formulate a theology of transformation that encompasses societal and political problems, no coherent, well-developed, accepted theological groundwork has emerged.

In this sense, the capacity of evangelicals to contribute to democratization in the public square of civil society depends on their own character and their moral and religious depth. Evangelical political leaders need evangelical vision, but one without a corporatist or triumphalist orientation. For instance, it would not be proper to create a Christian political party (interview 6) that fosters religious conflicts and group egoism. Instead, evangelical politicians need to embody the truth and implications of the Cross: operating humbly for others and pursuing a life of self-sacrifice for the common good. Chang Young-dal, a Protestant congressman, told me sadly that in political practice, Christian politicians often behave no better than their non-Christian counterparts. In his view, the power of evangelicals to play a transformative, positive role in politics lies in learning the spirit of the Cross.

Alexis de Tocqueville ([1835] 1956, 133) admonished us more than 170 years ago to approach the establishment of democracy as "the greatest political problem of our times." For Korean evangelicals, strengthening democracy—or, for that matter, approaching social and political issues based on the Christian gospel—may be the greatest religious problem of our times. Building democracy will be a long but worthwhile pilgrimage for evangelical Christians.

NOTES

Interviews

1. Kim Min-sok, MP, Sept. 26, 2000.
2. Paik Hwa-jong, editor of *Kookmin* daily newspaper, Oct. 9, 2000.
3. Chang Young-dal, MP, Oct. 28, 2000.
4. Kim Dong-wan, general secretary, KNCC, Oct. 30, 2000.

5. Kang In-Chul, professor, Nov. 13, 2000.
6. Son Bong-Ho, professor, Jan. 10, 2001.
7. Kim Nyong, professor, Jan. 12, 2001.
8. Lyu Hae-Sin, director of CEM, Feb. 2, 2001.
9. Ko Jik-Han, missionary, Mar. 3, 2001.
10. Soh Kyung-Suk, pastor, July 12, 2001.
11. Yi Man-Yol, professor, July 16, 2001.
12. Hwang U-Yo, MP, July 16, 2001.
13. Min Chong-Gi, professor, July 16, 2001.
14. Kim Young-Sam, former president of Korea, Aug. 9, 17, 2001.
15. Kim Dong-Ho, pastor, Nov. 6, 2001.
16. Soh Kyung-Suk, pastor, Jan. 10, 2002.
17. Cho Bae-Suk, MP, Mar. 22, 2002.
18. Yoon Hwan-Chol, civil activist, Mar. 22, 2002.
19. Soh Kyung-Suk, pastor, Apr. 10, 2002.

1. It is hard to define evangelicalism. However, in this chapter, the term "evangelicals" refers to those Christians who stress conversionism through Jesus Christ; biblicism, accepting the authority of the Bible; activism, advocating evangelistic activities; and crucicentrism, focusing on the redemptive ministry of Jesus Christ (Bebbington 1989, 2–19). They are distinguished from the so-called progressive group of Christians who put priority on social action over individual conversion through Jesus Christ in the Korean context. It could be argued that we can find evangelical Christians in the progressive Christian circles, as they participate in politics from their faith conviction in Jesus Christ. For evangelicals, social action is meaningful only in the light of evangelistic concerns. The term "evangelicals" may connote a wider sense than one expects.

2. Citations to personal interviews are cited by number, per the list above.

3. *Minjung* theology, influenced by the Latin American liberation theology of the 1960s, was developed around 1975 among a small group of Korean theologians. Etymologically, *"Minjung"* means the mass of the people, the masses, or just the people. *Minjung* theology is a political hermeneutics of the gospel and a political interpretation of Korean Christian experiences (D. K. Suh 1981, 19). *Minjung* theology reappropriates paradigms from the Bible, church history, and Korean history from the perspective of *Minjung*. This was the contextual Korean theology in progressive Christian circles aiming at applying the biblical message to the Korean context and alleviating the suffering of the poor arising from political and social oppression. Adherents argued that a rereading of the Bible made it clear that Jesus was a revolutionary who died for the oppressed. *Minjung* theology thus provided justification for, indeed mandated, Christians' participation in secular politics in support of democracy and the popular masses. For further detail, see So (1983) and Na (1988).

4. The Protestant pastors who led a Sunday service in the Blue House (mentioned by Kim Young-Sam 2001b, 385–387) were Han Kyung-Jik, Cho Yong-Gi, Kim Chang-Hwan, Kim Sam-Hwan, Park Cho-Jun, Kim Chang-In, Lim Young-Su, Kim Sun-Do, Kim Jin-Hong, Ok Han-Hum, Na Kyum-Il, Kim Ki-Su, Chang Cha-Nam, Yi Chung-Ik, Park Chang-Hwan, Chung Young-Hwan, Chung Young-Taek, Kim Dong-

Kwon, Kim Jun-Kyu, Choi Sung-Kyu, Song Tae-Kun, Sin Sung-Jong, and Son Sang-Ryul. These pastors are mostly well-known Protestant evangelicals leading large congregations.

5. However, there was some morning light in the democratization of party politics in 2002. In early 2002, major political parties, starting with the Millennium Democratic Party and the Grand National Party, made political reforms. According to these, the president of the party and the supreme council, the ruling decision-making committee, were elected by the members of the party. Also, in each party the candidate for the presidency was elected by both the members of the party and the Korean people who applied for participation in vote casting. The primaries were held across the nation to elect a candidate for president. In the case of Grand National Party, it decided to make its budget open to the public. These seem to be steps forward toward the democratization of party politics.

6. One of the noteworthy phenomena in evangelical participation in civil society was the establishment of the *Kookmin* daily newspaper in 1988 by the Yoido Full Gospel Church, a pentecostal church. Information highly controlled by the government hinders democracy. The political intervention of *Kookmin* has strengthened the role of the Yoido Full Gospel Church as well as the Protestant churches in the public square.

7. Kwon Chang-hee, the executive director of the CEM, told me that CEM was struggling to define the movement's identity. Yi Chung-sok (1997) made the following suggestions for the CEM: (1) the CEM has to find its identity and character: whether it is a personal ethics movement or social ethics movement and how to balance the two aspects; (2) the CEM needs more professionalization of organization; and (3) the CEM should be more pro-church by developing cooperation between the pastors and laity.

8. Soh has a strong Christian background. His great-great-grandfather became the first ordained pastor and, with Methodist missionary Rev. Underwood, set up the Saemunan Church, the first Protestant church in Korea. His family has attended the Saemunan Church ever since.

9. All the institutional elements of democratic governance (e.g., elections, an independent legislature, a freer press, and civil society) are in place in Korea, but prevailing attitudes toward power and authority tell another story. For individuals and institutions alike, to share or to delegate power (and hence prestige) in the zero-sum game is seemingly to lose it (Steinberg 1998, 82). In this setting, power becomes absolutely significant and tends to become personalized, which in turn breeds factionalism.

6

Consolidating Democracy: Filipino Evangelicals between People Power Events, 1986–2001

David S. Lim

"People Power" events in the Philippines were a significant model in the "third wave" of democratization in the 1970s and 1980s. How have evangelicals participated in consolidating democracy there? This chapter discusses evangelicals' role in People Power events from February 1986 to May 2001.

The first section sketches the political landscape and the role of religion in recent Philippine history and defines Filipino evangelicalism. Then I examine three kinds of evangelical involvement: participation in electoral processes, People Power uprisings, and civil society. I conclude by arguing that Filipino evangelicals have grown in political maturity and have helped develop democracy.

Background

Filipino Democracy

The first republic declared Independence from Spain in June 1898 and promulgated the Malolos Constitution in January 1899. Both were short-lived. The United States promptly colonized the Philippines. A 1935 Constitution was used from Independence in 1946 and revised in 1973. Claiming constitutional weaknesses and growing instability, President Marcos declared martial law in 1972 and suppressed democracy until political normalizations occurred in the early 1980s.

A new Constitution, drafted in 1986 and ratified in 1987, vests executive power in the president, who is also head of state. The Senate has twenty-four members; the House of Representatives not more than two hundred, mainly from legislative districts proportionate to population; a party-list system selects not more than fifty representatives from marginalized sectors—labor, peasants, urban poor, indigenous cultural minorities, women, youth—but not religious minorities. The Supreme Court, and subordinate courts, exercise judicial power. Local government units in each administrative area—province, city, municipality, and *barangay* (village)—include elected and appointed officials. Constitutional provisions ensure local government autonomy and a 1991 Local Government Code gives local government units responsibility for basic services in agriculture, health, social welfare and development, public works, environment, and natural resources. Constitutional and legal provisions were adhered to in the post-Marcos period, despite calls for a revolution or coup.

Yet, many political analysts consider the Philippines an "elitist democracy," like some Latin American democracies that ended military dictatorships through negotiated transitions based on elite consensus. Thompson (1996) thinks the "troubled nature of Filipino democratization" may produce "one of the worst structural situations of any of the new democracies outside Africa." The challenge lies not in maintaining the formal democratic system but in freeing it from elitist control. Stanmeyer (1999, 60–61) argues that "ruling powers...exert pressure on the mass media and [perhaps]...rewrite the Constitution to serve their own needs." The Philippines lack true or "popular democracy," government "of the people, for the people and by the people" (De Quiros 2001).

Filipino Religion and Democracy

The Philippines is the one sizable Asian nation with a Christian majority: 84 percent Roman Catholic, 8 percent Protestant (including Aglipayans or Filipino/Independent Catholics), 3 percent Iglesia Ni Cristo (INC), 3 percent Muslim, and 2 percent other.[1] Evangelicals (a subset of Protestants) are about 7 percent, just over 5 million in a population of 76.5 million.[2] The most visible evangelical group, the Jesus is Lord Church (JIL), whose influence extends far beyond its membership, has only 250,000 members, 0.03 percent of the population.[3]

Religion plays an active role in Philippine politics. Critical political rallies in recent years were held as religious assemblies or prayer meetings. Religious power has roots in the ancient past. Of old, shamans were consulted on matters of government; church and state were closely intertwined under Spanish colonial rule. Popular novels by the national hero, Dr. Jose Rizal—*Noli Me Tangere* (1887), *El Filibusterismo* (1891)—depict priests domineering over the community.

The Catholic Church was pivotal in opposing the Marcos dictatorship (1972–1986). Archbishop Jaime Cardinal Sin announced a "critical collaboration" against Marcos in 1978 and led the Catholic Bishops Conference of the Philippines (CBCP) in calling for an end to martial law. When Marcos held snap elections in late 1985, the Church gave all-out support to Corazon Aquino, assassinated Senator Benigno (Ninoy) Aquino's widow. The CBCP rejected the alleged Marcos victory as marred by massive vote buying, reckless violence, and systematic fraud. Cardinal Sin urged people to join the People Power uprising against him.

The cardinal endorsed House Speaker Ramon Mitra for president in the 1992 election. The religious sect INC, an important voting bloc, endorsed Eduardo Cojuangco. Mitra placed fourth and Cojuangco third; General Fidel Ramos, a former Marcos administration member and a Protestant, won; Bishop Eddie Villanueva, leader of JIL, gave him a last-minute endorsement and served as President Ramos's unofficial confidant.

In 1998, most religious leaders deemed Vice President Joseph Estrada unfit. The cardinal and CBCP energetically opposed Estrada's presidential bid. But INC and El Shaddai (a growing Catholic charismatic group led by Mike Velarde) supported him, and when Estrada won, Velarde became his official spiritual advisor.[4]

Religious groups were again active in late 2000, after Ilocos Sur Governor Luis Singson revealed Estrada's numerous illegal activities. Cardinal Sin and ex-President Aquino, who had successfully led People Power movements to block constitutional changes by Ramos (1997) and Estrada (1999), demanded Estrada's immediate resignation, leading rallies, celebrating masses, and offering prayers for the country's "salvation." Estrada had Velarde, INC, and Jesus Miracle Crusade (JMC) hold a counterrally for "national reconciliation," with a vast crowd dominated by El Shaddai and INC members.

Estrada's impeachment trial was blocked when eleven senators refused to open the controversial second envelope. Again, Cardinal Sin and Catholic clergy took center stage when crowds amassed at the Epifanio de los Santos Avenue (EDSA) Shrine from January 16 to 20, 2001. Catholic renewal groups—Couples for Christ (CfC), Handmaids of the Lord, Youth for Christ, Singles for Christ—were prominent during this People Power 2, which ousted Estrada.

After Gloria Macapagal-Arroyo became president and Estrada was arrested on plunder charges, Estrada loyalists marched to the EDSA Shrine to stage People Power 3. Again, the Catholic Church came out publicly, condemning *this* mass action, while INC supported it through its UHF channel Net 25 and radio station DZEC.[5] President Arroyo declared a "state of rebellion" when crowds attempted to besiege Malacanang Palace. INC and El Shaddai (probably constrained by circumstances) expressed support for the new administration despite their previous pro-opposition activities. May 14, 2001, senatorial elections became a plebiscite on the Arroyo administration, with the Catholic Church discreetly supporting all pro-administration candidates, while INC and El Shaddai campaigned for pro-Estrada Puwersa ng Masa candidates. Election results suggested the importance of religious endorsements.

Filipino Evangelicalism

Who are the Filipino evangelicals? One moment in 1989 first clearly defined evangelicalism in the public eye. As Philippine evangelicals prepared to host an international evangelical conference, Lausanne II in Manila, with a parallel Philippine Congress on World Evangelization in July, CBCP's pastoral letter "Hold Fast to What Is Good," read in all Catholic churches, began, "On January 22 to 24... Catholic Bishops... gathered in Tagaytay for a seminar on Fundamentalism. What brought us together was a serious pastoral concern about the increasing flow into our country of fundamentalist groups, preachers, TV programs, and the harm they cause to many of our faithful" (CBCP, 1989). The letter reflected awareness of increasing Catholic conversions to evangelicalism in the Philippines, as in Latin America, and their high-profile media exposure.[6] There were only 228 non-Catholic Philippine church groups before 1980 (Rose 1996b, 81),[7] but there were 23,400 Protestant congregations by October 1991 (DAWN 1991). The Philippine population grew at a rate of 2.5 percent a year; the Protestant population grew at a rate of 5.1 percent (G. W. Harper 2000, 251).

CBCP (1989) distinguished Protestants with whom they had "cordial relations" from those they considered fundamentalist:

> We must regretfully say that the fundamentalist sects, with their aggressive and sometimes vicious attacks on the Catholic Church, do not practice an ecumenism which we can trustingly reciprocate....
>
> Young people who have been raised Catholic are becoming Fundamentalists... in high school and college organizations, such as Young Life, Youth for Christ, Campus Crusade for Christ, Inter-Varsity, Teen Challenge, and the Navigators.

The newly organized Christian Leaders' Alliance of the Philippines (CLAP) issued an immediate response, "The Word of the Lord Stands Forever." CLAP had been reorganized in July 1988,[8] after evangelical clamor against alleged abuses of religious freedom displays of Catholic statues in public places and reported persecutions of evangelical children in Catholic schools, and the campus ministries mentioned were CLAP participants.

CLAP applauded Roman Catholics' adherence to ecumenical creeds and firm defense of Christ's deity and wished to maintain "friendly relations" and work together in nation building. They expressed appreciation for CBCP's declaring 1989 as Bible Year. But they dissented extensively from Catholic views on biblical authority and interpretation and differentiated themselves from fundamentalists, theologically *and* politically:

> If fundamentalist... mean[s] a person who believes that the Bible is the only authority, then we are not fundamentalists for we have a place for traditions, creeds and councils... subject to the supreme and final authority of Scripture. If fundamentalist means one who always interprets the Scripture literally without regard to the context, we are not fundamentalists for we believe in grammatical and historical exegesis. If fundamentalist means serving as a front for the CIA or Causa International... then we are not fundamentalists for we are nationalists who care deeply for the Filipino nation. (CLAP 1989, 1)

That theological differentiation had happened very early on. Fundamentalism was on its way out when the Philippine Council of Evangelical Churches (PCEC) was formed in 1965 (Vencer 1989, 48–49).[9] During PCEC's Second National Assembly in 1968, Chairman Fred Magbanua framed the debate: "Will [PCEC] be a Fundamentalist-separatist Council or an evangelical ecumenicity?" (Vencer 1994a, 17). Both camps wanted eventual membership in the International Council of Churches and World Evangelical Fellowship (Vencer 1994a, 17). The resignation of fundamentalist Rev. Antonio Ormeo, a founding PCEC vice chairman, confirmed the Assembly's direction.

The biggest political differences concerned anticommunism and a pro-Americanism touting free market capitalism, which fundamentalists vocally supported in an Alliance for Democracy and Morality (Sabreg 1991, 377).[10] But most evangelicals rejected simplistic anticommunist, pro-American rhetoric; many were committed to social justice, holistic ministry, and Filipino nationalism.[11] Attitudes toward charismatic gifts constituted another divergence. Fundamentalists deemed these cultic or heretical; evangelicals didn't. CLAP's president, Fred Magbanua Jr., and the secretary, David Lim, were "non-charismatic evangelicals"; Vice President Ramon Orosa and Treasurer Leo Alconga were "charismatic evangelicals."[12]

By the mid-1990s, "evangelicalism" became a technical term for individuals, churches, and organizations that belonged to the PCEC and the Philippines for Jesus Movement (PJM) or were sympathetic, as thousands of small unaffiliated "Full Gospel" congregations were. The 1998 centennial celebration of Protestant Christianity assumed that usage.

The PCEC comprises major "conservative evangelical" denominations—Christian and Missionary Alliance of the Philippines, Alliance of Bible Christian Communities of the Philippines, Conservative Baptists of the Philippines, the Baptist General Conference, Evangelical Free Church, Philippine

Baptist Mission of the Southern Baptist Convention (USA), Free Methodists, Church of the Nazarene, the Wesleyan Church—along with "classic pentecostal" denominations: Assemblies of God, International Church of the Foursquare Gospel (Foursquare), and Church of God-Pentecostal. Global evangelical bodies like the World Evangelical Fellowship and Evangelical Fellowship of Asia influenced PCEC's theology and history. Bishop Efraim Tendero has been PCEC's main spokesman since becoming the general secretary (later, national director) in 1993.

PJM comprises major indigenous pentecostals, or "charismatic evangelical" churches: JIL, Christ the Living Stone Fellowship, Take the Nations for Jesus Global Ministries, Inc., Jesus Saves Global Outreach, Love of Christ Ministries, and Universal Pentecostal Church. Founded in 1983 as a network, not a council of churches, PJM has ties with international pentecostal and charismatic bodies. Its leader, Bishop Eddie Villanueva, has been a key leader in Christ for Asia (originally Charismatic Fellowship of Asia).

Some ten thousand independent charismatic evangelical Full Gospel churches are registered with the government, with names like Jesus Loves You Full Gospel Church, Victory in Jesus Christ Congregation, Church of World Messianity, Bread of Life Christian Ministries, Jesus Is Alive Fellowship, Christ of All Ages Ministries, Jesus Reigns Ministries, Warm Body of Christ, and Jehovah Elohim the Lord of Glory Ministries. Each is self-governing, self-supporting, and self-propagating. They typically participate in PCEC- or PJM-sponsored activities and affiliated local ministerial fellowships, retaining a nonaffiliated status.

Non-Trinitarian groups affirming Christ's deity—"Oneness" groups like the United Pentecostal Church, "Fourth Watch," and JMC—are not counted as evangelicals; most evangelicals distance themselves from these groups. Both Catholic and Protestant churches consider INC an Arian cult.[13] Though some call it an evangelical sect, no evangelical group counts the INC as evangelical.

Evangelical sometimes includes evangelistically inclined and less politically left-leaning Protestant churches in the National Council of Churches in the Philippines (NCCP).[14] The centennial included them as "Biblical Christians" affirming "three irreducible minimums": (1) the supreme authority of the Bible in matters of faith and conduct; (2) salvation in Christ alone, through faith alone; and (3) belief in the Triune God (Tendero 1998, 5). Tendero counts many NCCP church people and groups as "Biblical Christians": "Government leaders like Fidel Ramos, Jovito Salonga and Neptali Gonzales, women leaders like Justice Flerida Ruth Romero and the late Betty Go-Belmonte, educators like Angel Alcala, Ricardo Gloria and William Padolina, and prominent artists like Gilopez Kabayao and Gary Valenciano ... made ... distinguished contributions for the betterment of our society" (6). He also praises NCCP universities and hospitals as Christian institutions.

Most evangelicals regard some NCCP denominations as fellow evangelicals but reckon others "ecumenical." The labels, also used by NCCP leaders and constituents,[15] accurately reflect theological and ideological differences. Evangelical-friendly NCCP churches include the Convention of Philippine Baptist Churches, Iglesia Evangelica Metodista en las Islas Filipinas, and the Salvation Army, itself a PCEC member. Ecumenicals include Iglesia Filipina Independiente (Aglipayan Church), United Church of Christ in the Philippines (UCCP), Iglesia Unida Ecumenical, Lutheran Church in the Philippines, United Methodist Church, and Episcopal Church in the Philippines. NCCP and PCEC have improved relationships since 1994 (Vencer 1994c, 27).[16] This chapter discusses only the leaders and members of evangelical-friendly NCCP churches who participate in PCEC and PJM activities, such as local ministerial fellowships, the National Church Planting Program, and March for Jesus.

Public perception of evangelicals was further clarified when the leaders of PCEC, PJM, CLAP, and the Philippine Congress on World Evangelization formed a united front for addressing national issues, called Christian Leaders Conference of the Philippines (CLCP), partly as an evangelical counterpart to CBCP (Charis 1994). From then on, following PCEC Director Tendero's lead, major evangelical churches typically designated their chief ministers "bishops."

Evangelicalism has a definite Protestant slant, but Filipino evangelicals do not confine the concept to Reformation Protestantism (Tendero 1994b, 12), including charismatic or pentecostal movements, and sometimes even Roman Catholic charismatic renewal movements, as part of their spiritual heritage: "The charismatic movement...spread outside the boundaries of 'official' evangelicalism. In 1966, there emerged a strong Catholic charismatic movement which, by 1980, flourished in over a hundred nations" (13).[17] Some evangelicals seek closer partnership with charismatic or even mainstream Roman Catholics, but most are wary; "renewed Catholics" have their own reservations (Harper 2000, 252–253).[18] Evangelical Catholics, marginal among Filipino evangelicals, are not included here.[19]

Filipino Evangelicals and Political Involvement

A growing minority of evangelicals were involved in People Power events in 1986, but most stayed aloof for five main reasons: (1) American mission heritages of pietistic theology (cf. Lim 2000); (2) continued American financial support and influence; (3) individualistic outlooks, emphasizing personal salvation and ignoring social or cultural issues; (4) concern for self-advancement due to low social status;[20] and (5) political naïveté. Like most Filipinos, they had no political experience beyond voting in elections.

Evangelicals became politically involved in three waves. First were "transformational" (or activist) evangelicals, predominantly educated and newly middle class, nurtured as students in the early 1970s by Inter-Varsity's "kingdom of God" paradigm, which led to the founding of the Institute for Studies in Asian Church and Culture (ISACC) in 1978.[21] They criticized Marcos and were present at EDSA 1.

A second wave arose as Christian development groups ministered among the urban poor. These groups helped "conservative evangelicals," particularly PCEC leadership, already exposed to international evangelical movements (especially the 1974 Lausanne Covenant), toward theological understanding that included sociopolitical involvement.

"Charismatic evangelicals" were a third wave, first visible in 1992. Their activist bent arose in the 1980s. Many of their leaders had activist or middle-class backgrounds and were theological optimists about transforming "the powers," having experienced God's supernatural power in personal and church life. They combined evangelistic zeal and political savvy, using mass media and street marches and rallies. In the 1998 elections, they displayed a lack of political sophistication, but, as People Power 2 and People Power 3 showed, they learned quickly.

Philippine Evangelicalism and Elections

Political scientists commonly define democracy as holding regular elections to transfer power to leaders (Dahl 1971). The Philippines held presidential elections in 1992 and 1998 and congressional elections in 1987, 1995, and 2001. Yet political analysts unanimously consider Philippine politics elitist, plagued with persistent poor governance and patronage politics, with an electoral culture of "gold, guns, and goons" (a common usage in public discourse). Misfits, cheats, and even criminals often win elections. Vote buying, violence, and both fraudulent and inept miscounting mar elections. Efforts to institute machine counting have been frustrated.

It's a liability to be labeled a traditional politician (or *trapo*, meaning "rags" in Filipino), yet such candidates continue to win elections. One convicted rapist was reelected to Congress, although unable to campaign from his prison cell. Political dynasties continue to dominate despite legal term limits. Almost all politicians claim to represent "new politics," but honest, or new, politics requires a stable electoral system and political parties with clear platforms. The multiparty system Constitution facilitates frequent party transfers based on personalities and patronage, worsening problems already evident in the earlier two-party system. No major presidential candidates in 1992 or 1998 had a clear political ideology.

Remarkably, Filipino voters remain optimistic about voting: nearly 75 percent think their vote makes a difference in determining what kind of government they get. All elections have an 85 to 90 percent turnout (Arroyo

1995, 6; Social Weather Stations [SWS] 2001a, 25). Filipinos may seek "saviors" to untangle complex problems they themselves need to solve, but they take their right to elect officials seriously.

Filipino Religion, Evangelicals, and Elections

The 1991 International Social Survey Program (Mangahas and Guerrero 1992, 2–6; Mangahas 1996, 2–4) rates Filipinos the most religious people worldwide, based on belief in God, daily prayer, attending religious services, and so on. Surveys of Roman Catholic countries in 1996 rated Filipino Catholics most religiously conservative (Mangahas 1997, 1–3). Filipinos hold the church in high esteem (Acuna 1991, 3; Mangahas 1991, 1; 1996, 5; SWS 1999, 154) but oppose church involvement in politics, especially electoral politics (Mangahas 1996, 3–5; 2001c, 13; Miranda 2000). Most ignore church endorsements, although poorer Filipinos are somewhat more influenced (SWS 2001a, 60).[22]

What role have evangelicals played? Evangelicals became prominent in the first post-Marcos presidential elections. Evangelical churches had grown markedly in the 1980s, and many leaders felt pressure to guide congregations politically. Despite their minority status, evangelicals undertook religious endorsements, electoral education, and partisan campaigns.

General Fidel Ramos won the 1992 elections. Ramos didn't hide his Protestantism, but he belonged to the UCCP Cosmopolitan Church and was not an evangelical as defined here.[23] He *was* evangelically influenced, openly taking Bishop Villanueva as his private chaplain.[24] The UCCP, and NCCP, advocating nationalism (read: anti-Americanism) and opposing economic globalization (liberalization and privatization), took a largely adversarial stance throughout his administration, as it had during Marcos's and Aquino's.

In 1992, Ramos was attacked over his military background. He needed Aquino's "anointment"[25]—and perhaps a little cheating—to win by a mere eight hundred thousand votes, with 24 percent of votes overall. These multiparty elections generated small parties, relying heavily on personal appeal. Cardinal Sin clearly, though obliquely, supported Ramon Mitra, the speaker of the House. One pastoral letter asked Catholics to repudiate Marcos-era "oppressors and plunderers" (Imelda Marcos and Danding Cojuangco) and those "who will oppose Catholic principles in their public acts" (Protestants: Ramos and Senate President Jovito Salonga). Another attacked Ramos for having commanded the Philippine Constabulary that enforced Marcos's martial rule (Timberman 1992, 112).

When Ramos assumed office, democracy was still very much under threat. The Aquino presidency had faced at least seven coup attempts, which hindered economic recovery from the Marcos kleptocracy. Aquino's administration ended with a serious energy crisis (Cortes 1999a), which it took

Ramos months to resolve. Overall, Ramos governed well, improving infrastructure and economic performance,[26] negotiating peace with communist and Muslim rebels, and professionalizing the military (Cortes 1999b). But he lost popularity in 1998 trying to change the Constitution to allow himself a second term after early poll surveys showed Estrada leading (Locsin 1998).

The 1998 presidential race initially included eleven major candidates, and Vice President Estrada took a runaway lead. (Imelda Marcos withdrew in favor of Estrada a month before the election.) Estrada was least acceptable to the political and economic elite, but last-ditch efforts to unite around a more qualified candidate came too late and failed to muster the consensus needed to support an alternative to Estrada and Ramos-backed Speaker Jose de Venecia. Emotions ran high, fueled by rumors of large-scale cheating to avert an Estrada victory. Cardinal Sin thought Estrada unfit for the presidency (Bacani 1998b), reportedly saying, "The most probable winner may be... disastrous for the country" (in S. Suh and Lopez, 1998a, 26). But the church's unwavering support for clean and honest elections provided stable ground during the fractious elections. Some religious groups, including evangelicals, endorsed specific candidates. CBCP wisely maintained neutrality while speaking boldly in defense of the sanctity of the electoral process (Karaos 1998). Despite the turmoil, the electorate preserved election integrity. Estrada won overwhelmingly, surpassing the closest contender by almost 20 percent. Religious groups opposed to Estrada, though disgruntled, accepted his electoral mandate.

Religious Endorsements

Evangelicals became more visible in the 1992 and 1998 campaigns. A vocal minority in 1992, they gained status by using media to express their views. Late in that campaign, JIL Bishop Eddie Villanueva strongly supported Ramos's candidacy.[27] Initially put off by Ramos's military background and inclined toward Salonga, a personal friend, Villanueva declined to endorse Ramos. But a week before elections, Villanueva was "led by the Lord" to endorse Ramos. His wife, Dory, "heard" Ramos's name out of nowhere; American Bob Wyner of Maranatha Ministries reported a voice telling him that Ramos (mispronounced RAY-mos) would be the next president and bless the nation, as he prayed for the Philippines on his flight into Manila. Dan Balais, PJM general secretary and chairman of the influential Intercessors of the Philippines (IFP), PJM's prayer arm,[28] supported Villanueva's choice on the spot. The key IFP leader in Mindanao, Rev. Ernie Abella, was already campaigning for Ramos as "God's chosen" (interviews with Villanueva and Balais).[29] But many evangelicals disliked this way of endorsing political candidates,[30] especially when PJM leadership gave Ramos an "anointing ceremony" after his victory.

These discomforts and fears were exacerbated in 1998, when Bishop Villanueva led PJM to endorse and predict success for Jose de Venecia, who eventually lost. PJM's leadership lost credibility. JIL endorsed de Venecia in April (Burgos 1998, 1). Villanueva then invited more than a thousand evangelical leaders to a dinner to hear him speak. Astonishingly, a placard using de Venecia's initials, JDV, proclaimed "Jesus Declares Victory." Villanueva claimed his staff did this without his knowledge (interviews with Villanueva and Magbanua). That meeting convinced many key leaders—Fred Magbanua,[31] Tendero, Jovie Galaraga—that de Venecia was "God's anointed." His written pledge "to all the brethren in Christ Jesus" may have made a big impact: "From the...moment...I received Jesus Christ as my LORD and SAVIOUR, it has become my conviction that a meaningful and purposeful service to my country and people can only be achieved if I submit my whole being to our God Almighty.... I will encourage and support all efforts and activities that will make the Philippines 'born again,' Renewed [sic] by God's Spirit nation...[and require]...use of the Holy Bible as the foundation of all teachings and seminars in all government institutions" (de Venecia, n.d.).

Evangelical leaders had laid hands on President Ramos in October 1997 and prayed God would move him to choose a successor "to fulfill God's glorious destiny for the nation." (Most thought Ramos would pick Gen. Renato "Rene" de Villa.) Another American, Bill Hamon, predicted that beginning with Ramos, the next three presidents would make the Philippines the "Gospel center of the world," and an evangelical businessman named Romy Salvador was ministering to de Venecia (interviews with Villanueva, Balais, and Salvador). Although no voice or prophecy provided "supernatural guidance," they reckoned that "God-given wisdom" and "common sense" showed the best prospect for advancing biblical Christianity and national prosperity as "God's choice." Even if the decision were unpopular, they should "seek the approval of God, not of man" (interviews with Villanueva and Magbanua).

Villanueva organized a nationally televised support rally at Rizal Park a week before Election Day. Comparing de Venecia to the biblical Joshua, Ramos read the Scripture "Be strong and courageous, for you will bring the Israelites into the land." Villanueva went further, declaring, "The president's choice is God's choice" (quoted in S. Suh and Lopez 1998a, 26).

Villanueva's later role in People Power 2 reduced disenchantment over his electoral endorsements, yet some think a public apology by the PJM leadership is still needed.[32] PCEC Bishop Tendero offered a written apology after the elections.

Some evangelicals distanced themselves publicly from such endorsements. "Election Prayer Watch '98" (a project coordinated by IFP, with PJM, and PCEC) cautioned, "Let us not succumb to the natural ways of the world in the preparation for the election.... Our choices must not be because of popularity of the candidates, nor their stature according to the world's standard.... Neither should we acknowledge the anointing of the Lord hastily without waiting on Him" (Operation Burning Bush 1998, 1, 6).

Dr. Melba Maggay criticized the hasty declarations in radio broadcasts on January 26, April 6, and May 4, opposing "this seasonal religious spasm of devotion by our officials, and the equally prophetic zealousness of some religious groups in politicizing not only religion, but in effect, politicizing God Himself.... God's holy name is used to serve political ends...making a travesty of the transcendent and the holy. It trivializes our Christian faith" (ISACC 1999, 103).[33]

Theologian David Feliciano (1998) debunked the belief that Ramos was God's anointed in ISACC's election issue of *Patmos*, and ISACC's executive director wrote the largest daily, criticizing Christian leaders "enamored with politics" who went far beyond "providing moral guidance":

> Some [even]... proclaim a... candidate as "God's anointed one"... not... in a quiet, well-reasoned pastoral tone but in the strident voices of politicians. They worked up the crowd which chanted the candidate's initials all throughout the meeting under the glare of television cameras....
>
> Is the Christian Church... helping in the transformation of our political habits of mass hysteria, of association with the great and mighty, and of sloganeering? Or is it being sucked unawares into traditional politics?... And, how do we use the name of God without being sacrilegious? (Juarez 1998; cf. ISACC 1999, 106)

After the elections, ISACC (1999, 104) complained that it "would be more empowering for people to make their choices without fear, favor, or pressure rather than deprive them of their chance to think for themselves," noting that SWS (Social Weather Stations) analysis (1997) showed "'no special pattern in the votes of charismatic groups' demolish[ing] the idea that there is a 'religious vote' among the 'born again'... groups."

A few "transformational evangelicals" tried to push the limits of church involvement in partisan politics. In 1991, the author, as academic dean of the Asian Theological Seminary (ATS) and board chair of its Center for Transformation Studies (ACTS), argued that democratic procedures can avoid divisiveness when churches become involved even in electoral politics:

> Churches should minister to... people of all political persuasions. But they also have a prophetic role—to apply the Gospel to social realities.... Christian maturity will be tested by our readiness to accept differences among fellow Christians.... [To] get church consensus... a Social (or Political) Action Committee... of church members... trained and/or working in government, law, business, and even the military... may be the best group to help work out the

agenda and processes for the church's participation in political affairs.

Churches... need... consensus (60–80% majority should be quite a consensus for non-compulsory recommendations!), otherwise the leaders would be speaking for themselves.... This means that churches as institutions will usually and inevitably lag behind their most prophetic voices. (Lim 1992, 8)

In 1998, my group (NCUT) held that a church may endorse candidates (but not require members to vote for them) *if* the endorsement came through a democratic process in that church. Otherwise, a church leader could at most campaign for his or her choice, making clear that it is a personal choice. In any case, language such as "God's anointed" and "chosen" should be avoided. CLAP agreed, opposing the religious bloc voting bill in 1995:

After a long process of political education, many Evangelicals may... [find] one political party comes closer to the Gospel.... However, this takes time [which]... results in more mature, more discerning voters. This is more participatory and therefore more genuine democracy.

While bloc voting is not part of our tradition, we do not prohibit others from acting this way....

What if the Roman Catholic Church wants to do the same thing...? We say, let them. Again, it will work only with those who do not want to make independent judgments, and prefer to work for narrow sectarian interests. ("Leaders Oppose Religious Bloc Voting Bill" 1995, 30)

Many evangelical leaders involved themselves in campaigns in 1992 and most supported Salonga. ACTS, with some NCCP friends, formed an *ad hoc* "Movement for Principled Politics" to prop up Salonga's faltering candidacy: "Principles, platform and performance—rather than money or 'winnability'—should take center stage in this electoral exercise. The candidates' integrity and track record should be accurately discerned... [avoiding] manipulative tools and disguises of politicians" (Movement for Principled Politics 1992, 9).

Rev. Jovie Galaraga, charismatic evangelical publisher of the monthly *Christian Journal*, included voter education in a twenty-page Easter edition (April 20, 1992) and three sixteen-page special weekly editions. The first issue already discreetly campaigned for Salonga (cf. pp. 4, 7); the final May 5 issue listed "candidates who we believe meet the biblical criteria of a leader for the nation" (p. 3).

PCEC consistently refuses to endorse candidates as a matter of policy ("Evangelicals Rally for May 11 Polls" 1992, 36) and rejects forming a Christian party (Vencer 1991c, 2), as churches should eschew partisan engagement:

"The church should refrain from being a king-maker.... [Church intervention] in the elections can be an admission of failure to teach the members the words and the morality of God.... Politicians should not seek the endorsement of any religious group.... It will lead to the increasing politicization of the church and the religious control of the state" (Vencer 1992c, 2). After the Ramos victory, PCEC criticized aspiring kingmakers and their endorsements: "In the election of a Protestant President, we give credit to our people, especially our Catholic countrymen for their refusal to vote along religious line" (Vencer 1992c, 2).

Partisan Involvement

The PCEC editorial noted that the individual "Christian can join a political party, serve as a political inspector, promote a political platform and even run for public office" and "must be interested in the welfare of the body politics [sic].... In this sense, every Christian should be a politician... to leaven society" (Vencer 1992c, 2). PCEC earlier argued that Christians who live their faith in office could improve government: "Any good Christian who is qualified should... seek government office in order to run that office in a Christian way and practice the principles of the Kingdom of God" (Dominguez 1987, 19).

In general, Filipino evangelicals do not object to clergy running for office, but hold that clergy should first discern their calling. Clergy running for office should take a leave of absence from the pastorate, or even resign (cf. Vencer 1992c, 2; Dominguez 1987, 19). Evangelical clergy are approached to run because of their proven leadership skills and integrity. Rev. Cornelio Dalisay (1987, 18), general secretary of the Philippine Evangelical Mission, responded: "I am being challenged to be a candidate for the mayorship and how I wish to... introduce true service, honesty and dedication to the people.... But because I am in the Lord's service, I have to think twice."

However, many did run for local posts and some for Congress. Twelve ran for House seats, four for governorships—including attorney Manito V. Lucero, pastor of Catanduanes Christian Congregations—and fifteen for mayoralties (*Far Eastern Economic Review*, April 23, 1992, 16). Almost all lost. But many won seats in local councils, as Grepor "Butch" Belgica (founder of Jesus the Vine Fellowship and Christians in Nation-Building) did in Manila.[34] PCEC reported four evangelical candidates for the Senate in 1992 (led by televangelists Rev. Ramon Orosa of Lord of Glory Ministries[35] and Vincent "Bingbong" Crisologo of the Catholic charismatic group Loved Flock) from the small Nacionalista Party.

In 1987 elections, four evangelical-friendly Protestants ran for the Senate: Jovito Salonga, chair of Aquino's Presidential Commission on Good Government; Neptali Gonzales, Aquino's secretary of justice; Leticia Shahani-

Ramos, UK ambassador; and Orlando Mercado, Salonga's protégé in the Liberal Party. The first two also served as Senate presidents. A few were already members of Congress, like agriculturalist Benjamin Bautista of Davao del Sur, who appointed itinerant evangelist Rev. Simeon Lepasana (1987, 18) his legislative assistant. In the 1994 *barangay* elections, many evangelicals won, including businessman Jess Crisologo in Manila. Attorney Daisy Fuentes became a congressional representative in 1995 and deputy speaker for Mindanao in 1998.

Electoral Education

Despite these high-profile involvements, most evangelical leaders simply tried to help a conscientious minority think through electoral issues. Most think "evangelical Christians will always be in the minority" (Vencer 1992a, 11) but can be a "significant minority."

Six months before the May 1992 elections, PCEC held an evangelical leaders' prayer meeting where Teodoro Benigno (1992), noted columnist and executive secretary of ex-President Aquino, discussed the situation. PCEC's *Evangelicals Today* devoted their February–March 1992 issue to electoral education, with six evangelical leaders discussing how to choose a president (pp. 7–9). The issue listed backgrounds, track records, and platforms of all seven candidates (pp. 16–19). A month before the elections, PCEC held a pastors' dinner fellowship with Commission on Election chair Christian Monsod on organizing citizens' assistance groups to deter cheating.

ISACC devoted a full issue of *Patmos* to voter education (vol. 7, no. 3, 1991), with articles by evangelical theologians and an article, "Civil Servants: What Could We Expect from Them?" by Patricia Sta. Tomas, chair of the Civil Service Commission. It invited readers to attend a January 1992 symposium recruiting volunteer poll watchers (p. 20). Anticipating 1998 elections, ISACC held an October 1997 Consultation of National Elections at the Philippine Social Science Center. Isabelo Magalit's (1998a, 20) keynote address emphasized, "Participatory democracy is a historical development that should not be resisted and for which we should be thankful.... Today we can no longer say that the choice of rulers is entirely in God's hands. In a democracy we have the awesome privilege of choosing those who rule over us."[36]

ISACC issued voter education publications for the lower classes, including a sixteen-page bilingual primer "Mga Kandidato sa Pagka-Pangulo: Siyasatin Natin" ("Presidential Candidates under Scrutiny") and a sixteen-page comic book, *Doon Po Sa Amin (There in Our Place)*.

PCEC and PJM organized May 2 prayer rallies in key cities. The largest aired for five hours over Christian radio ("Evangelicals Rally for May 11 Polls" 1992, 35). Magalit proposed biblical criteria for choosing candidates; Vencer called for the righteous to get involved and not abdicate their God-given role as salt and light (pp. 35–36), requesting "five specific duties": (1) pray for rulers and the electoral process; (2) urge everyone to vote; (3) work for clean, credible elections; (4) "promote good candidates" who "fulfill the Divine design for human rulers"; and (5) respect the verdict of the people (p. 36). Working for clean elections entailed volunteering for poll duties and reporting acts of fraud and terrorism.

In principle, all evangelical leaders agreed that religious identity should not be a criterion in choosing candidates. Vencer (1991c, 2) wrote: "To vote on religious grounds alone would be simplistic. Not all Evangelicals would be good politicians and not all non-Evangelicals would be bad public servants." In a later issue, he added, "If we vote for Evangelical candidates, it is because... [they] have the competence and the experience" (1992b, 4).

PCEC continued its "no endorsement" policy in 1998, but added criteria for choosing a president that hinted at support for de Venecia: (1) continuity with the previous administration; (2) ability: "expertise to forge alliance or form networks"; (3) personal advisers (cf. Proverbs 24:6); and (4) a "reasonable chance to win" (Vencer 1998, 24, 26, 31). PCEC (1998) joined the lobby for computerizing the May elections and distributed a primer on how to protect the sanctity of the ballot. Its March 24 prayer rally featured a National Citizens' Movement for Free Elections representative.

PCEC also joined an *ad hoc* Christian Coalition for National Transformation with the National Coalition for Urban Transformation (NCUT), Fellowship of Christians in Government (FOCIG), and ISACC (which hosted the planning sessions). The Coalition sponsored an April 17 "Economic Consultation for Churches," featuring Cielito Habito (chair of National Economic Development Authority) to emphasize issues rather than personalities. Knowing Estrada was unbeatable, they featured voter education, hoping to foster united evangelical advocacy on national issues. Some were very glad to have a Christian radio forum showing that evangelical leaders were by no means unanimous for de Venecia.

Maggay's (1998a, 1998c) *Patmos* editorial was published in a two-part series in the daily *Today*, April 12–13. Coolly noting Estrada's inevitable victory, she analyzed its roots as primarily cultural:

> Our system is a pure copy, ... in formal terms, of Western democratic processes. Not for us the so-called "Asian values," by which is meant ... dour subservience to a benevolent strongman.... We make a great show of our freedom-loving recalcitrance ... as witnessed to by EDSA....
>
> Yet we ... are ruled not by the reasoned logic of our formal political tradition, but by the complex web of interrelated networks of relationship where favors are sought and dispensed based on kinship and other ties.... There is nothing democratic about a system where

access to good jobs or justice or even mere services depends largely on who you know. (1998b, 3-4)

...While [our] democratic values...separat[e] us from our more regimented neighbors, we do not...share the culture of impersonality that has given birth to the democratic idea....The masses of our people do not relate to abstract institutions; they relate to people....

In a way...Erap [Estrada]...is a departure from...elite politics...[and] either a cause for rejoicing...as a sign of the potential power of the *pobres y ignorantes* who have always been at the margin of things, or a cause for dismay...[as] the deterioration of a political tradition that began with the [illustrious]...Osmena and Quezon. (1998c, 11)

She rejected "winnability" as a criterion, faulting the "gatekeepers'" use of poll ratings as prophecies to narrow many choices to a contest between "a philandering bobo and a smooth-talking *trapo*" (1998b, 5, 21-23).

Electoral education apparently got some leaders of ministerial fellowships deeply involved in monitoring and safeguarding elections through Operation Quick Count (OQC), the official citizen's arm of the Commission on Election, or National Citizens' Movement for Free Elections. In 1995, Rev. Jude Garcia of Las Pinas ministerial fellowship served as the chairman of the local OQC. Rev. Jonel Milan in Marulas, Bulacan, served as OQC chairman for Bulacan province in 1998 and 2001. Rev. Benedicto "Benny" Navarro of the Marikina Valley Ministerial Fellowship and the Marikina Moral Movement served as the OQC chair for Marikina City in 1998 and 2001 (interview with Navarro).

Philippine Evangelicalism and People Power

The most distinctive aspect of Filipino democracy was direct citizens' intervention, now called People Power. Here, People Power (capitalized) is used as a technical term for these events; the more sociopolitical usage, people power (lowercase), refers to empowering activities, especially of the poor. In the Philippines, the first usage is more common.[37]

When a significant segment of society believes the duly elected chief executive who refuses to resign has lost the moral authority to rule, massive protest may be the only recourse an agitated and oppressed populace retain.

The Philippine media labeled such mass actions People Power 1, 2, and 3 or EDSA 1 (February 22-25, 1986), EDSA 2 (January 16-20, 2001), and EDSA 3 (April 25-May 1, 2001), as the main events occurred on the main highway crossing Metropolitan Manila, named Epifanio de los Santos (after a heroic Supreme Court chief justice), generally called EDSA, where a large shrine to the Virgin Mary stands. More People Power events could yet happen, as most citizens do not trust the government to listen to public grievances.[38]

EDSA 1 was the culmination of events that led to the expulsion of Dictator-President Marcos. On a December 1985 American talk show, Marcos surprised everyone by calling for a "snap election" on February 7, 1986. Corazon Aquino was the candidate that opposition parties and "cause-oriented groups," and Cardinal Sin, favored.[39] After electoral fraud blocked Aquino's popular victory, Defense Minister Juan Ponce Enrile and Deputy Chief of Staff Gen. Fidel Ramos mutinied on February 22. When Marcos threatened to unleash the armed forces against them, Cardinal Sin broadcast an appeal for People Power to protect them. As tanks rolled down EDSA toward the defectors' camp, hundreds of thousands of Filipinos amassed to pray and stop them. In four days, the citizenry had swept Aquino into power. Marcos was whisked off to exile in Hawaii.

EDSA 2, fifteen years later, was a bloodless midcourse correction to an abusive presidency elected by popular vote. After ongoing presidential corruption was exposed, a fully televised impeachment trial was conducted, with witnesses putting their lives at risk. But when eleven senator-judges blocked examination of potentially decisive evidence against President Estrada on January 16, 2001, outraged citizens spilled into the streets and thronged to EDSA. Konsensiya ng Mamamayang Pilipino (Conscience of Filipino Citizenry; KOMPIL 2), a coalition of NGOs, coordinated these second EDSA actions, and the military and police broke ranks with the president. A four-day protest ended peacefully, despite the potential for violence. Supreme Court justices hastened to swear in the constitutional successor as the ousted president left Malacanang Palace. Though some Western press likened it to "mob rule," this was People Power at its best. Filipinos made democracy work; vigilance triumphed over complacency (e.g., Mydans 2001). But the quick, bloodless, and euphoric EDSA 2 transition still required legal vindication by the Supreme Court.[40]

True "mob rule," labeled "Mob Power" by *Asiaweek* (C. Bacani and Robles 2001), really occurred three months later. When the government moved to arrest accused ex-President Estrada on plunder charges on April 25, his loyalists tried to hinder it. After his arrest, they rallied at the EDSA Shrine for four days. A massive, mostly lower-class crowd agitated for the return of their disgraced leader. On the evening before May 1, Labor Day, about fifty thousand marched toward Malacanang Palace. The dispersal turned violent, although amazingly, only one policeman and three demonstrators were killed in the cross fire. "This was People Power gone tragically awry. The mobs were a legacy of Estrada's divisive rule—and another sad reminder that the country hasn't grown out of its chaotic political traditions" (Mydans 2001, 28). On May 1, the new president, Arroyo, declared a "state of rebellion" for several days, allowing police to detain alleged ringleaders without a warrant. The mobs quickly dispersed.

Filipino Religion and People Power

In all three events, Catholic and NCCP churches openly and actively supported what most have reckoned the democratic and responsible side (cf. Tate 1990; Racelis 1998, 172). Cardinal Sin, their most articulate spokesman, when installed as archbishop of Manila in 1978, had promptly opposed Marcos in a "critical collaboration," intentionally vague because of martial law. As the nation prepared for the February 1986 elections, Cardinal Sin personally "blessed" Aquino's candidacy. One week after the snap elections, the CBCP denounced them as "fraudulent." Cardinal Sin was among the first to call people to protect "our friends" in the rebel camp, and the Catholic Radio Veritas informed and encouraged the nation through the ensuing days.

For EDSA 2, the Catholic Church also took an early position, almost as soon as Governor Chavit Singson made his accusations. Cardinal Sin gave Singson sanctuary in his villa, encouraging him to "bring his crusade to its successful completion," and told Estrada to resign, as having lost the "moral ascendancy to govern." Over the next three months, priests denounced the president from pulpits, and CBCP organized or sanctioned street demonstrations.[41] The bishops mustered sixty thousand for a large anti-Estrada rally on November 4, where Cardinal Sin (2000, 7) remarked, "Mr. President, we want you to return to the grace of God. We are praying for you. The presidency is . . . a temptation for you, an occasion of sin. Resignation will be good for your soul." The president tapped religious groups—Catholic charismatic El Shaddai, as well as INC and JMC—to muster a million people at a counterrally the next weekend. The almost daily protests grew as the first trial day, December 7, approached. Estrada had the Filipino envoy seek Vatican intervention in early December, but she was rebuffed (Quiambao 2001). When the infamous Senate vote ignited EDSA 2, Cardinal Sin and ex-President Aquino appeared and spoke briefly at the EDSA Shrine to calm the crowds. The CBCP, joined by the charismatic Catholic CfC and mainstream NGO groups, called for Estrada's immediate resignation.

At EDSA 3 three months later, the Catholic Church again took a clear, visible stance. Estrada's predominantly poor supporters were backed by INC and El Shaddai. Cardinal Sin, CBCP, and CfC condemned rabble-rousing methods and desecration at the Shrine (cf. Reyes 2001).[42] (However, derogatory remarks used to describe the crowd caused the cardinal to apologize to the poor at the following week's celebrative mass and to promise that the church would prioritize pro-poor initiatives.)

Filipino Evangelicals and People Power

Where did the evangelicals stand?

When Marcos called snap elections in December 1985, most evangelicals took a conservative stance. Mainstream "pietistic" evangelicals argued that Romans 13 taught submission to authorities as appointed by God as long as they provide for religious freedom, although some admitted that civil disobedience might "sometimes be an option...after...exhaust[ing] all legal and constitutional processes" (Bautista 1991, 54). They hardly heeded the nationwide protests. But the People Power events gradually led many to work for further democratization. Evangelical participation increased in intensity and visibility in EDSA 2. Evangelicals calmly but actively and publicly joined the turmoil of EDSA 3.

EDSA 1

Some small evangelical groups began to criticize martial law as early as 1981; their June 5–6 "Novaliches Letter" (*Patmos* 3, no. 1 [1981]: 39–40) expressed grave concern over problems the Marcos regime had failed to address. Three groups (ISACC, Inter-Varsity Christian Fellowship [IVCF], and the Diliman Bible Church) signed a public letter condemning the August 1983 assassination of Senator Ninoy. The PCEC general secretary issued a statement denouncing all forms of sin, but also criticized public protest gatherings (excluding prayer rallies), endorsing only dialogue and media discussion as "the way of non-violence" (Vencer 1983, 12, 37). Maggay (1994, 37–38) later critiqued this stance: "Part of the reluctance of evangelicals to resist authoritarianism...stemmed from a concern to protect the freedom to worship and evangelize, as if it were something a government gives or takes away.... Paul may be in chains, but the gospel is unfettered. Communism, or any form of state pressure, [may]...threat[en] our missionary enterprises, but not...the gospel.... The Church...often...merely protect[s] its own cultic and evangelistic interests, removed from larger concerns of justice and righteousness."

During the snap elections, two charismatic evangelicals ran against the Marcos regime: businessman Narciso Padilla for president and radio commentator Roger Arienda for vice president. Considering this a "call" which some church leaders confirmed, they formed the Movement for Truth, Order and Righteousness Party, using a platform ISACC wrote at their request. Studying at Fuller Seminary, I wrote letters published in the evangelical monthly *King's Times* calling (in early December) for evangelicals to get involved in the snap elections and urging Padilla and Arienda (in January) to withdraw their candidacy and endorse the Aquino-Laurel ticket. Padilla and

Arienda did not withdraw and got a few thousand votes. There are no statistics on how evangelicals voted, but interviews with church leaders suggest most voted for Marcos.[43] PCEC issued a "Call to Sobriety" a week after the fraudulent February 7 elections, asking people to support soon-to-be-announced election results, which favored Marcos.

But on February 20, Rev. Fred Magbanua, the managing director of an evangelical radio company, Far East Broadcasting Company (FEBC), enlisted the help of CLAP, which decided to broadcast marathon programs to discuss civil disobedience. This helped spiritually prepare evangelicals for the unanticipated revolution. When EDSA 1 started on February 22, PCEC called for prayer meetings in churches, and its general secretary, Agustin "Jun" Vencer (1989, 78), visited EDSA and sent tents, food, and medicines to evangelical groups manning EDSA barricades. Eddie Villanueva, then an anchorman at DZAS/FEBC, urged people to go to EDSA as "peacemakers" to prevent violence and to bring food to share with others (interview with Villanueva). FEBC stations covered EDSA and provided crucial backup when Catholic Radio Veritas was forced off the air (Schwenk 1986, 27). Radio Veritas, expecting to lose its signal, urged listeners to tune to DZAS (Tate 1990).

On February 24, at the height of the crisis, a PCEC statement asserted that "our obedience to the State" was "subordinate... to God": "Where Caesar conflicts with Christ... Jesus is Lord. Divine law supersedes human law. Therefore our obedience is not absolute. Whenever government rules contrary to the will of God, then civil disobedience becomes a Christian duty.... After much prayer, we have arrived at the moral conclusion that the legitimacy of the present administration should be questioned" (Schwenk 1986, 13–14; cf. Vencer 1989, 79).[44] Jun Vencer read a February 28 statement on the radio:

> By Divine Providence... Mrs. Aquino and Mr. Laurel were placed at the actual helm of government. Consequently Mrs. Aquino and... her *de facto* revolutionary government are in control and in actual authority.
>
> On the basis of Romans 13, the leadership of the Council has concluded that our submission is to the actual government without regard as to the mode of its accession in power. We will, therefore, pledge our prayer and submission to President Aquino's government and will help in her efforts for reconciliation and nation building. (14–15)

Just before EDSA 1, Konsensiya ng Febrero Siete (KONFES, Conscience of February 7) issued a strong statement; however, only five groups out of some two hundred invited to sign did so: ISACC, IVCF, Diliman Bible Church, Faith Baptist Church, and First Free Methodist Church. Transformational evangelicals Melba Maggay (1994, 26–27) and Isabelo Magalit led

KONFES as the main evangelical group at EDSA and conducted worship services. ISACC issued calls to evangelicals over Radio Veritas and DZAS to go to the shrine and protest (86). Magalit (2000, 57–58) recently recalled "study groups that clarified how Christians should be involved in society" during martial law and the experience of witnessing "rampant cheating, vote buying, intimidation and coercion, ballot box switching, etc.":

> Many evangelicals were in a quandary. Can they respond to a call from Jaime Cardinal Sin? Would not participation in the barricades be equivalent to armed rebellion...? For many evangelicals, prayer was the main or only response. Some evangelicals joined the barricades.... We had no intentions of toppling the Marcos government by force of arms. We... protest[ed]... the conduct... of the February 7 election, but we went mainly to add to the civilian buffer so that a shooting war could be averted or postponed. We knew that our lives were at risk. We also believed in the safety of numbers but our faith was in God. We were unarmed, except for our Bibles and our hymnbooks!
>
> The people who manned the barricades in front of gate 2 of Camp Aguinaldo... under the banner of KONFES... [were] associated with ISACC and... students and young professionals from the Inter-Varsity Movement.

Although more church leaders promoted sociopolitical involvement after EDSA 1, conservative (PCEC) evangelicals mostly remained politically passive. But charismatic evangelicals became actively involved after Ramos's 1992 presidential election. Thus, the growing activist evangelical minority had important partners to work with (cf. Lim 1989, 31) at EDSA 2.

EDSA 2

Evangelicals, though still divided, were more visible in EDSA 2. The most prominent evangelicals joined the outcry for Estrada's resignation following Governor Singson's revelations. Many participated in EDSA 2 protests, though the EDSA Shrine, dominated by a giant Lady of Peace statue, was "too Catholic for evangelical comfort" and considered idolatrous, and a curse, by many evangelicals. I examine three groups in turn: transformational evangelicals, conservative evangelicals, and charismatic evangelicals.

TRANSFORMATIONAL EVANGELICALS. The Movement for National Transformation (MNT) campaigned for Estrada's resignation and urged participation in EDSA 2. Main movers included Rev. Rafael "Chito" Navarro, executive director of the Foundation for Transformational Development (TransDev);[45] Rev. Tony Sayson and Dr. Carissa Dimacali, both board members of TransDev and Asia Missions Network; Niels Riconalla, board chairman of FOCIG; attorney Raineer Chu of Art Medina; and the author (David Lim), representing NCUT's Political Advocacy Task Force. MNT cosponsored an October 17 "Workshop on Integrity in the Workplace" for evangelical pastors, business people, and media people, with ex-Senator Leticia Shahani, Congressman Roilo Golez, Ombudsman Aniniano Desierto, and Dr. Melba Maggay. MNT joined regular prayer rallies with NGO groups scheduled on Wednesdays in Makati City, and in an October 30 public statement called others to join, asking the president to repent and resign immediately: "We also call upon all Filipinos of good conscience to exercise their God-given constitutional rights to peaceful demonstrations of their indignation at... our national leaders... who dare to abuse their mandate by supporting corruption.... Popularity without competence and character will destroy our economy and society" (MNT 2000, 2). On November 11, before the impeachment trial ended, MNT convener Navarro (2000a, 1) urged evangelicals to demonstrate for Estrada's immediate resignation:

> Can we trust the congressional process and judicial system in our country to deliver justice... without pressure from the people through mass action?... Should Christians just withdraw into the prayer closet and let the brave opposition minority do the dirty work...? God has given the people the right to choose their leaders or to express their opposition through public demonstration.... God has ordained NOT the president, but the DEMOCRATIC SYSTEM.... The nation and Christians need to develop within them a national character that is morally strong. And this is only shaped by standing against evil.

He challenged the evangelical leadership not to "dissipate impact" by "calling for general prayers or general repentance" but to "call politicians to account for their specific misdeeds, as in the days of John the Baptist. This is not the time for safe homilies... [but] for a prophetic statement" (3).

Maggay and ISACC were actively involved in mass actions demanding Estrada's resignation soon after Singson spoke up. An early November open letter to ISACC (2000a) members, "Prayer for Erap's Removal from Office," urged them to:

1. Pray every day... that President Estrada will be removed from office.... The [serious] accusations against him... should have driven any one with a shred of integrity to vacate the office. But he struts about boasting and peddles empty dreams to the poor.
2. Lend your voice... be a conscience to our senators and congressmen.
3. Join rallies (prayer and protest).... Stand and be counted... exercising your right as a citizen... entitled to good government.

ISACC invited the public to a November 17 forum, "Why Societies Fail: A Second Look at Moral Leadership and Governance," cosponsored by IVCF and the University of Philippines–Coalition for the Urgent Resignation of Estrada. PCEC Director Tendero, NCCP General Secretary Sharon Duremdes, and Rev. Ernie Abella of Hope Services responded to speakers Edicio de la Torre (executive director of a government agency) and University of Philippines Professor Randy David (2001b, 15; see also Sycip 2001), whose characterization of Philippine society is much quoted: "a thin layer of rich and successful people floating in an ocean of abject poverty, an intellectual aristocracy... unable to dent the ignorance and superstition gripping the broad masses, a world-class managerial technocracy that can run giant firms in other shores but immobilized in its own by... an obsolete political culture, a people with a very high sense of the possible but neutralized at every point by a political leadership [seeking only]... what can be creamed off the earnings of a gambling culture."

Evangelical groups showed readiness to communicate prophetically, using cultural forms and media meaningful to masses of people. ISACC held a *Hari Nawa* (Wished-for King) worship in the Senate grounds, a version of *Simbang Gabi* (Evening Worship, a Filipino Christmas custom), on December 14, the eve of the impeachment proceedings. A lantern parade culminated in a worship service using Filipino liturgy, songs, chants, and *Kaloob* dancers: "This year, we are... highlighting the shadow side... of Christmas. We will celebrate... the coming of the true King, our Savior Jesus Christ, as a threat to the powers, particularly bad kings like Herod.... The Word of God has something relevant to say to our time... against moral corruption in our governance" (ISACC, 2000b). The gathering delivered an invitation letter to Senate President Aquilino Pimentel, read Esther 3 before him, and prayed for him.

At EDSA 2, ISACC led an *ad hoc* coalition Evangelicals for Justice and Righteousness (EJR), mainly KONFES veterans.[46] EJR led the January 18 evening prayer break[47] and EJR (2001) groups signed and e-mailed an "ISACC Statement on Erap Impeachment," asking "our people" to send protest letters to the eleven senators who voted against seeing the evidence, to join "the people power rally at EDSA," and to pray "for the removal" of Estrada, who "has lost all moral authority to govern."

Melba Maggay (2001, 2–3, 4–5) had also been at the microphone at the decisive moment at EDSA 2 and now used evangelical imagery and the vocabulary of the Filipino intelligentsia to describe that event:

> That fateful afternoon... leading... prayer for the nation... I sensed an electric excitement rippling through the crowd below. The vast crowd [was] parting like the Red Sea.... The black-clad Defense Secretary and the AFP [Armed Forces of the Philippines] Chief of Staff

were weaving their way... towards the stage. The rumors of the night before had become true: the military would go the way of the people if... EDSA [crowds rose] to a million. The entire military establishment, it was announced, had defected.

The crowd burst into a long and loud cheer, and... a native hymn of praise that is really more of a dancing jig: "Ako'y magpupuri sa Panginoon" [I will praise the Lord].... My own eyes filled with tears at the hand of [God's] mercy.... I was not alone in sensing that something more than people power was at work.... [Many] wore a look of wonder, stupefied... feeling that... we were part of a history that was not altogether our own making.... The scene seemed... a graphic picture of those mysterious moments when we hear the thud of God's footfall in human history and we stand transfixed, awed by the power of Him who is able to turn the hearts of people into water and make them follow Him like streams finding their way into the sea. Here... were a people fabled to be... disorganized or too indifferent... once again standing thickly side by side with their placards and prayers and a common sense of outrage... [and] hopes for... accountability and rectitude in public life....

This kind of direct democracy has yet to be analyzed and understood within our own categories. It is time we learn to reflect on our own political experience within our sociocultural meanings and not keep measuring it by the terms and tools of dominant political traditions.

... The decisive factor, both in the first EDSA and now, is this gentle show of solidarity by ordinary people... deep[ly] longing to see in our national life freedom and justice... within a tradition that has been there for centuries, erupting in such forms as Dagohoy's rebellion, Hermano Pule's religious subversion, or the katipuneros and bandoleros who staked themselves out and took the superior weaponry of Spanish and American soldiers with only raw courage....

Our tradition of revolt has... fus[ed]... political and religious impulses, rooted in an indigenous sense of spirituality and framed by a solidarity that displays itself in moments of a common sense of sorrow.... Manicured housewives... gave away dainty little baskets of sandwiches... simple folk... gave... boiled eggs or water or *pan de sal* to bedraggled watchers who kept vigil... entire families, rich and poor,... came with babies and children in tow, not wanting their little ones to be left out of so rich... a historic moment.... The liturgical sense... serves as center.... [A perplexed] Marxist sociologist... remarked to me after the first EDSA: "... This is the first time I have seen a revolution led by a statue of the Virgin Mary.

CONSERVATIVE EVANGELICALS. PCEC (2000a, 1) also issued statements to the press from early on, such as its careful October 18 "Evangelical Response to the Jueteng Scandal":

> The accusations of Governor Luis Singson against President Estrada are very serious. If... shown to be largely true... the President loses his moral authority to rule. He is no longer God's servant in promoting good and restraining evil. He should resign.... If he refuses... impeachment proceedings should be carried out.... Until the hearings and the investigation lead to a responsible conclusion, all people of good will should withhold judgment. This is the charitable thing to do. Let not the issue be muddled by mudslinging and rabble rousing, by violence and chaos in the streets. Anarchy is not God's will. We must respect the rule of law.

Another PCEC (2000b) statement on November 18 discussed threats of civil disobedience by some NGO radicals: "We call upon our countrymen to exert all forms of non-violent pressures on our legislators. In our judgment, this does not include such acts of civil disobedience.... Romans 13 is clear, and the situation is not parallel to what we find in Exodus 1, Daniel 3, or Acts 5."

On January 16, a late afternoon PCEC prayer rally began at Quezon Memorial Circle (People's Park), about five kilometers from the EDSA Shrine. At the news of the military defection, some participants went directly to the EDSA Shrine. PCEC (2001a) e-mailed and faxed its "Call to Prayer and the Quest for Truth" to member bodies, asking churches to organize intensive prayer meetings and join a January 19 Prayer Rally:

> We pray for peace.... Change... through peaceful non-violent means. Believers who join mass actions should seek to be a Christian witness.
>
> We appeal to the eleven Senator-Jurors to reconsider their decision... [and all involved] to continue this Constitutional process until justice is served.

On January 23, PCEC (2001b) issued a "Statement of Support for President Gloria Macapagal-Arroyo." The first subsequent issue of its official organ celebrated the grace of God over the nation ("People Power II" 2001; E. M. Feliciano 2001). These declarations appear to be addressed mainly to PCEC's own constituency.

CHARISMATIC EVANGELICALS. The most visible evangelical presence in the public media, as usual, was Bishop Villanueva of JIL. When Singson first made public revelations of corruption against his friend Estrada in early October, JIL's television station started following events closely. Two weeks later, Villanueva gave a bold one-on-one interview with Governor Singson on camera at a prayer rally in front of the Senate, where impeachment proceedings were to be held, sponsored by God's People's Coalition for Righteousness (GPCR), a new network of Villanueva's JIL church, Couples for Christ, the Association of Laity of the Catholic Church (Laiko, the Lay Movement arm of CBCP), a few more Catholic groups, and a Muslim-Christian advocacy group.[48] Dan Balais and other religious leaders were also on stage. Singson was then in hiding, making his appearance dangerous. The authorities stopped the rally early.

When Estrada's press secretary listed JIL as a participant in a November 14 pro-Estrada National Day of Repentance prayer rally, Villanueva held a high-profile press conference to deny it. In all subsequent public appearances he asked the president to resign immediately. During EDSA 2, Villanueva's church planned a big GPCR prayer rally at the People's Monument for January 20, calling all JIL churches in Luzon to send delegations (interview with Villanueva). Villanueva appeared at EDSA 2 as spokesman for JIL and GPCR. Events unfolded so swiftly that Villanueva apparently had no time to get PJM and PCEC/CLCP to come along (interview with Villanueva).

Balais, leader of IFP, repeatedly appeared publicly with Villanueva. He says he stood up as he did because of previous supernatural guidance. He had already been declaring to others that God would restore the nation. In October, he had had a vision of a bright light, representing Jesus, which took the presidential seat and swept it clean: God's holiness would bring judgment to Malacanang and mercy to the nation (interview with Balais). The November 2000 IFP prayer bulletin stated:

> God will expose & consume all forms of wickedness in the land. The line is drawn as iniquity reached its fullness.... This crisis & terrible shaking will pave the way for a dramatic change in spiritual... & moral climate.... Revival & prosperity will follow....
> Let us pray:
> 1. That... [any] transition of political leadership in our nation... would take place quickly and non-violently.
> 2. That upon seeing the hand of the Lord in these seasons of judgment and shakings, the... effect will be... FEAR OF THE LORD coming upon the leaders of the land.
> 3. That GOD'S RIGHTEOUSNESS, TRUTH AND JUSTICE will indeed become the foundations of Philippine society... the only Christian nation in the Far East. (Operation Burning Bush 2000, 1, 4)

Balais discouraged pastors from attending the November 14 National Day of Prayer and Fasting, as it seemed implicitly to support Estrada. Reflecting on Jeremiah 1:11–14, Balais declared in the January 2001 IFP bulletin, "Our nation is ripe for God's cleansing judgment... mercifully directed towards sin, corruption and the moral decadence of our people. On the surface, we see protest rallies, political unrest, economic crises, and major shakeup on our religious and governmental institutions; deep inside the soul of the nation is a desperate cry for righteousness... [and] spiritual transformation. A nation ripe for the Gospel of the Kingdom!" (Operation Burning Bush 2001, 1).

Evangelical support for Estrada was very slight, although a few evangelicals who had campaigned for his 1998 victory held a pro-Estrada view. At the November 14 rally, Roger Arienda proclaimed that people "should 'respect' the Estrada government... put in place by God himself" (quoted in Teodoro 2000, 9). Another pastor circulated a monograph entitled "Trial of the Two Servants of God," making parallels between the persecution of Estrada and that of Jesus Christ.

More important were conservatives who thought that evangelical churches, especially JIL, were too involved in politics, or even "unbiblical" to go against a democratically elected president. Villanueva's (2001, 3, 4) response invoked Thomas Jefferson and Edmund Burke, Rev. Pat Robertson, and biblical precedents!

> The Church in nature is non-partisan.... Christians... are called to bear with their government whenever possible. But... it is not wrong for Christians to make a stand and fight for their right just like in Saint Peter's time. He said, "We ought to obey God rather than men" (Acts 5:29).... Blind obedience to government is never right....
>
> That is why we in the JIL Church, PJM and GPCR... oppose... smut proliferation... legalization of gambling, bloc voting, and other devil-inspired bills.... [We must] ensure that God's principles in governance are... adhered to. Edmund Burke wrote, "It is necessary only for the good man to do nothing for the evil to triumph."

Evangelicals as a group had come far.

EDSA 3

When crowds started to gather after ex-President Erap Estrada's arrest on April 25, evangelicals became visibly involved again. This time, evangelicals were unanimous in opposing the pro-Estrada People Power rally. On April 27, two days after the start of EDSA 3, Bishop Eddie Villanueva, Bishop Efraim Tendero, Bishop Fred Magbanua, and Rev. Dan Balais issued a joint statement, published in the major dailies:[49]

> While we recognize the constitutional right of every citizen to free speech and assembly, we decry the demand of Erap's allies as without any legal anchor, let alone moral cause, manifest[ing] blatant and indecent disregard for the rule of law, reason and order. It is also a

wanton mockery of the spirit of Edsa People Power 2 which ousted an immoral and corrupt leader. The intent... [is] to destabilize [Pres. Arroyo's] legitimate government.

Remain calm and sober... and look up to God our "fortress and refuge and ever-present help in trouble."...

Finally, we reaffirm our all-out support to President Gloria Macapagal-Arroyo and her legitimate government in obedience to Romans 13 and I Timothy 2:1–5. (Villanueva, Tendero, Magbanua, and Balais 2001, 10)

This interspersing of biblical allusions and imagery with secular language displayed increased political maturity.

LITTLE PEOPLE POWER EVENTS IN 1997 AND 1999

Two less significant demonstrations, or little People Power events, against *cha-cha* (charter change), were mass actions against plans to change the Constitution by President Ramos in 1997 and President Estrada in 1999.[50] Both attempts were stopped by People Power rallies called by Cardinal Sin and ex-President Aquino, with strong NGO support. Evangelicals were involved in both.

CHA-CHA 1997. In 1997, although NGO groups were predominantly anti-cha-cha, evangelicals were quite divided. Most evangelicals seem to have been pro-cha-cha because of Bishop Villanueva's close ties with President Ramos, who wanted to amend the 1987 Constitution to permit a second term. PJM, supported by many PJM leaders, helped gather signatures favoring the change. PCEC issued no statement.

Bread of Life pastor Rev. Cesar "Butch" Conde, though anti-cha-cha himself, protested open church intervention in politics, particularly by Cardinal Sin, writing articles published as half-page ads in the major dailies. He quoted Ramos's (Catholic) secretary of budget and management, Salvador Enriquez Jr., rebuking the cardinal's strong statements: "What... great... sin could President Ramos have committed to deserve such vitriol and unkind words... except... that [he] happens to be a Protestant.... Cannot we be like many modern-day democracies that practice a high degree of tolerance of all kinds of religions?" (Conde, 1997b, 10).

Conde criticized the cardinal at the September 21 rally, emphasizing the separation of church and state. Clergy should be limited to spiritual and pastoral matters, leaving secular and political matters to the laity and avoiding direct political involvement, which he saw as divisive (Conde 1997a).

A significant minority, mainly transformational evangelicals, were openly anti-cha-cha. Several Christian leaders (including the author) called evangelicals to join "pro-democracy" groups for a rally at Rizal Park on September 21.

They believed that premature constitutional revision put nationalist and "authentic pro-people, pro-poor and pro-life provisions" at risk of being deleted or reduced by vested interests, and that constant constitutional change made the country unstable.

CHA-CHA 1999. In 1999, evangelicals were more united. Estrada intended to amend the Constitution, removing term limits of elected officials and opening the economy fully. (The Constitution prohibits foreign direct ownership of land and restricts the foreign share in local companies.) NGOs, joined by Cardinal Sin and ex-President Aquino, again strongly opposed cha-cha plans (Sprague and Lopez 1999). In an August 20 pastoral letter, the cardinal called the faithful to attend a prayer rally in Makati City.[51] That afternoon, Estrada countered with a half-million crowd at Rizal Park, announced as a birthday celebration for his advisor, Mike Velarde; Erap claimed this demonstrated support for his plans.

PJM, JIL, and PCEC strongly and publicly opposed the presidential initiative, also protesting the government cronyism and corruption that characterized Estrada's regime. But their voice was somewhat muted for fear of being seen as contrarian, having campaigned against Estrada in 1998.

Transformational evangelicals strongly supported the August 20 rally led by Aquino and Sin. They issued a public statement under the banner of Evangelicals for Justice and Righteousness, with ISACC, IVCF-Phil, and Christian Writers Fellowship as cosignatories (EJR 1999, 2):

> We view with alarm the return of insidious ills and forces that have blighted our lives during the Marcos regime. Cronyism, the muzzling of the press, and moves to amend the Constitution just to put a stamp of constitutional legitimacy on plots that essentially entrench favored political and economic interests are dangerous tendencies that must be resisted.... We deplore the ... moral malaise [of] ... a presidency ... adrift, tossed to and fro by every wind of cunning and corruption ... for lack of deep ethical moorings....
>
> To avert national disaster we call on our President ... to submit to ... public accountability.... God is King over the whole world and its rulers.... While the church and state are separate, both are subject to God and his laws.... The church ... has a prophetic duty ... to see ... that governance is in accordance with God's laws and ... original purpose ..., namely, to punish those who do wrong and praise those who do right." (1 Pet. 2:13–14)

SUMMARY OF EVANGELICALS AND PEOPLE POWER

Successive People Power events show growing political maturity among evangelicals. Consolidating Philippine democracy requires transformation of the polity itself to be able to choose good and competent officials. Many think People Power was necessary to control corrupt (1986, 2001) and abusive (1997, 1999) situations without violence and to correct abuse and misrule. A University of the Philippines law professor comments, "[People Power] is a check on the government. It's progressive because in order to be able to do that you have to convince millions of people.... We're not limited to the Western conception of democracy.... What we have is direct democracy" (*Today's Weekender Staff* 2001, 2). Most Filipino analysts hope that the People Power phenomenon has ended, arguing that People Power was necessary for a young democracy and that "direct action from the people" is no longer needed. Nonetheless, evangelicals remain ready to defend important political principles if need be. But preventing such needs by building up civil society is preferable.

Philippine Evangelicalism and Civil Society

Civil society is crucial for a nation's stability and democratic growth. Though People Power events indicate vital popular democracy most visibly and dramatically, the development of civil society is what adapts and maintains democratic processes and structures by building social capital—"features of social organization, such as trust, norms and networks that can improve the efficiency of society by facilitating coordinated action"—in a political culture (Putnam, Leonardi, and Nanetti 1993, 69; cf. Tocqueville 1956).[52]

"Civil society" here refers to voluntary associations, neither profit-oriented (businesses) nor political or bureaucratic (government), including all NGOs working for societal causes such as poverty alleviation, the environment, nationalism, social justice, education, and religion, as well as people's organizations, such as cooperatives and labor unions (Sicam 2001). Such groups "encourage debate on issues" (all too rare in the Philippines), "force government to be more transparent and get citizens to be involved in public issues" (Karaos 2001, 12).

NGOs in the Philippines are among the world's most organized.[53] Since EDSA 1, thousands of NGOs have organized civic action programs. The NGO community plays an important role in generating the "new politics" many long for. A "politics of issues and programs" has to start with changing the daily practices of bureaucrats, politicians, and ordinary citizens, by raising issues, finding and disclosing information, and holding decision makers accountable.

CBCP and NCCP churches have prominently articulated moral norms and taken leadership in development, justice, and peace concerns, advocating reforms and contesting abuses (cf. Racelis 1998, 172–175). They were deeply involved, often taking leadership in civil society, even before martial law.

Yet, frustration continues to linger: *How has civil society failed so badly that the poor could be manipulated to produce EDSA 3?* Civically involved people are a few in a large population; many reckon past efforts have been inadequate, particularly in educating and empowering the poor. Some suggest that civil society groups should organize, or ally with, a political party while pursuing issue-based coalitions and acting as pressure groups (Karaos 2001).[54]

How have Filipino evangelicals actively participated in civil society?

Evangelicals' role in enhancing civil society may have been their biggest contribution to consolidating democracy in the Philippines. Evangelicals have created and expanded social capital by increasing the pool of conscientious citizens, NGOs, and people's organizations and by contributing grassroots educators, political activists, community peacemakers, and skilled leaders and coalition builders. These civic contributions can be classified in eight areas: (1) personal civics, (2) poverty alleviation, (3) popular education, (4) political advocacy, (5) peace advocacy, (6) community organizing, (7) leadership development, and (8) pluralistic structure.

Personal Civics

For democracy to work, citizens must recognize their responsibilities and duties as well as claim rights and privileges. Yet, in the Philippines, an elitist culture fails to instill the value of individual initiative and moral living. The Catholic Church widely quotes Pope John Paul II's teaching that "democracy without values easily turns into open or disguised totalitarianism," and thus "authentic democracy must be founded on basic values like respect for the human person and human rights, for freedom, truth, justice, and the common good" (in Carroll 1996, 173–174). Yet the church often fails to inculcate such values, as is reflected in the poor moral fiber of the population.

Evangelicals have excelled in this arena, emphasizing the need for personal transformation in order to serve God and humanity. Filipino evangelicalism is widely recognized as producing conscientious citizens who have been taught to be individually responsible. The theology of the "priesthood of every believer" promotes personal responsibility, emphasizing conscience in making major and minor decisions. This enhances civic life in at least three areas: moral lifestyle, transformational outlook, and civic responsibility.

First, evangelicals encourage a *highly moral personal lifestyle*—honesty, diligence, and other virtues that uphold human dignity and social development—through evangelistic "calls to repentance." Evangelicals are admonished to be law-abiding citizens and practice good work ethics (E. Villanueva 1994a, 12). Business people like Bertram Lim pay taxes honestly and refuse to advertise liquor and cigarettes (Baui 1995). There is an emphasis on the family, the basic unit of society. For instance, Orosa (1993, 18) calls for family education after lamenting moral decline in Filipino culture. Evangelical leaders serve as informal counselors, providing timely and grassroots guidance to solve basic relationship problems, especially in marital and intergenerational affairs. These efforts lessen social burdens and build social capital. Training upright citizens helps create a moral environment and solid families and decreases vice and crime.

Second, evangelicalism fosters a *hopeful and optimistic outlook* in life and an entrepreneurial spirit and "can do" attitude, enhancing adherents' capacity to work for change. Evangelicals believe a righteous person can make a difference and impact society. This outlook is distinctive and quite countercultural! Filipino society tends toward a passive, laid-back, fatalistic attitude (*bahala na*). Evangelicals characteristically say, "To change the world, we must live a different lifestyle"; or "Following Christ is a call to spiritual revolution with personal and societal implications"; or "Personal transformation leads to a changed life which impacts the world." Evangelical emphasis on developing faith builds confidence in facing the future, trusting God for success, even for miracles. This increases willingness to take risks for a self-initiating and productive citizenry.

Third, evangelical faith emphasizes *caring for others*, especially for one's community: a life of love and good works. It advocates being generous, civic-conscious citizens who build sharing communities. Christians are called to be "salt and light" to the world and a "conscience of society" (e.g., Tendero 2001; Magalit 2001). Common teachings, such as "Like church, like people/nation," reflect this high sense of responsibility for community well-being (cf. PCEC 1987; Tendero 2001). Repeated calls for righteous living and for repentance for the "sins of the nation" also inculcate community responsibility.

Evangelicals' diligent, sober, and ethical lifestyles help them to rise to influential positions and to be tapped as candidates or appointees in government, especially where the rule of law is most valued within the bureaucracy.

Thus, evangelical commitment to evangelism and personal righteousness, which has often bordered on rejection of sociopolitical activism,[55] has nevertheless contributed to Philippine civil society. This replicates observations of some scholarly observers elsewhere that evangelical cultural characteristics—personal discipline, pragmatism, and competition—foster democracy (cf. Martin 1999a, 49).

But increasingly, Filipino evangelicals teach that evangelism and personal transformation should be supplemented by further participation in society. Even in conservative evangelical churches, compassion for the poor is leading to organized attempts at social betterment.

Poverty Alleviation

Over the past twenty-five years, evangelicals have generated a wide array of economic uplift programs. A great weakness of Filipino democracy is its failure to lift the masses out of poverty. The political system extends rights and freedoms, but economic vulnerability impedes the poor from meaningfully using these rights and secures short-term material benefits without shaping economic policies of long-term benefit (cf. David 2001a). Institutional structures that worked well for American democracy produce different outcomes in a highly stratified society where elites strengthen their power positions, "condemn[ing] the majority to continuing landlessness, poverty and powerlessness" (Racelis 1998, 165). Lack of significant agrarian reforms keeps the poorest, peasant, sector marginalized.

Poverty incidence remains essentially unchanged (cf. Mangahas and Guerrero 1992, 18; "ABS-CBN/SWS May 14, 2001 Day-of-Election Survey" 2001, 8). The Philippine Population Commission and the World Bank both estimated that 40 percent of the populace lived below the poverty line in 2000 (Coronel 2001, 12). As income gaps have widened, the government has failed to provide basic services the poor need to live productive lives.[56]

Hence, many see something to appreciate in EDSA 3. The movement showed the poor protesting their burden in a stunted economy. If properly harnessed, this sociopolitical discontent could produce lasting social change and economic growth. Evangelicals have been developing good infrastructure by which to help alleviate poverty by meeting basic needs and building structures that create opportunities for uplift.

Evangelical NGOs and Christian development organizations (CDOs) began to proliferate in the late 1970s.[57] World Vision started social welfare services with an orphanage in Mindanao in 1975, and then shifted to community-based programs in 1981. Christ for Greater Manila began ministry among street kids and later among prostitutes as well. Viv Grigg, a Navigators staff member, began Servants among the Poor, a ministry in the Tatalon slums, in 1978. After some incubation, ISACC was birthed in 1978. In 1980, PCEC founded Philippine Relief and Development Services, which for a time was the largest CDO. Relief operations, counseling services, medical clinics, educational services, income-generating projects, livelihood seminars, community development programs, and ministries to children at risk, prisoners, tribal minorities, and victims of disasters followed.

ATS began a postgraduate program focused on poverty in 1980. Since 1987, ATS has required a course in transformation theology, the evangelical counterpart to liberation theology. In the early 1980s, Jun Vencer, then with World Vision, sponsored training seminars for evangelical Bible school faculty to help them add community development to their curriculum. In 1985, ATS faculty and alumni formed the Penuel School of Theology to provide college-level training for pastors among the poor employing a "preferential option for the poor" paradigm. The Association of Bible Churches in the Philippines, renamed the Alliance of Bible Christian Communities in the Philippines in 1988, amended its bylaws to include "recovery and enhancement of evangelical responsibility, especially to the poor, based on sound biblical principles and adequate understanding of public issues" (*Evangelicals Today* [September–October 1988]: 43).

Since the 1990s, CDO microlending programs have been most visible. These formed an Alliance of Philippine Partners for Enterprise Development (APPEND) in 1991. The largest of its nine members is Tulay Sa Pagunlad, Inc., founded in 1981 by Christian (including charismatic Catholic) business people with the help of Australia-based Maranatha Trust. Ruth Callanta, a key early APPEND leader, cofounded the Center for Community Transformation in 1992, after being a top executive in the Philippine Business for Social Progress, the country's largest NGO, and served as an active member of the Presidential Commission to Fight Poverty under Ramos (1992–1998; cf. Lim 1995).

Early attempts at coalition building among CDOs started in 1988 with the Fellowship of Christian Urban Stewards, which evolved into Samahan ng mga Kristiyanong Organisasyong Pangkaunlaran (Association of Christian Development Organizations) in 1992. In 1998, they started an Alliance of Christian Development Agencies (ACDA); those ready to work with Roman Catholics formed NCUT. The shared vision is of churches catalyzing community transformation through people empowerment and poverty alleviation (see "Community Organizing" below).

In sum, since evangelical churches began tackling poverty issues a quarter-century ago, programs and networks have sought to span doctrinal lines, experiment with programs to assist those in immediate need, and build foundations for long-term economic uplift among the mass of Filipinos, especially the least advantaged.

Popular Education

Quality education is one primary route out of poverty; it also engenders high-quality political participation. U.S. colonial rule provided the infrastructure for mass education. By the 1970s, men and women both had high literacy and education rates. But about 46 percent still do not continue past secondary levels in education, and public education standards have greatly declined (Sycip 2001). The educational system needs standardization, with priority on popular education (Wallace 2001; Carroll 2001).

Roman Catholic religious orders and laity in the Philippines have set up quality schools mainly for higher social classes, leaving education of the vast poor majority an open field. The 1980s saw a proliferation of kindergartens and primary and secondary schools founded by evangelical churches, in partnership with educational CDOs. Most CDOs and many churches provide scholarship funds for the poor, not restricted to church members.

Mission Ministries Philippines, perhaps the most prominent educational CDO, begun in 1984 by ATS President Stewart DeBoer, helped start more than three hundred preschools among the urban poor in metropolitan Manila. There are parallels in the provinces. Buklod Biyayang Kristiyano (Channel of Christian Blessings) began a program in 1986 to enhance the capabilities of Christian Community Schools in Laguna province. Christ the Living Stone Fellowship in Rosales, Pangasinan, established Living Stone Christian Academy. Filipino evangelist Greg Tingson established a vocational school called Fortress College in his hometown, Kabankalan City in Negros Occidental, with courses in automotive, diesel, and electronics.

The Philippine Association of Christian Education (PCEC's Education Commission) established a government-recognized Philippine Graduate School of Christian Education, offering graduate degrees for administrators, teachers, and counselors at Christian day schools. Almost all Philippine evangelical Bible schools and seminaries offer Christian education programs.

Dr. Benjamin Tayabas, previously president of Pamantasan ng Lungsod ng Maynila ("University of the City of Manila"), a major university, leads the largest association of Christian schools, the Grand Alliance for Christian Education (GRACE). The Christian Teachers' Network (CTN) was founded in 1995 to promote quality teaching, led by Dr. Emmanuel Luna, dean of the University of Philippines Department of Social Work and Community Development. Since 1997, Christian school networks have held regular conferences to bolster high standards.

Political Advocacy

A democratic society needs open, honest governance and efficient bureaucratic procedures. Graft eats up funds for infrastructure building, destroys jobs, and inhibits investments. Philippine government spending has a 20 to 30 percent level of corruption, by conservative estimates (Wallace 2001).

Since the mid-1980s, several evangelical groups have provided political education and advocacy, pioneered by ISACC in 1978. Since their formation in 1986, PJM and IFP have fostered political discussion, including political education in prayer bulletins and prayer assemblies. ACTS and FOCIG, formed in 1989, addressed national issues: attempted coups (1987–1989), ouster of the U.S. military bases (1990–1991), confronting the economic crisis (1997–1998), and fighting government corruption (ongoing).

After failed coup attempts, several churches, ministries, and evangelical leaders started Moral Recovery or Value Formation programs for government agencies, especially the police and military: the Military Christian Fellowship (1989), Movement for the Restoration of National Democracy (1991), and the Philippine National Police-Value Formation Program (1992; cf. Vencer 1991b). PCEC's 1994 Moral Recovery training module highlighted love of God, patriotism, personal integrity, stewardship, family life, work ethics, and community life. They held weekly or even daily meetings in the workplace.

Beginning in 1991, annual March for Jesus rallies (formally begun in 1994) in major cities indirectly contributed to political education, addressing pornography (1991, 2000), gambling (1992–1993), lawlessness (1992), ecology (1993), AIDS education (1994), tax laws (1996), and the Asian economic crisis (1997).

Several evangelical groups focused on fighting corruption. Citizens' Battle against Corruption ran as a party-list candidate and won a seat in Congress (with 2.1 percent of the votes) in May 2001; Emmanuel Joel Villanueva, Bishop Villanueva's twenty-six-year-old son, was its congressional representative.[58] ISACC, FOCIG, and TransDev use newsletters and prayer letters to inform, educate, and mobilize constituents on political issues, particularly corruption. Together with ACDA and NCUT, they form the core of a newly organized coalition called Christian Convergence for Good Governance (CCGG), linked to the Citizens' National Network against Poverty and Corruption, a leading civil society antigraft coalition under chief executive officer Augusto "Steve" Legasto, himself an evangelical.

These activists used media contacts all along. Bishop Villanueva's church purchased and operated a television station (cf. S. Rose 1996b, 94). Even the conservative evangelical FEBC radio station DZAS has had a monthly Pakay-Talakay program to discuss contemporary issues since 1993. ISACC airs critiques on national issues, especially corruption and political abuses, in their radio programs (ISACC 1999, 9, 87–100; E. M. Feliciano 2000, 98–99), and devoted a full issue *Patmos* (vol. 15, no. 1, April 2000) to corruption in government. An anticorruption Web site, e-lagda.com, whose CEO, evangelical Enteng Romano, came to prominence during Estrada's impeachment trial, was an active CCGG member.

FOCIG's Action Center, founded in 1992, has a pool of lawyers ready to address corruption cases and became an accredited Corruption Prevention Unit of the Office of the Ombudsman in 1994 (FOCIG 1999, 22). Since 1997, they have pressed the Bureau of Internal Revenue to institute a service desk for taxpayers who want to pay the right amount of tax. In 1999, the Center began a weekly column in the daily *Pinoy Times*. Its December 2000 monthly prayer bulletin, *Prayer Focus*, requested, "Pray for...citizenry to be more vigilant and participative in the forthcoming May 2001 elections. Pray that God's wisdom will prevail in the minds and hearts of voters...our Local Governments to honestly and decisively allocate and disburse funds for the benefit of its constituents...God's mercy to bestow conviction of sins...for President Estrada and other government officials to repent." Evangelical political activists hold public forums with participants and resources from far beyond their own circle. For an October 2000 cosponsored workshop against corruption, TransDev (2001) started in January 2000 "conduct[ing] extensive research at the World Bank, the Philippine Center for Investigative Journalism, ISACC and other centers. We compiled three case studies that showed successes in eliminating corruption in public office." By promoting transparent and accountable governance, evangelical political action groups strengthen democracy.

Peace Advocacy

The country's peace and order have declined since the early 1970s. Various cause-oriented NGOs now combat crime and drug abuse. In 1992, Chito Navarro, head of PCEC's Church Growth Department, formed a Study Group on Lawlessness to examine its "spiritual, social, judicial, military/police, education and media aspects" (*Balikatan* 2, no. 3 [October–December 1992]: 3). Some churches joined the call to "adopt a cop" or "adopt a precinct," working with local police to decrease crime.

Communist and especially Muslim insurgency movements are the toughest peace-and-order challenge. Muslims have suffered from minority status and being treated with distrust, fear, and animosity by the Christian majority. Muslim communities in Mindanao are among the poorest in the nation (Vitug and Gloria 2000). Catholic and Protestant churches played a major role in the Mindanao peace process by upholding the right of Muslims to resources and decision making, especially in the newly established Autonomous Region of Muslim Mindanao. Their members have been urged to "love thy (Muslim) neighbor" and set aside centuries-old animosities.

Evangelicals have begun, albeit belatedly, to overcome their fear and apathy toward Muslims. When the Muslim issue was central in 1995, PCEC expressed full support for the peace process (*Evangelicals Today* 22, no. 7 [September 1995]: 32). A Christian and Missionary Alliance of the Philippines pastor, Absalom Cerveza, was a trusted friend of Nur Misuari, the main Muslim leader. Amid "total war" declared by President Estrada, evangelical leaders issued what became an official PCEC statement, the Davao Declaration, in September 2000: "We lament the injustices and racial biases committed against our Muslim and Lumad brothers and sisters in Mindanao. We also confess our lack of interest and depth in understanding the history of the conflict.... We are asking Government to redress injustice and to make up for the economic and political marginalization of Mindanao. We pledge ourselves to participate in the process of rectification" (*Evangelicals Today* 26, no. 5 [2000]: 30).

Community Organizing

Since the 1960s, the Filipino NGO community has accepted that alleviating mass poverty requires fundamental structural changes. Catholic and Protestant clergy and laity on the Philippine Ecumenical Council on Community Organization introduced issue-based community organizing as one approach.

They envisioned forming a "church of the poor," to press demands politically.[59] Some resulting "organizations of the poor" (NGOs and people's organizations) participate in local activism and policy debates. Such intermediary structures link poorer citizens to state and market and help protect people from naked power (Carroll 2001).

Evangelical ethos, which encourages participation and cooperation through voluntary associations (cf. Martin 1999a, 49), contributes in two ways: evangelicals have planted many autonomous local churches, and CDOs equipped these churches to do grassroots community organizing.

First, since 1980, evangelicals sought to "plant a viable church in every *barangay*." Despite falling short of the "every *barangay*" goal (DAWN 2001, 21–27), these efforts proliferated organized religious groups throughout the country, enhancing pluralism and strengthening democracy by its "inherent dividedness." Freston (2001) argues that evangelicalism's sectarian stance works against homogenizing forces in its cultural environment. Fukuyama (1999) rightly warns that "sectarianism can breed intolerance, hatred and violence." However, Filipino evangelicalism has overcome fundamentalist tendencies and developed an ethic of nonviolence that can keep in check potential socially destabilizing effects. Though many churches retain vestiges of exclusivist and authoritarian habits, most evangelical churches have moved toward being organized open communities with shared leadership and participatory processes (cf. E. Villanueva 1998, 263–265), "mini-democracies of God's people." The very structure of such community churches tends to lead to practicing transparency and accountability on a small scale.

Second, CDOs helped churches realize that transformative development must be participatory. Evangelical leaders included this idea in "Vision for the Nation," a statement presented to President Estrada on the August 1998 Centennial of Biblical Christianity in the Philippines: "A participatory community consists of people who take responsibility for their lives, and who are increasingly empowered to do so—Making decisions that affect their families and neighborhoods, their towns and cities, and the entire country, and being responsible for one another for 'each man is his brother's keeper.'"

As mentioned, the CDO networks ACDA and NCUT have gained expertise in community organizing by setting up model cooperatives, thrift banks, and other people's organizations. By developing training modules and seminar-workshops to teach these approaches, they have strengthened grassroots Filipino democracy.

Leadership Development

Evangelicalism's inherently decentralized structure tends to train and empower people to lead groups. Most evangelical church leaders, including Jun Vencer, Jun Ferrez, and Valmike Apuzen, came from very poor backgrounds.

These and many others rose to important positions within a decade. While the Catholic Church suffers greatly from lack of clergy—secular clergy and religious orders[60]—evangelicals, especially charismatics, effectively develop leaders through apprenticeship (on-the-job training), combined with flexible training seminars. Even in formal Bible schools and evangelical seminaries, low faculty-student ratios and practical skills training have produced generations of participatory congregational leaders.

Evangelical churches have a flurry of group activities that generate grassroots leaders and teachers: Sunday school classes, choirs, and fellowships for youth, men, and women, ministry groups such as medical teams, and community outreach. Concern for evangelism motivates leaders to reach out to friends and neighbors, thereby generating local networks, moral examples, and leadership skills where they live and work.

PCEC and PJM encourage formation of ministerial fellowships or pastoral associations in local communities (*barangay*, town, or city), especially since the early 1990s. Typically, officers rotate, chosen by regular elections and subject to term limits. These opportunities develop higher level leaders. On the national level, all leadership positions are filled through elections, which usually follow strict parliamentary procedure.

Freston (2001, 301) argues that active church members are apt to be more involved in their local communities and professional associations, which generates civic leaders. This pattern is common in the Philippines. Prominent evangelical business people, entertainers, professional athletes, police officers, military personnel, and politicians have been notable in fostering ideals of morality and service. Attorney Emmanuel Galicia, the "preaching lawyer," a pastor's son, having served as pastor of Davao Independent Baptist Church, became fiscal in the city court, and later city council majority floor leader. He was awarded Outstanding Prosecutor of the Country by the Integrated Bar of the Philippines in 1980 (Bubod 2001). Rosa Rosal, an active laywoman, has long led the Philippine National Red Cross. Washington Sycip became a well-respected elder in the business community, having founded an international firm of auditors and consultants known for its professionalism and integrity. Sycip (2001) vocally criticized "sins of the rich" that enlarge the gap between rich and poor.

This process blurs the lines between clergy and laity. Most leaders, from grassroots to national levels, especially among charismatics, never received seminary theological education. Many are business people and professionals, some remaining bivocational while serving as pastors of independent churches. Some denominations, such as the Pentecostal Churches of God Asian Mission, Inc., often raise up lay pastors (DAWN 2001, 85). Amid Catholic and Protestant charismatic renewal in the late 1970s, small charismatic fellowships with lay leadership sprouted all over. Cardinal Sin finally issued instructions, for example, requiring Roman Catholics to include prayers to the

Virgin Mary and receive supervision by Catholic clergy, which resulted in separation of Catholic and Protestant/evangelical groups. Nonetheless, despite conservative pressures, the clergy-laity divide was quite effectively broken.[61] The resulting decrease in Roman Catholic Church membership was the only major negative repercussion of this democratic and social capital–enhancing evangelical leadership growth.

Pluralistic Structure

The proliferation of autonomous evangelical religious units helps teach Filipinos to coexist tolerantly amid the growing diversity of modern society, which includes controversial religious allegiances. Wide internal diversity and debate among evangelicals, and mutual criticism of ecclesiastical positions and political stances, provide good practice in democratic living. This dialogic culture allows for dissent, even against leaders, and can be transposed into the broader society: "Dissent... [cannot] be dispensed [with] in the life of a nation. It is necessary... to ensure justice and relevance in... government. Undeniably, it will involve a certain amount of disorder" (Maggay 1994, 19).

Amid such pluralism, evangelicals became expert in networking and forming partnerships and coalitions.[62] This extends to involvements in civil society, as their relatively united stance in EDSA 2 and 3 illustrates. Smaller coalitions formed around various local and national concerns: ACDA, APPEND, CCGG, GRACE, and CTN. Coalitions and their member bodies also learned to work in partnership with like-minded international organizations.

This evangelical unity-in-diversity also manifests in reluctance to form separate associations of progressive churches, parallel to PCEC. Melba Maggay refused to countenance such a body after EDSA 1, thinking it unwise, especially as evangelicals were a small minority. PJM refuses to form another Evangelical Council of Churches parallel to PCEC. Independent churches and ministerial fellowships form various networks, but not as rivals to PCEC or PJM.

There is also growing confidence about working partnerships with other faith-based and non-faith-based groups in civil society and government. Two major coalitions, NCUT (mainly PCEC-related evangelicals) and GPCR (PJM-related evangelicals), are forming partnerships with prominent Roman Catholic and Muslim groups and leaders. These coalitions give all involved experience in working for the common good without compromising anyone's convictions.

Conclusion

Evangelicals are poised to play a significant "vocal minority" role in consolidating democracy as the Philippines enters the twenty-first century. Throughout the post-Marcos era (1986–2001), evangelical leaders have grown in their understanding and activity in Filipino politics and in their ability to work together for broad national goals.

In EDSA 1 (1986), evangelicals' pietistic heritage resulted in widespread conservatism and indifference toward sociopolitical involvement. Over the intervening years, conservative, charismatic, and transformational evangelicals' political involvement matured, as shown at EDSA 2 and 3.

Academics, economists, and business people have recently put forward concerns about long-term national development (Gonzales 2001; Ferriols 2001). "Yellow Paper 2," issued by people from many sectors who were prominent in EDSA 2, criticized Arroyo's failure to present a clear plan for the nation and considered poverty alleviation and good governance the top priorities.[63] Both are high on the agenda of evangelical social activists. For fifteen years, Filipino evangelicals have been moving in the directions these main civil society groups now advocate.

A recent major work by academics looking at scenarios for Philippine democracy to 2025 optimistically concludes: "The chances look good for the consolidation of Filipino democracy. The nation's cumulative democratic experience, including the recent and phenomenal expansion and strengthening of citizen's organizations in civil society, helps in the rebuilding and institutionalization of democracy.... Progress in economic development, if sustained, is conducive to democratic consolidation. The global democratic revolution provides it with a favorable external environment" (Abueva 2001, 216).

But some prominent opinion leaders question whether the cultural value system based on religious (read: Roman Catholic) upbringing negatively affects these prospects. Can Filipino evangelicalism help consolidate their "soft democracy"? Popular columnist Teodoro Benigno uses Samuel Huntington's 1993 thesis to show that the Latin American model the Philippines follows mires its democracy in poverty and elitism. Benigno (2001, 9) comments on "Yellow Paper 2," "Our top 30 economists and social scientists should have dismantled our democracy intellectually to find out why it doesn't work for us. Why we remain poorer than before, why the gap between rich and poor is getting wider, why we Filipinos remain hostage to our elite. Why we pray to the same God as the Protestants and Jews, and yet our religion has never played a central role in national progress. It has been a hindrance." Evangelical theologian David Feliciano (2001) took this up in a letter to the editor of the widest circulating daily:

> I wonder if Max Weber was right after all. In his book, "Protestant Ethics and the Spirit of Capitalism," he concluded that religion is a crucial factor in the development or non-development of a nation.... Certain Protestant values such as thrift, discipline, honesty

and hard work promote economic efficiency and advance businesses....

His theory appears incontrovertible. In Europe, countries with a long Protestant tradition definitely are more developed. England, Germany, Switzerland and Holland, to name a few, are more prosperous than those that are steeped in the Catholic religion such as Italy, Portugal, Spain, or even France. In the Americas, the United States, peopled by the Protestant pilgrims, is way, way ahead of its neighbors in South America which were colonized by Catholic Spain.

What does this say of our plight as a predominantly Catholic nation? Unless we work very hard, practice thrift, develop discipline and live honestly and simply, we will remain fossilized till doomsday.[64]

The variety and fluidity of Filipino evangelicals may indicate that they can be a force for democratic consolidation, modeling democratic processes in living and working together amid congregational pluralism and theological and ideological diversity. The alternative culture Filipinos need may benefit from this evangelical, bottom-up ethos of letting each member, no matter how ordinary, freely express views and work peaceably with those who share those views, to convince others. The CLCP (Section 1.3) provides space for PCEC, PJM, and independent churches to work out their political ideologies and action programs. Modeling how democracy should work may be evangelicals' best contribution to democratic consolidation in their nation.

Developing political organizations at the grassroots level can further enhance that contribution. As Maggay (1998b, 5, 21–23; 1998a) put it during the 1998 electoral campaign: as the poor are empowered—though "it may take another hundred years"—the nation is on its way to further democratization of access to traditional centers of power.

If evangelical churches and CDOs emphasize greater involvement with the poor, working as partners in transforming their communities to serve the needs of their neighbors, as well as plant churches among them, they will help produce a better-educated citizenry and more competent, diverse leadership and, hopefully, help break the curse of elite democracy, delivering the nation from any need for a People Power 4.

With less dependency on political, economic, educational, and/or religious elites, a truly popular democracy could evolve—a government of, for, and by all the people.

NOTES

Interviews

Balais, Daniel. February 1, 2001.
Jimenez, Ed. March 7, 2001.

Magbanua, Bishop Fred. March 18, 2001.
Navarro, Benedicto "Benny." September 27, 2000.
Salvador, Romy. March 6, 2001.
Tendero, Bishop Efraim. April 6, 2001.
Villanueva, Bishop Eddie. March 16, 2001.

1. A. These figures were derived from comparing the percentages of SWS polls of the electorate:

	June–July 1991	Dec. 1999	Dec. 2000	Apr. 2001
Religious Affiliations				
Roman Catholics	84%	86%	83%	84%
Aglipayans	4%	1%	2%	1%
Protestants (unspecified)	3%	1%	2%	2%
INC	3%	3%	3%	3%
Islam	1%	2%	2%	3%
Born again	—	1%	2%	3%
Seventh Day Adventists	—	1%	1%	1%
Baptist	—	1%	1%	1%
Charismatic	—	1%	—	—
Pentecostal	—	1%	—	—
Others	5%	2%	4%	2%

SWS surveys have consistently proven very valid and reliable. See "ABS-CBN/ SWS May 14, 2001 Day-of-Election Survey" (2001, 2); Abenir and Laylo (1996, 7–8).

2. DAWN (2001, 35) reports enumerate Protestant churches: PCEC = 28 percent, NCCP = 13 percent, Baptist = 16 percent, Independent = 19 percent, and Full Gospel = 24 percent. DAWN (2001) research reported 4.3 million Protestants in December 1997, and 26,700 *barangays* still without a Protestant church (Operation Burning Bush 1998, 4). Its December 2000 survey reported 5.5 million (7.2 percent of population) and twenty-six thousand *barangays* without a Protestant church (DAWN, 2001, 21–27).

3. Bishop Villanueva's political primacy is recognized by the public and among evangelicals. He was chief speaker at Rizal Park in the August 1998 centennial commemoration of Protestantism in the Philippines. His claim to influence more than a million votes may be true; many, especially charismatic evangelicals, take his views very seriously. This membership number exceeds G. W. Harper's (2000, 249) conservative estimate of 150,000 but is much lower than JIL's claim of two million internationally (262). Percentage based on SWS national survey of fifteen hundred registered voters April 19–23, 2001, lists the following "charismatic membership": Couples for Christ, 2 percent; El Shaddai, 1 percent; Charismatic Renewal Movement, 0.4 percent; Singles for Christ, 0.3 percent; JIL, 0.3 percent; Prex, 0.2 percent; GKK,

0.2 percent; Legion of Mary, 0.2 percent; Loved Flock, 0.2 percent; others, 3 percent; none, 92 percent (Mangahas 2001c, 2).

4. Despite reports to the contrary, Velarde did endorse Estrada, albeit quite subtly, particularly during a huge May 9 special rally aired over radio and television; see Bacani (1998a); Suh and Lopez (1998a, 24–25).

5. Senate President Aquilino Pimentel later revealed that intelligence reports estimated that 75 percent of the EDSA 3 crowd were INC.

6. S. Rose (1996b, 99) states that there were then twenty-seven religious TV shows on fifty-one spots for a total of forty-six hours per week, about thirty hours of which were "fundamentalist." But these thirty hours were all U.S.-funded and produced. Local preachers then could afford only radio airtime. Perhaps the visible witness of some "born-again" show biz personalities, such as Helen Vela of a top-rated radio and TV drama series and Gary Valenciano, a top concert singer then and now, was also of concern.

7. Explosive growth in the *number of* evangelical *groups* in the 1980s reflected the teachings of U.S.-based Ralph Mahoney and his *ACTS* magazine, which espoused the right of every gifted believer to form a "house church" in any place. Christian fellowships meeting in theaters, restaurants, and elsewhere proliferated. The author was then teaching that "a church by any name (and at any place) is still the church."

8. CLAP was first convened on February 20, 1986, by Rev. Fred Magbanua to address the postelection crisis, just before EDSA 1.

9. The Philippine Council of Fundamental Evangelical Churches officially changed its name in 1969 and incorporated as PCEC on March 3, 1970, with Florentino de Jesus as executive director (Vencer 1994a, 16–17).

10. The main anticommunist religious groups were the International Baptist Church, led by Rev. Gavino Tica; the Jesus Miracle Crusade, led by Rev. Wilde Almeda; and the Korean Unification Church cult and its political arm, CAUSA International (see S. Rose, 1996b, 97–98).

11. Cf. Isabelo Magalit's early writings in Inter-Varsity-Philippines' publications in the 1970s and David Lim's articles published in *Evangelical Thrust* in 1985 and 1986.

12. PCEC General Secretary Agustin "Jun" Vencer was busy preparing for the Lausanne Congress; Eddie Villanueva, national chairman of PJM, was not directly involved then.

13. "Arian" because INC denies the deity of Christ.

14. NCCP vision and mission statements commit NCCP to "work towards deeper understanding of ecumenism and mutual responsibility while growing in membership...[and] witness to the Good News of salvation through its prophetic role on issues affecting the powerless and its active engagement with the people towards the renewal of society."

15. Evangelicals refused to join the NCCP mainly because of its membership in the World Council of Churches (WCC), considered to be theologically liberal at that time. Filipino evangelicals today are still divided on this issue: some have become somewhat less wary of the WCC, but many still associate it with the apocalyptic "one world church of the Anti-Christ." On the historical and theological roots of this divide, see Vencer (1994c, 25–27).

16. Vencer says, "The... participation of PCEC in the Church-Military Liaison Committee and the National Ecumenical Consultative Committee has been due to... the NCCP. It has also endorsed the application of PCEC in the chaplaincy" of the Armed Forces of the Philippines, although "the government's pro-Catholic stand and the fear of key government officials to displease the Cardinal will probably keep the door closed to evangelicals for the chaplaincy for some time."

17. In the same issue, Ariel B. Costes (1994), director of Prayer Power Ministries, writes, "For having caused the thousands of Latin-speaking preachers worldwide to use local dialects and languages when they preach God's Word... for having influenced former bible-burning mobs of Catholics to love, purchase, study and incarnate the Scriptures whose 'Christ' used to be 'the dead Christ' are now exuberant [sic] and loyalists of the mega army of the Risen King and Lord of Lords, I pick out *Pope John XXIII*.... He galvanized... the inexhaustible energy of change that triggered the mega-religious-revolution of the 20th century. Now, there are more biblical believers among... Roman Catholics...! And the 'New Pentecost' is still growing, renewing and catalyzing!"

18. Isabelo Magalit, regional coordinator of the Asia Lausanne Committee for World Evangelization, suggested, anticipating Lausanne II, "Even Roman Catholics are welcome. I personally think, however that it may be difficult for a typical Roman Catholic to sign the Lausanne Covenant." Just after the 1989 "media war," evangelical publications included articles intended to promote rapport; cf. Claver (1990, 4). The *Christian Journal* published the Irish Catholic document "What Is an Evangelical Catholic?" entire in its April 20, 1992, issue.

19. Evangelicals continue to question many Catholic dogmas, especially as regards the *sole* authority of the Bible, justification by faith, papal infallibility, and the veneration of Mary and the Saints; cf. (Vencer 1994b, 15–16; 1995, 7).

20. Social class affects political stances. As evangelicalism augments the middle class, this may also assist Philippine democratic development. See Lipset (1959); Curtis (1997); Huntington (1991, 65–66).

21. They were joined by splinter groups from the Navigators: Lakas-Angkan and later REACH.

22. The survey shows that in the 1995 elections, only 32 percent voted for their church's endorsee; 49 percent did not vote accordingly; and 18 percent did not vote at all.

23. As PCEC head Tendero (1994b, 19) put it, "Let's pray... that God will raise up not just a President who happens to be a Protestant, but a President who has deep evangelical convictions, being prepared to really stand for the Lordship of Christ even in the highest public office in the land."

24. When Ramos's term began, Bishop Villanueva held private conversations with him at least monthly.

25. Aquino's endorsement of Ramos as the best candidate to continue her program of political stability and economic recovery was a bold move that defied her core supporters and the Catholic Church. Ramos had helped her overcome the coup attempts and had just formed the new Christian Democratic Party.

26. By early 1997, international magazines like *Time* and *Newsweek* were starting to call the Philippines the "new tiger of Asia," but then the July 1997 Asian economic crisis hit.

27. Villanueva's activism stemmed not just from his church's size and media exposure, but also from his activist background. He was a committed Marxist, propagating his convictions aggressively as a college professor at the Polytechnic University of the Philippines, before becoming an evangelical (interview).

28. Balais, a civil engineering graduate who became an evangelical in 1976 through the Jesus People ministry to hippies, became pastor of a megachurch called Christ the Living Stone Fellowship in 1983. IFP was born in 1986 right after EDSA 1 as a prayer movement for the nation, led by Violy Badua, a schoolteacher and administrator.

29. Abella, a former Methodist pastor in Davao City in southern Mindanao, had a charismatic experience and started the Hope of Asia megachurch. He also had an activist background and graduated from Silliman University's left-leaning School of Divinity.

30. One Asian Christian Charismatic Fellowship member complained in a letter to the editor, "JIL and the Coalition for the Body of Christ did not speak for the majority of born-again groups.... The supposedly solemn prayer rally turned into a political circus when Bro. Eddie Villanueva...[asked] God to intervene to make way for a De Venecia presidency" (Sambalilo 1998).

31. Magbanua claims he went into the meeting still deciding between Roco and Enrile (interview).

32. To this day, Villanueva and Magbanua, now PJM's treasurer, insist they would do the same thing if history were repeated. In their estimation, the Filipino people chose the wrong president, thereby postponing God's destiny for them (interviews).

33. Maggay, best known for her writings as an evangelical transformation theologian, received her Ph.D. in cultural anthropology and Philippine studies from the University of the Philippines and served as Inter-Varsity staff before founding ISACC in 1978 (cf. Whelchel 1998, 76).

34. Belgica became an evangelical while serving an eleven-and-a-half-year sentence for homicide. Released in 1976, he became a businessman, but soon went into church ministry.

35. As president of the Philippines Commercial and Industrial Bank at age thirty-one, Orosa was the youngest bank president and received a "Ten Outstanding Young Men" award in for business leadership. He founded and chaired Interbank in the mid-1970s.

36. A shortened version appeared in his column in *Evangelicals Today* (Magalit 1998b).

37. President Ramos called one of his programs "people empowerment," but 50 percent defined "people power" as mass action, 27 percent as "strengthening the political power of the majority," and 18 percent as both. Asked about satisfaction with how democracy has worked, 53 percent were satisfied, but 47 percent expressed dissatisfaction, and 38 percent said they might lose faith in peaceful ways of promoting democracy (Arroyo 1995, 1–2, 4).

38. A February 2001 Social Weather Station survey reported 64 percent saying they don't trust government. In an August 1994 survey, 66 percent said so (see Mangahas references).

39. See *Sunday Inquirer Magazine*, April 6, 1986, 8. The extreme left did not believe the election could remove Marcos and boycotted it. They were caught by surprise at the fast and relatively bloodless People Power event and left out of the final action. Most still believe that EDSA 1 was not a genuine revolution and continue to push people's struggle for liberation by radical means.

40. A significant minority, especially the poorest and the oldest, were not euphoric. A Pulse Asia survey from February 3–5, 2001, shows that 25 percent expected traditional oligarchic rule to prevail after EDSA 2. Among Class E, 44 percent expected continuation of the "tradition" of exploitation of the poor; 33 percent, continued illegal activities (gambling, prostitution, drugs); 28 percent, continued economic crisis (which further impoverishes the poor; Polo 2001).

41. Replying to accusations of Church interference, Archbishop Leonardo Legaspi, CBCP vice president, wrote, "Bishops [have] a pastoral imperative to work for the liberation of the oppressed, [although it is not their] responsibility to design practical political programs.... We live in a pluralistic society... [and] the faithful [are free] to subscribe to a plurality of views in political matters that do not contradict moral principles and Church teachings. It is the pastoral task of bishops not to give concrete prescriptions that preempt the laity's need to think and act... but to call for dialogue... that shapes the conscience of the faithful to pursue justice" (quoted in T. Bacani 2000, 9).

42. Senate President Aquilino Pimentel later revealed that intelligence reports showed that 75 percent of the EDSA 3 crowd were from INC (*Philippine Star*, May 25, 2001, 2).

43. This was mainly due to interpreting Romans 13:1–7 as teaching full submission to *all* ruling authorities. Evangelicals later debated extensively how to interpret this text (cf. Maggay 1994; Magalit 1998a, 1998b, 2000).

44. The response came a bit late because they had to ascertain the facts first (Vencer 1989, 80).

45. Chito Navarro was a senior management executive both in government and business, during which time he became an evangelical. He resigned from government in protest over electoral fraud in 1986 and became director of World Vision Philippines in 1987, international training coordinator for World Evangelical Fellowship in 1994, and general secretary of Asia Missions Network in 1997. In 2000, he cofounded TransDev, which works to alleviate poverty and fight corruption.

46. The EJR groups were ISACC, IVCF, ACDA, Reach, Samaritana, Open Doors Philippines, Mission Ministries Philippines, Christian Reformed World Relief Committee, and Kristianong Bayanihan Lingap sa Kabuhayan at Tagumpay. As many as forty evangelical Christian organizations may have been represented on January 19, as Efren Pallorina, regional coordinator for development of Open Doors Southeast Asia, claims.

47. They had this slot because Ed Jiminez knew KOMPIL organizers Vicky Garchitorena and Ding Deles from long involvement in development work as a Central Bank of the Philippines executive from 1978 to 1993 (interview).

48. GPCR was formed a few months earlier to launch an antismut campaign.

49. For example, *Philippine Star*, April 28, 2001, 8, reprinted in *Evangelicals Today* 27, no. 3 (June–July 2001): 33, with the title "Christian Leaders' Response to 'EDSA III.'"

50. For details, see *Far Eastern Economic Review*, May 20, 1997, 29.

51. Though Filipinos usually dislike church intervention in politics, a December 1997 SWS survey showed that 72 percent approved the church's opposition to cha-cha, and only 23 percent disapproved (SWS 1997, 48).

52. Putnam's research on the regional governments in Italy showed that voluntary associations foster institutional success in the broader society, and hence help consolidate democracy.

53. Budget Secretary Guillermo Carague's report to the National Ecumenical Consultative Committee held at the Evangelical Center, November 12, 1991; cited in *Evangelicals Today* (December 1991–January 1992): 33. He also revealed that international donations for the nation are channeled through the NGOs more than the government.

54. Karaos (2001) refers to the Brazilian Partido dos Trabalhadores as a political party built on a coalition of mass-based organizations that feed programs and platforms to the party leadership.

55. C. S. Lewis's remark, "He who converts his neighbor has performed the most practical Christian political act of all," is often quoted. So is Margaret Thatcher's remark: "There is little hope of democracy if the hearts of men and women in democratic society cannot be touched by a call to something greater than themselves. Political structures, state institutions, collective ideals are not enough. We parliamentarians can legislate for the rule of law. You the church can teach the life of faith" (quoted in Vencer 1998, 31).

56. For a brief, yet clear historical analysis of mass poverty in the Philippines, see David (2001a).

57. Bautista (1991, 91–92) notes that these CDOs emerged through the availability of foreign (mostly U.S.) funds, rather than arising from indigenous theological concern for the poor. However, involvement deepened understanding of poverty and led evangelicals to appreciate social implications of their faith.

58. He is the youngest member of Congress ever.

59. Racelis (1998, 168–172) gives a brief historical account of community organizing work in the Philippines in 1960–1986.

60. In 1990 there were only 5,319 priests and 7,908 nuns—one priest for every ninety-four hundred people (*Philippine Daily Globe*, July 14, 1990, 8). In 1996, the ratio was 1:20,000, and 1:30,000 in some areas (Fr. Reuters in *Philippine Star*, May 4, 1996), with about a third being foreigners. In 1990, JIL had five thousand pastoral workers for its three hundred thousand members; Cathedral of Praise had eight hundred workers in Metro Manila alone (Wourms 1992, 216; S. Rose 1996b, 99).

61. The two fastest growing charismatic groups are Catholic, yet led by businessmen: El Shaddai by Mike Velarde and Couples for Christ by Frank Padilla.

62. "Networking" here denotes a loose relationship of mutual help and coordination among groups; "partnership" denotes a strongly bonded relationship in which members covenant to share in decision making and resource development.

63. Many social critics feared President Arroyo might be unable to push any agenda through (especially in pursuing the plunder cases against Estrada). If so, it will suggest a failure to learn from EDSA 1. Cf. M. Villanueva (2001). Benigno

(2001) and others criticize the paper for lacking analytical depth and concrete proposals.

64. Woodberry's (1999) study suggests a strong correlation between Protestantism and the level of democratization in a society. This may change, because much decentralization and democratization have gone on in the Roman Catholic Church since Vatican II.

References

Abenir, Luis E., and Pedro R. Laylo Jr. 1996. "The 1995 Senatorial Election Surveys." *Social Weather Bulletin* 96, nos. 13/14 (July): 1–8.

"ABS-CBN/SWS May 14, 2001 Day-of-Election Survey." 2001. http://www.sws.org.ph/exit01/ex01rpts.htm.

Abueva, Jose V., ed. 2001. *The Philippines into the 21st Century*. Quezon City: University of the Philippines Press.

Acuna, Jasmin E. 1991. "Survey Data on Religion and Morality." *Social Weather Bulletin* 91, no. 22 (November): 1–8.

Aikman, David. 2003. *Jesus in Beijing: How Christianity Is Transforming China and Changing the Global Balance of Power*. Washington, D.C.: Regnery.

"Akhirnya Naro Melakukan Kudeta." 1995. *Gatra* n.p. October 21, 39–40.

Akkara, Anto. 2000. "Indian Churches Protest Against 'Price Tag' for Christian Conversion: Orissa Ordering Official Permission, Fees to Change Religion." *Christianity Today*.

Akkeren, Philip van. 1994. *Dewi Sri dan Kristus*. Jakarta: BPK Gunung Mulia.

Alegre, Alan C., ed. 1996. *Trends and Traditions, Challenges and Choices: A Strategic Study of Philippine NGOs*. Quezon City, Philippines: Ateneo Center for Social Policy and Public Affairs.

All India Federation of Organization for Democratic Rights. 1999. "Then They Came for the Christians: A Report to the Nation." Mumbai: All India Federation of Organization for Democratic Rights.

Almond, Gabriel Abraham, R. Scott Appleby, and Emmanuel Sivan. 2003. *Strong Religion: The Rise of Fundamentalisms around the World*. Chicago: University of Chicago Press.

Almond, Gabriel, and Sidney Verba. 1963. *The Civic Culture: Political Attitudes and Democracy in Five Nations*. Princeton: Princeton University Press.

---, eds. 1980. *The Civic Culture Revisited: An Analytic Study*. Princeton: Princeton University Press.

Alo, Teresita, et al., 1990. *The Iceberg and the Cross: Violence against the Church*. Manila: Justice and Peace Commission, Association of Major Religious Superiors in the Philippines.

Aloysius, G. 1998. *Nationalism without a Nation in India*. New Delhi: Oxford University Press.

Anderson, Benedict R. O'G. 1990. *Language and Power: Exploring Political Cultures in Indonesia*. Ithaca, N.Y.: Cornell University Press.

Anderson, Benedict R. O'G., and Ruth T. McVey. 1971. *A Preliminary Analysis of the October 1, 1965 Coup in Indonesia*. Ithaca, N.Y.: Monograph Series, Modern Indonesia Project, Cornell University.

An-Na'im, Abdullahi Ahmed, ed. 1999. *Proselytization and Communal Self-Determination in Africa*. Maryknoll, N.Y.: Orbis Books.

Arndt, H. W. 1971. "Banking in Hyperinflation and Stabilization." In *The Economy of Indonesia: Selected Readings*, ed. B. Glassburner. Ithaca, N.Y.: Cornell University Press.

Arnold, David, and David Hardiman, eds. 1984. *Subaltern Studies, III*. New Delhi: Oxford University Press.

---. 1985. *Subaltern Studies, IV (1985)*. New Delhi: Oxford University Press.

---. 1987. *Subaltern Studies, V*. New Delhi: Oxford University Press.

Arroyo, Dennis M., 1995. "Surveys of Satisfaction with Democracy, 1991–95." *Social Weather Bulletin* 95, no. 17 (September): 1–9.

Bacani, Cesar, and Raissa Espinos Robles. 2001. "Mob Power." *Asiaweek*, May 11, 28–30.

Bacani, Teodoro. 1987. *The Church and Politics*. Quezon City, Philippines: Claretian Publications.

---. 1998a. "Philippine Elections, AD 1998." *Manila Standard Today*, May 14, 8.

---. 1998b. "Questions from the Cardinal." *Manila Standard Today*, March 25, 8.

---. 2000. "Light for Healing." *Manila Standard Today*, November 23, 9.

Bachtiar, H. W. 1973. "The Religion of Java: A Commentary." *Majalah Ilmu-Ilmu Sastra Indonesia*, 5: 85–115.

Barrett, David B., George Kurian, and Todd Johnson. eds. 2001. *World Christian Encyclopedia*, Vol. 1. 2nd ed. Oxford: Oxford University Press.

Basu, Tapan, Pradip Dutta, Sumit Sarkar, and Tanika Sarkar, eds. 1993. *Khaki Shorts, Saffron Flags: A Critique of the Hindu Right*. New Delhi: Orient Longman.

Baudet, H., and I. J. Brugmans. 1987. *Politik Etis dan Revolusi Kemerdekaan*. Jakarta: Obor Foundation.

Baui, Jophen. 1995. "Bertram Lim: Christian Businessman." *Evangelicals Today and Asia Ministry Digest* 22, no. 5 (June): 4–5.

Bautista, Lorenzo. 1991. "The Social Views of Evangelicals on Issues Related to the Marcos Rule, 1972–1986." Master's thesis, College of Social Sciences and Philosophy, University of the Philippines.

Bayly, Susan. 1994. "Christians and Competing Fundamentalisms in South Indian Society." In *Accounting for Fundamentalisms: The Dynamic Character of Movements*, ed. Martin E. Marty and Scott R. Appleby. Chicago: University of Chicago Press.

Bebbington, David. 1989. *Evangelicalism in Modern Britain: A History from the 1730s to the 1980s*. London: Unwin Hyman.
Beech, Hannah. 2001. "Democracy Denied." *Time* (May 17) 34–35.
Beijing County Government. 1990. *Beijiang Xianzhi* [Beijiang County Gazetteer]. Yunnan: People's Press.
Bellah, Robert N. 1965. "Epilogue: Religion and Progress in Modern Asia." In *Religion and Progress in Modern Asia*, ed. Robert N. Bellah. New York: Free Press.
Belz, Mindy. 2001. "Caesar's Seminary." *One World* 3, no. 16 (January 27): 1–4.
Benigno, Teodoro C. 1992. "Smoldering Crises, 1992 Presidential Elections and the Political Scenario." *Evangelicals Today* (February–March): 10–14.
———. 2001. "Yellow Paper II: Splash in Shallow Waters." *Philippine Star*, July 6, 9.
Berger, Peter L., ed. 1999. *The Desecularization of the World*. Washington, D.C.: Ethics and Public Policy Center.
Bernas, Joaquin G. 1999. *A Living Constitution: The Ramos Presidency*. Manila: Anvil Publishing.
Bhargava, Rajeev. 1998. "Reflections of Democracy." In *Making a Difference: A Collection of Essays*, ed. Rukmini Sekhar. New Delhi: SPIC MACAY.
Bidwai, Praful. 1999. "Prejudice as 'Education.'" *Frontline* 16, no. 26 (December 11–24) 108–110.
Bloom, Irene, J. Paul Martin, and Wayne L. Proudfoot, eds. 1996. *Religious Diversity and Human Rights*. New York: Columbia University Press.
Boyd, Robin. 1971. *Church History of Gujarat*. Delhi: ISPCK.
Breman, Jan. 1974. *Patronage and Exploitation: Changing Agrarian Relations in South Gujarat*. Berkeley: University of California Press.
———. 1994. *Wage Hunters and Gatherers: Search for Work in the Urban and Rural Economy of South Gujarat*. New Delhi: Oxford University Press.
Brouwer, Steve, Paul Gifford, and Susan D. Rose. 1996. *Exporting the American Gospel: Global Christian Fundamentalism*. New York: Routledge.
Brown, Judith M., and Robert Eric Frykenberg, eds. 2002. *Christians, Cultural Interactions, and India's Religious Traditions*. Grand Rapids, Mich.: Eerdmans.
Bubod, Linda M. 2001. "He Could Never Be Bribed." *Evangelicals Today* 27, no. 3 (June–July): 17–19.
Budijanto, Bambang. 1997. "Socio-Religious Values and Participation: A Comparative Study of the Processes of Value-Change in Three Rural Javanese Hamlets and Their Relationship to People's Participation in Development." PhD diss., University of Wales.
Bureau of Democracy, Human Rights and Labor. 2000. *Annual Report on International Religious Freedom: China*. Washington, D.C.: U.S. Department of State.
Burgos, Jun. 1998. "Brother Eddie Backs JdV, but Junks Gloria." *Manila Standard Today*. April 21, 1998, 1, 12.
Burton, Michael G., and Jai P. Ryu. 1997. "South Korea's Elite Settlement and Democratic Consolidation." *Journal of Political and Military Sociology* 25, no. 1: 1–24.
Caplan, Lionel. 1983. "Popular Christianity in Urban South India." *Religion and Society* 30, no. 2: 28–44.

Carroll, John J. 1996. "Church and State: The Light of the Gospel on Public Issues." In *Looking Back, Looking Forward*, 1995, ed. Lorna Kalaw-Tirol. Manila: Foundation for Worldwide People Power.

———. 1998. "Philippine NGOs Confront Urban Poverty." In *Non-Governmental Organizations in the Philippines: Civil Society and the State*, ed. John J. Carroll. Honolulu: University of Hawaii Press.

———. 2001. "Restraining the Strong State." *Philippine Star*, July 20, 10; July 21, 12.

Casanova, Jose. 1994. *Public Religions in the Modern World*. Chicago: University of Chicago Press.

———. 1997a. "Catholicism in the United States of America: From Private to Public Denomination." In *Transnational Religion and Fading States*, ed. Susanne H. Rudolph and James Piscatori. Oxford: Westview Press.

———. 1997b. "Evangelical Protestantism: From Civil Religion to Fundamentalist Sect to New Christian Right." In *Transnational Religion and Fading States*, ed. Susanne H. Rudolph and James Piscatori. Oxford: Westview Press.

———. 1997c. "Globalizing Catholicism and the Return to a 'Universal' Church." In *Transnational Religion and Fading States*, ed. Susanne H. Rudolph and James Piscatori. Oxford: Westview Press.

Catholic Bishops' Conference of the Philippines. 1989. "Hold Fast to What Is Good." *Church Growth Challenge*, Supp. (January–March 1989): 1.

Central Government Visitation Team Second Detachment Nujiang Group. 1956/1981. "The Religious Situation in Nujiang." *Yunnan Mizu Qingkuang Huiji* [Collection in Minorities Situation in Yunnan]. Vol. 1. Kunmung, Yunnan: Yunnan.

Chae, Soo-Il. 1995. "Response to 'The Democratization Movement and Unification Movement of the Korean Church after the Independence.'" In *Hanguk Kidokyo wa Yŏksa* [Korean Christianity and History], Vol. 4, ed. Yi Man-youl. Seoul: Institute for the History of the Korean Church.

Chan, Joseph. 1998. "Asian Values and Human Rights: An Alternative View." In *Democracy in East Asia*, ed. Larry Diamond and Marc Plattner. Baltimore, Md.: Johns Hopkins University Press.

Chan, Kim-Kwong. 1987. *Towards a Contextual Ecclesiology: The Catholic Church in the People's Republic of China (1979–1983): Its Life and Implications*. Hong Kong: Phototech System.

———. 1992. "A Chinese Perspective on the Interpretation of the Chinese Government's Religious Policy." In *All Under Heaven: Chinese Tradition and Christian Life in the People's Republic of China*, ed. Alan Hunter and Don Rimmington. Kampen: Uitgeversmaatschappij J.H. Hok.

———. 2000. "Gospel and Opium" [in Chinese]. *Message: Bulletin of Hong Kong Christian Council*, no. 226 (September): 4–5.

Chand, Vikram K. 1997. "Democratization from the Outside-In: NGO and International Efforts to Promote Open Elections." *Third World Quarterly* 18, no. 3 (Summer): 543–561.

Chang, Hun. 1997. "Hanguk Minjuhwa 10nyŏn'Ŭi Chŏngtang Chŏngchi" [The Politics of Political Parties after the Ten Years of Korean Democracy]. In *Hanguk Sahoe wa Minjujuŭi: Hanguk Minjuhwa spinyŏnŭi Pyŏnggawa Pansŏng* [Korean

Society and Democracy: Assessments and Prospects of Ten Years of Democratization in Korea], ed. Jang-Jip Choi and Hyun-Chin Lim. Seoul: Nanam.
Chang, Yun-Shik. 1998. "The Progressive Christian Church and Democracy in South Korea." *Journal of Church and State* 40, no. 2: 437–465.
Charis News Services. 1994. "Leaders Summit: Nation-Building 'Body' Formed." *Evangelicals Today and Asia Ministry Digest* 21, no. 4 (April): 36.
Chinese Communist Party, Yunnan Frontier Research Office. 1956. "The Basic Situation of the Nujiang Lisu Autonomous Prefecture, 1956." *Lisuzu Shihui Diaocha*, 7–8.
Cho, Dae-yop. 1999. *Hanguk'Ŭi Simin Undong* [Korean Civil Movement]. Seoul: Nanam.
Cho, Hee-yon. 1990. "50, 60, 70 nyŏndae Minjok Minju Kwajong'Ŭi Chŏngae Kwajŏng'e Daehan Yŏngu" [Research on the Process of the National Democratic Movement in the 1950s, 1960s, and 1970s]. In *Hanguk Saheo Undongsa* [The History of the Korean Social Movement], ed. Hee-yon Cho. Seoul: Chuk San.
Choi, Chong-Chul. 1992. "Hanguk Kidokkyo Kyohoedul'Ŭi Chŏngch'ijŏk Taedo, 1972–1990" [The Political Attitudes of Christian Churches in Korea, 1972–1990]. *Kyŏngje-wa Sahoe* [Economy and Society] (Fall): 205–222; (Winter): 225–241.
Choi, Jang-Jip. 1996. *Hanguk Minjujuŭi'Ŭi Chogŏnkwa Chonmang* [The Conditions and Prospects of Korean Democracy]. Seoul: Nanam.
Choi, Jang-Jip, and Hyun-Chin Lim, eds. 1997. *Hanguk Sahoewa Minjujuŭi: Hanguk Minjuhwa spinyŏnŭi Pyŏnggawa Pansŏng* [Korean Society and Democracy: Assessments and Prospects of Ten Years of Democratization in Korea]. Seoul: Nanam.
"The Christian Employee." 1994. *Evangelicals Today and Asia Ministry Digest* 21, no. 2 (February): 25.
Christian Ethics Movement. 1997. *Kidokkyo Yuli Silchŏn Undong 10junyŏn Hwaltong Pokosŏ* [Christian Ethics Movement, 10th Anniversary Report].
Christian Institute for the Study of Justice and Development. 1987a. *Hanguk Kyohoe 100nyŏn Chonghap Chosa Yŏngu* [A Survey on the Entire 100 Years of the Korean Church].
———. 1987b. *Yuwŏl Minjuhwa Daetuzaeng* [June Democratic Great Struggle]. Christian Institute for the Study of Justice and Development, Report 2.
———. 1988. *Daetonglyong Sŏngŏ Tuzaeng* [Election Campaign for Presidency]. Christian Institute for the Study of Justice and Development, Report 5.
Christian Leaders' Alliance of the Philippines. 1989. "The Word of the Lord Stands Forever." *Church Growth Challenge*, Supp. (January–March): 1–3.
Chung, Chol-hui. 1995. "Hanguk Minjuhwa Undong'Ŭi Sahoejŏk Kiwon" [The Social Origin of the Korean Democratization Movement]. *Hanguk Sahoehak* [Korean Sociology] 29: 501–532.
Chung, Jin-hong. 1987. "Han'guk sahoe-Ŭi byŏndong-kwa kidokkyo" [The Change of Korean Society and Christianity]. In *Sahoe Byŏndong-kwa Han'guk-Ŭi Chongkyo* [Social Change and Korean Religion]. Seoul: Institute for Korean Thought and Culture.
Claver, Francisco S. J. 1990. "Interview." *Christian Examiner* 1, no. 3: 4.

Clifford, James, and George E. Marcus, eds. 1986. *Writing Culture: The Poetics and Politics of Ethnography*. Berkeley: University of California Press.

Cohen, Jean L. 1999. "American Civil Society Talk." In *Civil Society, Democracy, and Civic Renewal*, ed. Robert K. Fullinwider. Boulder, Colo.: Rowman and Littlefield.

Cohen, Jean L., and Andrew Arato. 1997. *Civil Society and Political Theory*. Cambridge, Mass.: MIT Press.

Comaroff, John L., and Jean Comaroff. 1997. *Of Revelation and Revolution: The Dialectics of Modernity on a South African Frontier*. Vol. 2. Chicago: University of Chicago Press.

Conde, C. L. 1997a. "Apology Meaningless." *Philippine Daily Inquirer*, October 18, 10.

———. 1997b. "Damasoism?" *Philippine Daily Inquirer*, October 6, 10.

Cooley, L. Frank. 1981. *The Growing Seed: The Christian Church in Indonesia*. New York: Division of Overseas Ministries, NCCUSA.

Copley, Antony. 1998. *Religions in Conflict: Ideology, Cultural Contact and Conversion in Late Colonial India*. New Delhi: Oxford University Press.

Corbridge, Stuart, and John Harriss. 2000. *Reinventing India: Liberalization, Hindu Nationalism and Popular Democracy*. Cambridge, U.K.: Polity Press.

Coronel, Sheila S. 2001. "Hothouse of Rebellion." *I Report* 7, no. 2 (April–June): 12–16.

Cortes, Rosario Mendoza. 1999a. "Corazon Cojuangco Aquino: 1986–1992." In *Philippine Presidents: 100 Years*. Quezon City, Philippines: New Day.

———. 1999b. "Fidel Valdez Ramos: 1992–1998." In *Philippine Presidents: 100 Years*. Quezon City, Philippines: New Day.

———, ed. 1999c. *Philippine Presidents: 100 Years*. Quezon City, Philippines: New Day.

Costes, Ariel B. 1994. "People Who Influenced Their Lives." *Evangelicals Today and Asia Ministry Digest* 21, no. 6 (June): 19.

Covell, Ralph R. 1995. *The Liberating Gospel in China: The Christian Faith among China's Minority People*. Grand Rapids, Mich.: Baker Books.

Cribb, R., ed. 1990. *The Indonesian Killings of 1965–1966; Studies from Java and Bali*. Clayton, Australia: Centre for Southeast Asian Studies, Monash University.

Crouch, Harold. 1978. *The Army and Politics in Indonesia*. Ithaca, N.Y.: Cornell University Press.

———. 1979. "The Trend to Authoritarianism: The Post-1945 Period." In *The Development of Indonesian Society*, ed. Harry Aveling. Queensland, Australia: University of Queensland Press.

Curtis, Gerald L. 1997. "A Recipe for Democratic Development." *Journal of Democracy* 8, no. 3: 139–145.

Dacanay, E. P. 2001. "Our Infinite Capacity to Turn Bread into Stone." *Philippine Star*, May 19, 10.

Dahl, Robert A. 1971. *Polyarchy: Participation and Opposition*. New Haven, Conn.: Yale University Press.

———. 1989. *Democracy and Its Critics*. New Haven, Conn.: Yale University Press.

———. 1997. "A Brief Intellectual Autobiography." In *Comparative European Politics: The Story of a Profession*, ed. Hans Daalder, Erik Allardt. London: Pinter.

———. 1999. "The Shifting Boundaries of Democracies and Governments." *Social Research* 66, no. 3 (Fall): 915–931.

Dalisay, Cornelio. 1987. "Should a Christian Join Politics?" *Evangelicals Today* (July–August): 18.
Dasan, Ebenezer. 2000. "Conversion and Persecution in South Gujarat." In *Conversion in a Pluralistic Context: Perspectives and Perceptions*, ed. Krickwin C. Marak and Jacob S. Plamthodathil. New Delhi: CMS/ISPCK.
David, Randy. 2001a. "Understanding Poverty." *Philippine Daily Inquirer*, July 15, A7.
———. 2001b. "Why Societies Fail: A Look at Governance and Moral Leadership." *Patmos* 16, no. 1 (April): 14–15.
DAWN (Development Action for Women Network). 1991. "DAWN Research Report." *Philippine Crusades Research*, November 5, 1.
———. 1998. "DAWN Congress Declaration 1998." *Evangelicals Today* 25, no. 2 (March–April 1998): 32–33.
———. 2001. "Harvest Force: Analysis and Trends." In *DAWN-Philippine Challenge*. Philippine Council of Evangelical Churches, Davao, Philippines: Philippine Challenge, Inc.
Dayag, Carijane C., and Ma. Glenda S. Lopez. 1993. "Are Filipinos Ready for Decentralization?" *Social Weather Bulletin* 93, no. 15 (August): 1–8.
Dela Rama, Jose C. 2001. "Social Justice and National Transformation." *Evangelicals Today* 27, no. 3 (June–July): 25–27.
Dena, Lal. 1996. *The Kuki-Naga Conflict: Juxtaposed in the Colonial Context*. Paper presented to seminar on "Dynamics of Identity and Intergroup in North-East India." Indian Institute of Advanced Study. Rashtrapati Nivas, Shimla.
De Quiros, Conrado. 2001. "Brute Lee." *Philippine Daily Inquirer*, March 5, A8.
Desai, Kiran, and Ghanshyam Shah. 2002. "Changing Profile of Gujarat MLAs." Paper presented to the conference on the "Sociological Profile of Indian MLAs," organized by Centre de Sciences Humaines, New Delhi, March 15, 2002.
Diamond, Larry. 1994. "Rethinking Civil Society: Toward Democratic Consolidation." *Journal of Democracy* 5, no. 3: 4–17.
Diamond, Larry, and Byung-kook Kim. 1998. *Consolidating Democracy in Korea*. Baltimore, Md.: Johns Hopkins University Press.
———, eds. 2000. *Consolidating Democracy in Korea*. Boulder, Colo.: Lynne Rienner Publishers.
Diamond, Larry, Juan J. Linz, and Seymour Martin, eds. 1995. *Politics in Developing Countries: Comparing Experiences with Democracy*, 2nd ed. Boulder, Colo: Lynne Rienner Publishers.
Diamond, Larry, and Marc F. Plattner, eds. 1996. *The Global Resurgence of Democracy*, 2nd ed. Baltimore, Md.: Johns Hopkins University Press
———, eds. 1998. *Democracy in East Asia*. Baltimore, Md.: Johns Hopkins University Press.
Diamond, Larry, Marc Plattner, and Yun-han Chu. 1997. *Consolidating the Third Wave Democracies*. Baltimore, Md.: Johns Hopkins University Press.
Dirkse, Jan-Paul, Frans Husken, and Mario Rutten, eds. 1993. *Development and Social Welfare: Indonesia's Experiences under the New Order*. Leiden, Netherlands: KITLV Press.
Dominguez, Arsenio. 1987. "Should a Christian Join Politics?" *Evangelicals Today* (July–August): 19.

Downs, Frederick. 1971. *The Mighty Works of God. A Brief History of the Council of Baptist Churches in North East India: The Mission Period 1836–1950*. Guahati, India: Christian Literature Center.

———. 1992. *History of Christianity in India, Volume 5, Part 5: North East India in the Nineteenth and Twentieth Centuries*. Bangalore: Church History Association of India.

Dunch, Ryan. 2001. *Fuzhou Protestants and the Making of a Modern China, 1857–1927*. New Haven, Conn.: Yale University Press.

Dye, Thomas R., and L. Harmon Zeigler. 1981. *The Irony of Democracy: An Uncommon Introduction to American Politics*. Monterey, Calif.: Duxbury Press.

Eaton, Richard M. 1984. "Conversion to Christianity among the Nagas, 1876–1971." *Indian Economic and Social History Review* 21, no. 1: 1–44.

Eckstein, Harry. 1966. *Division and Cohesion in Democracy: A Study of Norway*. Princeton: Princeton University Press.

Editorial Committee. 1985. *The General Situation of the Lancang Lahu Autonomous County* [in Chinese]. Kunming: Yunnan Nationality Press.

Edward, George. 2001. "The Mass Movement to Christ of the Maltos of Bihar: Its Causes and Consequences." PhD diss., South Asian Institute for Advanced Christian Studies. Bangalore, India.

Eisenstadt, S. N. 1965. "Transformation of Social, Political and Cultural Order in Modernization." *American Sociological Review* 30, no. 5 (October): 659–673.

Elwood, Douglas. 1986. *Philippine Revolution 1986*. Quezon City, Philippines: New Day.

Embree, Ainslie T. 1994. "The Function of the Rashtriya Swayamsevak Sangh: To Define the Hindu Nation." In *Accounting for Fundamentalisms: The Dynamic Character of Movements*, ed. Martin E. Marty and Scott R. Appleby. Chicago: University of Chicago Press.

End, Th. Van den. 1987. *Ragi Cerita: Sejarah Gereja di Indonesia 1500–1860* [The Yeast of the Story: Church History in Indonesia 1500–1860]. Jakarta, Indonesia: BPK Gunung Mulia.

Engels, F. 1878. "Anti Dühring." In *K. Marx and F. Engels On Religion* 1975 [translated from Russian]. Moscow: Progress Publishers.

Engineer, Irfan. 1999. "Conversions in Dangs." *The Hindu* [newspaper, India], January 23, 12.

Enthoven, R. E. 1975. *The Tribes and Castes of Bombay*. Delhi: Cosmo Publications.

"EU Draws a Parallel with Apartheid and Nazis: Modi Must Go." 2002. *The Daily Times* [India], March 22.

Evangelicals for Justice and Righteousness. 1999. "A Statement from Evangelical Filipinos." Fax from ISACC [Institute for Studies on Asian Church and Culture], Quezon City, Philippines, August 18, 1–2.

———. 2001. "ISACC [Institute for Studies on Asian Church and Culture] Statement on Erap Impeachment." E-mail, January 19.

"Evangelicals Rally for May 11 Polls." 1992. *Evangelicals Today* (June–July): 35–36.

Evangelicals Today & Asia Ministry Digest. Various issues. PCEC and Claris Communications, Quezon City, Philippines.

Feith, Herbert. 1962. *The Decline of Constitutional Democracy in Indonesia*. Ithaca, N.Y.: Cornell University Press.

Feliciano, David V. 1998. "'Anointing' Leaders." *Patmos* 13, no. 3 (April): 12–13, 26.
———. 2001. "Protestant Work Ethic Spells Progress." *Philippine Daily Inquirer*, July 28, A9.
Feliciano, Evelyn Miranda. 2000. *Unequal Worlds*. Quezon City, Philippines: Institute of Studies in Asian Church and Culture [ISACC].
———. 2001. "Seeds of Ruins Sprouting at EDSA II." *Evangelicals Today* 27, no. 1: 21–22.
Fellowship of Christians in Government. 1999. "*Celebrating 10 Years: Fiesta sa FOCIG.*" Quezon City, Philippines: FOCIG.
Fernandes, Walter. ed., *National Development and Tribal Deprivation*. New Delhi: Indian Social Institute, 1992.
Ferrez, Felipe S., Jr. 2001. "The Politics of Change." *Evangelicals Today* 27, no. 3 (June–July): 7.
Ferriols, Des. 2001. "Businessmen Propose Measures to Speed Up Economic Development." *Philippine Star*, July 4, B6.
"Fight against Corruption." *Foundation for Transformational Development*, 2001, 1st quarter, 2.
Filet, P. W. 1895. *Deverhouding Der Vorsten op Java tot de Nederlandcs-Indie* s. Gravenhage [now called The Hague, the Netherlands]: Martinus Nijhoff.
Flores, Philip C. 2001. "Obedience: The Key to National Transformation." *Evangelicals Today* 27, no. 3 (June–July): 20–21.
Foley, Michael W., and Bob Edwards. 1996. "The Paradox of Civil Society." *Journal of Democracy* 7, no. 3: 38–52.
Forrester, Duncan. 1980. *Caste and Christianity*. London: Curzon Press.
Freedom House. 2004. *Democracy's Century: A Survey of Global Political Change in the 20th Century*.
Freedom of Religious Belief in China. 1997. Beijing: Information Office of the State Council of the People's Republic of China.
Freston, Paul, 2001. *Evangelicals and Politics in Asia, Africa, and Latin America*. Cambridge, U.K.: Cambridge University Press.
———. 2004. *Protestant Political Parties: A Global Survey*. Aldershot, U.K.: Ashgate.
Fritschler, Lee J. 1969. *Smoking and Politics*. New York: Appleton-Century Crofts.
Frykenberg, Robert Eric. 1996. *History and Belief: The Foundations of Historical Understanding*. Grand Rapids, Mich.: Eerdmans.
———. 1999. "India." In *A World History of Christianity*, ed. Adrian Hastings. London: Cassell.
———, ed. 2003. *Christians and Missionaries in India: Cross-cultural Communication since 1500, with Special Reference to Caste, Conversion, and Colonialism*. Grand Rapids, Mich: Eerdmans.
Fu, Abu. 1994. "History on the Spreading of Christianity in Fugong." *Nujiang Wenzhi Ziliao* [Collection of Historical Materials in Nujiang]. Vol. 2. Kunming, Yunnan: Yunnan People's Press.
Fukuyama, Francis. 1999. *Social Capital and Civil Society*. Paper presented at the IMF Conference on Second Generation Reforms. Washington, D.C., November 8–9.
Fullinwider, Robert K., ed. 1999. *Civil Society, Democracy, and Civic Renewal*. Boulder, Colo.: Rowman and Littlefield.

Gallup Organization. 1984. *Hangukin'Ŭi Chongkyo wa Chongkyo Ŭisik* [The Religion and Religious Consciousness of Koreans]. Princeton, New Jersey.

———. 1988. *Hangukin'Ŭi Chongkyo wa Chongkyo Ŭisik* [The Religion and Religious Consciousness of Koreans]. Princeton, New Jersey.

———. 1990. *Hangukin'Ŭi Chongkyo wa Chongkyo Ŭisik* [The Religion and Religious Consciousness of Koreans]. Princeton, New Jersey.

Gasiorowski, Mark J., and Timothy J. Power. 1998. "The Structural Determinants of Democratic Consolidation: Evidence from the Third World." *Comparative Political Studies* 31, no. 6: 740–771.

"Gebrakan Para Mantan." 1995. *Gatra Magazine*. Jakarta. November 11, 22–24.

Geertz, Clifford. 1959. "The Javanese Village." In *Local, Ethnic, and National Loyalties in Village Indonesia* (Cultural Report Series No. 8), ed. G. William Skinner. New Haven, Conn.: Yale University Southeast Asia Studies.

———. 1960. *The Religion of Java*. Chicago: University of Chicago Press.

———. 1965. *The Social History of an Indonesian Town*. Cambridge, Mass.: MIT Press.

———. 1972. "Religious Change and Social Order in Soeharto's Indonesia." *Asia* 27: 62–84.

———. 1981. "Suparlan" [Foreword]. In *Abangan, Santri, Priyayi dalam Masyarakat Jawa* [Abangan, Santri, Priyayi in Javanese Society]. Jakarta: Pustaka Jaya.

———. 1984. "Culture and Social Change: The Indonesian Case." *Man* 19: 511–532.

Gener, Timoteo. 1999. "The El Shaddai Movement: Catholic Charismatic Renewal and Popular Religiosity in Lowland Philippines." *Phronesis* 6, no. 2: 3–44.

George, Alexander L. 1979. "Case Studies and Theory Development: The Method of Structured, Focused Comparison." In *Diplomacy: New Approaches in History, Theory and Policy*, ed. Paul Gordon Lauren. London: Free Press.

George, Alexander L., and Andrew Bennett. 2005. *Case Studies and Theory Development*. Cambridge, Mass.: MIT Press.

Ghosh, Partha. 1998. *The BJP and the Hindu Nationalist Movement*. New Delhi: Manohar.

Gilley, Bruce. 2001. "Power to the People." *Far Eastern Economic Review* (November 1) 34–36.

Gladdish, Ken. 1993. "The Primacy of the Particular." *Journal of Democracy* 4, no. 1 (January): 53–65.

Golwalkar, M. S. 1938a. "Presidential Address to RSS Members in Nagpur, December 28, 1938." *Indian Annual Register, Calcutta*, 2.

———. 1938b. *We or Our Nationhood Defined*. Nagpur, India: Bharat Prakashan.

Gomez, Raquel P. 2001. "Couples for Christ, a Pearl of Great Price." *Philippine Daily Inquirer*, July 1, D8.

Gonzales, Stella O. 2001. "Experts Alarmed Edsa II Gains 'Being Squandered.'" *Philippine Daily Inquirer*, July 4, A1–A18.

Gopinath, Vrinda. "EU Draws a Parallel with Apartheid and Nazis: Modi Must Go." *Indian Express* (Delhi), April 22, 2002.

Grafe, Hugald. 1990. *History of Christianity in India: Tamil Nadu in the Nineteenth and Twentieth Centuries*. Bangalore, India: Church History Association of India.

Greene, Jack P., and William Gerald McLoughlin. 1977. *Preachers and Politicians: Two Essays on the Origins of the American Revolution.* Worcester, Mass.: American Antiquarian Society.

Guha, Ranajit. 1985a. "The Career of an Anti-God in Heaven and on Earth." In *The Truth Unites: Essays in Tribute to Samar Sen,* ed. Ashok Mitra. Calcutta: Subarnarekha.

———. 1985b. *Elementary Aspects of Peasant Insurgency in Colonial India.* New Delhi: Oxford University Press.

———, ed. 1994. *Subaltern Studies, VIII.* New Delhi: Oxford University Press.

———, ed. 1998. *A Subaltern Studies Reader 1986–1995.* New Delhi: Oxford University Press.

Guillot, C. 1985. *Kiai Sadrach: Riwayat Kristenisasi di Jawa* [Kiai Sadrach: The History of Christian Expansion in Java]. Jakarta: Graffitti Press.

Guinness, Os. 2005. *Unspeakable: Facing Up to Evil in an Age of Genocide and Terror.* San Francisco: Harper.

Gujarat State Gazetteers: Dangs District. 1971. Ahmedabad: Government Printing, Stationery and Publications.

Gurudev, S. 1996. *Anatomy of Revolt in Northeast India.* New Delhi: Lancers Books.

Hadiwijaya. 1990. "Sala." In *Urip-Urip,* ed. Suwito Santosa. Surakarta, Indonesia: Museum Radya Pustaka.

Haggard, Stephan, and Robert Kaufman. 1995. *The Political Economy of Democratic Transitions.* Princeton: Princeton University Press.

Hahn, Bae-ho. 1997. "Assessing Kim Young-Sam Administration's First Four Years." *Korea Journal* 5, no. 2: 1–17.

Han, Sang-Jin. 1995. "Economic Development and Democracy: Korea as a New Model." *Korea Journal* 35, no. 2: 5–17.

Hansen, Thomas Blom, and Christophe Jaffrelot, eds. 1998. *The BJP and the Compulsions of Politics in India.* New Delhi: Oxford University Press.

Hanxin, Gao, and Heren Zhang. 1990. "The Religious Issues in Nujiang." *Nujiang Fanzhi (Internal)* 4, no. 12 (November): 21–22.

Hardgrave, Robert L. 1969. *The Nadars of Tamil Nadu.* Berkeley: University of California Press.

Hardiman, David. 1984. "Adivasi Assertion in South Gujarat: The Devi Movement of 1922–23." In *Subaltern Studies, III,* ed. David Arnold and David Hardiman. New Delhi: Oxford University Press.

———. 1985. "From Custom to Crime: The Politics of Drinking in Colonial South Gujarat." In *Subaltern Studies, IV,* ed. David Arnold and David Hardiman. New Delhi: Oxford University Press.

———. 1987a. "The Bhils and Shahukars of Eastern Gujarat." In *Subaltern Studies, V (1987),* ed. David Arnold and David Hardiman. New Delhi: Oxford University Press.

———. 1987b. *The Coming of the Devi: Adivasi Assertion in Western India.* New Delhi: Oxford University Press.

———. 1994. "Power in the Forest: The Dangs, 1820–1940." In *Subaltern Studies VIII,* eds. with David Arnold. New Delhi: Oxford University Press.

———. 1996a. "Farming in the Forest: The Dangs 1830–1992." In *Village Voices, Forest Choices: Joint Forest Management in India*, eds. with Mark Poffenberger and Betsy McGean. New Delhi: Oxford University Press.

———. 1996b. *Feeding the Baniya: Peasants and Usurers in Western India.* New Delhi: Oxford University Press.

———. 1998. "Origins and Transformations of the Devi." In *A Subaltern Studies Reader 1986–1995*, ed. Ranajit Guha. New Delhi: Oxford University Press.

———. 2002a. "Christianity and the Adivasis of Gujarat." In *Development and Deprivation in Gujarat. In Honour of Jan Breman*, ed. Ghanshyam Shah, Mario Rutten, and Hein Streefkerk. New Delhi: Sage.

———. 2002b. "Christianity and the Adivasis in the Dangs." In *Labour, Marginalisation and Migration: Studies on Gujarat*, ed. Ghanshyam Shah, Mario Rutten, and Hein Streefkerk. New Delhi: Sage.

Hardjono, Joan. 1983. "Rural Development in Indonesia: The 'Top-Down' Approach." In *Rural Development and the State*, ed. with David A. M. Lea and D. P. Chaudhri. London: Methuen.

Harper, Ann C. 2001. "The Iglesia Ni Cristo and Evangelical Christianity." *Journal of Asian Mission* 3, no. 1: 101–119.

Harper, George W. 2000. "Philippine Tongues of Fire? Latin American Pentecostalism and the Future of Filipino Christianity." *Journal of Asian Mission* 2, no. 2 (September): 225–259.

Harper, Susan Billington. 2000. *In the Shadow of the Mahatma: Bishop V. S. Azariah and the Travails of Christianity in British India.* Cambridge, U.K.: Eerdmans.

Hart, Gillian. 1986. *Power, Labor, and Livelihood: Processes of Change in Rural Java.* Berkeley: University of California Press.

Hastings, Adrian. 1997. *The Construction of Nationhood: Ethnicity, Religion and Nationalism.* Cambridge, U.K.: Cambridge University Press.

Hedlund, Roger, ed. 2000a. *Christianity Is Indian.* Chennai, India: Mylapore Institute for Indigenous Studies.

———, ed. 2000b. *Quest for Identity: India's Churches of Indigenous Origin: The Little Tradition in Indian Christianity.* New Delhi: ISPCK.

Hefner, Robert W. 1985. *Hindu Javanese: Tengger Tradition and Islam.* Princeton: Princeton University Press.

———. 1990. *The Political Economy of Mountain Java.* Berkeley: University of California Press.

———. 2000. *Civil Islam: Muslims and Democratization in Indonesia.* Princeton: Princeton University Press.

Heimert, Alan. 1966. *Religion and the American Mind: From the Great Awakening to the Revolution.* Cambridge, Mass.: Harvard University Press.

Heller, Patrick. 2000. "Degrees of Democracy: Some Comparative Lessons from India." *World Politics* 52 (July): 484–519.

Hluna, John Valnal. 1985. *Church and Political Upheaval in Mizoram.* Aizawl, Mizoram: Mizo History Association.

Hobbes, Thomas. [1651] 1996. *Leviathan.* ed. Richard Tuck. Cambridge, U.K.: Cambridge University Press.

Hoekema, A. G. 1997. *Berpikir dalam Keseimbangan yang Dinamis*. Jakarta: BPK Gunung Mulia.
Hong, Du-sung. 1992. "Chungsanchūng-Ūi sōngjang-kwa sahoe byōndong" [The Growth of the Middle Class and Social Change]. In *Han'guk-Ūi Kukkawa Simin Sahoe* [The Korean Nation and Civil Society], ed. Social Academy of Korea and the Political Academy of Korea. Seoul: Hanul Press, 255–278.
Horowitz, D. 1993. "Democracy in Divided Societies." *Journal of Democracy* 4, no. 4 (October): 18–38.
Hughes, Richard, ed. n.d. *The Primitive Church in the Modern World*. Champaign: University of Illinois Press.
Human Rights Watch. 1999. "Politics by Other Means: Attacks against Christians in India." New York: Human Rights Watch.
Human Rights Watch/Asia. 1997. *China: State Control of Religion*. New York: Human Rights Watch.
Hume, David. [1741–1742] 1994. *Political Essays*, ed. Knud Haakonsen. Cambridge, U.K.: Cambridge University Press.
Hunter, Alan, and Kim-Kwong Chan. 1993. *Protestantism in Contemporary China*. Cambridge, U.K.: Cambridge University Press.
Hunter, George G., III. 1992. "The Legacy of Donald A. McGavran." *International Bulletin of Missionary Research* 16, no. 4: 158–162.
Huntington, Samuel P. 1981. *American Politics: The Promise of Disharmony*. Cambridge, Mass.: Belknap Press.
———. 1991. *The Third Wave: Democratization in the Late Twentieth Century*. Norman: University of Oklahoma Press.
———. 1993. "The Clash of Civilizations?" *Foreign Affairs* 72, no. 3 (Summer): 2–26.
———. 1996. *The Clash of Civilizations and the Remaking of World Order*. New York: Simon & Schuster.
———. 1997a. "After Twenty Years: The Future of the Third Wave." *Journal of Democracy* 8, no. 4: 3–12.
———. 1997b. "Democracy in the Long Haul." In *Consolidating the Third Wave Democracies*, ed. Larry Diamond. Baltimore, Md.: Johns Hopkins University Press.
Im, Hyung-Baeg. 1996. "Korean Democratic Consolidation in Comparative Perspective." Paper presented at international conference on "Consolidating Democracy in Korea," Seoul, June, 19–20.
———. 2000. "South Korean Democratic Consolidation in Comparative Perspective." In *Consolidating Democracy in Korea*, ed. Larry Diamond and Byung kook Kim. London: Rienner.
Indonesian Christian Communication Forum (FKKI). 1997. "Info Forum Komunikasi Kristen Surabaya." *Jawa Timur* 6 (January): 1–9.
Inglehart, Ronald. 1988. "The Renaissance of Political Culture." *American Political Science Review* 82, no. 4 (December): 1203–1230.
Institute for Modern Society. 1982. *Hanguk Kyohoe Sōngjangkwa Sinang Yangtae'e Taehan Chosa Yōngu* [Research on Korean Church Growth and Faith Patterns].
Institute of Studies in Asian Church and Culture. 1998. *Presidential Candidates under Scrutiny: A Primer on Choosing National Leaders*. Quezon City, Philippines: Institute for Studies on Asian Church and Culture.

———. 1999. *Courage to Live These Days: Editorials That Matter.* Quezon City: Institute for Studies on Asian Church and Culture.

———. 2000. "Prayer for Erap's Removal from Office." One-page letter to Institute for Studies on Asian Church and Culture members.

Jaffrelot, Christophe. 1996. *Hindu Nationalist Movement and Indian Politics.* New Delhi: Penguin.

Jay, Robert R. 1963. *Religion and Politics in Rural Central Java.* New Haven, Conn.: Yale University Press.

Jayakumar, Samuel. 1999. *Dalit Consciousness and Christian Conversion: Historical Resources for a Contemporary Debate.* Oxford, U.K.: Regnum.

Jayal, Niraja Gopal. 2004. "Democracy and Social Capital in Central Himalaya: Tale of Two Villages." In *Interrogating Social Capital: The Indian Experience,* ed. Dwaipayan Bhattacharyya, Niraja Gopal Jayal, Bishnu N. Mohapatra and Sudha Pai. New Delhi: Sage.

Jenkins, Philip. 2002. *The Next Christendom: The Coming of Global Christianity.* Oxford: Oxford University Press.

Jiang, Ling. 1995. "A Brief Introduction to the Minority Groups in China: Lisu Nationality." *Mizu tuanjie* [Unity of Nationality] (October): 5.

Joshi, Satyakam. 1998. "Role of Forest Labour Cooperative Societies in Tribal Development." In *Tribal Situation in India: Issues in Development,* ed. Vidyut Joshi. Delhi: Rawat Publications.

———. 1999. "Tribals, Missionaries and Sadhus: Understanding Violence in the Dangs." *Economic and Political Weekly* (September 11): 2667–2675.

Joshi, Vidyut, ed. 1998. *Tribal Situation in India: Issues in Development.* Delhi: Rawat Publications.

Joshua, Thomas. 1996. "Christian Impact and Conflict Resolution in Manipur." in *Impact of Christianity on Northeast India.* Imphal.

Juarez, Florinda T. 1998. "Churches Being Sucked into Old Politics." *Philippine Daily Inquirer* (May 8): 12.

Kahin, George McT. 1995. "Soekarno tak Ingin Ada Pertumpahan Darah." *Tiras,* 47–52. Kang, In-Chul. 1996. *Hanguk Kidok Kyohoe-wa Kukka, Simin Sahoe* [Korean Christian Church and the State, Civil Society]. Seoul: Korean Institute for Church History.

———. 2000. "Religion and the Democratization Movement." *Korea Journal* 40, no. 2: 225–247.

Kang, Jung-In. 1997. "Kidokkyo wa Minjujuūi: Huntington'Ūi Europe Chungsimjuūi Pipan" [Christianity and Democracy: Criticism of Huntington's Eurocentrism]. *Sasang* (October–December): 258–285.

Kang, Mun-Gu. 1992. "Hanguk Sahoe'ui Minjuhwa, Sahoe Byŏnhyŏk and Pijibae Yŏnhap" [The Democaratization, Social Change, and the Ruled Coalition in Korean Society]. *Sahoi Bipyong* [Society Criticism], no. 7.

Kang, Wi Jo. 1997. *Christ and Caesar: A History of Christianity and Politics.* Albany: State University of New York Press.

Karaos, Anna Marie A. 1998. "Real Story of the Elections." *Philippine Daily Inquirer,* August 9, 12.

———. 2001. "Civil Society in the New Politics." *Philippine Daily Inquirer*, July 4, A9.
Kartodirdjo, Sartono. 1972. "Agrarian Radicalism in Java: Its Setting and Development." In *Culture and Politics in Indonesia*, ed. Claire Holt. Ithaca, N.Y.: Cornell University Press.
———. 1973. *Protest Movements in Rural Java: A Study of Agrarian Unrest in the Nineteenth and Early Twentieth Centuries*. Singapore: Oxford University Press.
Kepel, Gilles. 1994. *The Revenge of God: The Resurgence of Islam, Christianity and Judaism in the Modern World*. University Park: Pennsylvania State University Press.
Kim, Andrew E. 1995. "A History of Christianity in Korea: From Its Troubled Beginning to Its Contemporary Success." *Korea Journal* 35, no. 2: 34–53.
Kim, Byung-kook. 1998. "Korea Crisis of Success." In *Democracy in Asia*, ed. Larry Diamond and Marc. F Plattner. Baltimore, Md.: Johns Hopkins University Press.
Kim, Dong-chun. 1997. "1980nyŏndae Minjubyŏnhyŏk Undong'Ŭi Sŏngjangkwa Sŏngkyŏk" [The Growth and Character of the Democratic Transformative Movement in the 1980s]. In *Yuwŏl Minju HangjaengkwaHanguk Sahoe 10 nyŏn* [June Democratic Uprising and Ten Years of Korean Society], Vol. 1, ed. Federation of Academic Groups. Seoul: Dang Dae.
Kim, Ho-Gi. 1995. *Hyŏndae Chabonju'ui wa Hanguk Sahoe: Kukga, Simin Sahoe, Minjujuŭi* [Contemporary Capitalism and Korean Society: The State, Civil Society, Democracy]. Seoul: Sahoi Pipyong Sa.
———. 1997. "Minjuhwa, Siminsahoe, Siminundong" [Democratization, Civil Society, Civil Movement]. In *Hanguk Sahoe wa Minjujuŭi: Hanguk Minjuhwa sipnyŏn'Ŭi Pyŏngga-wa Pansŏng* [Korean Society and Democracy: Assessments and Prospects of Ten Years of Democratization in Korea], ed. Jang-Jip Choi and Hyun-Chin Lim. Seoul: Nanam.
Kim, Myung-Hyuk, ed. 1998. *Hanguk Pokumju'ui Songmyongso Moumjip* [Collections of the Statements of the Korean Evangelical Fellowship]. Seoul: Christian Literature Crusade.
Kim, Nyung. 1996. *Hanguk Chonchiwa Kyohoe-Kukga Kaldŭng* [Korean Politics and Church-State Conflicts]. Seoul: Sonamoo.
Kim, Se-Jung. 1999. "Chayu Minjujuŭiwa Kim Young-Sam Chŏngchi Kaehyŏk" [Liberal Democracy and Kim Young-Sam's Political Reform]. In *Hanguk'ŬiChayu Minjujuŭi* [Korean Liberal Democracy], ed Kim Suk-Kun. Seoul: Ingan Sarang.
Kim, Sun-Hyuk. 2000. *The Politics of Democratization in Korea: The Role of Civil Society*. Pittsburgh: University of Pittsburgh Press.
Kim, Sung-Gon. 1994. "90nyŏndae Hanguk Sahoe Byonhwa wa Kyohoe'ui Byŏnchŏn" [Korean Social Change in the 1990s and the Change of the Church]. In *The Christian Institute for the Study of Justice and Development, A Survey on Christians' Consciousness of Unification*.
Kim, Sung-Woong. 2000. "Congressmen and Religion." *Kukhoebo* [Bulletin of the National Assembly]. July, 65–69.
Kim, Yong-hak. 1989. "Elite Chungwŏn-e Itsŏsŏ'Ŭi Chiyŏk Kyŏkcha" [Regional Gap in Elite Recruitment]. In *Hanguk'Ŭi Chiyŏkjuŭi-wa Chiyŏk Kaldŭng* [Korean Regionalism and Regional Conflict], ed. Korean Association of Sociology. Seoul: Songwon Press.

Kim, Young-jin. 2000. "Ingan Sahoilul Modun Pulhwa, Pupaeeso Kuhaeya" [Should Save All Human Society from Disharmony and Corruption]. *Kukhoebo* [Bulletin of the National Assembly], July, 71.

Kim, Young-Sam. 2000. *Kim Young-Sam Hoegolok: Minjujuuilŭl Wihan Naŭi Tuzaeng* [Kim Young-Sam Autobiography: My Struggle for Democracy]. Vol. 1. Seoul: Haksan Sodang.

———. 2001a. *Kim Young-Sam Taetonglyong Hoegolok* [Kim Young-Sam President Autobiography]. Vol. 1. Seoul Chosen Daily Newspaper.

———. 2001b. *Kim Young-Sam Taetonglyong Hoegolok* [Kim Young-Sam President Autobiography]. Vol. 2. Seoul: Choson Daily Newspaper.

Ko, Tinming. 2000. *The Sacred Citizens and the Secular City: Political Participation of Protestant Ministers in Hong Kong during a Time of Change*. Burlington, Vt.: Ashgate.

Kodiran. 1971. "Kebudayaan Jawa." In *Manusia dan Kebudajaan di Indonesia*, ed. Koentjaraningrat. Jakarta: Penerbit Djambatan.

Kohli, Atul. 1991. *Democracy and Discontent: India's Crisis of Ungovernability*. Princeton: Princeton University Press.

Kong, Francis J. 2001. "Trusting Instead of Understanding." *Evangelicals Today* 27, no. 3 (June–July): 14–15.

Kusumodilaga, Wibisono Rusmiputro. 1990. "Perpindahan Kraton Kartasura ke Surakarta." In *Urip-urip*, ed. Suwito Santosa. Surakarta, Indonesia: Museum Radya Pustaka.

Lal, R. B. 1998. "Tribal Situation in Gujarat." In *Tribal Situation in India: Issues in Development*, ed. Vidyut Joshi. Delhi: Rawat Publications.

Lalsawma. 1994. *Revivals: The Mizo Way (A Gospel Centenary Souvenir)*. Calcutta: Printwell Offset.

Lama-Rewal, Stephanie Tawa. 2002. "Sociological Profile of Indian MLAs." (Seminar transcript available) Centre de Sciences Humaines. New Delhi, India.

Lambert, Tony. 1999. *China's Christian Millions: The Costly Revival*. London: Monarch Books.

Larson, George Donald. 1987. *Prelude to Revolution: Palaces and Politics in Surakarta, 1912–1942*. Holland: Foris Publications.

Latourette, K. S. 1929. *A History of Christian Mission in China*. London: SPCK Publishing.

Lawrence, Bruce B. 1998. *Shattering the Myth: Islam beyond Violence*. Princeton: Princeton University Press.

Lazarus, Sam, ed. 1992. *Proclaiming Christ: A Handbook of Indigenous Missions in India*. Madras: Church Growth Association of India.

"Leaders Oppose Religious Bloc Voting Bill." 1995. *Evangelicals Today* 22, no. 1 (January): 30.

Lee, Jeong-jin. 2000. "South Korean Presidential Power during the Process of Democratization: Chun Doo Hwan, Roh Tae Woo, and Kim Young Sam." PhD diss., University of Southern California.

Lepasana, Simeon. 1987. "Should a Christian Join Politics?" *Evangelicals Today* (July–August): 18.

Levine, Daniel H., and David Stoll. 1997. "Bridging the Gap between Empowerment and Power in Latin America." In *Transnational Religion and Fading States*, ed. Susanne H. Rudolph and James Piscatori. Oxford: Westview Press.

Li, Daoshing. "Survey on Christianity in Fugong," 1994, in Nujiang Weshi Ziliao [Collection of Historical Materials in Fugong] Volume 2. Yunnan: People's Press. 1082–1083.

Li, Fan. 2001. "Rural Power Play." *Asiaweek* (August): 1315.

Lijphart, Arend. 1977. *Democracy in Plural Societies: A Comparative Exploration*. New Haven, Conn.: Yale University Press.

Lim, David. 1985. "Towards a Christian Response to Communism." *Evangelical Thrust* 12 (November): 12–14.

———. 1986. "Why We Should Form an Evangelical Political Party." *Evangelical Thrust* 13 (August): 12–13, 20; 14 (September): 14–15, 18–19.

———. 1989. "Church and State in the Philippines, 1900–1988." *Transformation* 6, no. 3 (July–September): 26–32.

———. 1992. "How to Join Partisan Politics." *Christian Journal*, April 20, 8.

———. 1995. "Philippines: An Interview with Ruth S. Callanta." *Transformation* 12, no. 1 (January–March): 12–14.

———. 2000. "A Critique of Modernity in Protestant Missions in the Philippines." *Journal of Asian Mission* 2, no. 2 (September): 149–177.

Linz, Juan J., and Alfred Stepan. 1996. *Problems of Democratic Transition and Consolidation: Southern Europe, South America, and Post-Communist Europe*. Baltimore, Md.: Johns Hopkins University Press.

Lipset, Seymour Martin. 1959. "Some Social Requisites of Democracy: Economic Development and Political Legitimacy." *American Political Science Review* 53, no. 1 (March): 69–105.

———. 1994. "The Social Requisites of Democracy Revisited." *American Sociological Review* 59 (February): 1–22.

Lo, Clarence Y. H. 1992. "Communities of Challengers in Social Movement Theory." In *Frontiers in Social Movement Theory*, ed. A. Morris and C. Mueller. New Haven, Conn.: Yale University Press.

Locke, John. [1689] 1979. *An Essay Concerning Human Understanding*. ed. Peter H. Nidditch. New York: Oxford University Press.

Locsin, Teodoro L., Jr. 1998. "The Reason for Ramos' Defeat." *Today*, The Philippines, May 14, 9.

Lolly, R. R. 1985. *The Baptist Church in Manipur: A Historical Survey of the Mission Strategies and Development of the Baptist Church in Manipur, North East India, 1894–1983*. Imphal, India: Modern Printer.

Lumsdaine, David Halloran. 1993. *Moral Vision in International Politics: The Foreign Aid Regime, 1949–1989*. Princeton: Princeton University Press.

Luna, Emmanuel M. 2001. "Education and Nation Building." *Evangelicals Today* 27, no. 3 (June–July): 22–24.

Lyon, M. L. 1980. "The Hindu Revival in Java: Politics and Religious Identity." In *Indonesia: The Making of a Culture*, ed. James J. Fox. Canberra: Research School of Pacific Studies, Australian National University.

Madhab, J. 1999. "North East: Crisis of Identity, Security and Underdevelopment." *Economic and Political Weekly*, February 6.

Magalit, Isabelo F. 1995. "Why Bother with Society? The Biblical Basis." *Phronesis* 2 (March): 3–22.

———. 1998a. "A Biblical Framework for Christian Involvement." *Patmos* 13, no. 3 (April): 10–11, 18–20.

———. 1998b. "Why Bother with May 11?" *Evangelicals Today* 25, no. 2 (March–April): 10–11.

———. 2000. "Church and State Today." *Phronesis* 7, no. 2: 49–61.

———. 2001. "Salt of the Earth, Light of the World." *Evangelicals Today* 27, no. 3 (June–July): 9–11.

Maggay, Melba Padilla. 1994. *Transforming Society*. Oxford, U.K.: Regnum-Lynx.

———. 1998a. "The Curse of 'Winnability' on Worthy Bets." *Today*, Philippines, April 13, 11.

———. 1998b. "Our Changing Political Culture." *Patmos* 13, no. 3 (April): 3–5, 21–23.

———. 1998c. "Trends in Our Changing Politics." *Today*, Philippines, April 12, 11.

———. 2001. Untitled personal newsletter, January 24.

Mangahas, Mahar. 1991. "Who's Afraid of the Catholic Church?" *Social Weather Bulletin* 91, no. 4 (February): 1–6.

———. 1995. "An SWS Survey about the Pope." *Social Weather Bulletin* 95, no. 3 (February): 1–6.

———. 1996. "In Religiosity, We're No. 1." *Social Weather Bulletin* 96, no. 8 (April): 1–5.

———. 1997. "Why the Vatican Likes Filipino Catholics." *Social Weather Bulletin* 97, no. 21 (November): 1–4.

———. 2001a. "Acceptance of Gloria is Nationwide." February 16. http://www.sws.org.ph/feb01.htm.

———. 2001b. "Social Climate." February 26. http://www.sws.org.ph/-feb01.htm.

———. 2001c. *SWS Surveys Leading to the May 14, 2001 Elections*. Quezon City, Philippines: Social Weather Stations.

Mangahas, Mahar, and Linda Luz Guerrero. 1992. *Religion in the Philippines: The 1991 ISSP Survey*. Quezon City, Philippines: Social Weather Stations.

Mangahas, Mahar, Linda Luz Guerrero, and Gerardo A. Sandoval. 1999. "Opinion Polling and National Elections in the Philippines, 1992–98." Paper presented at WAPOR Regional Conference, Sydney, June 25, 1999. Quezon City, Philippines: Social Weather Stations.

Maningas, Ismael Ireneo. 1998. *Filipino Christian Morality*. Manila. St. Paul's: Makati City.

Manipur Baptist Convention Literature Committee. 1997. *The Manipur Baptist Convention: The First One Hundred Years of Christianity in Manipur: 1896–1996*. Imphal, India: MBC Literature Committee.

Manipur Naga Baptist Church Leaders' Forum. 1994. "Facts about the Naga Conflict." Imphal, India.

Marak, Krickwin C., and Jacob S. Plamthodathil, eds. 2000. *Conversion in a Pluralistic Context: Perspectives and Perceptions*. New Delhi: CMS\ISPCK.

March, James G., and Johan P. Olsen. 1995. *Democratic Governance*. New York: Free Press.

Marquand, David, and R. L. Nettler, eds. 2000. *Religion and Democracy*. Oxford: Blackwell.

Martin, David. 1999. "The Evangelical Political Upsurge and Its Political Implications." In *The Desecularization of the World*, ed. Peter L. Berger. Grand Rapids, Mich.: Eerdmans.

Marty, Martin, and R. Scott Appleby, eds. 1991. *Fundamentalism Observed*. Vol. 1. Chicago: University of Chicago Press.

———, eds. 1993a. *Fundamentalisms and Society: Reclaiming the Sciences, the Family, and Education*. Vol. 2. Chicago: University of Chicago Press.

———, eds. 1993b. *Fundamentalisms and the State: Remaking Polities, Economies, and Militance*. Vol. 3. Chicago: University of Chicago Press.

———, eds. 1994. *Accounting for Fundamentalisms: The Dynamic Character of Movements*. Vol. 4. Chicago: University of Chicago Press.

———, eds. 1995. *Fundamentalisms Comprehended*. Vol. 5. Chicago: University of Chicago Press.

Mastra, I. Wajan. 1970. "The Salvation of Non-Believers: A Missiological Critique to Hendrik Kraemer and the Need for New Alternative." PhD diss., Aquinas Institute of Philosophy and Theology, Dubuque, Iowa.

Mathew, George, ed. 2000. *Status of Panchayati Raj in the States and Union Territories of India*. New Delhi: Concept Publishing for Institute of Social Sciences.

Mayer, Peter. 2004. "Making Democracy Perform: Human Development and Civic Community in India." In *Interrogating Social Capital*, ed. Dwaipayan Bhattacharyya, Niraja Gopal Jayal, Bishnu N. Mohapatra, and Sudha Pai. New Delhi: Sage.

McVey, Ruth. 1965. *The Rise of Indonesian Communism*. Ithaca, N.Y.: Cornell University Press.

Meimban, Adriel O. 1999. "Ferdinand E. Marcos: 1965–1986." In *Philippine Presidents: 100 Years*, ed. R. M. Cortes. Quezon City, Philippines: New Day.

Meimban, Adriel O., and Rosario Mendoza Cortes. 1999. "Joseph Ejercito Estrada: 30 June 1998–." In *Philippine Presidents: 100 Years*, ed. R. M. Cortes. Quezon City, Philippines: New Day.

Mercado, Juan L. 2001. "Will Elections Abort Democracy's 'Third Wave'?" *Philippine Star*, May 14, 11.

Mills, J. P. 1941. "Remarks in the Census Report on the Naga Tribes." *Baptist Missionary Review* 47, no. 9.

Min, Chong-gi. 2000. "Hanguk'esō Chōngūi Chongchiga Kanūnghanga?" [Is the Politics of Justice Possible in Korea?]. In *2000 Minju Simin Academy* [2000 Democratic Citizen Academy]. Seoul: Christian Ethic Movement and Seoul City.

Miranda, Felipe B. 2000. "Right Now, Dare We Trust Anyone?" *Philippine Star*, October 24, 9.

Mitchell, William C. 1970. *The American Policy: A Social and Cultural Interpretation*. New York: Free Press.

Mitra, Ashok, ed. 1985. *The Truth Unites: Essays in Tribute to Samar Sen*. Calcutta: Subarnarekha.

Moghadam, Assaf. 2003. "A Global Resurgence of Religion?" Report prepared for the Weatherhead Center for International Affairs, Harvard University, March 30.

Moon, Yong-jik. 1996. "Che 15dae Kukhoeŭiwon Sŏngō Punsŏkkwa Chōnmang" [The Analysis and Prospect of the 15th Election for MPs]. *Uijong Yongo*, Seoul, 2, no. 1.

Morikawa, Shingo. n.d. "Citizens' Right and Democracy under the Constitution of the PRC." *Legal Forum: The Global Network for Chinese and British Lawyers*, www.enstar.co.uk/china/law/articles/legal_e.htm.

Mortimer, R. 1973. "Indonesia: Growth or Development?" In *Showcase State: The Illusion of Indonesia's "Accelerated Modernisation,"* ed. R. Mortimer. Sydney: Angus and Robertson.

——. 1974. *Indonesian Communism under Soekarno: Ideology and Politics, 1959–1965*. Ithaca, N.Y.: Cornell University Press.

Mosca, Graetana. 1939. *The Ruling Class*. New York: McGraw-Hill.

Mosse, David. 2005. *Cultivating Development: An Ethnography of Aid Policy and Practice*. London: Pluto Press.

Mou, Jiafu, and Qinhe Zhang, eds. 1999. *Religion and National Minority at the New Century: The Socio-Cultural Changes and Manifestation of Religion among the National Minorities in Yunnan* [in Chinese]. Kunming: Yunnan University Press.

Movement for Principled Politics. 1992. "An Appeal for Principled Politics." *Christian Journal*, April 20, 9.

Mubyarto. 1988. "Strategi Pembangunan Pedesaan"[Rural Development Strategy]. In *Pembangunan Pedesaan di Indonesia* [Rural Development in Indonesia], ed. Mubyarto and Sartono Kartodirdjo. Yogyakarta, Indonesia: Gajah Mada University Press.

Mubyarto, and Loekman Soetrisno. 1985. "Rural Development in Indonesia Past Experience and Future Policies." In *Rural Development, Capitalist and Socialist Paths*, ed. R. P. Misra. New Delhi: Naurang Rai Concept.

——. 1989. "Integrated Rural Development: Indonesia Dhaka, Bangladesh." Centre on Integrated Rural Development for Asia and the Pacific.

Muller-Kruger, Th. 1959. *Sedjarah Gereja di Indonesia* [History of the Church in Indonesia]. Jakarta: BPK Gunung Mulia.

Mydans, Seth. 2001. "People Power II: Not the Same Glow." February 5, *New York Times*.

Na, Yong-Wha. 1988. "A Theological Assessment of Korean Minjung Theology." *Concordia Journal* 14 (April): 138–149.

Nababan, S. A. E., ed. 1971. *Pergumulan Rangkap* [Double Wrestling]. Jakarta: General Secretary of Indonesia Council of Churches.

Namthiurei, M. 1972. *The Great Awakening: The Coming of Christianity in Zeliangrong Area, 1915–1971*. Manipur, India: Golden Jubilee Publication.

Nasution, Abdul Haris. 1995. "Catatan 50 Tahun Indonesia" [A Remark on Indonesia's 50th Year]. *Gatra*, Jakarta, Indonesia (August 19): 40–41.

National Alliance of Women [India]. 1999. *Violence in Gujarat: A Test Case for a Larger Fundamentalist Agenda*. Report of the Citizen's Commission on Persecution of

Christians in Gujarat. Available at http://www.hrsolidarity.net/mainfile.php/1999vol09no09/1892/.
National Council of Churches in the Philippines. 1989. *Report on "Exploring the New Religious Movements in the Philippines."* Quezon City, Philippines: Commission on Evangelism and Ecumenical Relations, NCCP.
Navarro, Rafael. 2000a. "Legal and Moral." Open letter, dated November 11, 3.
———. 2000b. "Theological Basis for Social Action." Unpublished manuscript.
Newhaus, Richard John. 1990. "Democracy: A Christian Imperative." *Transformation* 7, no. 4: 1–4.
Ngelow, Zakaria J. 1996. *Kekristenan dan Nasionalisme: Perjumpaan Umat Kristen Protestan dengan Pergerakan Nasional Indonesia 1900–1950* [Christianity and Nationalism: Christian Protestantism's Encounter with the Indonesian Nationalist Movement 1900–1950]. Jakarta: BPK Gunung Mulia.
Noll, Mark A. 1990. *Religion and American Politics: From the Colonial Period to the 1980s.* New York: Oxford University Press.
Noorani, A. G. 2000. *The RSS and the BJP: A Division of Labour.* New Delhi: Leftword.
Nuh, V. K. 2001. *Struggle for Identity in North-East India: A Theological Response.* Guwahati, India: Spectrum Publications.
O, Kyong-hwan. 1990. *Chonggyo Sahoehak* [Sociology of Religion]. Seoul: Seokwangsa.
O'Donnell, G. 1994. "Delegative Democracy." *Journal of Democracy* 5, no. 1. 55–69.
O'Donnell, Guillermo, and Philippe Schmitter. 1986. *Transitions from Authoritarian Rule: Tentative Conclusions about Uncertain Democracies.* Baltimore, Md.: Johns Hopkins University Press.
Ofreneo, R. Pineda. 1991. *The Philippines: Debt and Poverty.* Oxford: Oxfam.
Oh, John Kie-chiang. 1999. *Korean Politics.* Ithaca, N.Y.: Cornell University Press.
Om, Sung-chul. 1989. *Hanguk Kidokkyoin'Ŭi Chŏngchi Chamyŏ-e Daehan Yŏngu* [A Study on the Political Participation of Korean Christians]. MA thesis, Kukmin University, Seoul.
Operation: Burning Bush. 1998. "Election Prayer Watch '98." *Philippine Prayer Alert,* March.
———. 2000. "Our God Is a Consuming Fire." *Philippine Prayer Alert,* November.
———. 2001. "The Son of Righteousness Shall Arise with Healings in His Wings." *Philippine Prayer Alert,* January.
Orosa, Ramon. 1989. "A Voice in the Wilderness Speaks." *Asia Ministry Digest* (November–December): 2–4.
———. 1993. "Confronting the Spirit of Lawlessness." *Evangelicals Today and Asia Ministry Digest* 20, no. 10 (November): 15–18.
Pachauau, Lalsangkima. 2002. *Ethnic Identity and Christianity: A Socio-historical and Missiological Study of Christianity in Northeast India with Special Reference to Mizoram.* New York: P. Lang.
Pae, Sung Moon. 1992. *Korea: Leading Developing Nation: Economy, Democracy, and Welfare.* Lanham, Md.: University Press of America.
Pai, Sudha. 2001. "Social Capital, Panchayats and Grass Roots Democracy: Politics of Dalit Assertion in Uttar Pradesh." *Economic and Political Weekly* 36, no. 8 (February): 645–654.

Paik, Jong-kuk. 1994. "Hanguk Kidokkyoin'Ŭi Chŏngchi Ŭisik" [The Political Consciousness of Korean Christians]. In *Hanguk Kidokkyoin'Ŭi Chŏngchi Ŭisikkwa Minjuhwa* [The Political Consciousness of Korean Christians and Democratization], ed. Jong-kuk Paik. Seoul: Word of Life Press.

Pandian, M. S. S. 2002. "One Step Outside Modernity: Caste, Identity Politics and the Public Square." *Economic and Political Weekly* (May 4).

Park, Chan-wook. 1996. "15dae Kukhoeŭiwon Chongsŏn Kyolkwa Kaekwan" [An Overview of the Results of the 15th Election for MPs]. In *Che 15 dae Chongsŏn Punsŏk* [The Analysis of the 15th Election for MPs].

Park, Chung-shin. 2003. *Protestantism and Politics in Korea*. Seattle: University of Washington Press.

Park, Duk-hun. 2000. "Kidokkyoinkwa Siminundong'e Taehan Sinhakjŏk Kochal" [Theological Reflection on Christians and Civil Movement]. In *2000 Minju Simin Academy* [2000 Democratic Citizen Academy]. Seoul: Christian Ethic Movement and Seoul City.

Pathy, Jaganath. 1998. "Impact of Development Projects among Tribals." In *Tribal Situation in India: Issues in Development*, ed. Vidyut Joshi. Delhi: Rawat Publications.

Pei, Min xin. 1995a. "'Creeping Democratization' in China." *Journal of Democracy* 6, no. 4: 65–79.

———. 1995b. *From Reform to Revolution: The Demise of Communism in China and the Soviet Union*. Cambridge, Mass.: Harvard University Press.

———. 1998. "The Fall and Rise of Democracy in East Asia." In *Democracy in East Asia*, ed. Larry Diamond and Marc F. Plattner. Baltimore, Md.: Johns Hopkins University Press.

Pei, Min Xin. 1995. "People Power II: A Display of God's Might and Sovereignty." 2001. *Evangelicals Today* 27, no. 1: 19–21, 36.

Perkin, Harold. 2000. "American Fundamentalism and the Selling of God." In *Religion and Democracy*, ed. David Marquand and R. L. Nettler. Oxford: Blackwell.

Pettigrew, William. 1909. "Kathi Ksham: The Soul Departure Feast as Practiced by the NagasTangkhul, Manipur, Assam." *Journal of the Asiatic Society of Bengal* 5, no. 2.

———. 1910. "Ukhrul." In *Report of the Tenth Biennial Session (August)*. Gauhati, January 8–17.

———. 1922a. *Twenty-Five Years, 1897–1922*. Ukhrul Mission School. Ukhrul.

———. 1922b. "The Year in Manipur." *American Baptist Foreign Mission Society (108th Annual Report)*.

———. 1924. "Inspiring News from Manipur." *American Baptist Foreign Mission Society (110th Annual Report)*.

———. 1926. "Kangpokpi Station: Report of the North-East and Sadar Areas of Manipur State." February.

———. 1934. *Forty years in Manipur, Assam: An Account of the Work of Reverend and Mrs. William Pettigrew*. Imphal.

———. 2004. "Reports from the Ukhrul Field." *Assam Baptist Missionary Conference* Seventh Session, 1901–1902.

Philippine Council of Evangelical Churches (PCEC). n.d.-a. "The Christian and the National Elections: Some Principles and Guidelines." Quezon City, Philippines: PCEC.
———. n.d.-b. "Towards an Evangelical Response to the Current Ideological Unrest: A Study Paper." Quezon City, Philippines: PCEC.
———. 1987. "A Call to the Filipino People." *Evangelicals Today* (July–August): 48.
———. 1998. "The Bible and the May '98 Elections: Principles and Guidelines." Quezon City, Philippines: PCEC.
———. 2000a. "An Evangelical Response to the Jueteng Scandal." Leaflet, October 18. Quezon City, Philippines: PCEC.
———. 2000b. "Evangelical Response to the Leadership Crisis." *Evangelicals Today* 26, no. 6: 23.
———. 2001a. "A Call to Prayer and the Quest for Truth." E-mail, pcec@ailink.net, January 17.
———. 2001b. "Statement of Support for President Gloria Macapagal-Arroyo." *Evangelicals Today* 27, no. 1: 33.
Pinto, Stanny. 1999. "Land Alienation and Consciousness among the Vasavas of South Gujarat." PhD diss., Centre for Social Studies, Surat, India.
Poffenberger, Mark, and Betsy McGean, eds. 1996. *Village Voices, Forest Choices: Joint Forest Management in India.* New Delhi: Oxford University Press.
Polo, Jaime B. 2001. "Masa Negotiates Power." *Philippine Star*, June 5, 8.
Pringgodigdo, A. K. 1938. *Onstaan En Groei Van Mangkoenegorosche Rijk.* Batavia, Indonesia: Koninklije de Unie.
Punalekar, S. P. 1998. "Growth with Contradictions." In *Tribal Situation in India: Issues in Development*, ed. Vidyut Joshi. Delhi: Rawat Publications.
Putnam, Robert D. 2000. *Bowling Alone: The Collapse and Revival of American Democracy.* New York: Simon & Schuster.
———, ed. 2002. *Democracies in Flux: The Evolution of Social Capital in Contemporary Society.* Oxford: Oxford University Press.
Putnam, Robert D., Robert Leonardi, and Raffaella Y. Nanetti. 1993. *Making Democracy Work: Civic Traditions in Modern Italy.* Princeton: Princeton University Press.
Qin, Ning, ed. 1998. *Social and Cultural Changes: Christianity and National Minorities.* Kunming: Yunnan University Press.
Quiambao, Cecilia. 2001. "Church Is a Formidable Force in Political Life." *Bangkok Post*, January 30, 12.
Racelis, Mary. 1998. "Christianity, the State and Civil Society in the Philippines." In *Religion, Politics and Society in South and Southeast Asia*, ed. N. N. Vohra and J. N. Dixit. Delhi: Konark.
Rajendran, K. 1998. *Which Way Forward: Indian Missions? A Critique of Twenty-Five Years 1972–97.* Bangalore: SAIACS Press.
Ramos, Fidel V. 1996. *Break Not the Peace: The Story of the GRP-MNLF Peace Negotiations, 1992–1996.* Quezon City, Philippines: Friends of Steady Eddie.
———. 1999. "Challenge to the Free." *Asiaweek*, August 20–27, 54.
Remmer, Karen L. 1995. "New Theoretical Perspectives on Democratization." *Comparative Politics* 28, no. 1, 103–122.

Reyes, Roberto P. 2001. "EDSA, Shrine and History." *Philippine Star*, April 28, 10.
Ricklefs, M. C. 1979. "Six Centuries of Islamization in Java." In *Conversion to Islam*, ed. N. Levtzion. New York: Holmes and Meier.
———. 1981. *A History of Modern Indonesia*. London: Macmillan.
Roh, Chi-jun. 1995. *Hanguk'Ŭi Kyohoe Chojik* [The Organization of the Korean Church]. Seoul: Min Young Press.
Rose, Richard, Doh C. Shin, and Neil Munro. 1998. "Tension between the Democratic Ideal and Reality: The Korean Example." In *Critical Citizens: Global Support for Democratic Government*, ed. Pippa Norris. Oxford: Oxford University Press.
Rose, Susan. 1996a. "The Politics of Philippine Fundamentalism." In *Questioning the Secular State*, ed. David Westerlund. London: Hurst.
———. 1996b. "Spiritual Warfare: The Case of the Philippines." In *Exporting the American Gospel: Global Christian Fundamentalism*, ed. Steve Brouwer, Paul Gifford, and Susan D. Rose. New York: Routledge.
Rouffaer, G. P. 1931. "Vorstenlanden." *Adatrechtbundels*, 34.
"RSS Muddies Troubled Ayodhya Waters: Muslims' Real Safety Lies in Goodwill of the Majority, Says Bangalore Resolution." March 18, 2002. *Indian Express*.
Rudolph, Susanne Hoeber. 1987. *In Pursuit of Lakshmi: The Political Economy of the Indian State*. Chicago: University of Chicago Press.
———. 1997a. "Dehomogenizing Religious Forms." In *Transnational Religion and Fading States*, ed. Susanne H. Rudolph and James Piscatori. Oxford: Westview Press.
———. 1997b. "Introduction: Religions, States and Transnational Civil Society." In *Transnational Religion and Fading States*, ed. Susanne H. Rudolph and James Piscatori. Oxford: Westview Press.
———. 1999. "Is Civil Society the Answer?" Paper presented to Sri Lanka Ministry of Foreign Affairs, Sri Lanka, August 2, 26.
———. 2000a. "Civil Society and the Realm of Freedom." *Economic and Political Weekly*.
———. 2000b. "Is Civil Society the Answer?" Revised paper presented on August 2, 1999, as a lecture in the series sponsored by the Sri Lanka Ministry of Foreign Affairs to Celebrate the Golden Jubilee of Sri Lankan Independence.
Rudolph, Susanne H., and James Piscatori, eds. 1997. *Transnational Religion and Fading States*. Oxford: Westview Press.
Rustow, Dankwart A. 1970. "Transitions to Democracy: Toward a Dynamic Model." *Comparative Politics* 2, no. 3 (April): 337–363.
Ryu, Sung-min. 1990. *Hanguk Chongkyo Chidozadŭl'Ŭi Ŭisik-e Kwanhan Yŏngu* [Research on the Consciousness of Korean Religious Leaders]. Institute for Modern Society, Seoul.
Sabreg, F. T. 1991. "The Religious Right in the Philippines: A Preliminary Study." In *The Religious Right and the National Security Debate*. Manila: Tugon, National Council of Churches of the Philippines.
Sachedina, Abdulaziz. 2001. *The Islamic Roots of Democratic Pluralism*. Oxford: Oxford University Press.
Safdar Hashmi Memorial Trust. 2001. *The Saffron Agenda in Education: An Exposé*. New Delhi: SAHMAT.

Sajogyo. 1972. *Modernization without Development in Rural Java.* Bogor, Indonesia: Research Centre for Rural Sociology.
Salam, Solichin. 1970. *Sejarah Partai Muslimin Indonesia.* Jakarta: Lembaga Penjelidikan Islam.
Salonga, Jovito R. 1995a. "Reconciling My Christian Upbringing with My Political Career." *Phronesis* 2 (March): 23–34.
———. 1995b. *The Senate That Said No: A Four-year Record of the First Post-EDSA Senate.* Quezon City: University of the Philippines Press.
Samaria Forum. 1998. "Pernyataan Keprihatinan Sehubungan Dengan Peristiwa Kerusuhan di Surakarta 14–15 May 1998" [Concerned Statement Regarding the Riots in Surakarta on May 14 and 15, 1998].
Sambalilo, Jun M. 1998. "JIL Doesn't Speak for All Born-Again Groups." *Philippine Daily Inquirer,* May 8, 10.
Sanneh, Lamin. 1987. "Christian Missions and the Western Guilt Complex." *Christian Century* 104, no. 11: 331–334.
———. 1989. *Translating the Message: The Missionary Impact on Culture.* Maryknoll, N.Y.: Orbis Books.
———. 2003. *Whose Religion Is Christianity? The Gospel beyond the West.* Grand Rapids, Mich.: Eerdmans.
Santoso, David Iman. 1986. "The Indonesian Church between Crescent and Garuda." D.Miss. diss., Fuller Theological Seminary, Pasadena, Calif.
———. 1988. "The Relationship of Religion and State in Indonesia: Concepts and Realities." PhD diss., Fuller Theological Seminary, Pasadena, Calif.
Sarkar, Sumit. 1999. "Conversions and the Sangh Parivar." *The Hindu.* Online source.
Sartori, Giovanni. 1997. "Understanding Pluralism." *Journal of Democracy* 8, no. 4: 58–69.
Schmitter, Philippe C. 1999. "The Future of Democracy: Could It Be a Matter of Scale?" *Social Research* 66, 3 (Fall): 934–958.
Schwarz, Adam. 1994. *A Nation in Waiting: Indonesia in the 1990s.* Sydney: Allen & Unwin.
Schwenk, Richard L. 1986. *Onward Christians! Protestants in the Philippine Revolution.* Quezon City, Philippines: New Day.
Scott, Lindy. 1995. "The Political Significance of the Protestant Presence in Latin America: A Case Study from Mexico." *Transformation* 12, no. 1: 28–33.
Sekhar, Rukmini, ed. 1998. *Making a Difference: A Collection of Essays.* New Delhi: SPIC MACAY.
Serra, Renata. 2001. "Social Capital: Meaningful and Measurable at the State Level?" *Economic and Political Weekly* 36, no. 8: 693–704.
Shah, Ghanshyam, Mario Rutten, and Hein Streefkerk, eds. *Development and Deprivation in Gujarat: In Honour of Jan Breman.* New Delhi: Sage.
———. 1998. "Divided They Stand." In *The BJP and the Compulsions of Politics in India,* ed. Thomas Blom Hansen and Christophe Jaffrelot. New Delhi: Oxford University Press.
———. 1999a. "Conversion, Reconversion and the State: Recent Events in the Dangs." *Economic and Political Weekly,* February 6, 312–318.

———. 1999b. "The Other Side of the Dangs." *The Hindu*. February 2.

———, eds. 2004. *Labour, Marginalisation and Migration: Studies on Gujarat, India*. New Delhi: Sage.

Sheth, Pravin N. 2000. "Gujarat." In *Status of Panchayati Raj in the States and Union Territories of India*, ed. George Mathew. New Delhi: Concept Publishing for Institute of Social Sciences.

Shin, Doh C. 1998. *The Evolution of Korean Support for Democracy during the Kim Young Sam Government* (Studies in Public Policy, No. 297). Glasgow: Centre for the Study of Public Policy, University of Strathclyde.

———. 1999. *Mass Politics and Culture in Democratizing Korea*. Cambridge, U.K.: Cambridge University Press.

Shiraishi, Takeshi. 1997. *Zaman Bergerak: Radikalisme Rakyat di Jawa 1912–1926*. Jakarta: Grafitti.

Sicam, Paulynn P. 2001. "Who Anointed Civil Society to Be Guardians of the Public Welfare?" *Philippine Star*, March 8, 13.

Sigmund, Paul, ed. 1999. *Religious Freedom and Evangelization in Latin America: The Challenge of Religious Pluralism*. Maryknoll, N.Y.: Orbis Books.

Simao National Minorities Affairs Bureau Editing Committee. 1993. *The Study on Traditional Culture of Lahu in Simao*. Kunming: Yunnan People's Press.

Simao Prefecture Government. 1990. *National Minorities in Simao*. Kunming: Yunnan Nationality Press.

Simatupang, T. B. 1982. "Doing Theology in Indonesia: Sketches in Contextual Theology." *Bulletin of the Commission on Theological Concerns* 3, no. 2 (August).

Sin, Cardinal Jaime. 2000. "Resignation Will Be Good for Erap's Soul." *Today*, Philippines, November 5, 7.

Singh, Amar Kumar, and M. K. Jabbi, eds. 1996. *Status of Tribals in India: Health, Education and Employment*. New Delhi: Har-Anand Publications.

Singh, S. K. 2000. "Panchayats in Scheduled Areas." In *Status of Panchayati Raj in the States and Union Territories of India*, ed. George Mathew. New Delhi: Concept Publishing for Institute of Social Sciences.

Sjahrir. 1986. *Basic Needs in Indonesia: Economics, Politics and Public Policy*. Singapore: Institute of Southeast Asian Studies.

Skaria, Ajay. 1999. *Hybrid Histories: Forests, Frontiers and Wildness in Western India*. New Delhi: Oxford University Press.

Skocpol, Theda, and Morris P. Fiorina, eds. 1999. *Civic Engagement in American Democracy*. Washington, D.C.: Brookings Institution Press.

Smith, Christian. 1998. *American Evangelicalism: Embattled and Thriving*. Chicago: University of Chicago Press.

———. 2000. *Christian America? What Evangelicals Really Want*. Berkeley: University of California Press.

Smith, Donald E. 1974. *Religion and Political Modernization*. New Haven, Conn.: Yale University Press.

So, Nam-dong. 1983. *Minchung Sinhak Tamku* [An Exploration of Minjung Theology]. Seoul: Hangilsa.

Social Weather Stations (SWS). 1997. "SWS Report Survey: December 1997 National Survey." Quezon City, Philippines: Social Weather Stations.

---. 1999. "SWS Survey Sourcebook: Fourth Quarter 1999." Quezon City, Philippines: Social Weather Stations.

---. 2001a. "Filipino Voting Attitudes and Opinions: Selected Findings from SWS 1984–2001 National Surveys." Quezon City, Philippines: Social Weather Stations.

---. 2001b. "SWS Survey Sourcebook: Second Quarter 2001." Quezon City, Philippines: Social Weather Stations.

Soh, Kyung-suk. 2001. "Hanguk Sahoe'Ŭi Munjewa Kidokkyo Sahoe Undong'Ŭi" [The Problems of Korean Society and the Role and Direction of Christian Social Movements]. Unpublished manuscript.

Son, Bong-ho. 1997. "Kidokkyo Yuli Silchŏn Undong'Ŭi Sijak" [The Beginning of the Christian Ethics Movement]. In *Kidokkyo Yuli Silchŏn Undong 10junyŏn Hwaltong Pokosŏ* [Christian Ethics Movement 10th Anniversary Report], ed. Christian Ethic Movement. 20–26.

---. 1998. "Hanguk Chŏngchiwa Kidokkyo Siminundong" [Korean Politics and the Christian Civil Movement]. Paper presented at the first symposium of Christian Institute for Politics, June 19.

---. 2002. "Hanguk-esŏ'Ŭi Kidokgyowa Chŏngchi" [Christianity and Politics in Korea]. Paper presented at the international symposium on Christianity and Politics held by the Institute for Church Growth, March 22.

Son, Ho-chol. 1995. *Haebang 50nyon'Ŭi Hanguk Chŏngchi* [Korean Politics after 50 Years of Liberation]. Seoul: Sae Gil Publishing.

Sprague, Jonathan, and Antonio Lopez. 1999. "The Battle Lines Form." *Asiaweek*, September 3, 28–29.

Stanmeyer, Anastasia. 1999. "More and More, the People Get Their Say." *Asiaweek*, August 20–27, 60–61.

Stark, Rodney. 2001. *One True God: Historical Consequences of Monotheism*. Princeton: Princeton University Press.

State Administration on Religious Affairs [China]. 2000. "Rules on Administration of Religious Activities of Aliens in China." September 26, People Republic of China.

Steenbrink, Karel A. 1993. *Dutch Colonialism and Indonesian Islam*. Amsterdam: Rodopi.

Steinberg, David. 1997. "Civil Society and Human Rights in Korea: On Contemporary and Classical Orthodoxy and Ideology." *Korea Journal* 37: 145–165.

---. 1998. "Korea: Triumph and Turmoil." *Journal of Democracy* 9, no. 2: 76–90.

Stoll, David. 1990. *Is Latin America Turning Protestant?* Berkeley: University of California Press.

Stout, Harry S. 1977. "Religion, Communications, and the Ideological Origins of the American Revolution." *William and Mary Quarterly* 34, no. 4: 519–541.

Suh, David Kwang-Sun. 1981. "A Biographical Sketch of an Asian Theological Consultation." In *Minjung Theology People as the Subject of History*, ed. Yong Bock Kim. Singapore: Commission on Theological Concerns.

Suh, Sangwon, and Antonio Lopez. 1998a. "(Nearly) a Done Deal." *Asiaweek*, May 15, 24–25.

---. 1998b. "Revving for a Hard-Fighting Last Lap." *Asiaweek*, May 8, 24–26.

Suhartono. 1991. *Apanage dan Bekel: Perubahan Sosial di Pedesaan Surakarta 1830–1920.* Yogyakarta, Indonesia: Tiara Wacana.

Sumartana, Th. 1982. "A Personal Reflection." *Bulletin of the Commission on Theological Concern* 3, no. 2.

———. 1997. "Kiprah Gerakan keagamaan dalam Politik Praktis." *Refleksi* 20, no. 2: 5.

Sumual, Nicky. 1981. *Pantekosta Indonesia.* Manado, Indonesia: Tanpa Penerbit.

Sutarman. 1988. "Sadrach's Community and Its Contextual Roots: A Nineteenth Century Javanese Expression of Christianity." PhD diss., Vrije Universiteit, Amsterdam.

Suwondo, Kutut. 1999. "Kepemimpinan Indonesia Pasca SU 1999." *Journal of Society and Development Studies* 1, no. 2: 1–11.

Sycip, Washington. 2001. "Impoverished Democracy." *Asiaweek*, February 2, 25.

Tano, Rodrigo. 1987. "Current Issues in Theology for Filipino Evangelicals." *Evangelicals Today* (July–August): 6–8.

Tate, C. Neal. 1990. "The Revival of Church and State in the Philippines: Churches and Religion in the People Power Revolution and After." In *Religious Resurgence and Politics in the Contemporary World*, ed. Emile Sahliyeh. Albany: State University of New York Press.

Tawney, R. H. 1962. *Religion and the Rise of Capitalism.* Gloucester, Mass.: P. Smith.

Tendero, Efraim M. 1994a. "Running with the Vision." *Evangelicals Today and Asia Ministry Digest* 21, no. 7 (July): 18–19, 28.

———. 1994b. "The Worldwide Evangelical Movement: A Historical Sketch." *Evangelicals Today and Asia Ministry Digest* 21, no. 6 (June): 12–13.

———. 1998. "Why Biblical Christianity?" *Evangelicals Today* (August–September): 5–6, 15.

———. 2001. "Transforming the Nation." *Evangelicals Today* 27, no. 3 (June–July): 5, 11.

Teodoro, Luis. 2000. "The Government They Deserve." *Today*, November 13, 9.

Thompson, Mark. 1996. "Off the Endangered List: Philippine Democratization in Comparative Perspective." *Comparative Politics* 28, no. 2: 179–205.

Tien, Ju-K'ang. 1993. *The Peak of Faith: Protestant Mission in Revolutionary China.* Leiden, Netherlands: E. J. Brill.

Tilly, C. 1978. *From Mobilization to Revolution.* Reading, Mass.: Addison-Wesley.

Timberman, Dave. 1992. "The Philippines at the Polls." *Journal of Democracy* 3, no. 4 (October): 110–124.

Ting, K. H. 1999. *Selective Works on Theological Construction, Vol. 1.* Nanjing: Nanjing TSPM/CCC.

Tizon, Albert. 1999. "Revisiting the Mustard Seed: The Filipino Evangelical Church in the Age of Globalization." *Phronesis* 6, 1: 3–26.

Tjitrohoepojo. 1939. *Serat Najokatomo: Perpustakaan Reksopustoko Mangkunegaran* th.M.Metz, Mangkoenagaran. Rotterdam: Nijgh & Ditmar.

Tocqueville, Alexis de. 1840. *Democracy in America*, trans. Henry Reeve. New York: J. & H. G. Langley.

———. [1835] 1956. *Democracy in America*, ed. Richard D. Heffner. New York: Mentor.

Today's Weekender Staff. 2001. "Instant Revolution Pinoy Flavor." 412 (May 6): 1–2.

Truman, David. 1951. *The Governmental Process.* New York: Knopf.

U.S. Department of State. 2000. *2000 Annual Report on International Religious Freedom: India*. Washington, D.C.: Bureau of Democracy, Human Rights, and Labor, U.S. Department of State.

Utrecht, Ernst. 1974. "The Military and the Elections." In *Indonesia after the 1971 Elections*, ed. Hong Lee Oey. London: Oxford University Press.

Van der Veer, Peter. 1994. "Hindu Nationalism and the Discourse of Modernity: The Vishva Hindu Parishad." In *Accounting for Fundamentalisms: The Dynamic Character of Movements*, ed. Martin E. Marty and Scott R. Appleby. Chicago: University of Chicago Press.

Van Niel, Robert. 1984. *Munculnya Elit Modern Indonesia*. Jakarta: Pustaka Jaya.

Varshney, Ashutosh. 2002. *Ethnic Conflict and Civic Life: Hindus and Muslims in India*. New Haven, Conn.: Yale University Press.

Vencer, Agustin B., Jr. 1983. *A Biblical Framework for an Evangelical Response to the Current Socio-Political Unrest in the Philippines*. Quezon City, Philippines: PCEC.

———. 1989. *Poor Is No Excuse*. Exeter, U.K.: Paternoster.

———. 1991a. "The Church and Relief." *Evangelicals Today* (August–September): 4–7.

———. 1991b. "National Value Transformation: A Christian Responsibility." *Evangelicals Today* (June–July): 2–7.

———. 1991c. "The 1992 National Elections: A Christian Responsibility." *Evangelicals Today* (August–September): 2–3.

———. 1992a. "Christian Duties to Government and Society (Part 2)." *Evangelicals Today* (April–May): 11–13.

———. 1992b. "On Evangelicals and Politics: An Interview with Dr. Jun Vencer." *Evangelicals Today* (April–May): 2–4.

———. 1992c. "A Protestant President and a National Agenda." *Evangelicals Today* (June–July): 2–4.

———. 1994a. "The Evangelicals in the Philippines: A Brief History of the Philippine Council of Evangelical Churches." *Evangelicals Today and Asia Ministry Digest* 21, no. 8 (August): 16–17.

———. 1994b. "The Evangelicals in the Philippines: A Brief History of the Philippine Council of Evangelical Churches (PCEC)." *Evangelicals Today and Asia Ministry Digest* 21, no. 9 (September): 14–17.

———. 1994c. "The Evangelicals in the Philippines: A Brief History of the Philippine Council of Evangelical Churches (PCEC)." *Evangelicals Today and Asia Ministry Digest* 21, no. 10 (October): 25–27, 32.

———. 1995. "Comments on Evangelicals-Catholics Together." *Evangelicals Today and Asia Ministry Digest* (April): 7–8.

———. 1998. "The May 1998 National Elections: A Christian Responsibility." *Evangelicals Today* 25, no. 2 (March–April): 24–26, 31.

Verghese, B. G. 1996. *India's Northeast Resurgent: Ethnicity, Insurgency, Governance, and Development*. New Delhi: Konark Publishers.

Verkuyl, J. 1990. *Ketegangan antara Imperialisme dan Kolonialsime Barat dan Zending pada Masa Politik Kolonial Etis*. Jakarta: BPK Gunung Mulia.

Villanueva, Eddie. 1994a. "On Being a Good Citizen." *Evangelicals Today and Asia Ministry Digest* 21, no. 8 (August): 12.

———. 1994b. "The Supernatural Dimension." *Evangelicals Today and Asia Ministry Digest* 21–22 (November): 8–9.
———. 1998. "Jesus Is Lord Church." In *The New Apostolic Churches*, ed. C. Peter Wagner. Ventura, Calif.: Regal.
———. 2001a. "On the Role of Church in Politics." Unpublished manuscript. Jesus Is Lord Church, Bocaue, Bulacan, Philippines, 4.
———. 2001b. "Without Legal Anchor nor Moral Cause." *Philippine Star*, April 28, 10.
Villanueva, M. Val A. 2001. "Burden of 3 EDSAs." *Philippine Star*, July 5, 8–9.
Vitug, Marites D., and Glenda Gloria. 2000. *Under the Crescent Moon: Rebellion in Mindanao*. Manila: Ateneo Center for Social Policy and Public Affairs/Institute for Popular Democracy.
Wallace, Peter. 2001. "Does the Philippines Have a Chance?" *Philippine Star*, July 20, 10–11; July 21, 12.
Walls, Andrew F. 1996. *The Missionary Movement in Christian History: Studies in the Transmission of Faith*. Maryknoll, N.Y.: Orbis Books.
Walzer, Michael. 1965. *The Revolution of the Saints: A Study in the Origins of Radical Politics*. Cambridge, Mass.: Harvard University Press.
Ward, Ken. 1974. *The 1971 Election in Indonesia: An East Java Case Study*. Monash Papers on Southeast Asia No. 2, Monash University, Australia.
"Wawancara A. M. Fatwa: Sistem Kepartaian Sekarang Belum Kondusif." 1995. *Tiras*, Indonesia, November 9, 46–52.
"Wawancarra Letjen (pur.) Sayidiman Suryohadiprojo" [Interview with Lieutenant General (Ret.) Sayidiman Suryohadiprojo]. 1995. *Forum Keadilan*, Jakarta, November 6, 80–84.
Weber, Max. 1910. *Prostesantische Ethik und der Geist des Kapitalismus*. Translated as *Protestant Ethic and the Spirit of Capitalism* by Talcott Parsons. Foreword by R. H. Tawney. New York: Scribner.
Webster, J. C. 1992. *The Dalit Christians*. New Delhi: ISPCK.
Wendt, Alexander. 1999. *Social Theory of International Politics*. Cambridge: Cambridge University Press.
Whelchel, James. 1995. *The Path to Liberation: Theology of Struggle in the Philippines*. Quezon City, Philippines: New Day.
Wickeri, J., ed. 2000. *Love Never Ends: Papers by K. H. Ting*. Nanjing: Yilin.
Willis, Avery T., Jr. 1977. *Indonesian Revival: Why Two Million Came to Christ*. South Pasadena, Calif.: William Carey Library.
Wingate, Andrew. 1999. *The Church and Conversion: A Study of Recent Conversions to and from Christianity in the Tamil Area of South India*. New Delhi: ISPCK.
Woodberry, Robert D. 1999. "Religion and Democratization: Explaining a Robust Empirical Relationship." Paper presented at the annual meeting of the Religion Research Association.
———. 2004. "The Shadow of Empire: Christian Missions, Colonial Policy, and Democracy in Postcolonial Societies." PhD diss., University of North Carolina, Chapel Hill.
Woodberry, Robert D., and Timothy S. Shah. 2004. "The Pioneering Protestants." *Journal of Democracy* 15, no. 2: 47–61.

World Bank. 1990. *World Development Report: Poverty.* New York: Oxford University Press.

Wourms, Michael. 1992. *The J.I.L. Love Story: The Church without a Roof.* El Cajon, Calif.: Christian Services Publishing.

Wuthnow, Robert. 1996. *Christianity and Civil Society.* Valley Forge, Penn.: Trinity Press International.

———. 1999. "Mobilizing Civic Engagement: The Changing Impact of Religious Involvement." In *Civic Engagement in American Democracy*, ed. Theda Skocpol and Morris Fiorina. Washington, D.C.: Brookings Institution Press.

Xaxa, Virginius. 2001. "Protective Discrimination: Why Scheduled Tribes Lag Behind Scheduled Castes." *Economic and Political Weekly* 36 (no. 29): 2765–2772.

Xin, Tong. 2000. "One Can Not Rewrite History." In *Reference Materials for Works on Catholic Church* (Series 2, Internal Material) [in Chinese], ed. Editorial Committee of State Religious Affairs Bureau. Beijing: Religious Culture Press.

Xu, Yongfu, Qigui Zhou, and Zongcu Du. 1998. "Actively Lead the Religious Believers to Serve Socialism by Constructing Two Civilizations: Survey of the Christian Church in Gaoziba." *Zongjiao*, nos. 41–42: 68–70.

Yamamori, Tetsunao, and Chan Kim-kwong. 2000. *Witnesses to Power: Stories of God's Quiet Work in a Changing China.* Carlisle, U.K.: Paternoster.

Yamane, David. 1997. "Secularization on Trial: In Defense of a Neosecularization Paradigm." *Journal for the Scientific Study of Religion* 36, no. 1: 109–122.

Yi, Chung-sok. 1997. *Kiyunsil Sipnyŏn Pyŏngkawa 21segi Chŏnmang* [The Evaluation of the Ten Years' CEM and Prospect for the 21st Century]. In *Kidokkyo Yuli Silchŏn Undong 10junyŏn Hwaltong Pokosŏ* [Christian Ethics Movement 10th Anniversary Report], ed. Christian Ethic Movement. 28–42.

Yi, Kap-Yun, and Moon Yong-jik. 1994. *Hanguk'Ŭi Minjuhwa: Chŏngae Kwajŏngkwa Sŏnggy Ŏk* [The Democratization of Korea: Its Process of Development and Character]. Korean Association of Politics, Papers from International Workshop, 11, 19.

Yi, Man-yol. 1989. "Segye Kidok Kyohoessa'esŏ'Ŭi Hanguk Kidokkyo" [Korean Christianity in the History of World Christianity]. In *Hanguksa Simin Kangjoa* [Citizen Lecture for Korean History], Vol. 4.

———. 1991. *Hanguk Kidokkyowa Minjok Ŭisik* [Christianity in Korea and National Consciousness]. Seoul: Chisik Sanŏpsa.

———. 1997. "Changno Daetonglong'e Taehan Kidae wa Chajŏl" [Expectations and Discouragement about Elder President]. *Christian Academy* (November–December).

Yi, Sang-gyu. 1995. "Haebanghu Hankuk Kyohoe'Ŭi Minjuhwawa Tongil Undong" [The Democratization Movement and Unification Movement of the Korean Church after Independence]. In *Hanguk Kidokyowa Yŏksa* [Korean Christianity and History], Vol. 4, ed. Man-youl Yi. Seoul: Institute for the History of the Korean Church.

Yim, Hyuk-baek. 1997. "Chiyŏndoigoinnŭn Minjujuui'Ŭi Konggohwa" [The Consolidation of Delayed Democracy]. In *Hanguk Sahoewa Minjujuŭi: Hanguk Minjuhwa sipnŏnŭi Pyonggawa Pansŏng* [Korean Society and Democracy: Assessments and Prospects of Ten Years of Democratization in Korea], ed. Jang-Jip Choi and Hyun-chin Lim. Seoul: Nanam.

Youngblood, Robert L. 1993. *Marcos Against the Church: Economic Development and Political Repression in the Philippines.* Quezon City, Philippines: New Day.

Yu, Sok-chōn, and Byong-young Park. 1992. "Hanguk Haksaeng Undong'Ūi Kujowa Kinūng" [The Structure and Function of the Student Movement]. In *Sahoe Undongkwa Sahoe Kaehyōklon* [Social Movement and Theory of Social Reform], ed. Sang-jin Han and Jong-hoi Yang. Seoul: Chon Ye Won.

Zerinini-Brotel, Jasmine. 2002. "The Political Elite in Uttar Pradesh, 1952–2000: A Sociology of the Governing Classes." Manuscript.

Index

Aaron, Sushil xii, xiii, 9, 12–14, 15, 16, 27–31, 38, 39, 90, 87–129
Abella, Ernie 244, 258, 281n29
activism xii, xiii, 7, 22, 25, 39, 99, 232n1. *See also* Bebbington, David
Adivasi Bhoomiheen Kisan Hakk Sanrakshan Samiti (Association to Restore Land Rights of Adivasi Peasants) 117
adivasis 12–16, 91–93, 87–129, 131–153. *See also* tribal peoples
advocacy for marginalized groups. *See* evangelical Christianity: democratizing effects of
Africa vii-xiv, 3, 5, 6, 10, 21, 41n3
agency among marginalized people groups. *See* democratization: revitalized agency
Aglipayan Church (Filipino Independent Catholics) 236, 241, 278n1
Agung, Sultan 161
Ahn, Byung-Moo 200
Alcala, Angel 240
alcoholism and drug use and sales 57–59, 66–71, 82n30, 104–105, 107–110, 118, 125n13, 127n43
Alconga, Leo 239
Aliran thesis 158, 180. *See* Geertz, Clifford
Alliance of Bible Christian Communities in the Philippines 239, 268
Alliance of Christian Development Agencies (ACDA), Philippines 269, 271, 273, 275, 282n46
Alliance of Philippine Partners for Enterprise Development (APPEND) 269
Almeda, Wilde 279n10

Almond, Gabriel 8
Amos for Gujarat (AG) 90, 98, 103, 110, 112–113, 115–116, 123
Anglicanism vii, xi, 104
 in South Korea 214, 226
Ansor (Nadhlatul Ulama's youth organization) 162
Apok, C. 141, 144
Apuzen, Valmike 273
Aquino, Benigno (Ninoy), Senator 237, 254
Aquino, Corazon Cojungco-, President of the Philippines (1986–1992) 237, 243, 248–249, 252–255, 263, 264, 280n25
Arato, Andrew 132
Arianism 240, 279n13
Arienda, Roger 254–255, 262
Arroyo, Gloria Macapagal-, President of the Philippines (2001-present) 237, 252, 260, 263, 276, 283n63
Asheemanand, Swami 114, 119
Ashram Shala 95, 97, 98
Asia Missions Network 257, 282n45
Asia vii-xiii, 3–42, 121, 186
Asian Institute for Civil Society Movements, South Korea 226
Asian Theological Seminary (ATS) 246, 268, 269
 Center for Transformation Studies (ACTS) 246–247, 270
Assam, India 133–134, 136, 143
Assemblies of God Churches xi
 in Fugong, China 84n37
 in Indonesia 168
 in the Philippines 240
 in South Korea 226

318 INDEX

Association of Bible Churches in the Philippines 268
authoritarianism and autocratic rule 43–44, 65, 79–80, 156–157, 162–163, 185–189, 191–192, 209–211, 235–237, 254
Azariah, Bishop V.S. 36, 100

Badua, Violy 281n28
Baipidezai village, China 10, 11, 67–72
Balais, Daniel 244–245, 261–262, 281n28
baptism 62–64, 85n51, 104. *See also* government control of religion
Baptists 137, 139
  in Indonesia 168, 170
  in Northeast India (indigenous) xiii, 133, 141–142, 144–146,
  in Northeast India (American) 134–135, 137, 142
  in the Philippines 239, 240, 241, 255, 274, 278 nn.1–2
Bapu, Morari 89
Barisan Tani Indonesia (Indonesia Farmers Front) 162
Barnabas, C.S. 103
Barrett, David x
Bautista, Benjamin 249, 283n57
Bebbington, David 7, 22, 39, 41n7, 98, 232
Belgica, Grepor 248, 281n34
beliefs. *See* religion and religious worldviews
Benigno, Teodor C. 249, 276, 283n63
Berger, Peter xii, xv, 22
bhagats 105–107, 109, 111, 114, 127n44
Bharati, Shankaracharya Vidya Narsingh 89
Bharatiya Janata Party (Indian People's Party, BJP) 89, 114, 121–122, 124n4, 124n6, 125, 129n60, 136n56, 150. *See also* Hindutva
Bhargava, Rajeev 97
Bhil people group 88, 93–95, 97, 108, 111, 113, 118
Bhineka Tunggal Eka (Diversity But One, motto of Indonesia) 178
Bible translation 7, 28, 68, 70, 127–128nn48–49, 138, 167
biblicism x, 7, 22, 99, 232n1. *See also* Bebbington, David
BJP. *See* Bharatiya Janata Party
Bread of Life Christian Ministries, Philippines 240
Breakfast Prayer Meeting of the National Assembly, South Korea 215
Breman, Jan 89
bridging capital. *See* social capital: bridging
Buddhism xv, 7, 20, 25, 62, 162, 207
  Buddhist political movements in South Korea 201, 215, 218
Buddhists 12, 15, 31, 53, 120, 166, 199, 200–203, 214–215, 218–219
Budijanto, Bambang xii, xiii, 9, 15–16, 19, 26–27, 31, 33–34, 36–37, 39
Burke, Edmund 262

Callanta, Ruth 269
Calvinism 22, 29, 208
Campus Crusade for Christ 223, 238
capital, social. *See* social capital
Caplan, Lionel 104
Carague, Guillermo 283n53
Cárdenas, Lázaro 211
Carter, Jimmy viii
Casanova, José 26
caste 6, 13–16, 22, 34, 43, 92, 120–121, 123. *See also* Nadar caste
Catholic Action 189
Catholic Church, Catholicism, etc. *See* Roman Catholic
Catholic Committee for Justice and Peace, South Korea 190
Catholic Farmers Federation, South Korea 190
Catholic Labor Youth Coalition, South Korea 189
Catholic Priests' Association for Justice, South Korea 201
CDOs (Christian Development Organizations) 273, 277
Center for Community Transformation, Philippines 269
Center for Strategic and International Studies (CSIS), Indonesia 160, 164, 182n22, 182n24
Central Academy of National Minorities, China 60
Central Axe (a parliamentary faction), Indonesia 157, 158
Cerveza, Absalom 272
Chachet, Frans Lion 181n10
Cha-Cha People Power events 263–264
Chaeya movement, South Korea 189, 192, 216
Chan, Kim-Kwong xii, 5, 6, 9–12, 14–16, 19, 27–31, 38, 39, 43–86
Chand, Vikram xvii
Chang, Hun 204
Chang, Young-dal 231
charismatics and charismatic churches xi, 6
  charismatic renewal movements 168, 241, 274, 278n3
  in Indonesia 164–166, 168, 169, 170, 171, 175, 183n31
  non-charismatic evangelical churches, Indonesia 169
  non-charismatic evangelicals, Filipino 239
  in the Philippines 239, 240, 242, 247, 256, 260–262, 274, 278n3
  Catholic 248, 253, 269, 274, 283n61
Che, Jung-Ku 200
Chen, Shaoying, 61–65, 76
China viii, ix, xii, 4, 6, 10–12, 14, 19, 28, 43–86, 120
China Christian Council (CCC) 45–49, 51, 52, 54, 73–75, 77, 78, 81n3, 81n5, 82n9, 85n51
Chinese Communist Party (CCP) 43–47, 49, 51–54, 57, 60, 62, 65–66, 71–73, 79–80, 82n17

United Front Work Department (UFWD) 47, 50, 82n13
Chinese People's Political Consultative Conference (CPPCC) 51-53, 62, 65, 82n17, 83n19
Cho, Bae-Suk 215
Cho, Yong-Gi, Pastor 203, 208
Cholla, South Korea 204-205
Christian Coalition for National Transformation, Philippines 250
Christian Coalition for Producing Democratic Government (CCPDG), South Korea 202
Christian Committee for Fair Elections (CCFE), South Korea 218-220, 226
Christian Convergence for Good Governance (CCGG), Philippines 271, 275
Christian Democratic Party, Philippines 280n25
Christian Embassy, South Korea 206
Christian Ethics Movement (CEM), South Korea 218-222, 226, 231
Christian Federation of Social Movements, South Korea 226
Christian Institute for Politics, South Korea 215
Christian Institute for the Study of Justice and Development (CISJD), South Korea 193, 200-201
Christian Leaders' Alliance of the Philippines (CLAP) 238-239, 241, 247, 255, 279n7
Christian Leaders' Conference of the Philippines (CLCP) 241, 261, 277
Christian Teachers' Network (CTN), Philippines 270, 275
Christianity. *See also* church; democracy: evangelical influence; evangelical Christianity; evangelicals; evangelicalism
  contextualization of 70, 109-110, 258
  growth and diffusion of 10, 27, 30-32, 44-45, 49, 51, 61, 165, 167
  local histories of 63, 66, 88-91, 99-100, 133-140, 236
  minority status 6-9, 89, 122, 124, 160, 186-187, 236, 278
Chu, Raineer 257
Chun, Doo-hwan, President of South Korea (1980-1988) 191, 194, 197, 210-211
Chun, Ho-jin 190
Chun, Ki 200
Chun, Pil-sun 187
Chung, Chol-hui 189
Chung, Ju-Young 207
Chung Hyun church 202
church. *See also* Christianity
  centralization, authoritarianism, and failure to delegate 115-117, 228-231
  discord and fragmentation among churches 15, 131-132, 142, 144, 228 (*see also* social capital: bridging)
  confrontations with political authorities 33-36, 51-56, 63-65, 73-78, 110-115, 118-119, 145-151, 192-194, 251-265
  involvement in politics (questionable) 34, 160, 203, 244-249
  involvement in politics (prophetic) 32, 34-35, 40, 145-151 (*see also* church: confrontations with political authorities)
  as peacemaker 15-16, 69, 145-150, 174-176, 272
  political failures and omissions of 15, 76-78, 115-118, 146-147, 211-214, 228-231, 245-247
  as school of democracy 21, 30, 39, 53, 55, 60, 102, 109-110, 111-115, 164-166, 173-177, 225-226, 229, 266-267, 273-275
  separation from politics 35, 187-188 (*see also* separation of church and state)
Church of North India 98, 116
Church of South India 105
Church Peace Council, India 147
Cigong, China 61-65
Cigong Christian Temporary Gathering Point, China 64
Citizens' Coalition for Economic Justice (CCEJ), South Korea 218-219, 222-226, 231
Citizens' National Network against Poverty and Corruption, Philippines 271
citizenship. *See also* civil society; democratization; social capital
  activities teaching citizenship 8-9, 18-20, 38, 275
  character development 17-18, 37-40, 102-103, 209-211, 216-217
  electoral education 141-142, 173-174, 176-177, 218-222, 249-251
  leadership development 11, 29, 32, 39, 52-53, 55-56, 99, 113-115, 272-275
  teaching civic participation 17-19, 132-133, 173-174, 216-226, 265-275
civil disobedience 71, 73, 75, 192f., 254-255, 260, 262-263
Civil Movements for Social Reform and Christians' Participation, South Korea 226
Civil Service Commission, Philippines 249
civil society 9-11, 45, 131-153, 195, 197, 216-226, 265-275. *See also* citizenship; democratization; social capital
  church foundations for 17, 51-56, 73-78, 131-138, 173-177
  church networks in 6, 60-72, 76-77, 195-197
  networks as an element of 27-31, 37-40, 216-226, 265-275
  role in democratization 212-214
Clifford, James 90
Cohen, Jean 132

colonialism x, xiii, 37, 123n2
   British, in India 8, 93–94, 100, 123n2, 125n17, 133–140, 149 (*see also* divide and rule)
   internal, in India 98, 110–111, 113–114, 122–123, 129n63, 149–150
   Japanese, in Korea 186, 187, 207, 216
Comaroff, Jean and John 137–138
communism 24, 43–44, 49, 71–72, 74, 162, 254, 272. *See also* Chinese Communist Party; Marxism
Communist Party (PKI), Indonesia 156, 158, 162, 167–168
community organizing. *See* evangelical Christianity: democratizing effects of
Conde, Cesar 263
Confessing Church 73
confrontation with authorities, by evangelicals. *See* church: confrontations with political authorities
Confucianism 22, 46, 174, 207, 219
Confucius 26
Consultation of National Elections, Philippines 249
contextualization 89
conversion xi–xii, 66, 67, 71, 89, 100, 106, 108, 119, 166, 176
conversionism 7, 22, 99, 232n1. *See also* Bebbington, David
Corbridge, Stuart 123
Costes, Ariel B. 280n17
Couples for Christ (CfC), Philippines 237, 253, 261, 278n3, 283n61
Crisologo, Jess 249
Crisologo, Vincent 248
Crozier, Dr. 139
crucicentrism 7, 22, 99, 232n1. *See also* Bebbington, David
Cultural Revolution, China 44, 52, 74
culture of questioning 25, 111
Curtis, Gerald L. 225

Dahl, Robert A. 7, 209
Dalisay, Cornelio 247
Dalits (untouchables) 92, 120, 123
Dangi Christians 28, 97–98, 101–103, 104–119
Dangis 12–14, 87, 93–97, 104–111
Dangs, India 28, 30, 87–129
Daniel, K. 103
Dasan, E. 89
Davao Declaration, Philippines 272
David, Randy 258
de Venecia, Jose 245, 250, 281n30
de Villa, Renato 245
DeBoer, Stewart 269
Degar (Montagnard) xiii
Deles, Ding 282n47
deliverance, from oppressive conditions 13, 105, 107, 109, 125n13, 260. *See also* exorcism, healings
democracy ix, xii–xv, 3–5, 7–9, 10, 17–18, 20–21, 31, 37–40, 43–44, 46, 49, 54–55, 60, 79, 88, 97, 118, 123, 132–133, 176, 179, 186, 195, 204, 207–209, 211, 216–217, 220, 226–227, 229, 230–231, 235, 249, 251, 257, 264–268, 270, 273, 275–277
   evangelical influence upon, direct 9–10, 18, 32–37, 40, 59–60, 163–67, 188–215
   evangelical influence upon, indirect 9, 27–32, 37–40, 44–46, 216f.
   impact of Christianity: hypotheses 3–4, 6, 26–32
   liberal 21
Democratic People's Coalition (Minjuju'ui Kukmin Yonhap), South Korea 189
Democratic Liberal Party, South Korea 202, 211
Democratic Party, South Korea 201
Democratic Recovery People's Committee, South Korea 189
democratic transition and consolidation 3, 17, 32, 37, 43, 191–194, 265–275
democratization ix-x, xii, xv, 4, 8, 10, 12, 21–22, 24, 34, 35, 38, 42n13, 44–46, 51, 56–58, 65–69, 72, 108–109, 132, 158, 168–178, 185–233, 216–226, 235, 249–251, 254, 265–275, 277, 284n64. *See also* democratization, elements of; democratic transition and consolidation
   assisting marginalized groups 3, 10–11, 28, 31, 56f., 67f., 69, 71, 99–100, 111–115, 137, 267–269, 272–273
   civil society 29n3–31, 72, 273–275
   economic development 22, 56–60, 67–68, 98–104, 111–113, 177, 222–225, 267–269
   effects of religious worldviews 11–14, 30
   indirect 8, 26–32, 40
   political influence upon 11, 60–80, 186–188, 192–193, 200–204, 208–209, 270–272
   revitalized agency 10–12, 27, 30–31, 100–101, 172–173
   role of mass protests in 33–35, 140f., 145f., 151, 188–199, 251–256
   third wave of ix, 235
Dena, Lal 139
Desierto, Aniniano 257
Dhale, James 142, 150
Dhinakaran, D.G.S. 126n25
Diamond, Larry 216
Diliman Bible Church, Philippines 254–255
Dimacali, Carissa 256
Ding, K. H. (Kuang-hsun), Bishop (also as Ding Guangxun) 50, 82n13
divide and rule policies 14–15, 35, 139, 149, 163–164. *See also* fragmentation in society
Downs, Frederick 142
drug trade, Moreh, India 149
DZAS radio station, Philippines 255–256
DZEC radio station, Philippines 237

INDEX

East Asia, in general 196, 198, 225
East India Company 66, 91, 94
East Timor 6, 157
Ebenezer, Michael 103, 117
economic development 9, 10, 35, 37–38, 56–60, 66, 76, 102, 111–113, 156–157, 197–198, 223, 250, 267–269, 276. *See also* evangelical Christianity, democratizing effects of
ecumenical and evangelical Christianity 49, 92, 120, 164–166, 177, 187–192, 196–197, 218–219, 222–224, 238–239, 272–273, 279n14, 280n16, 283n53
ecumenism 92, 120, 238, 279n14
EDSA (Epifanio de los Santos Avenue Shrine) 242. *See also* EDSA1; EDSA2; EDSA3 (People Power events)
EDSA 1 251–252, 254–256, 259, 265, 275–276, 281n28, 282n39, 283n63
EDSA 2 251–254, 256–262, 275, 276, 282n40
EDSA 3 251–254, 262–263, 265, 268, 275, 276, 282n42, 282n49
educational efforts, evangelical. *See* evangelical Christianity, democratizing effects of: educational efforts
Edwards, Bob 229
egalitarianism 3, 7, 21, 30. *See also* evangelical Christianity, democratizing effects of: egalitarian effects
El Shaddai (Catholic charismatic group), Philippines 237–238, 253, 278n3, 283n61
Engineer, Irfan 126n31
Enrile, Juan Ponce 252
Enriquez, Salvador Jr. 263
Epifanio de los Santos Avenue (EDSA) Shrine 237. *See also* EDSA
Episcopal Church in the Philippines 241
equality. *See* egalitarianism
Erap. *See* Estrada, Joseph
Estrada, Joseph, President of the Philippines (1998–2001), called Erap 237–238, 244, 250–253, 256, 262, 264, 271–273
Ethics and Public Policy Center (EPPC) xvi
ethnicity 131–153
Evangelical Church of India 98
Evangelical Council of Churches, Philippines 275
evangelical Christianity, democratizing effects of 3, 5, 7–8, 23, 27, 42n13, 44, 51, 55–56, 80, 87f., 118–120, 122–123, 132, 148, 227
  advocacy for marginalized groups 16, 24, 39, 43, 80, 99, 110–111, 115, 117–119, 148–149, 164, 168, 250, 257, 261, 265–266, 270–272
  augmenting skills 11, 28, 70–72, 100, 103, 111–113, 266–270
  building inter-group cooperation 18–19, 31, 39, 52–53, 108, 137–139, 140–144, 146–147, 165, 169, 174–175 (*see also* social capital: bridging; discord and fragmentation among churches)
  community organizing 30–31, 38–39, 111–115, 140–142, 272–273
  educational efforts 13, 39, 59–60, 70–71, 93, 95, 97–98, 109–110, 135–136, 167, 177, 269–270
    women's education 112
    vernacular education 59–60, 70–71, 109–112
  egalitarian effects 30, 43, 107, 110, 118–120. *See also* egalitarianism
  literacy and literacy efforts 11, 13, 22, 28–29, 31, 59–60, 70–72, 82, 92, 95–96, 99, 109–113, 116, 118–119
  overcoming dysfunctional behaviors 57–58, 65, 82n30, 108–109
  poverty and poverty alleviation 12, 30, 39, 56–60, 70–73, 92–95, 99–101, 111–113, 147, 175–178, 222–226, 267–270
evangelical ethic xii. *See also* Weber; protestant ethic
Evangelical Fellowship of India (EFI) 145, 151n4, 152
Evangelical Fellowship of India Commission on Relief (EFICOR) 142
evangelical political participation. *See* political participation: evangelical
Evangelicalism and Democracy Project 12
evangelicalism vii, x, xii-xiv, 4, 7–9, 10, 14–16, 29
  characteristics of x, 7, 22, 43, 99, 232n1
  in China 10, 50
  evangelical theology 104, 160, 173
  global viii, xiv-xv
  in India 87–88, 90–93, 103, 110, 118–123
  in the Philippines 19, 241, 266, 273, 276, 280n20
  in South Korea 18
evangelicals viii, ix, xii-xiv, 18, 35–36
  conservative evangelicals 256, 260
  in India 103, 111–112, 116, 131–153
  in Indonesia 164–166, 168–78, 175, 177, 179
  in the Philippines 39, 235–284
    transformational 241–242, 246, 256, 263–264
  in South Korea xi, 185–186, 190–191, 195–197, 199, 203–206, 215–217, 219, 221–223, 225–231
  Third World 43
  in the United States 91
Evangelicals for Justice and Righteousness (EJR), Philippines 258, 264
evangelism 100–103, 113, 175, 177–178, 187, 219, 221, 267
evangelistic missions 177
evangelists 104, 106, 109, 112, 116, 137
evangelization 107, 181n9
exorcism 84, 106, 109. *See also* healings: power encounters

322   INDEX

Falungong 78. *See also* government control of religion
Fan, Chenguang 81n5
Far East Broadcasting Company (FEBC) 255, 271
Federation of Christian Youth for the Defense of Democracy, South Korea 189
Feliciano, David 246, 276
Fellowship of Christian Urban Stewards, Philippines 269
Fellowship of Christian Youth, South Korea 200
Fellowship of Christians in Government (FOCIG), Philippines 250, 257, 270, 271
Fernandes, Sujatha xii, xiii, 9, 14–16, 27, 31, 34–35, 39, 131–153
Ferrez, Jun 273
Fieldstead and Company xvi
Foley, Michael W. 229
Forest Labor Cooperative Societies (FLCS), Dangs, India 95–96
Fortress College, Kabankalan City, Negros Occidental, Philippines 270
Foundation for Transformational Development (TransDev), Philippines 256, 271, 282n45
fragmentation in society 131–133, 136–141, 143, 145, 147–149. *See also* church: discord and fragmentation among churches; divide and rule
Freedom House report (2007) ix
Freston, Paul viii, xvii, 7, 22, 143–144
Fritschler, Lee J. 194
Fugong County, Yunnan, China 10–11, 14, 56–60, 65, 80, 83n26
Full Gospel churches, Philippines 239–240, 278n2
fundamentalism 7, 20, 23–24, 26, 85n46, 91, 98, 187, 238–240, 273, 279n6

Galaraga, Jovie 245, 247
Galicia, Emmanuel 274
Gandhi, Mohandas Karamchand ("Mahatma") 95, 97–98, 109–110, 129
Gandhian movements and workers 95, 97–98, 109–111
Garchitorena, Vicky 282n47
Garcia, Jude 251
GCW. *See* Gujarat Christian Workers
Gedangan Forum, Salatiga 166
Geertz, Clifford 158, 180
global South vii-xii, xiv, xvi, xixn10, 20
Gloria, Ricardo 240
Go-Belmonte, Betty 240
God's People's Coalition for Righteousness (GPCR), Philippines 261–262, 275, 282n48
Golez, Roilo 257
Golkar, Indonesian political party 157–158, 162–163, 173, 180

Golwalkar, M.S. 124n4
Gonzales, Neptali 240, 248
government control of religion 6, 10, 20, 42–54, 62–65, 73–76, 78, 81n2, 81nn7–8, 82n9–11, 89–90, 119–123, 123n2, 123n4, 124n6, 128n52, 128n57
Grand Alliance for Christian Education (GRACE), Philippines 270, 275
Grand National Party (GNP), South Korea 203
Grigg, Viv 268
Guangdong Province, China 61ff. *See also* Yangshan County, China
Guided Democracy, Indonesia 156
Guillot, C. 166
Gujarat, India xii, xiii, 5, 9–10, 12–14, 28, 31, 36, 39, 87–123
Gujarat Christian Workers (GCW) 12, 13, 88, 90, 98–106, 108–119, 123
Gujarati Christi Seva (Christian Service for Gujarati, GCS) 111
Gutzlaff, Charles 66

Habibie, Jusef (B. J.), President of Indonesia (1998–1999) 157, 166, 171, 182n28
Habito, Cielito 250
Haggard, Stephen 198
Hahn, Bae-Ho 209
Halmodi, India 107
Ham, Suk-Hon 200
Hamengkubuwana I, Sultan 161
Hammond, Laurie 136
Hamon, Bill 245
Han, Kwang-Ok 203
Han, Yong-San 203
Han Chinese 72–73, 83
Handmaids of the Lord, Philippines 237
Haokip, Hawlngam 146
Hardiman, David 89, 93, 106, 111
Harper, Susan Billington viii
Harrison, Lawrence 22
Harriss, John 123
Hastings, Adrian 138, 144, 147
Hatfield, Mark viii
healings 29, 105–107, 110
  power encounters 11, 13–14, 29–30, 62f., 64, 70, 102, 104–108
  role in leading to faith 31–44, 69–70, 104–108, 109
Hebei Christian Council, China 12, 52, 53, 82n15
Hebei Pastoral Training Center, China 52
Hebei Province, China 12, 51–53, 79
Hebei Religious Affairs Bureau 83n19
Hebei Religious Regulations 53
Hefner, Robert W. 26, 158
Henan Province, China 77
Higgins, J.C. 139
Hinduism xv, 7, 20, 89, 109, 122, 131, 133–134, 150, 162
Hindus xiii, 14–16, 24, 26, 88–90, 98–99, 111–112, 115, 121–123, 138, 141, 150, 166

Hindutva 36, 38, 122, 124. *See also* nationalism, Hindu
Hobbes, Thomas 20
Hockey, S. 145–146
Holiness Church, South Korea 193, 226
Honam, South Korea. *See* Cholla
Hong, Young-gi xii-xiii, 9–10, 15, 16–19, 27, 32–34, 36–39
Hong Kong 63, 75
Hong Kong Christian Council 83n23
Horam, Ringkahoa 149
house churches 82n18, 107
Hsu, Shuicun 63
Hu, Benxun 83n19
human rights 25, 145, 173, 175, 191, 197, 226
Hume, David 20
Hungkyo, Valley Rose 143, 150
Huntington, Samuel P. 26, 195–197, 276
Hwang, Woo-Yea 215

Iglesia Filipina Independiente/Aglipayans. *See* Aglipayan Church
Iglesia Ni Cristo (INC), Philippines 236–238, 240, 253, 279n13, 278n1
Ikatan Cendekiawan Muslim Indonesia (Indonesia Association of Muslim Intellectuals) 157
Ikatan Pendukung Kemerdekaan Indonesia (The League of the Upholders of Indonesia's Independence) 163
illiteracy 70–72, 88, 92–93, 95–97, 103f. *See also* literacy; educational efforts, evangelical
Im, Hyung-Baeg 198
imperialism xii, 149
In, Myung-Jin 192, 200, 203
India viii, xii-xiii, 4, 6, 32, 35, 60, 87–129, 131–153
  Indian Central Government 15, 90, 112, 134, 139, 142, 147–151, 153
India Missions Association 99
individualism xii, 136
Indonesia viii, xii-xiii, 6, 16, 33–35, 155–183
Indonesia Democratic Party of Struggle (PDIP) 157–158, 169, 175
Indonesian Christian Communication Forum (FKKI) 164, 182n26
Indonesian Council of Churches 166–167
Industrial Mission Committee, South Korea 189
industrialization 188, 198
Institute for Studies in Asian Church and Culture (ISACC) 242, 246, 249–250, 254–258, 264, 268, 270–271, 281n33, 282n46
Institute on Culture, Religion and World Affairs (CURA) (Boston University) xvi
Insulinde 162, 182
Intercessors of the Philippines (IFP, prayer arm of PJM) 244–245, 261, 270, 281n28

interfaith forum, Indonesia 174–177
inter-group cooperation 18–19, 31, 39, 52–53, 108, 137–139, 140–144, 146–147, 165, 169, 174–175. *See also* social capital: bridging
International Church of the Foursquare Gospel, Philippines 240
International Council of Churches 239
International Fellowship of Evangelical Mission Theologians (INFEMIT) vii, viii
Inter-Varsity Fellowship (International Fellowship of Evangelical Students, IFES) 36
  Indonesia Inter-Varsity Fellowship 165
  Inter-Varsity Movement, Philippines 238, 254–256, 258, 264, 279n11, 281n33, 282n46
Intervide forum, Yogyakarta, Indonesia 166
intolerance and tolerance 20–21, 23–24, 26, 73, 80, 121, 140, 144, 149, 229
Iralu, Niketan 146, 149, 150
Islam xv, 7, 16–17, 20, 24–26, 89, 121, 133, 158, 162–163, 178, 278n1. *See also* Muslims

Jakarta, Indonesia 156–157, 164
Jansz, P. 167
Japanese Colonialism. *See* Colonialism, Japanese
Java 155, 157, 160, 166–167, 174, 181nn9–10
Jefferson, Thomas 262
Jesuits 98
Jesus is Lord Church (JIL), Philippines 236, 240, 244–245, 260–262, 264, 278n3
Jesus Miracle Crusade (JMC), Philippines 237, 240, 253, 279n10
Jews 276
Jharkhand, India 121
Jiangxi Bible School, Central China 12, 53–56
Jiangxi Christian Council 53, 55, 83n20, 83n23
Jiangxi Province, China 53–55, 79
Jiangxi Religious Affairs Bureau 55
Jiminez, Ed 282n47
Jin, Rev. Yun Peng 52–53
John Paul II, Pope 121, 266
Johnson, Todd x
Joshi, B.N. 128n56
Joshi, Satyakam 126n31
Joshua, Thomas 149, 150
Justice Politics Forum, South Korea 220

Kabayao, Gilopez 240
Kahin, George McT. 156
Kamaleson, Samule 126n25
Kang, In-Chul 195
Kang, Ku-Chul 200
Karaos, Anna Marie A. 283n54
Karen people group xiii
Kartasura, Indonesia 161–162
Kashung, Rev. 145, 148–150
Kasimo, J. 159

Kaufman, Robert 198
Kebatinan (Javanese religion) 162, 174
Kim, Chae-hyun 193
Kim, Chang-Hwan 208
Kim, Chang-In 202
Kim, Dae-Jung, President of South Korea (1998–2003) 197, 200–207
Kim, Dong-Wan 200, 202
Kim, Hyung-tae 192
Kim, Il-Sung, Prime Minister and President of North Korea (1948–1994) 207
Kim, In-soo 219
Kim, Jong-Il, Leader of North Korea (since 1994) 207
Kim, Jong-Phil 202–203, 215
Kim, Jung-Kwon 215
Kim, Myung-hyuk 190
Kim, Ok-Son 207
Kim, Sang-Kun 202
Kim, Su-han, Cardinal 189
Kim, Sung-hun 192
Kim, Young-Jin 215
Kim, Young-Sam, President of South Korea (1993–1998) 10, 18, 33, 38, 197, 200–210, 211–214, 216, 227, 230
Konsensiya ng Febrero Siete (Conscience of February 7, KONFES) 255–256, 258
Konsensiya ng Mamamayang Pilipino (Conscience of Filipino Citizenry, KOMPIL) 252, 282n47
Korea Student Christian Federation 222
Korean Evangelical Fellowship (KEF) 191, 197, 200
Korean Federation of Civil Society Groups 221
Korean National Association of Christian Pastors (KACP) 226
Korean National Council of Churches (KNCC) 192, 196–197, 200, 202, 223
Korean Students Christian Fellowship 200
Korean Women's Groups Coalition 200
Kuhn, Isobel and John 84n37
Kuki people group (Northeast India) 15, 136, 139, 142–147, 149
Kuki National Army (KNA) 143, 147
Kuki National Front 143
Kuki National Organization 143
Kuki Punitive Measures (KPM) 139
Kukna (Konkana) people group, India 88, 93, 108, 113, 118
Kwangju, South Korea 190, 193
Kwangju Christian Committee for Mission Freedom, South Korea 193
Kwangju Uprising, South Korea 190
Kwangju YMCA 193
Kwon, Chang-hee 233n7
Kyungbuk (North Kyungsan) Province, South Korea 205
Kyungnam (South Kyungsan) Province, South Korea 205
Kyungsan Province, South Korea 204, 205

Lahu people group 28, 30, 66–73, 79, 84nn42–43
Lancang Lahu Autonomous County, China 66, 70
Lal, R.B. 96
Laltlanmawii, Vice Chairman 144
Las Pinas ministerial fellowship, Philippines 251
Latin America vii-xiv, 3, 5, 7, 10, 21, 189, 198, 238, 276
Laurel, Mr. 254–255
Lausanne, Covenant and movement 36, 99, 190, 227, 231, 242
    Asia Lausanne Committee for World Evangelization 280n18
    Lausanne Congress 279n12
    Lausanne II, Manila 238
Le Jolle, Mrs. 166
leaven effect 10, 40, 45–46, 53, 56, 60, 72–73, 76, 78, 80
Lee, Hoi-Chang 203, 215
Lee, Jeong-Jin 212
Lee, Kuan Yew, Prime Minister of Singapore (1959–1990) 26
Legaspi, Leonardo 282n41
Legasto, Augusto 271
Lepasana, Simeon 249
Leung, Mrs. 63
Lewis, C.S. 283n55
Liangmai 142
Liberal Party, South Korea 187
Liberal Party, Philippines 249
liberation movements 31
liberty 7, 8, 10, 21
Lim, Bertram 266
Lim, David xii, xiii, 9, 17–20, 27, 32–34, 36–39, 257, 279n11
Lipset, Seymour Martin 20
Lisu people group 28, 30, 56–60, 70, 83n24, 84n36
literacy and literacy efforts 11, 13, 22, 28–29, 31, 59–60, 70–72, 82, 92, 95–96, 99, 109–113, 116, 118–119. See also illiteracy
    use of vernacular and literacy 59–60, 70–71, 109–112
    women's literacy programs 112
Lo, Clarence Y.H. 224
Locke, John 20
Lok Sabha (lower house of Indian Parliament) 151n4
Longhua County, China 51
Lucero, Manito V. 248
Lugo, Luis viii
Lumad people group 272
Lumsdaine, David H. xii-xiii, xvii, 25, 3–42
Luna, Emmanuel 270
Lungmuana, Rev. 141, 144, 149
Lutherans xi, 120, 241

Macapagal-Arroyo, Gloria. *See* Arroyo, Gloria Macapagal
macropolitical effects. *See* democracy: evangelical influence upon, indirect
Magalit, Isabelo 249, 255–256, 279n11, 280n18
Magbanua, Fred Jr. 239, 245, 255, 262, 279n8, 281nn31–32
Maggay, Melba Padilla 32, 246, 250, 254–255, 257–258, 275, 277, 281n33
Maharashtra, India 107
Mahoney, Ralph 279n7
Manila 244, 248–249, 251, 253, 268, 283n60
Manipur, India 5, 120, 131, 133–135, 138–140, 142–145, 147, 149–150
Marcos, Ferdinand, President and dictator of the Philippines (1965–1986) 19, 33, 36, 194, 235–237, 242–243, 252–256, 264, 282n39
Marcos, Imelda 243–244
Marikina Valley Ministerial Fellowship and Moral Movement, Philippines 251
Martin, Bernice 22
Martin, David xi, 22, 143
Marx, Karl 66
Marxism 25, 281n27
Marxism-Leninism 25, 46
Mastra, I. Wajan 159
Masyumi (Indonesian Political Party) 158, 162
Mataram, Indonesia 161
Mathur, Om, BJP leader 89
Maxwell, Colonel 135
McCulloch, Political Agent 139
McGavran, Donald 108
Megawati Soekarnoputri, President of Indonesia (2001–2004) 155, 157, 158, 164, 171
Mencius 27
Mennonite churches, Indonesia 167–168, 170
Mercado, Orlando 249
Methodists xi
   in the Philippines 240, 241, 255, 281n29
   in South Korea 186, 187, 188, 192, 226
Miao people group 70
micropolitical effects. *See* democracy, evangelical influence upon, indirect
Milan, Jonel 251
Military Christian Fellowship 270
Millennium Democratic Party (MDP), South Korea 203, 215
Mills, J.P. 136
Min, Chong-gi 221
Mindanao, Philippines 244, 249, 268, 272
Minjung theology 188, 189, 200, 222–223, 225, 231, 232n3
Minjung movement, South Korea 200, 216, 222–223
Misbach, H. 162
Mission Ministries Philippines 269, 282n46
mission schools 98

missionaries xiii, 23, 61, 66, 70, 83n26, 91, 98–99, 133–139, 159, 166–167, 186, 195
Mitra, Ramon 237, 243
Mizo National Front (MNF), India 147–148
Mizoram Kohran Hruaitute Committee (Committee of Church Leaders in Mizoram, MKHC), India 141
Mizoram, India xiii, 5, 120, 133, 134, 140, 141, 142, 148
modernization and Christianity 91, 118, 196
Modi, Narendra 89, 124n6
Moi, Daniel arap vii
monotheism 71
Monsod, Christian 249
Moon, Ik-Hwan 200
Moon, Yong-jik 196
Moral Recovery programs, Philippines 270
Morrison, Robert 66, 84n37
Mosse, David 91, 125n14
Movement for National Transformation (MNT), Philippines 256, 257
Movement for the Restoration of National Democracy, Philippines 270
Muslim-Christian advocacy 261
Muslims 20, 26, 35–36, 39, 89, 121–122, 156, 159–160, 163–166, 169, 171, 173–174, 176–178, 180n8, 182nn20–21, 182n28, 236, 272, 275. *See also* Islam
Myongdong Cathedral, South Korea 189, 197

Nadar caste 99–100, 122, 126n25. *See also* caste
Naga people group 15, 136–139, 142, 144–149
Nagaland, India xiii, 5, 120, 133–134, 140–143, 146, 149–150
Nahdlatul Ulama (Revival of Ulama, NU) 157–158, 162–163, 183n32
Nanjing Treaty, China 66
National Association of Protestant Elders, South Korea 203
National Church Planting Program, Philippines 241
National Citizens' Movement for Free Elections, Philippines 251
National Coalition for Urban Transformation (NCUT), Philippines 250, 257, 269, 271, 273, 275
National Council of Churches, South Korea 189–190
National Council of Churches in the Philippines (NCCP) 240–241, 243, 253, 265, 278n2, 279nn14–15
National Economic Development Authority, Philippines 250
National Ecumenical Consultative Committee, Philippines 280n16, 283n53
National Mandate Party, Indonesia 183n32
National Minority and Religious Affairs Bureau, Yunnan Province, China 66

326   INDEX

National Pastors' Federation for Justice and Peace Practice, South Korea 192
National People's Congress, China 65
National Prayer Network (NPN) 165
National Reawakening Party 183n32
National Socialist Council of Nagaland (NSCN), India 143, 147–148
National University Students Federation, South Korea 200
nationalism(s) 23–25, 43, 47, 186, 265
 cultural 122
 Filipino 239
 Hindu 88–89, 118–123 (see also Hindutva)
Navarro, Benedicto 251
Navarro, Chito 257, 272, 282n45
Navarro, Rafael 256
Navigators, the, Philippines 238, 280n21
Nayak, Chhotubhai and Ghelubhai 110
Nazism 24–25
New Korean Democratic Party 197
New Order regime, Indonesia 155–157, 160, 162–163, 173–174, 181–182nn14–17
Ngurhnema, Rev. 141
North Korea 187, 207, 216, 223
Northeast India xii-xiii, 5, 9, 14–16, 32–35, 131–153
NU. See Nadhlatul Ulama

O'Donnell, Guillermo 213
Oh, Chung-Il 200, 202
Operation Quick Count (OQC), Philippines 251
Orissa, India 121, 141
Ormeo, Antonio 239
Orosa, Ramon 239, 248
Oxford Centre for Mission Studies (OCMS) vii

Padilla, Frank 283n61
Padilla, Narciso 254
Padolina, William 240
Pae, Sung Moon 194, 196
Paek, Wan-Gi 207
Paik, Hwa-Jong 203
Paik, Jong-kuk 206
Pakubuwana II 161
Pallorina, Efren 282n46
Pancasila 178
panchayats 98, 113–114
Panikkar, K.M. x
Park, Chan-Wook 204
Park, Chong-Chan 207
Park, Chong-Chul 36, 191, 198, 201
Park, Chung-Hee, Leader of South Korea (1961–1979), 188
Park, Duk-hun 221
Park, Hyung-Kyu 200
Parkindo (Christian Party), Indonesia 163
Parmusi 163
Parsis 95
Partai Demokrasi Indonesia (Indonesian Democratic Party, PDI) 163–164, 182nn24–25

Partai Nasional Indonesia (Nationalist Party, PNI) 158, 162–163
Partai Persatuan Pembangunan (United Development Party, PPP), Indonesia 163
Partai Serikat Islam Indonesia (Indonesian Islamic League Party), Indonesia 163
Partido dos Trabalhadores (Brazil) 283n54
patriotism 43, 47
Peace Democracy Party, South Korea 204
peacemaking. See church –as peacemaker
Pentecostal Churches of God Asian Mission, Inc. 274
pentecostals and pentecostal churches viii, x-xi, 6, 88, 98, 233n6, 240
 in Indonesia 164–165, 168–169, 171
 in the Philippines 240–241, 278n1
Penuel School of Theology, Philippines 268
People Power 19, 191–194, 241–242, 251–265
 People Power events 19, 235, 237, 251–265 (see also Cha-Cha People Power events; EDSA)
People's Coalition for Democracy and National Unification, South Korea 189
People's Coalition to Protect Korean Agriculture 224
People's Movement Coalition for Democracy and Reunification (PMCDR), South Korea 200
People's Movement to Win a Democratic Constitution, South Korea 192
People's Party, South Korea 202
persecution, religious 6–7, 10, 24, 27, 53, 55–62, 73, 89f., 118–123, 123–125n3–11, 128, 129n141, 163–164, 166
Perti (Pergerakan Tarbijah Islamijah/Islamic Educational Movement) 163
Pettigrew, William 135–136, 138
Pew Charitable Trusts viii, xvi, 5
 Pew Forum on Religion and Public Life viii, xi, xvi
Philippine Business for Social Progress 269
Philippine Center for Investigative Journalism 271
Philippine Congress on World Evangelization 238, 241
Philippine Council of Evangelical Churches (PCEC) 239–242, 245, 247–250, 254–256, 260–261, 263–264, 268, 270, 272, 274–275, 277, 279n12, 280n16, 280n23
Philippine Council of Fundamental Evangelical Churches 279n9
Philippine Ecumenical Council on Community Organization 272
Philippine Evangelical Mission 248
Philippine Graduate School of Christian Education 270
Philippine National Police-Value Formation Program 270

Philippine National Red Cross 274
Philippine Population Commission 268
Philippine Relief and Development Services 268
Philippines for Jesus Movement (PJM) 239–241, 244–245, 249, 262–264, 270, 274–275, 277, 281n32
Philippines viii, xi-xiii, 4, 6–7, 10, 16, 19–20, 32–33, 35, 39–40, 194, 235–284
Phillips, Mrs. 166
pietistic theology 160, 241
Pimentel, Aquilino 258, 279n5, 282n42
PJM. *See* Philippines for Jesus Movement
pluralism 3–4, 11–12, 16, 22, 39, 41–44, 46, 65, 79–80, 176–179, 194, 228–229, 266, 273, 275, 277
  cultural 115
  democratic 4, 26–27, 41n12
  political, fostered by churches 18–19, 28, 33–35, 79–80, 118, 179–180, 275
  social 79, 229
Policy of Freedom and Religious Belief, China 46–47
political activism viii, xii, xiv-xv, xviiin2, 21
political corruption 33, 77, 141, 147, 270–272
political institutionalization 33, 39, 113–115, 173–174, 211–214, 227, 231, 265–266
political participation, evangelical 9, 17, 31, 38
  by Christians, in elections 18, 19, 32, 87, 199–204, 242–249
  by churches 32–35, 76–78, 140f., 145–146., 151, 163–166
  endorsements 17, 200–203, 244–248
  improper or opportunistic 17, 19, 33, 40, 165–166, 203–204, 244–249
  long-term development of 27, 190–194, 216–217, 243–251
  maturity of 17, 77–78, 98–103, 190–191ff., 256, 261–262, 264–265
  noninvolvement, proper and improper 34–35, 165–166, 188–191, 254, 264–265
  principled 173–174, 176, 192–194, 246–248
  theological and biblical basis 36, 103, 160, 177–178, 188, 208–209, 214–216
    other texts considered (Exodus, I Samuel, Daniel, Acts, etc.) 22, 73, 172, 192, 230, 260, 262 (*see also* civil disobedience)
    Romans 13 considered 35, 37, 166, 170–172, 179, 182n28, 333, 254–255, 260, 282n43
  theological rethinking 16–17, 27, 36–37, 52, 54, 60, 73–74, 88–89, 101–105, 145, 165–170, 188–191, 222, 227, 230, 256–263, 275–277
political parties 10–12, 18, 43–47, 89, 118–123, 150, 162–163, 173–174, 201–207, 248–249
  Christian involvement in 187–188, 199–204, 248–249
Political Watch, South Korea 226

politics 9, 19, 36, 88, 131–153, 155–183, 187, 191, 199. *See also* political participation
  historical patterns, recurrent 15, 65–73, 91–93, 99–101, 132–140, 149–150, 159–160
  mass political protests (*see* protests, mass political)
  politics, presidential 17–19, 33f., 177–178, 206–214, 254–263
  role of religion in 18–19
Popular Movement Headquarters for the Attainment of a Democratic Constitution (Minju Honbop Jaengchyi Kukmin Undong Bonpu), South Korea 192
Posleyabhai 107
poverty and poverty alleviation. *See* economic development; evangelical Christianity, democratizing effects
power encounters (perceived as supernatural) 62, 106. *See also* healing
Prabhakar, Dan 103, 117
pragmatism 43, 79, 267
Prayer Power Ministries, Philippines 280n17
Presbyterians xi
  in India 133, 141, 144
  in South Korea 186–187, 193
    Hap-tong Churches 188, 202, 226
    Chuung Hyun Church 208
    Kaehyuk (Reform) Churches 193, 204
    Kijang Churches 188, 192, 226
    Tong-hap Churches 187, 192, 226
    Saemunan Church, 192
    Taegu Tong-hap churches 193
Presidential Commission on Good Government, Philippines 248
proselytism xiii, 66
Protestant ethic xii, 22–23. *See also* Weber; democratization: economic development; evangelical Christianity: democratizing effects
Protestant theology 23
Protestantism x, xi, 6, 7, 20–24, 27, 276
  conservative 88
  European 29
  evangelical xi, 4, 9, 21–23
  global South x
  in India 102
  in India (in the Dangs) 89
  in Indonesia 16–17, 159, 177
  in Latin America 28
  in the Philippines 19
  in South Korea 186, 200, 207 (*see also* Minjung theology and movement)
Protestants ix, xi, 6, 10, 185, 195. *See also* Christianity; church; evangelicals
  in China 44–50, 53–54, 56–57, 61, 63, 65, 67, 72–73, 75, 78–79, 85n46
  evangelical 12, 14, 31, 132, 218 (*see also* evangelicalism; evangelicals)
  in South Korea 218

Protestants (*continued*)
  in India 15
  in Indonesia 164, 166, 181n14
  liberal 189 (*see also* ecumenical and evangelical Christianity)
  in the Philippines 19, 236, 238, 240, 263, 272, 275–276, 278n1
  in South Korea 17, 190, 194–195, 198–202, 214–215, 218–219, 226, 228
    Korean Association of Protestant Churches 197
protests, mass political 33–36, 40, 76f., 122, 147–148, 165–166, 186, 191–194, 251–265
Public Security Bureau, China 75
Pule, Hermano 259
Putonghua (Mandarin Chinese) 68, 70
Putnam, Robert 8, 23, 41, 108, 132, 140, 225, 265, 283n52

Qin, Ning 71, 85n46
Qingyuan Christian Council 63, 64
Qingyuan People's Congress, China 64

Racelis, Mary 283n59
Radio Veritas (Catholic), Philippines 255, 256
Rais, Amin 183n32
Rajya Sabha (upper house of Indian Parliament) 151n4
Ramakrishna Mission, India 150
Ramos, Fidel, President of the Philippines (1992–1998) 10, 19, 33, 237, 240, 243–246, 252, 263, 269, 280n24, 281n37
Rashtriya Swayamsevak Sangh (National Volunteers Organization, RSS) 88–89, 119, 121–122, 123n4, 124n6, 150. *See also* Hindutva
REACH, Philippines 280n21, 282n46
Reform and Open Policy, China 44, 46, 66, 69
Reformed Theological Seminary, South Korea 222
regime of attraction 109
regionalism 38, 204–206
Rekso Roemekso, Indonesia 161
religion and religious worldviews
  beliefs, impact of 13–14, 21, 29
  in China 46–50
  historical influence on politics 19, 158–160, 236–238, 241–242
  in Indonesia 158–159
  influence on culture 185
  worldview, effects on daily life 30, 31–32, 118
Religious Affairs Bureau (RAB), China 47, 49, 54, 62, 64–67, 81n8, 82n10
religious enthusiasm, reactions to 20
religious freedom. *See* government control of religion
Republican Party of India (RPI) 120

research design, methods 4–6, 45, 81n1, 85n48, 90–91, 126n31, 151n1, 151n4, 152, 155, 185, 231–232, 232nn1–2
research design, hypotheses and conclusions 4–10, 29, 43, 45–46, 87–88, 90–91, 132–133, 151n4, 155, 166f., 185–186, 194–195, 235–236, 275–277
Rhee, Syngman, President of South Korea (1948–1960) 187
Riconall, Niels 257
Rizal, Jose 236
Robertson, Pat 262
Roh, Tae-woo, President of South Korea (1988–1993) 194, 200–202, 205, 210
Roman Catholic Church 143, 266, 284n64
  in Indonesia, Catholic Party 162, 163
  in the Philippines 236–238, 247, 266, 274–275, 280n25
    Association of Laity of the Catholic Church (Laiko, the Lay Movement arm of CBCP), 261
    Catholic Bishops Conference of the Philippines (CBCP) 237, 238, 241, 244, 253, 265, 282n41
    charismatic renewal movements 237, 241
  in South Korea 189–190, 201, 218
Roman Catholicism ix, x, 6, 7, 24, 243, 277
  in East Timor 171
  in Indonesia 16
  in the Philippines 19, 276, 280n16
Roman Catholics 12, 31, 44, 49, 53, 189
  in India 15, 90, 98
  in Indonesia 159, 166, 177
  in the Philippines 236–238, 240–241, 243, 253, 269, 272, 274–275, 278n1, 280n17
  in South Korea 192, 197–198, 200, 202, 214–215, 218, 219
Romano, Enteng 271
Romero, Justice Flerida Ruth 240
Rongmai 142
Rosal, Rosa 274
Rose, Susan 279n6

Sachedina, Abdulaziz 26
Sadar, Manipur 137
Sadrach, Kyai 166, 181nn9–10. *See also* Wulung, Tungal
Sajogyo 156
Salonga, Jovito 240, 244, 247, 248
Salvador, Romy 245
Salvation Army 192, 241
Samahan ng mga Kristiyanong Organisasyong Pangkaunlaran (Association of Christian Development Organizations), Philippines 269
Samaria Forum, Surakarta, Indonesia 166
Samaritana, Philippines 282n46
Samraj, M. 103
Samuel, Vinay vii, viii, xvii, xviii
Sangh Parivar 121, 122

INDEX 329

Sanneh, Lamin 110
Santosa, Iman 165
Sarekat Rakyat (Populace League), Indonesia 162
Sarekat Tani Islam Indonesia (Indonesia Muslim Farmers Front) 162
Sayson, Tony 256
school of democracy argument 21. *See also* church: as school of democracy
secularization and desecularization 26
Sekber-Golkar (Sekretariat Bersama Golongan Karya, Joint Secretariat of Functional Groups) 157–158, 162–163, 173, 180n6. *See also* Golkar
Semarang, Indonesia 167
Sena, Shiv 120
Senepati, founder of Mataram, Indonesia 161
Seoul Labor Movement Coalition, South Korea 200
Seoul National University (SNU), South Korea 191, 198, 219
separation of church and state 35, 49, 74, 187, 196, 263–264
Serikat Islam (Islamic League, SI) 161–162
Se-Ung, Ham 200
Seventh Day Adventists 168, 170, 278n1
Shabri Kumbh 89, 114
Shah, Ghanshyam 89
Shahani-Ramos, Leticia 248–249, 257
shahukars 93, 94, 95, 111
Shintoism 186, 207
Sikhs 120, 122
Simao City, China 67, 84n41
Simao National Minorities and Religious Affairs Bureau, China 84n41
Sin, Jaime, Cardinal 33, 36, 236–237, 243–244, 252–253, 256, 263–264, 274
Sin Myong Church, South Korea 207
Singh, Emil Jeba 126n25
Singles for Christ, Philippines 237, 278n3
Singson, Chavit 253, 256–257, 261
Singson, D. 149
Singson, Luis 237
Skaria, Ajay 89
So, Ui-Hyun 201
social activism 102
social capital 15, 19, 22, 31, 40. *See also* Putnam, Robert
    bridging 8, 15, 31, 39–40, 52–53, 81, 103, 108, 111, 137–139, 143, 145=146, 174–177, 218–219, 222–226, 272–273 (*see also* inter-group cooperation; church: discord and fragmentation among churches)
social disenfranchisement xii, 93–103
Social Gospel Movement 189
social identity 45, 172–173
social liberalization 80
social transformation 44
Soeharto, Major General, President of Indonesia (1967–1998) 17, 33, 34, 155–158, 160–166, 171, 173–175, 178, 179, 181n15
Soekarno, President of Indonesia (1948–1967) 155–157, 160, 171, 182
Soekarnoputri, Megawati. *See* Megawati
Soh, Kyung-suk 218, 222–225, 228, 231, 232
Solo, Indonesia 160–161, 167. *See* Surakarta
Somang Church, South Korea 214
Son, Bong-ho 218, 219, 221–222, 228, 231
Son, Myung-Sun 208
South Korea viii, xi-xiii, 4–6, 10, 16–19, 32, 34–36, 38, 40, 75, 185–233
Staines, Graham 121, 141
Standard Committee of the Associations, India 142
Stanmeyer, Anastasia 236
State Administration for Religious Affairs (SARA), China 47, 81n8
Sudarshan, K. 89
Sumartana, Th. 159
Surabaya, Indonesia 164, 174
Surakarta, Indonesia 9, 16, 157–160, 155–183. *See also* Solo
Surat, India 88, 90, 93, 96–97, 102
Sycip, Washington 274

Taegu Cheil Church, South Korea 193
Take the Nations for Jesus Global Ministries, Inc., Philippines 240
Tamenglong, India 139, 143
Tamil Nadu, India 100, 104–105
Tangkhul Nagas, Ukhrul, India 135–136, 138
Taoism 62
Tawney, R.H. 21, 27
Tayabas, Benjamin 270
Teen Challenge, Philippines 238
Tendero, Efraim 240, 245, 262, 280n23
terrorism 24, 25
Thatcher, Margaret 283n55
theology of transformation 103, 116, 165, 221, 225, 231, 242, 268, 271, 281n33
Thompson, Mark 236
Three-Self Patriotic Movement (TSPM), China 48–49, 52, 54, 73–75, 77–78, 85n51
Tica, Gavino 279n10
Ting, Bishop. *See* Ding, K.H., Bishop
Tingson, Greg 270
Tocqueville, Alexis de xi, 8, 10, 20, 22, 27, 31, 38, 41, 227, 231
tolerance. *See* intolerance and tolerance
Tomas, Patricia Sta. 249
Tong-hap churches. *See* Presbyterians, South Korea
Torre, Edicio de la 258
Touthang, Dino L. 142, 151n4
trapo 33, 242, 251
tribal regions 56–60, 65–73, 87–130, 131–154, 272
tribal peoples 6, 10–12, 14–16, 28–42, 89–101, 104f. *See also* adivasis

Trinity, doctrine of the, and non-Trinitarian belief 68, 71, 240
Trulock Theological Seminary, Imphal, India 149
Tulay Sa Pagunlad, Inc., Philippines 269

UCCP. *See* United Church of Christ of the Philippines
Underwood, Rev. 233n8
Unification Democracy Party, South Korea 204
United Church of Christ in the Philippines (UCCP) 241, 243
United Liberal Democrat Party (ULDP), South Korea 203, 215
urbanization 188
USA vii-viii, xiv, 21, 35–36, 44, 85n46, 121, 171, 187, 190, 195–196, 216, 222, 227, 235, 269, 277

Vacation Bible School 99
Vajpayee, Atal Behari, Prime Minister of India (1996, 1998–1999, 1999–2004) 121
Valenciano, Gary 240, 279n6
Value Formation programs, Philippines 270
Van Andel, H.A. 167
Vanvasi Kalyan Parishad (a VHP affiliate) 89, 119
Varli people group 93, 113, 120
Varshney, Ashutosh 26
Vatican 253
Vatican II 284n64
Velarde, Mike 237, 264, 283n61
Vencer, Agustin B. 249, 250, 255, 268, 273, 279n12, 280n16
Verba, Sidney 8
VHP. *See* Vishwa Hindu Parishad
Victory in Jesus Christ Congregation, Philippines 240
Villanueva, Eddie 237, 240, 244–245, 255, 260–263, 271, 278n3, 279n12, 280n24, 281n27, 281n30, 281n32
Villanueva, Emmanuel Joel 271
Villanueva, M. Val A. 283n63
violence 89, 91, 121, 163–164. *See also* persecution, religious
Vishwa Hindu Parishad (World Hindu Confederation, VHP) 88–89, 114, 124n4, 124n6, 125n11

Wahid, Abdurrahman, President of Indonesia (1999–2001) 155, 157–158, 171
Walzer, Michael 20
Warm Body of Christ, Philippines 240
Weber, Max xii, 10–11, 20–23, 27–31, 38, 276
Wesleyan Church, Philippines 240

Westminster Graduate College, South Korea 221
Williams, Theodore 126n25
witchcraft, belief in, in India 105–106
Wong Cilik ("small people") 163
Woodberry, Robert D. 22, 195, 225, 284n64
World Bank 268, 271
World Council of Churches 279n15
World Evangelical Fellowship 239, 240, 282n45
World Vision India 111
World Vision International 98, 103, 126n25, 268
World Vision Philippines 282n45
Wulung, Tunggul 166. *See also* Sadrach
Wungnaoshung, Rev. 148
Wyner, Bob 244

Xaxa, Virginius 92
Xiadade Village, China 67–69
Xinjiang Uygur Autonomous Region, China 45
Xu, Yongan, 84n41

Yang, Madame 11, 73–76, 80
Yangshan County, China 11, 61–65
Yangshan People's Hospital, China 63
Yanjin Seminary, Beijing 52
Yayasan Kerukunan Persaudaraan Kebangsaan (The Harmonious Brotherhood Nationhood Foundation), Indonesia 164
yeast. *See* leaven effect
Yi, Byung-Sung 207
Yi, Chung-sok 222
Yi, Kap-Yun 196
Yi, Man-Sin 200
Yi, Man-yol 218, 219, 228
Yi, Myung-soo 219
YMCA, South Korea 190
Yogyakarta, Indonesia 155, 161
Yoido Full Gospel Church, Seoul 203, 214, 233n6
Yong-bok, Kim 200
Young Life, Philippines 238
Youth for Christ, Philippines 237, 238
Yunnan Province, China 56, 66, 71, 85n46
Yunnan Theological Seminary, China 60
YWCA, South Korea 190

Zaihmingthana, Rev. 141, 146, 148
Zen, Ze-kiun, Cardinal Joseph ix
Zendings, 159, 166
Zhang, Caixian 68
Zhao, Zhi-en 81n3
Zoroastrianism 95